The 1001 Most-Asked Questions About
The American West

Photo by Charles Belden. *Courtesy Western History Department, Denver Public Library.*

THE 1,001 MOST-ASKED QUESTIONS ABOUT THE AMERICAN WEST

With Answers
by

Harry E. Chrisman

SWALLOW PRESS   OHIO UNIVERSITY PRESS
CHICAGO   ATHENS, OHIO   LONDON

This book was designed as a class project in typography at the School of Art, Ohio University, faculty advisor, Richard Bigus. Graphic design students deserving special mention are: Stephen Horn, Dale Roberts, Mary Smith, and Sue Spalding.

Frontispiece photo by Charles Belden. *Courtesy Western History Department, Denver Public Library.*

Copyright © 1982 by Harry E. Chrisman
All Rights Reserved
Printed in the United States of America

Library of Congress Cataloging in Publication Data

Chrisman, Harry E.
    1001 Most-Asked Questions about the American West.
    Includes index.
    I. West (U.S.)—Miscellanea.   I. Title.
II. Title: One thousand one questions about the American
West.   III. Title: One thousand and one questions about the
American West.
F591.C49   978   82-6337
ISBN 0-8040-0382-3   AACR2
ISBN 0-8040-0383-1 (pbk.)

Swallow Press Books
are published by
Ohio University Press
Athens, Ohio

This book is dedicated

with

deep affection

to the Great West of my youth,

a land that spawned one of the most Romantic eras

ever known.

No man or woman

was ever to ride across the Western Earth

or to sleep beneath its star-lanterned skies,

without feeling the majestic spirit

which spoke to its Native People

and to its wild things.

Other Books by Harry E. Chrisman

Lost Trails of the Cimarron
The Ladder of Rivers: The Story of I.P. (Print) Olive
Butcher's History of Custer County, Nebraska (Ed.)
Fifty Years on the Owl Hoot Trail (With Jim Herron, Sr.)
The Fighting Railroad Mayer, by Earl Walker (Ed.)
When You and I Were Young, Nebraska! (with Berna Hunter
    Chrisman)
Boss Neff in the Texas and Oklahoma Panhandle (Ed.)

Contents

Introduction ————————————— xi

Chapter 1   Wild and Domesticated Animals,
            Fowls, Reptiles, and Insects of
            the West ————————————— 1

Chapter 2   Business and Commerce in the
            Pioneer West ————————————— 45

Chapter 3   Cattlemen and Cowboys ————————— 63

Chapter 4   Culture in the Frontier West ——————— 93

Chapter 5   Folklore ————————————— 117

Chapter 6   Indians ————————————— 131

Chapter 7   Geographical Locations and
            Geological Formations ——————————— 179

Chapter 8   Lawmen, Outlaws, Gunfighters ——————— 199

Chapter 9   The Military ————————————— 237

Chapter 10 Pioneer Life ————————————— 271

Chapter 11 Tack and Equipment ————————— 291

Chapter 12 Towns, Territories, Transportation,
            and Communication ——————————— 303

Acknowledgements

I wish to acknowledge the great help that has always been given me by the capable staff members at the state historical societies of Colorado, Oklahoma, Nebraska, Texas, North Dakota, South Dakota, New Mexico, Kansas, and Wyoming. Wherever I have gone in quest of answers to questions that have come up in my writings, the staffs of these state institutions, their libraries, and their museums, have always been most helpful. And at no time have I needed and used their facilities more than in the preparation of this book.

I would like to thank Mr. Marion Stevens, former publisher of *The West* magazine. Some materials included in this volume first appeared in earlier form in "The Roundup" page of that publication which I edited during the years 1965-1971.

My thanks go also to Donna Ippolito, my editor at the Swallow Press, for her constructive criticism and great help in improving the content of the book. I also wish to thank Shari Schartman, production manager at Swallow Press for her great help.

Finally, to all those relatives and friends who encouraged me to compile this volume, my warmest thanks.

H.E.C.

Introduction

For more than forty years in newspaper and magazine work, I have been answering questions about the American West, particularly the Old West, for readers. No matter how unusual the question or how difficult it was to track down a reply, I always attempted to do so. On the other hand, though the question might at first appear to be obscure or arcane, the response was often common knowledge to someone who had been reared in the Old West.

I began to notice, as the years went by, how frequently certain questions were repeated. Seeing this, I started to select these "repeaters" and jot them down with the idea of one day collecting them in book form. Many questions kept me on my toes: "Can a horse trail his own kind by smell, as does a dog?", "What did the term "gillflirted' mean in reference to a mare?", and "Without surgical instruments how would an Indian extract a foreign object from the eye of another?" I've even had questions concerning whales, from people living near the waters of former whaling areas in the Oregon-Washington district: Readers of my column, "Roundup Time," published in the late sixties and early seventies in the national monthly magazine *The West*, often posed some of the most difficult queries.

In this book, I have concentrated on those puzzlers, compiling more than a thousand questions about the American West whose answers are often difficult to find. While I did not leave out Wild Bill Hickok, Custer's Last Stand, and Bat Masterson, those characters and events have been dealt with comprehensively in many other books and sources. Further, wherever necessary and wherever possible, the material has been updated to 1981.

While a single-volume work on the American West cannot hope to be comprehensive, it must be as accurate and authentic as the author can make it. The nature of language on the frontier of this country, as the nation was forming, meant that a subject might go by various names, depending on the region where the action was taking place. For example, an orphan calf in Texas might be called a "doughgie," whereas in Arizona it would be called a "leppie," and in Oregon by still another name. Such variations in language, terms, and definitions, in the passing of more than three-quarters of a century since the demise of the range cattle industry, have imposed their challenges to anyone attempting such a work. So my answers are subject to correction by readers with special expertise or access to materials not available to me in my research.

In my efforts to provide correct answers to all questions, I have also drawn on a personal store of knowledge gained from a boyhood spent on a ranch and a young manhood riding after cattle and horses as a cowhand and a wrangler, closely associated with the men who spoke and used the Western language from earliest training.

Like so many Westerners, I have a special feeling for the land, its history, and the pioneer people who have shaped it. Together with the many fascinating items of fact, lore, and information included herein, it is my hope that in my 76th year I have also communicated my lifelong affection for what is to me one of Earth's special places—the American West.

Harry E. Chrisman
10245 W. 14th Avenue,
Denver, Colorado 80215

We go eastward to realize history

and study the works of art and literature,

retracing the steps of the race.

We go westward as into the future, with

a spirit of enterprise and adventure.

Thoreau

Photo courtesy Fort Niobrara Wildlife Refuge, Valentine, Nebraska.

Q. *Is the longhorn cattle species apt to become extinct?*
A. No. Many wildlife and park herds are now protected. Further, commercial ranchers have found them to be a good investment, and are growing them for beef purposes. The longhorn has earned the respect of everyone associated with them.

1 WILD and DOMESTICATED ANIMALS, FOWLS, REPTILES, and INSECTS of the WEST

When my mother dedicated the story of her pioneer life, which extended from 1879 to 1900 in central Nebraska, she penned the following:

> This book is dedicated with love and affection to the good sod of the prairies, the nutritious buffalo and bluestem grasses, the bountiful wild game, the ample rainfall, the horned cattle, the bronco ponies, the wild fruits and the timber from the canyons— without which our lovely state of Nebraska could never have been settled.

Her dedication set forth the pioneer's feeling of debt and gratitude for the elemental things without which they could never have survived those first bitter years on a new land, many of them without the tools and finances to feed, clothe, and shelter their families. In this quote from her book, *When You and I Were Young, Nebraska*, we note she speaks first of the "good sod of the prairies," for from this sod were constructed the humble shelters that protected the Great Plains pioneer from fierce blizzards that swept the land. Second come the nutritious grasses, which constituted the food for their work animals, and then she gives thanks for "the bountiful wild game." It was this latter, the wild game and migrating fowls, that provided a much needed food source for their families.

So many questions have been asked about the domestic animals and wild game of the Old West that perhaps only a comprehensive encyclopedia could answer them all. Here we take up the most commonly asked questions.

The Horse, being the chief source of power, and an animal that all rode or used for fast transportation in the premotorized age, generates the greatest interest among domestic animals. The questions run from simple queries about how to tell a horse's age to quite complicated, ofttimes unanswerable, questions con-

concerning the thought processes of the equine species (a subject beyond my competency!).

Next come questions about cattle. The cattle industry and its way of life attracted not only those who actually lived it on the Western range but those who today avidly study its history. The longhorn and the buffalo, both so numerous on the Plains, are now rarities, thus arousing even further interest in them as symbols of the Old West.

And so it goes with the rest of the animals, domesticated and wild. Though the life of the Old West is gone, through our many questions about its native animals we may gain insight into the problems of survival that still confront both animal and human on this planet.

HORSES

Q.   *Why does a colt appear so ungainly at birth and during its first few weeks of life?*

A.   A colt does appear to be all legs when born, for the legs, from the knees down (cannon bones) are as long as they will ever be in life. However, within a matter of a few weeks, the colt gets its balance and its capacity for handling itself, and the seeming ungainliness soon disappears.

Q.   *When does a colt shed its baby teeth? When has it filled its mouth with mature teeth? Can a horse's age be accurately judged after it becomes a "smooth mouth," that is, without cups in its teeth?*

A.   A colt sheds at age two-and-a-half years. At four-and-a-half years all the foal teeth are gone, and the horse has a full mouth of teeth at age five. Expert horsemen can judge a horse's age even after it is smooth-mouthed, that is, after age ten. At twelve years, the indentation in upper jaw teeth becomes enlarged; at fifteen, the nippers in the upper jaw become round; at eighteen, the nippers in the lower jaw are triangular in shape; at twenty, the corner teeth have become triangular. At twenty-five, the middle teeth of the lower jaw are twice as thick as they are broad; However, many irregularities make judgment of age more difficult as the animal ages. An expert horseman can also tell if a horse's teeth have been "worked over" to add cups and make the animal appear younger than it actually is.

Q.   *Are the horses disappearing in the country? Will the equine species become extinct?*

A. No. In 1915 there were 21 million horses in the nation. Though no census is now taken on horses, knowledgeable private sources state that there were approximately 7.7 million horses in the nation by the 1970s. Most animals are private riding horses on ranches and small farms and ranchos. It is estimated there are now about 12 million horses.

Q. *Is it possible that wild horses will become extinct?*

A. It is doubtful. There are still areas, such as deep in the gorges of the Grand Canyon, to which man can barely penetrate, yet where wild horses still exist. So long as man cannot reach them with saddle horses to catch and handle them, they will remain free. Other bands of wild horses, such as those in northern Wyoming, have developed human friends who have fought legal battles to keep them alive by preventing horse hunters from getting to them. Yet, generally speaking, the wild horse, or mustang, is a thing of the past.

Q. *What can we do to help the wild mustangs that are being so ruthlessly exterminated by horse hunters, dog feed people, and others?*

A. We should encourage others to protect the better mares and foals, as well as to urge the U.S. government to keep good seed stock. In the event the nation is ever confronted by a land war, without horse or mule power, we would face a perilous situation, for much fighting would be done in the mountains where even jeeps and trucks cannot travel or haul matériels of war. Further, draft horses can always be used on farms and the government should see that good stallions are maintained on the range, as were the remount studs in the 1920s and early 1930s. Current gasoline shortages are forewarning us now. The simplest manner to dispose of the poorest stock is for government hunters to shoot them where they range and salvage the meat for sale to canners. To stop the canning of horse meat for dog, cat or fox food, we must remember that all we have to do is to *stop buying canned meat labeled "horse meat."*

Q. *Did wild horses ever become so numerous in the West as to interfere with the work of the cattle roundups?*

A. Yes. It has been told that in places the wild horses ran ahead of the circle-riders to a point where the wild horses scared the cattle back upon the roundup riders, causing a day's gather to be lost. Will Barnes, in an article, "Wild Horses," in *McClure's* magazine, 1908-1909, told of this incident. A New Mexico rancher said afterward that about 200 head of wild horses were involved in the incident.

Q. *Where did the name "mustang" originate?*

A. From the Spanish *mesteño.* The horse trappers in early Texas days were called *mesteñeros.* They trapped the wild horses by driving them into stout circular corrals with wide "V" catch-wings.

Q. *What is meant by "mouthing a horse?"*

A. Examining his teeth to tell his age.

Q. *What sort of horse is called a stewball?*

A. The term is usually "stew bald." It's a black and white spotted animal, sometimes also called stewballed.

Q. *Is the pinto horse, as we know it today, chiefly an American breed?*

A. While the pinto as we know it is chiefly an American breed, it dates back to antiquity, its distinctive color patterns appearing on Egyptian tombs of 3,400 years ago. Two distinct strains of markings distinguish the pinto, according to the Pinto Horse Association of America, Inc. There is the *tobiano* and there is the *overo*. The tobiano predominates in North America and Europe—a basic white with overcolorings in large spots. The overo pattern is basically a dark or roan, with white overmarkings. The term pinto is derived from the Spanish *pintado*, meaning "painted." The paint hoss was prized by the American Indians who loved color as well as the fine disposition and fleetness of foot of these attractive animals.

Q. *What does it mean to "spell" a horse?*

A. To permit it to rest a few minutes, get its breath, after a hard pull or long run.

Q. *What, on a horse, is called a chestnut?*

A. The small, bony outgrowth just below the point of the hock, on the inside of the animal's hind legs.

Q. *What is the difference between a bay and a sorrel?*

A. A bay is a red, or dark-red, with a black cannon bone, mane, and tail. The sorrel is more of an orange-red, with a light mane and tail. Most horsemen speak of light bays and dark bays, yet some call a bay a chestnut. The chestnut is properly a moderate brown, yellower and duller than a toast brown. The color of a horse's points often carry down into the legs, the dark bays having almost black legs below the knee and hock, the sorrels a lighter color. "According to Mohammedan myth," Texas author, teacher, and folklorist Frank Dobie once wrote, "the first horse that God created—created as a matter of course out of the Wind—was a bay, or perhaps a chestnut, with a star in its forehead, the sign of glory and good fortune." So the bay, which some call a chestnut, seems to be the perfect color for a horse.

Q. *When a colt is born, which part of it comes first?*

A. Normally, a colt comes into the world head first and with his front feet. Mama breaks the covering sack, licks him clean, and in a few hours he's on his feet and nursing.

Q. *How can we make owners provide winter shelter and food for their animals? Many have only a windbreak, or a board shed. The animals stand within and suffer terribly in storms.*

A. In Colorado, in 1973, livestock owners were taken to court and fined for such abominable practices. Perhaps a flood of letters to horse magazines and livestock publications would help call attention to this problem.

Q. *I have heard and read that horses have been on the North American continent since prehistoric times. Then I read that Spaniards were the ones to introduce them as late as the thirteenth century into Mexico and South America. Which is true?*

A. Both. The three-toed horse of prehistoric times was a small animal not much more than two or three feet in height. It became extinct eons ago. It was not until the Spanish Conquistadores brought horses to this continent that they became known to the American Indian and used by him.

Q. *Can a saddle horse actually be "hackamore broke" and still perform as well as one broken to the bridle and bit?*

A. Yes, but it requires a skillful horsebreaker to do it, for it is difficult to teach an animal to respond quickly to the touch of the rein on its neck (neckreining) without a bridle bit in its mouth. Once learned, however, an intelligent horse acts as well without a bit as with one and enjoys more comfort.

Q. *Does the horse have the faculty of trailing his kind by smell, as does a dog and other animals?*

A. Yes, this trait has been observed in some horses, principally those from mustang stock, saddle animals, and range-bred horses. As a boy I observed range animals, both mares and studs, that could trail other horses this way. When turned from a corral, with no other horses in view, they would run in circles, sniffing the air with head high. Once the odor from the band was detected, or the ground scent of their trail, the freed animal would set out at a lope to reach them. I never observed this trait in draft animals, possibly because there was no occasion for one to be separated from the others. Wild cattle in Texas were also most gifted with picking up scent.

Q. *What sort of a horse is called a "stumpsucker?"*

A. The term is applied to an animal that chews wood, such as its manger or stall timbers, or, when left in wooded areas, chews on a tree limb or stump. The need for salt or other required body chemicals is thought by some to be the cause of this. Others feel that it is a result of nervousness. One man told me that his father cured a stumpsucking mare (it is also called cribbing) by making his wife keep her chickens out of the barn where the mare was stalled. Their presence caused the animal's nervousness, he thought.

Q. *Was there actually a White Stallion of the Plains, as described in many stories?*

A. There is reason to believe there was a basis for the many stories of the white stallion, the first of which was related as early as 1844 by Josiah Gregg in his *Commerce of the Prairies.* Frank Dobie tells of the white mustang in his work *The Mustangs.* Most wild horses were bays, sorrels, and blacks. They were not paints or pintos, contrary to the popular notion that the Indians caught their mounts from wild bands of mustangs. By the 1870s and 1880s, according to the mustangers, the animals were bred down to regular colors of browns, bays, sorrels, a few buckskins and claybanks and greys. The wild mustangs were descended from the Spanish horse stock, a blend of North African Barb, Arabian, Norse, and other breeding. The "white stallion" story continued to appear in such works as *Trail Drivers of Texas,* where old cowboys told of chasing (but never catching) the white stallion. Seems in most of the stories the white stud had a preoccupation toward suicide when the chase grew too hot for him.

Q. *In the United States, is there any county where horses outnumber humans?*

A. We know of one—Jefferson County, Colorado—and there surely are many others over the West.

Q. *What was the age of the oldest saddle horse ever recorded?*

A. There are no accurate statistics on this matter. However, Black Kid, owned by Frank Benton of Burns, Colorado, lived to nearly forty years. At age thirty-eight, Black Kid would shake hands, though rheumatism had crippled him. Superior, another Colorado horse, owned by Du Bois Brothers of Denver, reached age thirty-two. Sonfield, a fine Morgan stud, lived past age thirty in Mount Vernon, Washington. About forty years for a horse is equal to 105 or 110 years for humans. That's long enough for either!

Q. *In trailering my horse, how frequently should I take him off the trailer?*

A. Every two to four hours is best. Many animals cannot urinate while on a trailer, and kidney trouble or bladder infection can result from inattention to an animal's natural needs.

Q. *When trailering a single horse in a double-horse trailer, which side should he be placed on?*

A. Keep the single animal on the left stall. This permits him to ride on the "high" side of the trailer, behind the driver, since all highways are constructed so as to peak in the middle. An animal is nervous, doesn't ride well or get rested on the right side, the "low" side.

Q. *When did the famous Midnight horses die—Midnight and Five Minutes to Midnight?*

A. Midnight, famous bucking horse, born 1910, died in 1936. Five Minutes to Midnight, born 1924, died in 1947. The pair were buried on the old Verne Elliott Ranch, near Platteville, Colorado. (The bodies have since been removed to Oklahoma City.) Over the original graves were these inscriptions:

Midnight
Under this sod lies a great buckin' hoss,
There never lived a cowboy he couldn't toss;
His name was Midnight, his coat black as coal,
If there is a Hoss Heaven, please God, rest his soul.
                    —by a cowboy.

Five Minutes to Midnight
Again the Reaper
Has visited the corral.
He took
Five Minutes to Midnight,
The cowboys' pal.
                    —a cowboy.

Q. *What were the bloodlines of Midnight, famous bucker?*
A. Jim McNab, who owned Midnight as a colt and broke him, says he was sired by Billy, a part-Morgan-Percheron stallion, and a badly spoiled dam that had thoroughbred blood, "a real good one." Midnight was foaled on the Doorkey Ranch, near Fort MacLeod, Alberta, Canada. He was first presented formally as a bucker at the Fort Mac-Leod Rodeo in the year of 1924 where he threw every rider up to the finals when an Indian boy, Pete Bruisehead, drew him, made a qualified ride, and won on him. Midnight's signature was a fast running-buck, "hit the ground hard on front feet, turn hindquarters sideways and kick at the same time as front feet hit the ground." As McNab described it, "the rider got hit in the belly with the saddlehorn about the same time he was hit in the seat with the cantle."

Q. *What was a bell mare?*
A. A mare who had a bell strapped to her neck and who was used to toll the other horses when needed. Horses like to follow a leader, and usually an older mare was selected to carry the bell.

Q. *Did the Plains Indians, before the advent of the white man in numbers, practice the custom of gelding (castrating) their horses before breaking them to ride? Or was the practice adopted only after the Indians saw the white men do it?*
A. Prior to arrival of the Spaniards, the Indians had no horses to geld. The Spaniards, arriving with Cortez in 1519, had eleven stallions and five mares. So these men were riding studs, not geldings. Frank Dobie, in *The Mustangs*, wrote: "The time at which the Spaniards began castrating non-breeding stallions, and bulls alike, seems to be undeterminable. About the close of the eighteenth century Felix

de Azara found stockraisers on the Pampas castrating *potros* (unbroken males) at the age of two years and riding only geldings." This offers a clue, not a solution or complete answer, to the question. Castration took care of the business of trying to ride quarrelsome, contentious, and frisky studs. By 1830 we know that Californians were gelding their saddle animals. Since the Indians obtained their saddle horses from the Mexicans by trade and theft, and not from De Soto and others in the sixteenth century, as is sometimes reported, it is reasonable to believe that by the early seventeenth century the Plains Indians were following the custom of gelding saddle horses to make them more tractable and useful for buffalo hunting and warring with other tribes.

Q. *Though we bred our snow white mare, Dolly, to a snow white Arabian stud, we failed to get a white colt. Why?*

A. Colts are born with a dark coat, later turn white or gray. Perhaps your colt will lighten up and become a blond! Of course there is the matter of genetics, and we sometimes get a color we do not prefer.

Q. *I saw a mule that was said to be locoed. Did you ever see a locoed mule?*

A. Strangely enough, though I have bought and sold hundreds of mules, I've never seen one that was locoed. It is no doubt a possibility that mules would eat loco weed, if starving, but mules were not allowed to run so much on the range, where loco weed might exist, as were horses. Also, there are fewer mules. And mules, to anyone who knows their habits, are notoriously fussy about their diet.

Q. *Is it true that a horse broken by Indians was better than one broken by cowboys?*

A. An "Injun-gentled" horse was highly prized by Indians. The Indians went about the breaking of horses by gentling them as colts and working with them patiently. The cowboys rode a horse until he was exhausted, if necessary, to get him to stop bucking. However, many cowboys were noted for breaking broncs to be gentle-broke and useful as cow horses, not just to be ridden. Cowboys never prized an Indian horse, for the Indian mounted on the right side, and that would be almost heresy to any cowhand. Indians were not so particular, they raided and stole what they could get from the ranches, split the ears at the top, cut long hairs off the tail, painted symbols on the horse and decorated him as they did themselves.

Q. *Was Comanche, the horse that survived the Battle of the Little Big Horn, Lt. Col. G.A. Custer's mount?*

A. No, the horse was issued to Capt. Myles Keogh, also killed in the battle.

Q. *I am puzzled by the origin of mules, jacks, burros, asses, and so forth. Where does each fit into the natural scheme?*

A. The jack and jennet are a natural pair; they are asses, male and female. The stallion and mare (equines) are another natural pair, male and female. If you cross a mare with a jack, the result is a mule (a hybrid, which does not reproduce its kind except in rare cases). Cross a stallion with a jennet and you get what is called a hinney (also a hybrid). The big castrated mule is best known for heavy work, hauling freight wagons, etc. But the common burro (the ass), the smaller product of the crossing of the ordinary jack-jennet, has been carrying man's burdens since Biblical times. The registered Spanish jack is small, jet black, and has clean white points under the belly and a mealy white nose. He has fine action and class. His big brother and sister, the registered Mammoth jack and jennet, are larger, have good white points also, but are slower and stronger. The latter is the jack that generally fathers the large work mules. The stallion and mare, when mated, bring the horse colt. Female mules are referred to as "Mollies"; the male mule as a "Jack-mule."

Q. *What is a set-fast?*

A. A sore on a horse's back that fails to heal, usually caused by a poor saddle.

Q. *Who brought the first cattle into Arizona?*

A. Coronado, the Spaniard. Father Kino, the Spanish missionary, later brought 700 head into that area about 1700 A.D.

Q. *What is meant by a "baskettail" in horses?*

A. Wild horses, or those that run loose for any length of time, encounter brush, weeds, tall grasses, thistles, devil claws, sandburs, and other growing plants. As they get these thorns and trash wound up in their tails, and as the hair grows longer, it wads up into a large bunch, veritably appearing like a bushel basket. When the animals are caught up, the tails are thinned out with a knife blade, cutting away the hair and trash.

Q. *Have Morgan and Arabian horses (fairly well matched in weight and both versatile breeds) ever been matched in competitive racing, endurance runs, or weight-pulling?*

A. We cannot be certain that such competition has not been thought up. However, it appears likely that *individuals* from both breeds would show superiority in various events. However, such individual superiority would not necessarily apply to the breed.

Q. *How was bronc riding conducted in the early shows of the 1880s?*

A. Generally, as on ranches, the riders roped the horses from the bunch in the corral. The rider was helped to mount outside, in front of the assembled crowd, and the horse turned loose with a couple of pick-up riders sent after him. The rider "rode until the finish," that is, until the horse quit bucking.

Q. *Why is a good cutting horse usually a not-so-good roping horse?*

A. A top cutting horse always stays behind the animal he is working, to get it out of the herd or into some place desired by the rider. But the top roping horse has to carry its rider up behind and alongside, and even ahead of the animal to be roped. It is a difficult adjustment for the horse to make, if used for both purposes. Some animals adjust to it. Others do not.

Q. *I have heard it remarked that Charles M. Russell, the cowboy artist, "idealized" the horse and "glamorized" him in his paintings. Is the remark true or false?*

A. Russell dealt chiefly with the northern range horse and the Indian horses of the north country. These animals, whose ancestors may have been the small, Texas mustang, did develop into bigger-boned, taller animals than their cousins who stayed in the south. Since the range grass of Montana was far more nutritious than the grasses in the south, the animals grew bigger, and their work helped them develop into animals that might be said to have been "glamorized" by Russell's deft touch. But actually the horses looked pretty much as he painted them.

Q. *I have a good four-year-old quarterhorse, well broke to ride, and I want to make a roping horse of him. But he is afraid of the rope. What must I do?*

A. Unless you, yourself, are a fair roper and have trained animals before, I would advise you to turn him over to a professional trainer. If you work him yourself, be patient, swing your rope slowly, teach him that no harm will come to him from the rope.

Q. *From what source did the American quarterhorse spring?*

A. As early as 1880, according to one old-time Texas rancher, there was an interest in breeding up the best qualities of several types of riding horses to produce an animal that preserved the better qualities of each breed, particularly for working cattle. The stock from which the quarterhorses spring was, however, being bred up in Virginia and the Carolinas at least two centuries earlier than this. So from these animals, and from the tough and wiry mustang stock, eventually came the horse we call the quarterhorse— fast for a quarter of a mile, greatly favored for cutting, roping, rodeo work, and general pleasure riding on ranches. For more information you may write the American Quarterhorse Assn., Box 200, Amarillo, Texas.

Q. *What sort of a shoe did the Westerners use for preventing horses from slipping on icy roads?*

A. In the East, an easily changeable shoe called the Crampon had been invented by M. Anelli, London, England. But this shoe never found favor in the West. Westerners preferred an iron, nailed-on horseshoe, one that had sharp cleats and was strong enough to assure a wagon horse or driving horse secure footing on ice, in mud, or on slick rock. The Western saddle horse was shod with a smaller and lighter shoe, yet one that gave long service on rocky trails. The draft animals that hauled freight (yes, even the oxen) were kept shod the year round, or so long as they were being hitched and driven. The ox shoe, as most understand, was two half-shoes, one for each toe (the cloven hoof) of the ox. The shod ox foot resembled a pair of parentheses, ( ).

Q. *Can you name a truly good horse trainer who is living today? Where has he worked and demonstrated his abilities?*

A. Glen Randall, a former Nebraskan, has trained some of the great horses seen in many motion picture films such as Ben Hur. He also trained horses used by film star, Roy Rogers. Randall worked in Hollywood for years.

Q. *What was the practice of "soring" horses?*

A. To make a saddlehorse or harness horse pick up its feet higher, some trainers practiced "soring." This was the act of damaging with a hot iron, a tight shoe, or a knife the tender part of the animal's foot (the frog) so that the animal put its feet down gingerly and picked them up quickly because of the pain. Western cattlemen and cowboys never used such methods, and though it was frequently practiced by trainers of blooded horses, many horsemen frowned upon it as they did upon the "docking" of an animal's tail.

Q. *What did the term "gillflirted" mean when speaking of a mare?*

A. The term is from archaic Scottish, meaning a "giddy or shameless girl." The word was used in the Old West to describe the condition when the partition between the anus and the exterior of the mare's vagina had been torn and damaged by accident or through intemperate breeding as a filly.

Q. *Was "creasing," that is, shooting a horse slightly across the top of the neck, used widely in the Old West to capture wild horses?*

A. This is, I believe, almost an old wives' tale. The only persons who ever wrote of "creasing" an animal to capture him were those who also told of killing the animal accidentally in their effort to "crease" him. "Creasing" would require better marksmanship than the ordinary horse hunter possessed. Further, there were many better ways of capturing, without injuring, wild horses.

Q. *How early in history did man use the horse in his wars?*

A. Man's inhumanity toward his fellow man is no greater than has been his exploitation of the innocent equine. The earliest records of the Egyptian pharaohs and the kings of Babylonia and Assyria show their soldiers in chariots pulled by horses. It would be safe to say that the horse, man's greatest servant, has died by the tens of thousands, perhaps even millions, in wars of conquest since the dawn of history.

CATTLE

Q. *How large were the biggest wild cattle of (a) the Texas longhorn breed, (b) the wild cattle of ancient Europe?*

A. We know from eyewitness accounts of the old cattle days and from present stock in the wildlife preserves at Cache,

Oklahoma, and Valentine, Nebraska, that the longhorns may often weigh upwards of 1700 pounds and stand fifteen to sixteen hands in height at the withers. The European wild cattle of antiquity, the massive Aurochs (extinct by 1627 A.D.), stood six and seven feet in height and probably exceeded a ton in weight, according to scholars. Some Central Asian Aurochs are still preserved in the Soviet Union.

Q. *How many longhorn cattle passed through Abilene, Kansas, in 1867? In 1868?*

A. In 1867, 35,000 head; in 1868, 75,000 head, according to Joseph McCoy, the man who established the original shipping yards at Abilene in 1866-67. During the peak years which followed, hundreds of thousands of head were being shipped from that point to the packing houses, bringing on the great banking boom and packing industry at Kansas City. (McCoy authored *Historic Sketches of the Cattle Trade of the West and Southwest*, published 1874.)

Q. *Is it true that the cattle on the trail drives would sometimes stampede without reason?*

A. Longhorns had their own reasons for running. Like most wild animals, they ran out of fear—when they were surprised, they just "lit out." Often cowboys didn't ever learn what had scared them. Charles M. Russell, the cowboy artist, once had a herd start running when wild geese flew up from the prairie ahead of them. He wrote, "Nobody knows why they run but the cows, an' they won't tell."

Q. *What is the origin of the name "maverick" as applied to unbranded cattle?*

A. There are many stories, but the following is the one generally believed by descendants of Samuel A. Maverick, a lawyer who was living at Decrow's Point on Matagorda Bay (Texas) in 1845. A neighbor, Tilton, owed Maverick a fee—about $1,200—and could not pay. So he turned 400 head of longhorn cattle over to pay the debt. The cattle were supposed to be watched over by a Negro family, but they failed to brand the calves annually, so the offspring matured without marks. Eleven years afterward, Maverick sold the herd to Toutant Beauregard, "range count," that is, whatever number of animals the buyer could find. Beauregard, while no doubt getting his money's worth, failed to find all the "unbranded" cattle he had expected, for neighbors had been slapping their own brands on the likely twos and threes they found unbranded. Thus, any unbranded calf or cow or steer was called a "maverick," and this name followed cattle from Texas to Montana.

Q. *What is a* cabestro?

A. That is Spanish for a bell ox. One ox was usually belled when a herd grazed together to make it convenient for the herder to find them easily when in brush or trees.

Q. *Were Texas longhorns mean? Would they attack people afoot?*

A. "Curious" would be a better word than "mean." Artist Frank Reaugh told of setting up his easel many times on the Texas prairie land, only to have the wild cattle come so close they would flee in distress when he made a sudden movement. The cows, with calves, would fight anyone offering them danger. And the bulls, guarding the herds, had to be watched. Most Texas cowboys liked to be on a horse when around the cattle. However, the cattle were not mean.

Q. *What is a leppy?*

A. A motherless calf, the same as a "doughie" (dōgie), or "poddy."

Q. *Where may I get information on buying longhorn cattle today? Also buffalo?*

A. Write to Refuge Mangager, Fort Niobrara National Wildlife Refuge, Hidden Timber Route, Valentine, Nebraska. As the herds need to be thinned annually, some animals become available for fanciers who wish to raise longhorns.

Q. *An old trail driver told me that steers had pals, just like men have and that they trailed together, bedded down in the same area, and acted like close friends. Is this true?*

A. Yes, two or three old cowmen, among them Old John Kirkpatrick, Cody, Wyoming, have told me the same. I have observed the same among steers in feed lots. Animals apparently share some of the same instincts as humans, among them being the love of friends.

Q. *On the cattle range, what type of animal did they term a "sleeper"?*

A. A sleeper was a calf that had been earmarked but was not branded. At roundup time, the only way ownership could be determined was to watch which cow the calf followed.

Frequently it was observed that the earmark on the calf did not match the brand ownership shown on the cow. This meant someone had earmarked the calf with the hope that the calf would be passed over during the round-up and that, later, the thief could put his own brand on the calf which bore his earmark.

Q. *When the sixteen Western states, in 1880, had only about thirty-five percent of the cattle in the United States, why then do we think of the Old West as "cattle country."*

A. Probably because of the methods used in handling cattle in large herds; because of the open range system in handling them; because of the great spring and fall roundups, where cowboys, mounted on swift horses, were given a romantic and adventurous role. The farms of the East had nothing to match such color and excitement.

Q. *Were calves ever force-fed from their mothers on the range? How was it done?*

A. Yes, when calves are born out of season and arrive in cold weather, they become chilled and cannot get on their feet to nurse standing. Cowboys learn to rope the cow, throw her gently, and bring the calf to her to nurse.

Q. *Why did cattle "mill" at times while crossing rivers?*

A. Cattle, when scared, turn their heads toward the center of the herd for safety. This causes them to jam up tight together and get into a milling motion. It was most difficult for riders to break up these milling patterns, once they had become well established among the frightened animals. Often many head died by drowning before the mill was opened up and the animals turned toward the river bank again.

Q. *Why did Texas cowmen call the little calves "doggies"?*

A. The pronunciation of this word as used by Western cattlemen is "doughgies," rather than "doggies." It is my personal belief that the dialect of Texas gave us this variant pronunciation and spelling. The term usually used in the Southwest is leppies, meaning little orphan calves. This latter name may have come from the Mexican *vaqueros* who referred to poor children who ran the streets half-naked as *leperos*, or "leppies."

Q. *What was an "estray" on the cattle range?*

A. The word was used more after the free-range days had passed. It referred to an animal such as a horse or cow that had strayed from its home and was taken up and held for its owner by another. The stray animals were usually advertised in the local newspapers in columns titled "Estrays."

Q. *What was a "freemartin," as referred to by cowmen?*

A. Occasionally an infertile, or imperfectly sexed, female calf is born as part of a twin male-female combination. Such a heifer is called a freemartin.

Q. *Where did the expression "Holy Cow!" come from?*

A. The term no doubt derives from the fact that in India the cow *is* a holy animal, according to their religious views, and is treated with great respect and dignity.

Q. *Explain how they "flank," or wrestle down, a calf before they brand it.*

A. When the calf is dragged to the branding fire by the roper and his horse, a cowboy grabs it by the scruff of the neck with his left hand and reaches over its back and grabs it by the flank with his right. Using both knees as a fulcrum for leverage, he quickly flops the calf onto the ground on its side. The flanker will usually throw the calf from the *opposite side* to which they will brand it, thus bringing it down for the iron man to affix the brand. (Or they simply turn the calf over while on the ground, if the wrong side is up, for brands are carried by different ranchers on different sides.) A second man grabs one hind leg and places his foot behind the calf's other hock to hold down the rear end. Some flankers grab the rope on the neck or hind legs, and when the calf is down, quickly loosen the rope and toss it off.

Q. *Beef prices are so high now. Are we producing as many cattle as we did ten years ago, say, in 1970?*

A. Latest figures show an increase in production from 1960 to 1975, then a falling-off in production through 1978. All cattle on farms exceeded 132 million in 1972. This figure dropped to just over 116 million in 1978 *(Statistical Abstracts of U.S., 1979).*

Q. *What does it cost to keep a cow for a year on a Western ranch?*

A. It would depend on the area, northern range or southern, and the type of care given the animal. From $100 to $150 in these inflated (1981) times would be an educated guess. About $60 to $80 in normal times.

Q. *What are the productive, calf-bearing years of the average Western range cow?*

A. Most females start reproducing at age three. Ranchers usually cull their old cows at ten years of age, depending on market conditions. Over the nation, about eighty percent of the females calve annually; twenty percent fail to reproduce.

Q. *Who introduced the Aberdeen-Angus breed of cattle to the U.S.?*

A. George Grant, a native of Banffshire, Scotland, brought the first bulls of this breed to Victoria, Kansas, in 1873. By 1876 the Aberdeen-Angus of both sexes had been introduced into Canada by Professor Brown of Ontario Agricultural College. Black Angus cattle are good keepers and good foragers. They bring sturdy calves with small heads which permit easier delivery from the mothers. The beef is tasty and the animals are quiet and easily handled on range or farm. For all these reasons, Black Angus soon became popular with U.S. and Canadian ranchers.

Q. *When was the Hereford crossed with the longhorn breed?*

A. The Herefords first reached America in 1817 when Henry Clay of Kentucky imported two cows and a bull. They gained favor rapidly and by the 1870s the breed had reached Texas. Some were crossed with longhorns. The result was a robust animal, but with the passing of open range conditions, a better breed of beef animal, "with less hoof and horn," was desired. Breeders turned away from the longhorn to Whiteface Herefords, Angus, and shorthorns. Today the Hereford is the most popular on Western ranges, outnumbering all other breeds combined. The longhorn is, of course, now only maintained in wildlife refuges, along with the buffalo, and on a few ranches.

Q. *What is the gestation (pregnancy) period of (a) the cow; (b) the mare; (c) the rabbit; (d) the ewe?*

A. The cow has a gestation period of 281 days (average) but limits of 210 days to 353 days. The mare, 336 days, with a limit of 264 to 420 days. The rabbit, 31 days with limits of 30 to 35 days; the ewe (sheep), 151 days, with limits of 135 to 160 days.

Q. *What is meant by the expression, "The cattle sulled on us"?*

A. Old cowboys used the expression as we would use "balk,"

meaning to stop and refuse to move. Cattle often sulled at rivers, or crossing old trails, or places where they were afraid to walk, as in lowlands where danger of bogging presented itself.

Q. *What single book was most influential in getting cattlemen interested in the trans-Missouri country as range land for their cattle herds?*

A. There were several influential publications of the post-Civil War years, but no doubt Dr. Hiram Latham's *Trans-Missouri Stock Raising*, subtitled "The Pasture Lands of North America," published in Omaha in 1871, inspired most of the early bankers and cattlemen to attempt ranching enterprises in the Western range country. In Latham's work was a letter over the signature of Alexander Majors of the late firm of Majors, Russell, and Waddell explaining how cattle could be winter-ranged anywhere and make a fine gain in weight. This, stated Majors, had been his personal experience in wintering his work oxen over a period of twenty years on the Plains. Another testimonial by John Iliff, a Denver rancher and butchershop operator, lent credence to this belief. The great blizzards of the 1880s lay ahead, and until ranchers had experienced this full fury of nature on the Great Plains, the idea that cattle needed no extra food or winter shelter prevailed.

SHEEP

Q. *Here in the East, we think of Wyoming as cattle country, but I am told there are more sheep than cattle in the state.*

A. According to the 1980 *Statistical Abstract of U.S.*, Wyoming has 1,105,000 sheep; 1,300,000 cattle.

Q. *Do you believe that a* weed *killed those 1,200 sheep near the nerve-gas testing place in Utah a few years ago?*

A. There *is* a weed on the Western ranges called *halogeton* which is poisonous to hungry sheep. If they gorge on this weed, they die, for the weed has the effect of withdrawing the calcium from their bodies. The U.S. Army recently admitted that the death of the first 5,000 sheep *was* from the nerve-gas it was testing. However, these latter deaths of sheep did *not* occur in that same proximity to the testing area.

Q *I know, comparing sheep to cattle, that the ewe is the
cow, the lamb the calf, and the ram the bull, or male. But
what is a "wether?"*

A. In your analogy the wether is the steer, a male sheep castrated before reaching maturity.

Q. *How can I tell a sheep from a goat?*

A. Though related distantly, the sheep is a stockier animal,
generally with a heavier coat of white wool and not bearded on the chin as are male goats. While the horns of the
goat are quite distinctive, the horns in old male sheep
are generally flatter, and laterally coiled and flattened.

Q. *Were sheep ever trailed like cattle were in the Old West?*

A. Yes. Sheep have been trailed to and from California from
Midwestern states. Edward N. Wentworth in some of his
excellent pamphlets has described these long drives in
some detail, using the drover's journals to clarify dates
and places. As early as 1540 the Spaniard, Coronado,
crossed into what is today the state of Arizona with 500
head of cattle and several hundred head of sheep and
goats. No doubt many of the sheep accompanied his
expedition as far as the great bend of the Arkansas River
but apparently were used up for food, for there is no evidence that the animals survived and proliferated on the
Great Plains.

Q. *When was the sheep industry started in California?*

A. Father Junipero Serra, with Portola's overland expedition,
reached the Bay of San Diego in July 1769. He is reported
to have brought 400 head of livestock with him and to
have taught the Indians how to care for the cattle and
sheep. The animals increased greatly, and, by the year
1800, California was estimated to have 74,000 cattle,
24,000 horses, and 88,000 head of sheep. At the time the
Spanish missions were at their zenith, it is estimated some
321,000 sheep were in existence.

Q. *Were the range fights between cattlemen and sheepmen as
vicious as they have been reported?*

A. Yes, there was much disputing about range land between
the two parties. Sheep ate the grass down to the roots,
thereby depriving the cattle and horses of food. Race
hatred entered into the matter, too, for many of the early
sheepmen on the Southwestern frontier were Mexicans.
While the government range was free to all, the cattlemen

seemed to feel they held first rights to it, even in instances where the Mexican owners had preceded them.

BUFFALO

Q. *Are the buffalo now increasing in the nation?*

A. Commercial growers of buffalo make that claim. However, there are said to be but 15,000 of the animals in the country, and 10,000 are owned by commercial interests that are offering the animals for sale for human consumption. (Total U.S.-Canada buffalo population is estimated at 30,000.) So it would appear that again, the plight of the American Bison is something to be concerned with, and the Great Plains animal's future is insecure. We should again think of giving the buffalo the utmost in protection and not be guided too much by statistics from those who still prey upon this species for a profit.

Q. *Fifty or more years ago a thriving herd of buffalo roamed free on a large island in Great Salt Lake, Utah. What happened to them?*

A. That herd was introduced to Antelope Island in 1892, a herd of seventeen cows and bulls, taken there on an old-time cattle boat. The herd increased in a few years to about 500 head. Today, about sixty head may be observed near the state park boundary fence. The herd is privately owned and on private property.

Q. *What did buffalo meat cost on the Great Plains in the 1860s?*

A. *The Wyandotte* (Kan.) *Gazette* reported that "buffalo sandwiches at one dollar apiece" were sold to travelers in December, 1867. Actually, one could have all the buffalo meat one wanted simply by killing the animal and butchering it. But first a buffalo had to be shot and that was not the easiest thing to do.

Q. *What was the weight of an average, mature buffalo bull?*

A. About a ton (2,000 lbs.). The mature cow would weigh just a little more than half of that.

Q. *Is there any proof that prehistoric Indians used a technique of driving buffalo off cliffs to kill them during their hunts?*

A. In northwestern Colorado, in 1978 or 1979, a site was located that is proving to be such a place. It is on the ranch of Charles Frasca, northwest of the Pawnee Pass, west of Sterling, Colorado. So far the bones of at least 100 head of buffalo have been uncovered at the site, and members of the Smithsonian team are still at work there unravelling this mystery of the past. The buffalo are of the prehistoric type, from an era 9,000 years past. The mass of bones lies at the base of a deep arroyo, where the buffalo were driven from the height and then systematically slain and their meat appropriated. Though Frasca, the ranch owner, had known of the bones since 1936, he was unaware of the significance of the find. The bones are twenty-five to thirty percent larger than those of the present buffalo, and with greater horns. Eden spear points have also been found in the bones, indicating that not all the animals died from the fall over the cliff.

Q. *What did the Indians call buffalo chips?*

A. Some called them after the French name *bois de vache.* In each Indian tongue there was no doubt a name for them.

Q. *Could a Spanish or Mexican matador kill a buffalo in fair fight?*

A. The evidence is all against it. A buffalo beat several fighting bulls at El Paso in fair contest, battering the bulls until they were dizzy. Bob Yoakum, a Pierre, South Dakota, saloonkeeper, sponsored this event in January, 1907. He offered to bet $1,000 cash that the bull could beat any matador, but officials wouldn't permit the fight to take place. Nor is there any record that any matador offered to fight the buffalo! The buffalo's heavy skin armor on the neck and the shoulder alone would probably turn any sword thrust a matador might make. (A bullfighter would aim his sword point to such a high spot in an effort to reach downward toward the heart.) A "fair fight" precluded all the preliminaries that take place in the bull rings of Mexico and Spain, where the neck muscles of the bull are partially paralyzed by the *banderillos* before the matador steps into the ring. A half-paralyzed and tortured Spanish bull is one thing; an angered and fit, ready-to-fight American buffalo is another.

Q. *Why is the American bison called a "buffalo?" We know that the carabao, or water buffalo, properly deserves that name.*

A. The English language is a growing tongue. Though improperly called "buffalo" by early explorers, the animal is now called by both names through popular usage.

Incidentally, Buffalo, New York, was not named after the buffalo, but after the French name given the stream, "beautiful flow," our present-day Niagara River.)

Q. *Is a buffalo tongue a different color than the cow's tongue?*

A. The cow tongue is white; the buffalo tongue black. People who have tasted both say the buffalo tongue is better.

Q. *Of buffalo killed on the southern Plains during the most active of the hunting years, 1872-74, what proportion were killed by the Indians?*

A. It has been estimated that white hide hunters slew 3,698,730 buffalo to the possible 150,000 taken and used by Indians, both for their own use and trade.

Q. *I read where an old check blank found in a Dodge City drug store showed that "Brick" Bond killed more than 6,000 buffalo in sixty days, November 1, 1874, to January 1, 1875. Is this possible?*

A. The author once asked Bob Rath, son of Charles Rath, the old Dodge City hide buyer and freighter, about these figures, for they seemed incredible. Bob also thought the figures had been stretched out of all proportion to the facts, for this would have meant that Bond killed "stands" of *more than 100 animals each day!* This does not match up to accurate, first-hand reports and figures found in the old diaries of such experienced buffalo hunters as Henry H. Raymond, Wright Mooar, Tom Nixon, Jim Cator, and others. Nixon's was thought to have been the largest single kill in one "stand," 204 buffalo. Jim Cator estimated he had killed 16,000 buffalo over four years. A "kill" of more than 100 animals in a stand was a rare bit of luck and skill. Frank Collinson and Vic Smith are two men remembered for having performed this feat. While Brick Bond was an experienced hunter, the figures attributed to him were not set down or known by him, and he never made such a claim for himself.

Q. *Why were there no laws to protect the buffalo?*

A. In 1875 both Colorado and Kansas passed legislation concerning buffalo slaughter for hides only. But it was too late. The vast southern herd had already been effectively destroyed. The Texas legislature, that year, was also considering a statute to protect the remaining buffalo. But Gen. Phil Sheridan appeared before a joint assembly at Austin and discouraged such legislation. He took the position that it would help to subdue the Plains Indians to kill off their food supply. The previous year a bill was pigeonholed by President U.S. Grant, after having been ratified by Congress. By the time men with an interest in saving the buffalo came along, such as Charles Goodnight and Charles J. (Buffalo) Jones, only a few animals remained. These were ultimately confined in zoos, parks, and refuges.

Q. *Could a rattlesnake kill a buffalo?*

A. Charles J. (Buffalo) Jones thought not. He wrote: "While domestic cattle are stricken down by the deadly venom of the rattlesnake, the buffalo receives the snake's long fangs in its long hair and wool which sheathe the buffalo's head and legs, and [the buffalo] trample the serpents into the earth with their sharp hooves." I once saw a buffalo cow with a calf at her side strike out with *both front feet*, and leave a snake twisting in its death throes. (Whether it was a rattler or not, I wasn't able to observe. The cow was plainly on the prod, so I kept the high fence between us!)

Q. *What was the total number of buffalo slaughtered on the Great Plains?*

A. Col. Richard Dodge estimated the number of hides shipped from the Western states in 1872-74 to be 1,378,359 on the Santa Fe Railroad alone! However, buffalo were being slaughtered in 1868-69 and 1870-71, though perhaps not in such great numbers. So great was the demand for hides that by 1884-85 the species was threatened with extinction. An estimated four million head of the big animals was said to be grazing between Fort Larned and Fort Zarah in the late 1860s. Since that entire area was subjected to the hide slaughter, all the buffalo died under the rifles. By 1889 there was said to be only 541 buffalo left in the United States. Since there were estimated to be 60,000,000 buffalo on the continent in 1492, when Christopher Columbus came to the islands of the Caribbean, we can judge that in a period of 500 years, that was the total of buffalo destroyed by the white man, chiefly for their hides, and by the American Indians who used the entire carcass for food, lodging, and clothing. Buffalo hides were used for the heavy factory belts that drove the steam machines of the early Industrial Revolution, as well as for fur coats and robes for the populace.

WILD ANIMALS

Q. *Why are bighorn sheep considered such a hunter's delight?*

A. Because of their rarity. They are becoming so scarce that so-called conservationists, like one California taxidermist, have led hunting parties into forbidden areas (California has outlawed bighorn hunting, as have many states) for fees as high as $3,000 a sheep! The bighorn's beauty and his elusiveness have made him a target for every idiot who owns a rifle and has no understanding of what an "endangered species" means. Many of the illegal hunters of bighorns are millionaires. *Perhaps a fine of a few hundred dollars is no obstacle to them.* A prison term might stop the slaughter.

Q. *What has caused the threat of extinction to the bighorn?*

A. The bighorn sheep has two natural enemies: wolves and man. Since the wolves have been practically exterminated already by man, the bighorns had a chance to live and thrive in number. But that was denied them when game laws failed to give them adequate protection until recently. It is estimated that two million bighorns ranged the West before the white man arrived. Today, there are less than 15,000 desert and mountain bighorns left. There are perhaps 20,000 to 30,000 Dall and stone sheep left in Canada and Alaska. If something is not done to protect all of them, they too will be exterminated by so-called sportsmen who pursue them in helicopters, airplanes, and snowmobiles. With their normal environment being occupied by man, this is truly an endangered species.

Q. *Does a doe (female deer) ever have antlers?*

A. Strangely enough, they do. An old Colorado guide and hunter told me he had seen this phenomenon twice, one doe wearing eight-inch antlers, the second with a six-inch pair. Since he saw but two in his life, they must indeed be rare.

Q. *What is the difference between animals' horns and animals' antlers?*

A. A deer has antlers. Antelope and cattle have horns. The skull adornments called horns are usually possessed by both male and female as permanent features, being composed of bony projections from the animal's skull. The horns are covered with a hard substance known as keratin. Antlers, which are pure bone, are shed annually. (Normally only the male deer possess them; however, as stated

above, there are rare instances of females with antlers.)
Horns, on the other hand, are not shed.

Q. *What is the best way to hang up a deer for skinning?*

A. Most hunters slit the skin between tendon and hock and thrust a stout limb across, then hang the animal by hind legs, head down. But I have been told by guides that this is wrong, that it's better to make a tripod and hang the deer by the head. This keeps the head clear of blood and offal—important if you're planning to save it.

Q. *How many deer are killed on highways by cars in the U.S.?*

A. I have never seen national statistics on this. The state of Nebraska provided these figures a few years ago: 1,120 in one year; 1,112 in another. If the kill figure tops 1,000 in one state, the death rate must be considerable over the nation—as high or higher than the human death figure on highways.

Q. *I shot my first deer in Maine last year, cleaned it, and brought it straight home in a pickup truck. It was a fine buck, but the foulest tasting meat I ever tried to eat. What happened?*

A. If the meat hadn't spoiled over a matter of days, you may have cut into the musk glands, found between the hocks and hooves of the deer. That taints the meat, for you often get the musk on your hands or skinning knife while working with the animal. These glands are directly below the hock, have no hair on them, and are leathery stiff. The best thing to do is cut off the deer legs at the hocks and watch out for those glands! Failure to clean and bleed the animal promptly can also cause taint.

Q. *I shot a nice buck at rutting time. The meat tasted sour. What should I have done?*

A. **First, I feel there should be no hunting in the rutting season. Leave the animals to reproduce their kind, and we'll all have better hunting in the future.** The buck's testicles should have been immediately, but carefully, removed.

Q. *I have heard that there are places in the West where one may hunt elk without a license and at any time of the year. Is this so?*

A. Yes, there are *private herds* whose owners permit you to come on to their property, and some will even guarantee you an elk. It costs, but you always return home with the game.

Q. *Do elk always travel downhill to find cover when hunted, as my friend, who has trailed them, tells me?*

A. Better not believe it. *Usually* they go *up* a mountain, unless during extremely bad snows and cold weather, for the hunters are coming after them *from below.* Most all game animals will go either direction, or any direction, to avoid danger when they sense or smell it.

Q. *Are bears in the national parks as dangerous as news stories would indicate? Several years ago two girls were reported killed by a bear.*

A. Yes, you can depend on it. A bear is a *wild* animal. Because bears learn to waylay cars in order to beg for food along the highways in Yellowstone and other national parks, tourists come to regard them as tame animals. But bears are temperamental, easily frightened, and will bash in your skull with a blow from one of their great paws as easily as look at you. Never feed them in parks; never try to play with them; stay at least twenty or more yards distant. If a female has cubs, leave her strictly alone. Only fools and tenderfeet feed bears in parks anymore. Ask any park ranger.

Q. *What is the most fantastic bear story you ever heard?*

A. Oddly enough, the strangest I ever heard was the true story of a bear killed by William H. Jackson, the famous photographer, during the Hayden Expedition to explore the Rocky Mountain region of the West. Jackson spied a big silvertip grizzly watching him and Dr. Hayden from over a fallen log. Jackson took aim, fired. The bear never moved, though Jackson knew he had hit him. The two men carefully approached. The bear's head still rested on the tree trunk. When he touched the bear's head with his rifle barrel, the animal fell backward, dead. An examination revealed that Jackson's bullet had penetrated the bear's *left nostril,* leaving no mark, but entering his skull and killing him instantly. Now that's an *unusual* story!

Q. *How dangerous is the cougar to man?*

A. The cougar (called a mountain lion in the West) is actually a rather timid animal, fearful of man and dogs, though, if starving, it will attack either. Classified as a predator, the cougar has been hunted to the point of becoming another endangered species. Almost extinct in the East and Midwest, the cougar ranges in the wild, broken, or mountainous country of the West. Its main food has been deer, now thinned out by hunters. Without man's help and sympathetic attention, this big and beautiful cat will become extinct.

Q. *Are there any true lobo wolves left in the West? Where did they get that name?*

A. The name *lobo* came from the Spanish, meaning wolf; *lobato*, young wolf. The name was applied to many wolves in the West—gray wolves, timber wolves, etc. The true lobo wolf did once range the Rocky Mountains and Great Plains areas from Great Slave Lake in Canada to Mexico and Texas. Its ferocity and danger to the livestock business nearly caused its extermination by ranchers. The true lobo is built somewhat along the lines of a husky dog, as we know them today, and wears a heavy coat of fur with a soft underfur. The lobo is a powerful animal, measuring sometimes nearly six feet from nosetip to tail-tip. Strangely enough some of the few remaining true lobos are maintained at the Lobo Wolf Park near Kane, Pennsylvania. In the ealy 1800s, my mother saw lobos in the Cedar Canyons, near Anselmo, Nebraska, and recounted how they could drag down full-grown cattle, then not touch them, but leave them there to "ripen" a few days before eating them. It was believed that these lobos drifted south with the great blizzards of 1880-81 and 1888, along with the Snowy White Owls that appeared in Nebraska at that time. If any true lobos remain in the West, they are in the wilderness areas in the Rocky Mountains or in the great parks of the national park system. Gray wolves, timber wolves, and coyotes still are seen on the Great Plains and in the foothills of the Rockies.

Q. *How large is the footprint of an ordinary lobo wolf?*

A. About four-and-a-half-inches long. The smaller prairie wolf, or coyote, has a footprint half this size. The prairie swift, or "kit fox," has a print about half that of the coyote.

Q. *What is the correct pronunciation for the word "coyote"?*

A. In the Midwest they say kī′yŏt. In the Southwest, and as used by motion picture people, they say kī yŏt′ee.

Q. *Do coyotes prey on newborn calves to the extent ranchers claim?*

A. Possibly. But it depends on the rancher telling the story. One rancher, Charles H. Greathouse, ranched for years in

New Mexico. When his cows calved, he would find baby calves dead. Their little bodies would be eaten by coyotes. Greathouse started riding herd, day and night. Then he found out why the calves were dying: they were infected with a navel disease, his veterinarian told him. The doctor gave him a quart of iodine and suggested that when the calf came he paint the navel, where the umbilical cord had been severed, with the germ-killer. "After that," Greathouse said, "... I lost no more calves." So it is apparent that the coyote has been blamed, even when the fault is not his own. Naturally, a coyote will feast on a dead calf. But doesn't man, too?

Q. *What makes coyotes yelp so much?*

A. They are communicating.

Q. *Are coyotes as destructive of sheep and cattle as many ranchers testify? What about the many game wardens who also poison them? Will present practices end in the total extermination of all such animals as skunks, badgers, coyotes, and wolves?*

A. No. The normal diet of coyotes consists of rabbits, field mice, and other such small rodents and prairie fowl. The official then heading up the government agency charged with the poisoning of wild animals appeared on a TV news program in 1972. He stated that were it left to him, personally, he would end much of the poisoning program of the so-called predators. True, some control measures are necessary in some few areas, but we now face the prospect of gaining a continent and losing all the wild game on it. There is no excuse for killing all wildlife simply because it is in the interests of sheep-growers and cattlemen. These people use *the public lands* (under the Taylor Grazing Act) and should remain accountable for the welfare of nature's own wildlife while doing so. President Richard Nixon placed a ban on the poisoning of coyotes in 1972, but ranchers have made strenuous efforts to get this law repealed. Greater care in the husbandry of their herds would help ranchers prevent losses of livestock, a great amount of which is wrongly blamed on the coyote. Newborn, young, and sick livestock should be watched over and cared for in responsible fashion to prevent losses.

Q. *A female deer is called a doe. What is a female fox called?*

A. A vixen. The young are called cubs.

Q. *Is the prairie dog of the dog family, or is it a squirrel?*

A. The prairie "dog" is actually one of the marmot family, sort of a cousin to the woodchuck, or groundhog. These creatures are thick-bodied, gnawing and burrowing fellows, with short, bushy tails. They are edible (many pioneer families have had to eat them to survive), but the meat is not particularly palatable.

Q. *What is the significance when prairie dogs meet and seem to kiss? We saw this in the Black Hills last summer at the Prairie Dog Park.*

A. It is their sign of recognition, for males and females alike seem to practice the habit. It has been observed that if one animal from a distant part of the dogtown appears at another part, he is chased away as an intruder. However, if they are from the same part of the town, they "kiss," open-mouthed, heads side-by-side, as a form of recognition and identification.

Q. *Where did the name "prairie dog" originate, and by whom?*

A. In 1742 Louis and Francois Verendrye, in Montana, called the little fellows *petite chien*, or "little dogs." However, it is recorded that Lewis and Clark were the first white men to collect specimens from which a scientific description was made possible. The small barks, or chirping, may have made the Frenchmen think of dogs.

Q. *Do prairie dogs travel far from their burrows?*

A. Their range seems to depend upon availability of forage. If grass roots are scarce, they ramble as far distant as two or three miles in a day. Their usual range, with adequate forage, is a matter of yards from the safety of the burrow. In flood periods they have been known to move several miles from the old town.

Q. *Are the little prairie dogs as destructive as some Western ranchers believe?*

A. It depends. A dogtown requires several acres of grassland to exist. Eventually, because they feed on grass roots in winter, that area will become almost devoid of grass. As the area becomes less productive of grass, the dogtown dwellers work over into the adjacent areas where there is better grass. Now the short-term way of thinking about this is to destroy all the dogs with poison so they cannot do this. However, in the long-term way of looking at it, which more and more soil conservationists and intelligent ranchers are beginning to understand, it is best to permit the dogtowns to survive, so long as they do not get too large. For when they move from one area, they leave it well-aerated from their tunnels, just waiting to catch and store the rainfall. The new grass that seeds and develops there generally comes up *much better* than in the older grassy areas. The U.S. Dept. of Agriculture issued a bulletin that shows how prairie dogs consume Russian thistle (tumble weeds), which is unsuited for either cattle or horses. A dog's stomach was found to contain 20,000 seeds of poisonous knotweed. In one Montana area seventy percent of the animal's feed was poisonous loco weed. In May, the dogs' stomachs contain cutworms to the extent of thirty-five percent of their diet. So the prairie dogs work *for* ranchers, not against them.

Q. *Are there still badgers in the West?*
A. Yes, many of them still live on the Plains and along the watercourses. The badger is most self-sufficient and self-reliant; he can fight off dogs and coyotes. He is a digger with sharp, long claws; he can even fight off an enemy while digging an escape hole! His hide, though pretty, is not particularly valuable, so man does not trap or hunt the badger extensively. He offers little trouble to humans, sometimes living quite close to towns and villages.

Q. *How much damage do badgers inflict on farms and ranches?*
A. Very, very little. A predator, the badger hunts nights for prairie dogs, ground squirrels, mice, and other small rodents and animals. He may occasionally dig into an irrigation canal, but he destroys hundreds of gophers that would do ten times the damage he may do to that same canal. Incidentally, his name comes from the "badge" markings on his European cousin.

Q. *Is the bite of a badger poisonous?*
A. Not usually. But many wild animals are subject to rabies, and any bite should be carefully treated by a physician if possible.

Q. *How long do animals live—for example the horse, dog, cat, etc.?*
A. The horse, 23 years; dog, 14 years; cat, 13 years; elephant, 48 years; rabbit, 6 years; an eagle, 35 years; turtle, 100

years. These are all approximate ages. Many live longer, others die sooner.

Q. *I know the beaver played an important role in the development of the West. Can you tell me a bit about this animal, since I have never seen one?*

A. The beaver has a rich brown pelt, with soft underfur. Its pelt became a trade of the seventeenth, eighteenth, and nineteenth centuries. The pelt was bartered for muskets, blankets, tobacco, knives, and other trade goods throughout the American West and western Canada. Hudson's Bay Company reported that in twenty-four years, three million beaver pelts were sold on the London market alone. The adult animal is about three to four feet in length, weighs thirty to seventy pounds, has a humped back and a rather broad head with mouth containing front teeth designed for cutting down trees and eating bark. Its tail is about a foot in length, flat, and about six inches in width, designed as a prop for holding the animal erect as he gnaws on trees, and an excellent rudder in swimming. He also applies the tail as an alarm system when visitors come to his ponds. The beaver is a great builder of dams, the dams providing him a home .and a place where he may store the logs upon whose bark he will feed during the cold winter months. He has fairly good eyesight, and his lips are so formed that he can chew underwater without getting water in his mouth. There are automatic water-valves on his nose and ears that close when he goes under water, and he can remain submerged for up to fifteen minutes and more. His feet are webbed for swimming, and he is a peaceful, hardworking, and industrious animal, of little danger to anyone. Considering the travail man has put his kind to in the past, the beaver now deserves our help and aid to survive.

Q. *Why does a raccoon wash its food in water before eating?*

A. This animal does not have salivary glands, so prewashing food aids its digestion, according to some who have studied its behavior. It is also possible that the raccoon enjoys clean food and does not like gravel and sand in its teeth!

Q. *Have you ever seen a brown skunk?*

A. No, but a color photo of one was sent to me by the Homer Jeffreys, Pocatello, Idaho. They photographed it along the U.S.-Canada line. Experts report that only about one out of 250,000 of the animals may be brown, with the usual accompanying white stripes.

Q. *Is it true that skunk bite in frontier times always gave the white man rabies but didn't affect the Indians?*

A. The skunk bite, like that of a dog, causes rabies only when the animal is infected with the disease. If a skunk has rabies and bites an Indian, the Indian will suffer the same as a white man.

Q. *What is a prairie gopher?*

A. A small rodent four to five inches in length that lives in burrows on the plains and is harmless. It feeds on grass, seeds, and roots and is colored a dark gray with black stripes down the back.

Q. *Where did the term "varmints" come from?*

A. Probably from the word "vermin." Westerners called many of the predatory animals varmints, usually "varmi'ts."

Q. *What do woodrats use to make nests in places like northern New Mexico, where little but skunkbrush or other shrubs grow?*

A. The rat nests you see that are built up four to five feet in height are usually built of horse pellets (dung). They also use what leaves, grasses, etc., they can find and work them in for winter feed.

Q. *How can kangaroo (desert) rats exist without water?*

A. They don't. The metabolic action of their system takes the moisture from seeds, stems, leaves, or the occasional insect they devour. They also obtain any dew that forms, and their kidneys are so extremely efficient that their urine is reported to be four times as concentrated as that of humans. The rat's system is so constructed that water in the bladder is reabsorbed and used over and over for the body's needs. This is an example of the operation of natural selection, nature selecting only the species that can exist in that particular environment and that can, over periods of time, perfect its physical resources to meet the environmental requirements.

Q. *Where can I buy jackrabbits (preferably Great Plains jacks) for coursing with hounds?*

A. Such black tail jacks (Kansas-Oklahoma) run about sixty dollars a dozen; possibly more today. If six to eight females are included, the price will be even higher, perhaps

$100 a dozen. Check the ads in western and hunting magazines. There are several suppliers of jacks for this purpose.

Q. *How can I tell if the rabbits I hunt and use for food have the disease* tularemia?

A. A veterinarian tells me that they have spots on their livers if infected. The rabbits should be dressed out with gloves on your hands until you know if there is infection in your area. Many other rodents have this disease, and woodchucks, gophers, squirrels, coyotes, foxes, and porcupines have been known to be carriers of it. Even partridge and grouse have carried it. The disease is commonly referred to as rabbit fever, though not restricted to rabbits. It is extremely contagious to humans.

Q. *Is there any animal or bird life in Death Valley?*

A. Yes. Though summer temperatures have been recorded as high as 134.6° F. (as of July 1913), much life persists there. There are twenty-six species of animals, including kit fox, kangaroo rat, and coyote. There are many kinds of reptiles, spiders, and insects. There are 230 species of birds in the Valley! And there are such fish as the little pipfish in Salt Creek. The existence of these birds, reptiles, and fowls is so tenuous, and their survival so threatened, that no human should kill *any* species in that arid land. Nature has the ecology finely balanced there, and the passing of any species might endanger all.

Q. *What species of wildlife are apt to become extinct in the West because of present practices in hunting?*

A. The grizzly bear is losing ground, as well as the mountain lion. Javelinas (wild pigs) are threatened in Arizona. Bighorn sheep and Rocky Mountain goats are threatened as well. Among birds the masked bob white, the whooping crane, the kirtlands warbler, and the peregrine falcon are in danger. It seems the human animal is the greatest predator of all. A few years ago a man told me that he and his brother had taken 1,500 bass out of a *stocked* Colorado lake in one year! You and I paid for the rapaciousness of these two fishermen.

Q. *What do you think about the rapid depletion of wild game over our nation? Can a state like Colorado accommodate 160,000 hunters or more each year? What does the future hold?*

A. First, game and fish departments have been too free in

their issuance of out-of-state permits. One winter in Colorado I spoke with eight elk hunters who had not found a single elk or deer in the mountains. It is my belief that hunting as a pastime will eventually be forbidden by both state and federal law. Why? Because hunting is as outdated in modern civilized life as is the mummification of the dead. In the past, when hunting wild game supplied the family table, it was an economic necessity. Today only the destruction of the remaining species can result.

Q. *Are modern vehicles a threat to wild animals in the back or wilderness areas?*

A. Definitely. Running wild animals such as deer and elk through deep snow has been practiced by many non-hunters, and this will kill wild animals. Snowmobiles, helicopters, jeeps, trucks, airplanes, motorbikes, and skis—coupled with a lack of good sense—invalidate for wildlife its proper place on this earth. Much of the wildlife on the Western scene may soon join the buffalo, unless measures are taken soon. With the passage of legislation to totally outlaw hunting, any overstocking on the ranges and in the wooded areas and mountains could be taken care of by a new government service devoted to scientific thinning of herds, with the meat marketed to the general public through a government meat supply service at prices comparable to other meats. These profits would help defray the costs of control of wildlife and its protection, supplanting the license fees from private hunters once used to support game wardens.

Q. *What is it best to do when you find young animals or fowl lost in the woods without their mothers?*

A. *Leave them alone. Don't touch them!* Leave a bit of food nearby if you have it. Most "abandoned" young animals and birds have mothers who are only temporarily away from them, most likely out searching for food. Do not leave your scent near the young. Nature has a way of "taking care of its own." Do as little as possible to disturb this natural balance.

REPTILES

Q. *How long is a rattlesnake?*

A. The prairie rattler will rarely exceed forty-five inches, less than four feet. But the Texas diamondback will grow up to six feet. Bullsnakes get even bigger, up to seven and eight feet. The latter are not poisonous but are a real pest to chicken raisers for they delight in newborn chicks. My mother once lost a complete setting of fourteen little chicks before she spied the five-foot bullsnake and chopped off its head to rescue the chicks. They were all crushed and dead, of course.

Q. *Is the hog nose snake dangerous?*

A. No, it will not bother humans, and its bite is not poisonous.

Q. *How wide is the range of the prairie rattlesnake?*

A. This species will range a mile or more when hungry, searching for field mice, newly born rabbits, and smaller reptiles. Heat pits in front of its eyes permit it to find its prey, and it detects odors with its forked tongue. Left alone, it will leave other creatures (its natural prey excepted) alone. Disturbed and made to fear, it will strike with its deadly poison.

Q. *I need a rattlesnake band for a hatband. What will one cost? Also, do the number of rattles on a snake determine age?*

A. A western supply house gave me these figures: tanned, $25; untanned, $10. No, there is no connection between age and number of rattles.

Q. *What is the record number of rattles found on a rattlesnake?*

A. I do not know if this is a record-breaker, but it will do until one comes along. While hunting with his father in 1969, Alan Darty, age eleven, Winter Park, Florida, killed a five-foot three-inch rattler that had twenty-three rattles and a button.

Q. *How may one distinguish the "friendly" from the "deadly" type of coral snake?*

A. There is an old rule, given in verse by the old *Boy Scout Handbook* which goes: "Red and black, friend of Jack; Red and Yellow, kill the fellow." But let's change that word *kill* to *watch* the fellow! Many, many harmless snakes, in fact snakes that are *valuable* to man, are killed for no reason whatever. Simply because a snake is a snake is no reason for its death. I lived among rattlesnakes for many years. We killed only those that were near the house and barns. Very few cattle or horses are bitten by rattlers, and most of them survive. If you do not like snakes, stay away from where they live! It's that simple. They, too, have their place in the scheme of things.

Q. *Where does a toad come from?—the sort we see on the prairies of the Midwest and West.*

A. The toad undergoes a metamorphosis (change) from the tadpole you see in backwaters of streams or in freshwater lakes (rain-water). The toad must mature from a tadpole before the small pools of water dry up. Thus, the eggs hatch quickly, within a couple of days. Then the mouth of the coming toad develops in another day or two and the tadpole feeds on small organisms in the pool. The tiny toad soon emerges from this changing creature and begins its life on earth. By this time the tail has been absorbed into the growing body of the toad as food itself. The full-grown toad is then in existence and feeds on insects, worms, and vegetables.

Q. *I once heard an old man who had lived in the West in the 1870s tell that he had seen it "rain frogs." How true is his statement?*

A. I cannot speak for this old gentleman, but I have personally seen such a shower of frogs near Big Springs, Nebraska. They came in a heavy rainstorm one night, and when I saw them falling on the hood of the truck I was driving, I stopped and picked up several from the pavement. They were all alive and started hopping immediately after they lit, showing no injuries whatever. I would estimate that several thousand fell in the length of time I made the observation and over an area of a quarter of a mile. They were small, three-quarters of an inch to an inch-and-a-quarter across, with complete development of legs. Many to whom I have told this fact refused to believe it. But I have read since where a postman, in early times, had such a rainfall of frogs on his top buggy during a rainstorm.

Q. *How do the little land turtles, such as we see crossing the highways in the West, survive the cold winters of the plains?*

A. These are called box turtles. They dig into the sandy earth or into leaf mold in winter. Many occupy holes left by badgers, skunks, and rabbits. They come out of hibernation about April, then, after a period of relative quiet, begin mating in May or June. Eggs are laid from June to July and require a bit more than two months to hatch.

These turtles eat grasshoppers, and they also like vegetation, including poisonous mushrooms. However, the Plains Indians of Kansas and Oklahoma feasted on the turtles without harm and claimed the cooked meat was a delicacy.

FOWL

Q. *Do you feel it is sportsmanlike for hunters to use detailed topographic maps, drawn up by fish and wildlife departments, of the dancing (mating) grounds of the wild grouse and then for hunters to build blinds and go there to shoot the birds?*

A. These so-called sportsmen who make a practice of such "hunting" are no doubt the kind of people who brought forth the expression "shooting fish in a barrel." Fortunately, not many sportsmen stoop to such practices.

Q. *Why does the pheasant population fluctuate so greatly on the central Plains area?*

A. The Michigan Department of Conservation offers some pertinent information on this matter, gained through a study of fourteen of the Midwestern states. Many factors appear involved. Reduction in pheasant population came about because of deteriorating habitat caused by the spread of suburbs, highways, and intensification of agriculture. Clean farming, early and high-speed mowing, herbicide spraying, and fall plowing helped decimate the birds' numbers. Federal programs to keep wildlife cover and feed on the ground are available to farmers and ranchers and should be adopted by them. However, no move should be made to establish bounties on predators, and hunters instead should turn to other game to help the pheasants restock.

Q. *Are the migratory fowls, such as ducks and Canadian geese, undergoing any threat to their survival as a species today?*

A. I certainly think so. To begin with, their nesting areas (marshy lands and swamps) are being taken over by urban residential developments. For example, the Denver Federal Center—a great, sprawling development in a former marsh area—stands today on what was once a nesting and resting place for migratory fowls.

Another example comes from eastern Colorado where there is a great oil development. Around the oil installations are large "sludge pots," small lakes of dirty oil and distillate that, to a bird, appear as clear lakes on which it may rest during migration. The ducks and geese that land there *have been dying by the tens of thousands!* This has been going on since 1969, though the oil companies have been ordered to clean up these miserable bird-traps. Some progress has been made to date, but the sight of the beautiful Canadian geese and Mallard ducks struggling to free themselves from these death pits is tragic. The great oil spills along our seacoasts are equally disastrous to sea birds.

Q. *How long is the tail of the pheasant? I shot one that measured twenty-seven-and-one-half inches. Is that a record?*

A. The Nebraska Game Commission reported one tail that measured thirty-and-five-eighths inches in length. There may be even longer ones than that on record.

Q. *Is the bird called the roadrunner, or chapparel cock, a sacred bird to the Indians?*

A. The roadrunner was a medicine bird to the Comanches and the Cheyennes. Its feathers and skin reportedly had the power to keep evil from the Indian lodge, much as our own ancestors thought the horseshoe did for the sod and log home, if placed over the doorway. The Indians had these feathers on their person when they went in to battle, and they were considered powerful medicine.

Q. *Why is it almost impossible to find anyone who owns an old Indian war-bonnet willing to sell it? Are feathers that expensive?*

A. Even worse than that. It is against the law to traffic in eagle feathers, for the bald eagle is now a protected species. Hunting from airplanes, ranchers and others have destroyed scores of eagles. Curbing sales of their feathers helps protect the birds against such unfair hunting practices and gives them a chance to survive.

Q. *When you mention a group of geese on the ground you call it a "gaggle of geese." What do you call them when they are in flight?*

A. A skein of geese.

Q. *I have heard that the sandhill cranes have a mating dance. What is it like?*

A. The males stand in circles, walk or strut up and down before their beloved. They raise and lower the wings, toss sticks and bits of grass with their bills, bow to the females, and preen before them.

Q. *Of what value is a turkey buzzard, ecologically speaking?*

A. The turkey vulture, it is true, cheats other creatures out of the carrion they feed upon. But they too die, and their bodies are then consumed in the ecological process by the insects, worms, beetles—yes, and even coyotes and small rodents. Nothing is lost in the ecological process, each animal and human creature contributes its body in the final reckoning with nature's inevitable process.

Q. *What was the commonest flying bird of the central prairies?*

A. The meadowlark was most common, as was the curlew. The latter is now quite rare. Perhaps in numbers, the small sparrows now would rank first.

Q. *Where do migrating fowl find water today, say, in western Kansas or Oklahoma?*

A. In normal years, particularly in the wetter years, the Western prairies are dotted with freshwater lakes throughout those regions. Wild animals and fowl assemble around the lakes. In drier years, the great river systems offer water to migratory fowls, for those systems are but a day's flight apart through most of the prairie lands.

Q. *What species of bird is called the "killdeer"?*

A. The killdeer is a plover and is said to inhabit the prairie areas from the Yukon to Peru and Chile. At breeding time in the spring the bird's call sounds like a shrill KILL-DEE, KILL-DEER! It has a beautiful trill at the end. The killdeer makes no nest; the young hatch on the ground in grasses in the lowlands. Soon the young are out hunting insects and bugs like their elders.

Q. *I have heard that the passenger pigeon once numbered in the billions in the U.S. Is it a rare species today?*

A. It truly is *rare*—for it is extinct! The last one died in a zoo in 1914, it is said. Commercial hunting of this lovely bird caused its extinction. It is my belief, after watching the abundant numbers of several species decline in the past fifty years, that other species are direly threatened, such as the curlew, the sandhill crane, and many species of the Pacific birds who are dependent upon the rookeries of the islands and atolls that have been taken over for military purposes by the various nations, several being atom-bombed into total uselessness.

Q. *Do poisons set to kill predatory animals affect bird life?*

A. Yes. Near the Valentine (Nebraska) Fish Hatchery, a flock of six wild turkeys was found dead, poisoned by the pest exterminating company that had been engaged to kill rats at the nearby city dump. The firm used corn, treated with the highly toxic poison "1080," which biologists at the University of Nebraska Veterinary Science Department found in the turkeys' digestive tracts. The killings were "totally unnecessary," according to the same commission, since a poison such as warfarin could have been used on the rats without harm to birdlife. However, such poisons remain in the animal carcasses, and these are often eaten by other animals.

Q. *Does a hawk kill a rattlesnake by picking it up and dropping it from a great height?*

A. No. The hawk is master of the snake right on the ground. The hawk attacks by holding its wings high so that the snake, when it strikes, hits only the tips of the wing feathers. After the snake strikes, the hawk leaps upon it with its talons, pins the reptile to the ground, then tears its head apart with its beak, effectively destroying the snake so it may no longer strike with its venom. Such an attack on a snake by a hawk has been recorded on film; otherwise it might seem incredible that such a relatively light bird could immobilize and destroy a five-foot rattlesnake. Imagine what an eagle would do!

Q. *Was the great snowy owl numerous on the Plains?*

A. No, this beautiful bird appeared only at rare times from its northern home in Canada when severe blizzard conditions seemed to bring them south of the Canadian border into the northern tier of states. My mother saw them in 1882-83 in central Nebraska and again in 1888. They were two feet in height, with a wing spread of sixty inches. They fed on rats, mice, and smaller birds.

INSECTS

Q. *Before the age of modern medicine, how did the Indians treat the stings and bites of blister bugs, red ants, wasps, yellow jackets, and bees?*

A. Working with Sioux Indians while running a potato digger as a youth, I watched them apply the simplest of all remedies to mosquito bites, stings from insects, and scratches. They would simply pick up some fresh earth, spit on it, make a mud poultice, and hold it on the injured place for a few minutes. When stung by a yellow jacket, I tried their remedy. It worked! When possible, they always added a dab of fresh cow manure to the mud-pack.

Q. *Were there honey bees on the plains when the settlers first came West?*

A. No, the honey bee was transported from the Old World. But there were many, many species of native bees. Most of the native bees did not store honey and they were not the social insects that the honey bee is observed to be. They lived solitary lives in their individual nests.

Q. *Who discovered the mosquito to be the carrier of yellow fever (malaria)? Was there much malaria on the frontier?*

A. Dr. Carlos Finlay of Havana, Cuba, in 1881 had assigned this role to the mosquito, *Aedes Aegypti.* However, it took Dr. Walter Reed, with his advanced scientific methods, to establish Dr. Finlay's theory beyond a doubt, in 1898. Dr. William Gorgas later followed up these two men's discoveries with practical control measures. By this time the Western frontier had been settled, malaria or no malaria. But the "ague" and "swamp fever" were always terrible sicknesses to be reckoned with, particularly by frontier families living along turbid river systems and near meandering streams; for where mosquitoes lived, there malaria fever wracked their pioneer settlements with death and sickness, the mosquito never being suspected as the cause.

Q. *How did the pioneers fight off the plague of locusts (grasshoppers) in 1874-75?*

A. The 'hoppers won; all the pioneers could do was attempt to burn them or to drive them temporarily off plants with tree-limb switches. Nothing stopped the grasshoppers, which ate even the horse collars, pitchfork handles, and other places where salty sweat from the animals and humans had soaked into the objects. Cornstalks were consumed down even with the ground and all gardens eaten up.

Q. *How many eggs would a grasshopper lay?*

A. From fifteen to seventy-five, depending on the species.

Q.   *When does a grasshopper start hopping?*
A.   Almost as soon as it is born.
Q.   *How many species of grasshoppers are there?*
A.   Entomologists have identified nearly two hundred in one state alone—Kansas.
Q.   *What causes the great swarms of grasshoppers such as I saw in North Dakota in the early 1930s?*
A.   Several factors are needed to cause the 'hoppers to swarm. Migratory hoppers are solitary creatures; they live alone until they become crowded. Crowding may not occur for many generations, then certain conditions may exist that create millions, billions, of them—a surge in births, a curtailment in deaths. Weather conditions help cause these. If natural enemies fail to thin them out, they swarm and migrate, searching for the solitude they have lost.
Q.   *Why was the scarab beetle (our Western tumblebugs) a sacred object to the Egyptians?*
A.   That we don't know for certain. The dung beetle has been studied, however, and we know that he rolls up a ball of cow or horse dung until he has made a fair-sized ball, sometimes an inch in diameter. Then he digs a hole beneath the ball and lowers it into the ground to feed its young. Dung comprises his total diet, and it is known that the beetle can ingest enough manure in a day to equal his own weight. Perhaps this act of returning dung to the earth, then drawing his own sustenance from the waste, influenced the Egyptians in their respect for this humble creature. Modern man is today learning that recycling of waste materials is the scientific thing to do. If dung can maintain the life of this species of beetle, perhaps, in our new thinking, waste materials will help prevent our own destruction in the ages to come.

Photo courtesy Russ Langford, Golden, Colorado.

Q. *Did Pawnee Bill (Major Gordon Lillie) ever take his wild west show to Europe before affiliating with Buffalo Bill?*

A. Yes. He took his Historical Wild West, Mexican Hippodrome, Indian Museum and Grand Fireworks show to Europe in 1894 to the Fine Arts Exhibit at Antwerp. The above photo shows a portion of his showmen at Church's Inn, in Wales, quaffing ale. Numerically identified are: 1. Pawnee Bill; 2. (?) Wheeland; 3. Tony Esquivel; 4. Tex Williams; 5. Cherokee Bob; 6. Black Heart, Arapahoe Chief; 7. Bronco Billy Irving; 8. (?) Webb; 9. Tom Dumphy; 10. Mexican Charley.

BUSINESS and COMMERCE in the PIONEER WEST

If one were asked to compile a list of the ten best books concerning the American West, somewhere within that listing would be Josiah Gregg's *Commerce of the Prairies, or the Journal of a Santa Fe Trader*, published in two volumes in 1844. The actual *business* of the Old West had been, from the time the fur traders crossed the Rockies and commenced trading with the Indians, the art of *commerce*. In particular there was a great trading of steel and metal goods such as knives and guns for the precious beaver pelts that brought silver and gold at the St. Louis market.

Gregg's visit to Santa Fe in 1831 was a tour made in behalf of his frail health. His health regained, he made four more trips with the Santa Fe traders, serving as a bookkeeper and clerk for their activities, a profession that brought him into closest touch with business practices as they had developed along the old trails to Santa Fe, Chihuahua, and Aguascalientes.

No doubt the questions his friends and neighbors asked upon his return from these trips influenced Gregg to write his famous work. Today, most of the questions asked of Gregg are immaterial to present social and economic activities, yet the old mines of Tombstone, the yellow gold from Montana territory, and the great cattle drives of the 1870s still fascinate all who are interested in finance and commerce.

The business and commerce of pioneer times is, in many instances, still the business and commerce of today.

Q. *Approximately what profit was made by traders who took merchandise down the old Santa Fe Trail from Missouri?*

A. There was an old saying, "Duty on American goods goes one-third to the trader, one-third to the officials, and one-third to the Mexican government." After the duty was paid, traders probably took fifty to seventy-five percent profit, sometimes more. Mexican silver *pesos* were accepted for trade goods and taken to Missouri at a time when our nation was on a very poor paper money standard. This metallic money meant something and helped put Missouri on a sound money basis. This factor alone made many Santa Fe traders rich.

Q. *What type of hand printing press did they have in the days of Horace Greeley when he was advising young men to "Go west"?*

A. Greeley himself learned on the old two-pull Ramage press. The Washington hand-press and other types of platen presses accompanied the wagon trains westward.

Q. *What was the real purpose in organizing the Lewis and Clark Expedition to go up the Missouri River to the West Coast in 1804?*

A. After President Thomas Jefferson made the Louisiana Purchase, paying France $23,313,000, it was necessary to explore this vast domain to see what he had bought. Congress was asked for $2,500 to pay the expedition's expenses. Most of the men of the party were on the U.S. Army payroll, so personnel cost was small. The money was spent mostly for supplies and trade goods.

Q. *How early did trappers search for furs along the Colorado River of the West?*

A. Jim Baird of Missouri went trapping there as early as 1812, looking for beaver. Following his imprisonment in Mexico, he wrote in 1826, "... beaver is the most precious product this territory produces."

Q. *Who was Manuel Lisa and for what was he so famous in the West?*

A. Lisa was a Spaniard who, along with two Frenchmen, Pierre and August Chouteau, organized the Missouri Fur Company. They built Fort Lisa, on which site Omaha, Nebraska, presently stands. He was a guiding spirit in the development of the fur business in the West.

Q. *Did the Hudson Bay Company make any contribution, other than to the fur business, in developing the western portions of Canada and the United States?*

A. Yes, that company also formed the Puget Sound Agricultural Company in 1839. They established two enormously successful farms, one at Cowlitz, in present Lewis County, Washington, which, in 1841, produced 41,000 bushels of wheat, 4,000 of oats, and other crops such as barley, peas, and potatoes. The farm operated until 1854, when armed

American settlers took possession and the British withdrew. Nothing of the Cowlitz farm remains today.

Q. *What caused such a furor of exploration along the West Coast of North America in the early sixteenth century?*

A. It was largely economic in origin. The British Parliament had offered 20,000 pounds sterling for the discovery of a western entrance to a strait around North America. English mariners, the best of their day, had been finding many pelts such as those from the sea otter, during their quest. The furs brought great profits to them in Canton, China. So both trade and exploration boomed simultaneously.

Q. *I am interested in Indian pottery. Where, in the West today, may I see good displays?*

A. The finest Indian pottery may be seen at museums and in private collections in New Mexico, Arizona, Nevada, and California. The Philbrook Art Center, Tulsa, Oklahoma, contains the Clark Field Collection of 600 of the finest examples from Taos, Santa Clara, Santo Domingo, San Juan, Maricopa, and Tesuque pueblos.

Q. *What is the best-selling pottery made by New Mexico Indians?*

A. Probaby the Jemez (pronounced hay'mess). It is richly colored, inexpensive, and thus popular with tourists. Though the pieces break easily because Jemez tends to be poorly fired, the pottery is very attractive.

Q. *I found a Lea & Perrins Worcestershire Sauce bottle along the Santa Fe Trail. Could it be very old?*

A. It could be, for the company's bottles date back to 1823.

Q. *I found a bottle in a dry stream near Virginia City, Nevada, labeled: "Aerated Waters, Cantrell & Cochrane's, Dublin-Belfast." What did it originally contain?*

A. You found a ginger ale bottle that was made in England. Its thick glass withstood carbonation pressure. The bottles were laid on their side when packed, so the cork kept wet and held the contents. The bottles now bring ten to twenty dollars among old bottle collectors.

Q. *Where may I obtain information on how to construct a log cabin or an old fort in authentic Western tradition?*

A. Contact the National Park Service, Washington, D.C. They reconstruct old forts, cabins, and lodges, and may be able to provide you with architectural drawings and other information.

Q. *Was any barbed wire manufactured in Kansas?*

A. Yes, Kansas has had several manufacturers of wire. The earliest were South Western Fence Company, Topeka, 1879, and the Consolidated Barbed Wire Company, Lawrence, 1878.

Q. *What were the early contributing factors to the opening up of the barbed wire business of the West?*

A. The development of the telegraph in the late 1830s is said to have given impetus to the wire industry of that early time. Then the manufacture of hoop skirts, believe it or not, opened up another market for wire in the late 1850s and early 1860s. From that point on, "bobbed wire" fences, and the telephone and power lines crossing the continent took precedence.

Q. *We hear much talk of rescuing the Western ecology. Do you think anything will actually be done to cooperate with nature?*

A. Perhaps a catastrophe of some sort may jar lawmakers and money-makers enough to awaken them to what is transpiring throughout the West. We do not appear to have an economy that can operate within nature's bounds. If all of us were aware of the dangers of pollution, and the extermination of wildlife, it is possible we might forestall our end many centuries. But it will require the concentrated efforts of all of us to halt the damage already done, much less restore the lands and animals.

Q. *Has our farm population shrunk as much as some reports would have us believe?*

A. Possibly even more than we want to believe. In 1920 the farm population comprised 11.6 percent of the nation's total. Today it is approximately 4 percent, and the rural movement into the urban centers is growing. Big industrial firms are entering now into large-scale food production (which, incidentally, provides them a lush tax write off). The small farm is doomed.

Q. *What gold coin was used principally to pay for cattle in the trail-driving days?*

A. Both the Double Eagle (twenty dollars) and the eagle (ten dollars) pieces were used extensively. Weight meant a lot, when trail drivers carried money in saddle bags. A twenty dollar gold piece was twenty times lighter than carrying twenty silver dollars.

Q. *What was the common value of table salt in the old Southwest in prepioneer days, 1825-35?*

A. A dollar a bushel was the retail price at Santa Fe and Taos for the salt freighted northward from the Salt Flats between the Rio Norte and the Pecos rivers.

Q. *How may I learn to shoe horses as a trade?*

A. There are many advertised schools that teach the craft; however, the best way to learn is to practice it. Find a good horseshoer (farrier) and hire out to him with the understanding he will teach you the trade.

Q. *How much would a farmer produce in Civil War days?*

A. In 1863 a farmer produced enough to feed and clothe himself and his family (usually four more persons). Today's farmer must feed and clothe forty-three persons, yet he does it with motorized machinery in half the time spent by the Civil War farmer.

Q. *What was "steam shearing" like in the early sheep country?*

A. The steam plants were shearing sheds using steam power to drive the clippers that sheared the sheep. They were much faster than the hand-driven shears formerly used.

Q. *Mexicans (Chicanos) claim their antecedents were most important to the development of the Southwestern states. What did they do to merit distinction?*

A. First, the North American cowboy learned the basics of his trade from the Mexican *vaqueros.* Second, Francisco Lopez discovered gold near Newhall, California, in 1842, six years before James Marshall's discovery at Sutters Mill. Third, the Mexicans, not the Spaniards, taught the incoming immigrants from the East how to farm under irrigation. Thus, we have the Southwest's basic industries— cattle raising, mining, and farming.

Q. *Who conceived the idea of blasting underground oil formations in the sands, rocks, and gravels to collect the oil so it could be pumped from a well? Can oil from Western shale be satisfactorily collected in this manner?*

A. Col. E.A.L. Roberts, of Mexican War and Civil War service, while watching shells explode in water, thought up the principle to increase oil production and to start it again after it had ceased to flow into the well. On January 2, 1865, he brought six torpedoes to Titusville, Pennsylvania. On January 21, he exploded the first one in the "Ladies Well" there. It was a success, and thereafter nitrogylcerine and other explosives, up to atomic bombs today, have been used to collect the oil in sands and gravels below the surface. The recent atomic tests in Colorado were an adaptation of this old process, attempting to boil the oil from the shale rock formations and gathering it for pumping. It has not been proven entirely feasible because of water shortages and other problems.

Q. *What value is placed on the oil shale lands of the Colorado Plateau? How much oil is locked up there?*

A. Several years ago, the Oil Shale Advisory Board of the U.S. estimated there to be two trillion barrels of oil locked up in these rock formations. More recent estimates even exceed that figure. The U.S. Geological Survey puts the amount of oil at 3.9 trillion barrels.

In the 1940s the U.S. Government erected a pilot plant at Rifle, Colorado, to determine whether or not oil could be successfully extracted from the shale. When this proved possible, further determination was made as to the optimum size of a plant operation that would be economically feasible. The government then stepped aside and offered the U.S. oil companies the opportunity to develop this promising source of oil for the American people. Several oil companies did enter into agreements with the government, made a few half hearted efforts, then abandoned the project. (The big oil companies were focused on cheaper oil to be obtained from the Middle East.) The government continued its research and experiments, continuing to build pilot plants which proved oil could be successfully extracted from the shale. However, years passed by, and no oil came from this rich resource on the Colorado Plateau.

Pulitzer Prize winners Donald Bartlett and James Steele, from the *Philadelphia Inquirer*, spent a year examining the U.S. energy debacle and the failure of the shale oil industry. Their findings, recently published again by the *Chicago Tribune* (December 16, 1980), detail the failure of the nation's oil interests to function effectively.

Since the private oil companies did not develop the resource, the Colorado Plateau shale oil lands might just as easily have been operated through public ownership. It is interesting to note that, had this occurred, by this time the nation would have seen enough income from it to (a) pay off the national debt, (b) pay off the interest on the national debt, (c) put as much gold back into the vaults of Fort Knox as is presently held by the U.S., and (d) make available gasoline at fifty cents per gallon for the next 100 years! Two trillion barrels of oil, figured at the present Middle East oil price of thirty to forty dollars a barrel, represents considerable wealth.

Though the major oil companies continue to dabble in this area, often releasing press reports of grand things to come, it may be a long time before the Colorado-Wyoming-Utah shale oil lands are tapped. Until now the money for research and development has been provided mainly by the American taxpayers, though we have yet to realize any benefit from this great national resource located on public lands.

Q. *Is the U.S. today the largest producer of cattle?*

A. No. United Nations records show that in 1979 India had 181,651,000 head of cattle against the United States' 110,864,000 head. India, of course, is not a competitor in beef production because of their religious scruples against the slaying of the sacred animals.

Q. *What was animal hair used for in industry during early times?*

A. For stuffing mattresses and upholstered furniture; later, when this use declined, the auto industry stuffed car cushions with it. Today, animal hair is used for air-filtering purposes in some types of air-conditioning.

Q. *Who built the Great Smith auto? There is one at the Museum of the Kansas Historical Society.*

A. Dr. Clement Smith of Topeka built it about 1908. H.A. Hackney, great-nephew of Smith's, is reported to have built another vehicle from this design.

Q. *How did they get rennet for cheese-making in early times?*

A. At the old Cheesecake Ranch on the Oregon Trail they would allow a calf to fill its stomach with milk, then butcher the calf, take out its stomach, wash it, and hang it to dry. When dried, it held the rennet. The rennet was then used to curdle the milk.

Q. *I have heard that the first municipally owned packing house started up in Paris, Texas. True?*

A. According to author James Farber, this is true. After a disastrous fire in 1916, the concept of large-scale community enterprises to take up slack in unemployment sprang up there. Their slaughterhouse filled an important need for their people, and it was a "first" for the nation.

Q. *A friend who was in Alaska last year brought back a coin. It reads: "Good for a Dollar– Hemrich Packing Co., Kukak Bay, Alaska." What is its value to collectors?*

A. The coin, or token, is called a Bingle. It has a value up to sixty dollars on the ten dollar Bingles, about thirty-five on the five and one dollar tokens. They were issued because of shortage of legal tender or coin.

Q. *Do screwworms threaten the Western cattle industry today as they did back in the 1880s?*

A. Yes, to some extent. The larvae of the screwworm fly imbed under the animals' skin, forming deep sores which are difficult to treat. Great hope was held out for the use of the sterile screwworm fly as a biological deterrent. However, this approach failed to keep up with the influx of fertile flies. One of the worst recent screwworms infestations occurred in 1968 in the American South and Southwest. The old screwworm must be watched as closely today as in yesteryear.

Q. *Was the custom of work-swapping as common on the Great Plains as in the Kentucky mountain country?*

A. Probably even more so. The lack of a horse, ox, or mule demanded that the settler without an animal trade work for the use of an animal on his own land. The man owning the animals would get several days' work from the other for the use of a team for a day. At a log-raising on the Plains (putting up the heavy ridge-log on a sod house) the neighbors usually came and made a picnic of the day, plus donating man-power and horse-power. Women, too, swapped work at quilting bees and during canning time. Harvest time was a general swap-work period throughout an area.

Q. *Will you give me a brief description of a Western livery and feed barn? I am a writer of "Western stories" and have never seen such.*

A. There were several different designs, however the most common were built in the standard rectangle with a pitch roof. Each had an "office" at one side of the front, near the large sliding doors where the teams entered. The center space to the rear had stalls on each side where from six to twenty teams could be sheltered, depending on the barn's size. A grain bin and tack room for harness and saddles was usually at the rear of the office. There was a large hay mow above, and the hay was forked down to the horses in overhead mangers. Frequently a buggy shed was constructed at one side of the barn. At the rear was a "wagon yard" and an exercise corral with the ever-present manure pile. In the corral was usually a windmill, with the water tank where the animals could water. Freighters and stage teams usually accounted for the establishment's steady income. Cowboys and townspeople also kept their teams and rigs there. The livery barn was a most popular place in the small villages, second only to the town's hotel. There was little theft of horses or equipment from the old-time livery barn.

Q. *When was meat first shipped in refrigerated boxcars?*

A. As early as 1872 refrigerated beef was shipped east from Salina, Kansas. The Marquis de Mores built a packing plant at Medora, North Dakota, in the 1880s; however his plan to use refrigerated cars in which to ship the beef appeared to be a failure and the venture was discontinued. It was not until 1881 that Gustavus F. Swift, with ten new refrigerator cars, proved to American railroad owners (who had fought the idea) that it would profit them to carry dressed beef.

Q. *Has anyone in authority come out against the use of pesticides in the West?*

A. Yes, Nebraska's Game Commission director has said: "The evidence against these chemicals is so overwhelming there is no longer any doubt of the need to end their use." He cited evidence of traces of DDT in the state's fish, which humans consume. Among the killers are Heptachlor, Lindane, Aldrin, Endrin, Dieldrin, and Chlordane. DDT was the worst of the lot.

Q. *Is there danger in re-use of pesticide barrels?*

A. Definitely. At least three cases of poisoning have been reported when boys bathed in a used Parathion barrel. The poison was *not* swallowed; it penetrated through the skin.

Q. *I would like to invest in Canadian land close by my home state, Minnesota. What should I expect to pay for a forty-acre plot, with timber, on or near a lake?*

A. Some forty-acre plots were offered a few months ago in the Rainy River area at $1,000 each. This was a bargain then, and I doubt it could be obtained so cheaply now. The taxes on such land run as low as twenty-five cents per acre. The land is new, but not "primitive," and one should expect to put up improvements on it to realize its full potential as vacation-type property.

Q. *How was it possible for a small, weak nation like the U.S. in the old days to force a big nation like Russia out of California and the West Coast area?*

A. It was not the power of the U.S., but the strength and prestige of Great Britain with whom we, at that time, had treaties, that made the Monroe Doctrine workable. Russia found 54°–40° acceptable as the southern boundary of Russo-America.

Q. *I am interested in homesteading land in the West. What land is available?*

A. There is some poor land available in some Western states; also in Alaska, some fair lands. Write the Bureau of Land Management, Washington, D.C.

Q. *Was there trade between Utah's Mormons and California? What did they exchange?*

A. In November 1847, the Mormons sent an expedition southwest to find a route to California. They brought back cattle, seeds, horses, grain feeds, etc. They paid with money and a few trade items. This opened up a lively exchange between the two states.

Q. *An uncle in Utah has asked me to come live with them and work in a uranium mine. I am unemployed. Would you say this is a good move for me?*

A. No. Stay out of uranium mines, unless you are looking for lung cancer. There are already one hundred uranium miners dead from lung cancer and an Atomic Energy Commission biochemist estimates that out of the few thousand miners engaged in uranium mining, an eventual death toll of a thousand miners will be established. It is known that a more vigorous and expanded research into uranium mining standards must be made by the responsible government officials and by the mining companies before uranium mining will be safe for you or any other prospective miners.

Q. *I am a Michigan man, twenty-four years of age, a factory employee. I want to go West and work in the open, on a ranch. What is the best way to get in touch with an employer?*

A. A want-ad in the *Denver Post*, or a Cheyenne paper, will help. Be certain you can be satisfied with hard work and wages that may seem low to you. Ranching, working with livestock, is hard work. Yet many Westerners find a freedom one cannot find in the confines of an industrial city, and an opportunity to eventually be "one's own man." Be sure you want this. Then strike out!

Q. *Is there a radium cave where one can rid one's self of arthritis?*

A. Several such caves have started up since the uranium boom of the 1950s. One is west of Denver, in the mountains. But it is doubtful if your pains from arthritis will be cured in such a cave. Yet the trip West in the open air may help!

Q. *What is the story behind the construction of the bank at Vernal, Utah?*

A. The trustees of the Bank of Vernal, organized in 1903, decided a few years later to constuct a brick building to house the institution. W.H. Colthorp, the president, discovered it would cost less, by $1.45 a hundredweight, to have the bricks mailed parcel post than to have them freighted in by either train or wagon. Astounded postal officers were soon staring at thousands of bricks, all wrapped in neat bundles of fifty pounds each and addressed to the Bank of Vernal. The bricks traveled from Salt Lake City to Price, Utah, to Mack, Colorado, and on to Vernal, a distance of 407 miles. A new postal regulation resulted: No one may mail more than 200 pounds by parcel post in a single day! But the Vernal bricks were delivered and the bank was soon under construction. It stands there today.

Q. *When did the cattle industry in Montana begin to assume its importance to that state? What brought it about?*

A. The beef industry was important to the state even as early as the mining era, 1865-66. In the year 1865, mining reached its peak ($18,000,000), then began to decline. Many ex-miners (and also the capital from successful mining enterprises) then entered into the cattle business. The state's nutritious grasses assured success. By 1880 the Montana census showed nearly 500,000 head of beef cattle on the range. The influx of settlers and demand in the East for meat made cattle raising a most important industry there.

Q. *How did branding affect the sale of hides?*

A. In 1886, at the Convention of the Tanners Association of America, a series of discussions disclosed that branding caused a loss of $15,000,000 a year to the stockmen of the Great Plains. The *Laramie Boomerang* (Wyoming) estimated that an animal branded on its side was worth two dollars less than an unbranded one. *The Colorado Live Stock Record* stated that a large brand on a good horse would lessen its value by fifty dollars. With the introduction of fenced pastures, branding became less needed and many ranchers with enclosures began to put "hair brands" on their livestock, a mark that burns the hair but not the hide and is used while shipping. Also notching an ear was practiced.

Q. *On a Western tour last summer I was appalled at the smog that hangs over entire mountain valleys in California and in Colorado, not just over the metro areas of large cities. What is being done to correct it?*

A. Cars, trucks, and diesel engines are the real culprits. Industrial wastes contribute a share. The only hope appears to rest with Congressional action creating stiff laws that force auto manufacturers to put smog control units on every vehicle they manufacture.

    Then, if this doesn't stop the pollution, other steps must be readied and taken. There is great danger to forests, grasslands, and to humans from this air pollution.

Q. *What proportion of beef sold in the United States goes into ground beef (hamburgers)?*

A. It is estimated that four billion pounds of beef is annually ground into hamburgers. This is about one-fifth of the total production.

Q. *How many bushels of grain could be threshed in a day using the old steam-engine-separator combination (threshing rig)?*

A. Warren Bomberger, Sargent, Nebraska, who owns a Case engine and separator, says such a rig was capable of threshing about 1,600 bushels of wheat daily. The engine required almost a ton of coal daily to perform this task with a head of 75 pounds of steam pressure. When new, such an engine used a pressure of 150 pounds. Such rigs came into use about 1890 and passed into limbo in the

early 1930s. The separator was pulled from farm to farm
by the engine and did custom threshing. The wheat had
been cut, usually with a binder, and bound into bundles.
These were hauled in the field from the shocks and fed
into the separator. The straw from the operation was left
in stacks, sometimes to be used for livestock bedding and
even feed, but often simply to be burned.

Q. *What caused Buffalo Bill's financial troubles? He had
made more than a million dollars, I understand.*

A. William F. ("Buffalo Bill") Cody made many unfortunate
investments, and he was generous to friends and acquaint-
ances. When the Wild West show business declined in the
early decades of the twentieth century, probably because
of disinterest in Indians and cowboys, Cody was left high
and dry. He had developed his Scout's Rest Ranch at
North Platte, Nebraska, and his TE Ranch, near Cody,
Wyoming, but by 1916 he was working for others (Sells-
Floto Circus). He was old and ill, and his death came in
1917, in Denver. He is buried west of there on beautiful
Lookout Mountain. A Cody museum is at the gravesite,
which is visited by tens of thousands of tourists even
today. Another larger Buffalo Bill museum is at Cody,
Wyoming.

Q. *Are old Gold Stocks or Gold Mine Certificates of any
value?*

A. Yes. Antique dealers buy and sell them, not for their face
value but as mementoes of the gold era in the West.

Q. *Did Death Valley Scotty actually own a gold mine? I
have heard he sold stock in a mine.*

A. Yes, Scotty sold shares in the "Death Valley Scotty Gold
Mining and Developing Company." The capital stock indicated on the certificates was $2.5 million. They bore the
date 1913, but there is no evidence to indicate that Scotty
ever had a mine, other than from his friend and "partner,"
Alfred Johnson, wealthy Chicago insurance man, who put
up the cash for everything Scotty had, including his desert
castle in Death Valley. Scotty's stock certificates showed
Thomas A. Watt as "president" of the company and
L. Smith as secretary. The stock was listed at one dollar a
share and was incorporated under the laws of Arizona.

Q. *Where did our word "dollar," for the old-time silver dollar, originate?*

A. From the German word *Taler*, the name given the first

large-size European silver coin. The Taler was issued as a substitute coin for the gold florin and found immediate success among tradesmen.

Q. *Can you supply a physical description of William S. Body, discoverer of the Body mining district in 1859 and after whom the town of Bodie is named?*

A. The only description of Body (the way his name was spelled) we have ever seen was printed in the *Bodie Free Press*, November 3, 1879, following his death. Body's remains had been exhumed from the mountaintop where they had rested for twenty years and were returned to the town of Bodie for tribute and reburial. The *Free Press* at that time wrote: "The skull, which had been carefully cleaned, [was] polished like a billiard ball. . . ." Body was otherwise described as a man ". . . whose heart was right but who was not always constant." Body had perished in a blizzard about 1859–60.

Q. *Why did the mines at Tombstone, Arizona, quit producing?*

A. The Tombstone mines were gold-silver producers, fifteen percent gold to eighty-five percent silver. They were flooded out when water was struck at depth. The nearby Bisbee and Clifton (Morenci) mines are copper producers, open pit mines that are still active. Other mines in that area, such as the Johnny Pearce Mine at Pearce, Arizona, just ran out of gold ore.

Q. *Whose likeness is the womanly face on the old-time silver dollar such as were minted prior to 1922?*

A. The model was Anna W. Williams of Philadelphia. She was selected in 1878 by the British sculptor George Morgan, who was commissioned to do the design. Morgan thought her profile the most beautiful he had ever seen and no doubt selected it because of its resemblance to the classic Greek profile. Those dollars have since been called the "Morgan Dollar" by numismatists.

Q. *Can you tell me anything about a placer mining area called Cornucopia, near Elko, Nevada?*

A. An 1881 map showed it as northwest of Elko, near the bend of the South Fork of the Owyhee River, about where Deep Creek reservoir is today.

Q. *How was a miner's washboard (to clean clothes) made?*

A. A pine slab was marked off with horizontal lines and then the lines were notched across with saw and pocketknife to emulate the ridges of a manufactured washboard. It was crude but effective, and a few may be seen today in Western museums.

Q. *Where did the old mining town of Silver Plume, Colorado, get its name?*

A. The first ore discovered there was shaped like a feather, hence the odd name.

Q. *How did they get the enormous dredges (some of which are still to be seen) on to the mountains near Breckinridge, Colorado?*

A. The two great scows you see there today were built there on the stream. The machinery came mostly from California and was installed on the boats.

Q. *Is there or is there not a Lost Dutchman Mine in the Superstition Mountains?*

A. I would say it is *most doubtful.* Millions have been spent by experts trying to locate this will-o-the-wisp mine. The Dutchman himself is reported to have said he had no mine there. Almost annually some group or individual claims to have found the Lost Dutchman or the Adams Diggin's. They may have located something, but they never find those two lost ones!

Q. *What size was the largest gold nugget found in the Black Hills of South Dakota?*

A. Potato Creek Johnny, a mining character, was said to have picked up a seven-and-one-half-ounce nugget on Potato Creek. That stream was so-named because miners there were so poor all they could afford to eat was potatoes. Johnny was a diminutive, bearded fellow who often took part later in the "Days of the '76" celebrations held at Deadwood.

Q. *When was gold first discovered in the Columbia River drainage, east of the Cascades?*

A. In 1852, Angus MacDonald, the trader at Fort Colville, reported a gold strike. Other discoveries were made at the mouth of the Pend d'Orielle River about this time. The larger rush to Colville came in 1855.

Q. *What years were the ten dollar gold pieces coined in Oregon, and by whom? What is their value today?*

A. The so-called Beaver Coins of Oregon were minted in 1849. The Oregon Exchange Company made them. Their value today is out of sight—perhaps $5,000 to $7,000, if in fine to uncirculated condition.

Q. *Has the continued pressure for a raise in the gold price had any influence on gold mining and prospecting in the West today?*

A.   Definitely. There is now more activity in the Sierra Nevada Range and in the Rockies than for the past thirty years. The gold price has risen spectacularly, and has had its corrections from $100 an ounce to $800, and back to under $500. Almost every specialist predicts that as the dollar weakens, gold will continue to rise. This, of course, has induced mining companies to open up older mines and to search for new ones. Gold, which could not be profitably mined at $35 and $50 a troy ounce, can make a fine profit at today's prices. Inflation, which appears to be with us for several more years, makes gold more precious. Any flight from the dollar inspires more and more confidence in the yellow metal. Silver, likewise, which is also mined with gold, has also become higher in price.

Photo courtesy Mrs. George Hledik, Roundup, Montana.

Q. *Were the old-time range cowboys as "wild and woolly" as depicted in Western fiction books?*

A. Those range men loved a card game, a drink and friendly companionship as much as our workers and businessmen do today. But they could get together, as Frank (Doc) Hagadone and his Montana pals have done in the photo, and enjoy a card game on a saddleblanket in great comfort and with restraint.

3 CATTLEMEN and COWBOYS

The American Cowboy is still unknown to most Americans, despite the fact that his life, work, and play have been delineated in tens of thousands of stories, books, films, and TV dramas. Unfortunately many of those who write of the cowboy, play him in films, or direct others representing him, really have little firsthand knowledge.

The actual cowboy of the cattle range, those men who lived with their herds and knew no other life, were a breed apart from the heroic figures we fictionalize on the screen or in the "Western" novel. The originals were basically herdsmen, with a loyalty first to the animals they tended, second to the boss who paid them, and last to themselves and their best fortune. Their dress was homespun of linen, cotton, wool, and, of course, leather, plus an assortment of light hardware that was strictly utilitarian in purpose. They smelled of cow and horse dung, and seldom bathed. They wore beards that easily became nests for lice, fleas, or other vermin and provided secure foci of infection for barber's itch. Their underclothes were changed periodically, spring and winter, and were washed when occasion permitted. They also wore the burns and scars from the sun's rays and the blisters from the cold as we today wear our pallid complexions from indoor work throughout the changing seasons. Their eyes, rarely peering through glasses and always seeming to range far out over the open spaces of the prairie lands, developed deep wrinkles at the corners. Their lips, generally closed tight against dust, developed a tight setting that gave them the stern appearance that has been overdeveloped in the characters played by well-known actors on the screen. In sum, one would find nothing romantic or glamorous in the appearance of an old-time genuine cowboy.

It is at a deeper level that one finds the specialness of his character. To those of us who were foaled in the West by fathers who rode after cattle and whose earliest memories include fast "horseback" rides astride the boottops of fond and kindly uncles, the old-time cowboy was no Man of Mystery. He was at any given moment a stern and driving father or a generous and comradely companion. He was loyal to the ranch boss under whom he worked, and equally demanding and expectant when he became a boss or property owner himself.

The cowboy of old has become a symbol, an image. The symbol is a fair-haired, handsome, youthful, well-dressed, well-groomed, guitar-twanging imitation. We like him, we enjoy his adventures.

But we loved the original.

Q. *Was Will James, the author of* Smoky, *and many other cowboy books, actually a working cowboy?*

A. James made his living "ridin' and ropin'" for several years, which is to say he earned the name of "cowboy" honestly. He was a fine wrangler and, like Charles Russell, was deeply interested in portraying honestly the cowboy and wrangler, particularly the Bronc Peeler. It is too bad that in his autobiographical work, *Lone Cowboy*, he falsified his origins, seemingly because of an inner belief that to be a "true westerner" one had to be foaled in the Old West. Though this did not detract from *Lone Cowboy* as a fine book, it did put Will James (a native of Quebec, Canada, whose real name was Joseph-Ernest-Nephtali Dufault) in the defensive position that apparently preyed upon him until his death in September 1942. It was, as wrote his biographer, Anthony Amaral, in *Will James, The Gilt Edged Cowboy*, "... a lie that began with the lightness of a snowflake in James' mind and turned into an avalanche." I recommend Amaral's book to all interested in the *true* Will James.

Q. *What was the first cattle brand registered in Texas?*

A. Richard H. Chisholm's brand was registered at Gonzales, March 4, 1832. It was an HC Bar and is thought to be the earliest. The Texas brand registration law did not become effective until 1838, though the DeLeon brand is said to have been used on the Aransas River (Corpus Christie region) as early as 1806.

Q. *I have heard that Pancho Villa, the Mexican revolutionary, had a complicated brand resembling a "Death's Head." True?*

A. Yes, like many Mexican brands it was a most complicated work and did resemble a human skull.

Q. *What is the "freezing" system of branding animals?*

A. It is termed the *cryogenic technique,* or cryobranding. Wide-faced copper irons are used. They are chilled in dry ice. The hair is then clipped and skin-surface wetted with a solution of ninety-five percent ethyl alcohol before applying the iron. The contact of iron on the skin freezes the cells that produce pigmentation, so the hair falls out and is replaced with *white hair.* The advantages of cryobranding are said to be less hide damage, absence of pain, and a more legible brand that can be read from a distance.

Q. *What brand did Theodore Roosevelt use on the Dakota ranch he owned?*

A. Teddy used two brands: the Maltese Cross, on his Chimney Butte Ranch, ten miles south of Medora, North Dakota, and the Elkhorn Brand on his range, thirty-five miles above Medora on the Little Missouri River.

Q. *Where may I purchase old branding irons?*

A. Most museums in the West have a few to sell, particularly the privately operated museums. You might also make contact with private collectors who deal in Western relics, through Western magazines.

Q. *What was a Swallow Fork brand?*

A. It was a V-shaped cut in a steer's ear, resembling the swallow's tail. Ear-marks were used in conjunction with the regular brands burned on animal's hides.

Q. *What was the Jingle Bob brand?*

A. The jingle bob was an ear mark, rather than a brand, in which the ear was split on the steer and the lower, lesser cut left to dangle. John Chisum used this mark in New Mexico, along with his famous Fence Rail brand, which was a burned brand that extended from the animal's front shoulder on the left side and continued straight back and across the hip. Chisum also used a horseshoe, or U brand.

Q. *It has been said that the XIT brand was the most difficult brand on the range for a rustler to work over or change. Is this true?*

A. No, there were many brands more difficult to change. The late Bob Jones, a ninety-two-year-old cowman of Boulder, Colorado, who ranched in the Neutral Strip

(Oklahoma Panhandle) and in Texas, told me that the most difficult brand of all to change was the Churn Dash Bar brand, its bar resembling the churn dash handle.

Q. *What were the various ear marks called?*

A. They were overslope, underslope, crop, grub, underbit, overbit, swallow fork, and jingle bob.

Q. *What was a dewlap in branding?*

A. A dewlap is an incision made in the loose skin of the brisket, letting a piece three or four inches hang down loose.

Q. *What was a wattle in branding?*

A. A wattle is an incision made, usually on the skin of the neck. The loose piece is wadded back up and tucked into the wound, as to make a lump under the hide when it heals.

Q. *What are the names of some of the most unusual brands that you have seen?*

A. The Scissors, Picket Pin, Round or Rolling Swastika, Two Up and Two Down, Crossed S, Gold Spectacles, Low Key, Crawfish, B Hourglass B, Chain C's, Pollywog Triangle, Buckhorn (this is similar to Teddy Roosevelt's Elkhorn), Flying Blocks, and the Ampersand brand.

Q. *When did the practice of bull grappling, as we see it in Spain and Mexico, start?*

A. Wentworth and Towne in *Cattle & Men* ascribe the practice to about the middle of the Bronze Age, 2500 to 1400 *B.C.*, at the Palace of Minos, legendary king of Crete, at Knossos. The event was then of religious, rather than just sporting, nature and the challengers were *women* as well as men!

Q. *Where was the world's longest fence line built? When?*

A. In Australia, in 1963, at a cost of more than two million dollars. A woven-wire fence was completed to keep out the dingoes (wild dogs) from the sheep herds. This fence is 3,500 miles in length!

Q. *What is the barbed wire called that has a one-eighth inch zig-zag strip of flat metal, then two parallel wires woven in beside it?*

A. From your description I believe you are thinking of what is called "Champion," or "Ricrac," as described in most wire catalogs. Edward M. Crandell patented it in 1879 and 1880.

Q. *Why does the cowboy, or this image we have of him, seem to be an outstanding symbol of pure Americanism?*

A. Professor Hal Bridges, in the *New York Times Book Review*, put it tersely when he said:

> The cowboy seems to be rapidly becoming our chief symbol of Americanism. He stands for a region never alienated from the rest of the nation by Civil War, a region comparatively remote from the European civilization that so strongly influences the East. He is, it appears to me, beginning to eclipse Uncle Sam.

Many Western writers have been trying to establish this point for years—the American Heartland is the vast Mountain-Plains range upon which the American Cowboy played out his role in history.

Q. *Tell me something about the Dakota Old-Time Cowboys Association.*

A. This is the *Tri-State Old Time Cowboys Association* (Nebraska-South Dakota-Wyoming) but it welcomes men who have cowboyed in whatever state. It is a nonprofit group, and membership costs only one dollar. They have more than 1,000 members. Annual social roundups are held at Gordon, Nebraska, in May and August. Write Tri-State Old Time Cowboys Assn., Frank L. O'Rourke, Secty.-Treas., Rt. 1, Chadron, Nebraska, for particulars.

Q. *Is there a school for cowboys somewhere in the West?*

A. Yes, several. One is the Mountain States Ranch School, west of Laramie, Wyoming (Rex Route), on the Little Laramie River. It is on the property of the 91 Ranch. The great need for qualified ranch hands prompted the establishment of the school. They train young men to raise cattle, horses, and crops for profit. Modern, efficient range management and care and breeding of livestock are in the curriculum. The school in the past has accepted a federal grant of aid.

Q. *Who organized the first cattlemen's association in Wyoming?*

A. The Albany County stock growers met on April 15, 1871,

and organized the Wyoming Stock and Wool Grower's Society. Later they changed the name to Wyoming Stock Grazers. Later a group met and formed the present Wyoming Stock Grower's Association in 1872. The earlier organization was then dissolved.

Q. *Was the term "cowpoke," as used by Mari Sandoz in her works, an actual term used to describe cowboys in the early days?*

A. No, that is a late journalese term. Cowboys did refer to themselves as "cowpunchers," this term having arisen out of their loading work at shipping time, "punching" cattle into the stock cars on the railroads.

Q. *Was "Buffalo Vernon," the old rodeo man, the son of James Averill and "Cattle Kate," who were lynched in Wyoming in 1889?*

A. No, there is no evidence to support such a statement. Those who knew Buffalo Vernon, the rodeo star, deny the story. James Averill and Ella Watson (later dubbed "Cattle Kate" by the Bothwell gang who hung them), were never married and had no children. He came to Horsecreek Pasture and filed on a homestead February 24, 1886. Ella came there from Kansas and filed on nearby land March 24, 1888. Both claims were on the range used by A.J. Bothwell. Averill had a small store and Ella worked part-time for him. Bothwell wanted them off the land. Averill stood up against him, terming the cattlemen "land grabbers" in open letters published in the press. Bothwell summoned John Durbin, Tom Sun, R.M. Galbraith, Bob Connor, E. McLain, and another cowhand, and they went to Averill's home and hung the pair. The cattlemen used every effort to defame the injured parties and bring disgrace upon them. But the truth eventually came out. It was a sordid and selfish act on the part of Bothwell.

Q. *Is it true that all cowboys were bowlegged?*

A. No, this is another of the half-truths that Western writers have played up for so long. If riding started at a most tender age and was continued through a lifetime, it might help warp the legs a bit. The thing is that *all cowboys look bowlegged,* since their chaps and pants shape themselves to the contours of the saddle and horse. My legs are straight, and I rode from the age of four years up to twenty. My father rode from age five to thirty-five, and his legs were straight. But yes, to keep the record straight, *some* cowboys *did have bowed legs!*

Q. *Where did the term "ginning cattle" (to worry or excite them) come from? Was it like "chousing the herd?"*

A. One old cowman said the expression came from Texas, and he likened young, rough cowboys in action to the way in which a cotton gin tore up the cotton fibers in extracting the seeds. In handling cattle, or roping calves for the branding fire, a quiet, methodical manner was preferred, for it was possible to get more work done that way than in exciting, "chousing," the herd.

Q. *How was the game called "chicken-pulling" played?*

A. I believe this was originally a Mexican sport where a rooster was buried in the sand, leaving only its well-greased head and neck sticking out. Riders would swoop down on horseback, seize the chicken's head, pulling the bird from the sand. If the head came off, chicken dinner!

Q. *Has there ever been a book about trail driving written by actual Texas trail drivers?*

A. Yes, *The Trail Drivers of Texas* is its title. It is a rare book, but libraries with a top Western selection will have it. Within its pages are hundreds of stories, written by trail men, relating their experiences in the sixties, seventies and eighties, bringing the vast herds up the Texas trails to markets and to the northern ranges. It was originally two volumes; published in a second, revised edition in one volume by Cokesbury Press, Nashville, Tennessee, in 1925.

Q. *Was the antagonism of Kansas settlers to Texas cattlemen, because of the Spanish fever the Texas cattle brought with them, as virulent as Western writers portray it?*

A. Even more so. The tick on the Texas herds (which were immune to fever) caused death among the Kansas settlers' herds. Even the northern cattlemen guarded the trails and eventually had legislation passed to prevent Texas herds passing across their range.

Q. *What and where was the "Comanche Cattle Pool"?*

A. In 1880, ranchers who held cattle in the Cherokee Strip banded together and organized the Cherokee Strip Live Stock Association. One of the cattle "pools," where cattlemen ran their cattle together on the same range, was this Comanche Cattle Pool, branding CP, in the north-

central part of the strip, and running over into Kansas.
The Comanche Pool was organized that year, 1880, by
Jesse Evans, R.W. Phillips, Wylie Payne, and Maj. Andrew
Drum. The pool encompassed 4,000 square miles of good
cattle range and held 84,000 head of cattle. The pool was
broken up in 1886.

Q. *I am a boy, ten years old, with black hair and eyes. My*
brother, who is seventeen, tells me there are not any cow-
boys anymore. Is he right?

A. No, son. Your brother is wrong. Men in the West still
"work cattle," as they call caring for them. The men ride
horses and carry out many of the same tasks the old-time
cowboy worked at. Raising cattle is pretty much the
same, year in and year out. True, the old, free-range days
are gone, and trail driving is no more. But as long as ten-
year-old boys with black hair and black eyes still live and
enjoy reading of cowboys, there will be cowboys. For a
cowboy is a necessary part of a boy's life.

Q. *Is there any record of a woman riding in a cattle stampede?*

A. L.B. Anderson, Sequin, Texas, told of seeing a lady riding
side-saddle, who was swept into a longhorn stampede,
while he was on a trail drive, passing near a small town.
He wrote: "Seeing the cattle gaining, that woman swung
herself *astride* and pulled off a race that beat anything I
ever saw. She outdistanced everything in that herd and
rode away safely." Apparently, to see this distinguished
horsewoman shift from the lady-like sidesaddle position
to the more practical "clothespin position," as polite
women then called it, was really amusing to old cowboy
Anderson.

Q. *How many Negro cowboys were there in the old West?*

A. They were probably in their racial proportion to the
number of whites in the business. One estimate, given by
Durham and Jones in *The Negro Cowboy*, states that
approximately 5,000 Negro cowboys were trail drivers to
the estimated 40,000 white drovers. Almost every other
trail herd had one or two blacks among the crew, either
wrangling the *remuda*, acting as cook, or riding the drag.
Many were considered top hands. However, when the
books and stories were written about trail driving, they
were "fenced out."

Q. *In their book* The Negro Cowboy, *authors Durham and*
Jones imply that there were many thousands of black

cowboys on trail drives. Why havn't we heard more of them in books and stories?

A. The Negro cowboy has been fenced out of his proper place in Western literature, just as the black man has been in many other phases of American life. Fortunately, this exclusion is being rectified somewhat in Western literature today. Many thousands of Negro cowboys rode the Chisholm and Western cattle trails.

Q. *Can you tell me anything about the Negro cowboy, Bones Hooks?*

A. Matthew (Bones) Hooks was a Texas Panhandle cowboy. He came to Clarendon, Texas, in 1886. Bones was a bronc stomper of note, but his name has been established because of his good work for racial peace and his love of children. In Amarillo, Texas, Hooks helped establish the Dogie Club for underprivileged Negro boys. Mr. Hooks died in 1909.

Q. *Who was Bose Ikard?*

A. He was a Negro cowboy employed by Charles Goodnight for several years. Ikard died in 1929. Goodnight erected a monument to him with the legend: "Served with me on the Goodnight-Loving Trail; never shirked a duty or disobeyed an order; rode with me in many stampedes; participated in three engagements with Comanches; splendid behavior."

Q. *What is the story of the Negro cowboy who brought his master's body home from a trail drive?*

A. The black man was George Glenn. He had accompanied his employer and trail boss, R.B. (Bob) Johnson, to Abilene, Kansas, on a trail drive. There, Johnson fell ill and died. The body was placed in a sealed metal casket and temporarily buried at Abilene in July, 1870. The following September, when the herd had been delivered to the northern range, Johnson's body was disinterred, placed on a Studebaker wagon, and Glenn drove the wagon back to Texas. There was no railroad south from Abilene at that time. The road brand of this outfit was the Scissors. Some have said that, in a false bottom of the wagon, more than $50,000 in gold had been hidden away, which George Glenn delivered to the cattle owners whose animals had made up the Scissors herd.

Q. *In your judgment, who was the most interesting Negro cowboy of the Old West?*

A. Many were most interesting—Sam Johnson, Bose Ikard, Willis Peeples, Bill Pickett, George McJunkin, as well as many who were known only as "Nigger John," "Nigger Pete," etc. But for me, Jim Kelly, Print Olive's "bad nigger" represents the best in the black man among white men—maintaining his dignity, his pride in himself and his people, doing his work among other men, and taking his orders and carrying them out to the letter. I wrote what I learned about him in my book *The Ladder of Rivers: The Story of I.P. (Print) Olive*, published in 1962. Jim Kelly never backed down from any other man, black or white. He stayed in Nebraska, after the Olives left, and lived into his seventies. He was buried at Ansley, Nebraska, in 1912, receiving a fine tribute by the editor of the *Custer County Chief*, Broken Bow, Nebraska.

Q. *I have heard that the south Texas brush-poppers were the cream of the old-time ropers. Just how good were they?*

A. Rev. Bruce Roberts of Uvalde, Texas, once related a story of the steer roping at the San Antonio Exposition, in 1902 or 1903. Two teams competed, the Prairie Team against the Pear Eaters. The latter team were brush poppers. They lost, tying nine rough longhorn steers in 9 minutes, 54 and 4/5 seconds. The Prairie Team made it in 9 minutes, 49 and 3/5 seconds. Lou Blackaller of the Pear Eaters made the best individual time, tying three steers in 2 minutes, 29 and 3/5 seconds. That's how good they were! Rodeo time is now faster, but there are no shows today where big, wild, and dangerous Texas longhorns are being dealt with.

Q. *Why did James C. Dahlman, former mayor of Omaha, change his name when he came north with a trail herd from Texas?*

A. It was rumored that Dahlman, whose Texas name was James (Jim) Murray, had had trouble in a gunfight and sought to put time, distance, and a change of personality between himself and the Texas Rangers. Dahlman was Omaha's mayor for twenty years, and was a well-respected man under either name.

Q. *Who was Billy Binder, and what was he known for in the West?*

A. Billy was one of the finest horsebreakers that ever lived. He was with rodeo shows many years. He broke horses

for the British Army and for the U.S. in World War I.
Billy died a few years back at age ninety-four. He was
then living with a son at Southboro, Massachusetts. He
was a well-liked cowboy and had worked and ridden in
the Nebraska Sandhills.

Q. *What happened to Divine, the CY ranch foreman who
helped clean out the Hole-in-the-Wall gang?*

A. R.M. Divine, after about fifteen years in Wyoming, returned to his Missouri home, then later moved to Kansas,
where he died and was buried.

Q. *Where was the Beer Mug ranch?*

A. There may have been several; however, as early as 1880
there was one located about twenty miles northwest of
Medicine Bow, Wyoming. It was owned by Massingale
and Ross. Jim Ross was sheriff of Carbon County, 1884–
1888. The early ranch was a meeting and gathering
ground for roundup crews. The ranch is, I believe, still in
existence and under the same name.

Q. *What was tie-fast roping?*

A. In the early days of "cowhunting" in the brushy mottes
and thickets of Texas, the Mexican *vaqueros* and cowboys left one end of their rope tied to the saddle horn.
This guaranteed them a longhorn, even though the rider
might be swept off his horse in the initial struggle with
the animal. They took this method of roping north with
them during trail driving days. On the grassy plains, in the
north country, however, the cowboys took a wrap of two
or three "dallies," as they called them, around the saddle
horn. Occasionally they lost their rope for a few minutes,
but there was usually some other cowhand there to rope
the animal and rescue it for them. To tie a cow quickly in
the brush, the tie-fast method enabled the rider to get off
fast and get his longhorn under control.

Q. *What area constitutes today's "average ranch" in the
Southwest ranch country of Texas, New Mexico, Arizona?*

A. A recent example: 11,640 acres; 225 head of cattle;
capital investment of $187,000; gross income of $16,264.
This permitted interest at 4.1 percent (pretty low!) on
investment and ended up with a *loss* of $1,537 annually.
It is not a pretty picture, but is perhaps much rosier than
what it will be in future years as inflation continues. But
remember, this is not the large corporate farm-ranch

operation subsidized in the millions by the federal
government. It represents an average, conservative ranch
operation, with a man-wife-family working and striving
to succeed. This is why we have the farm (ranch) dissatis-
faction, and so many small operators quitting their farms
and ranches.

Q. *What do Western cattlemen today pay for grazing cattle
on federal lands?*

A. Just a few years back the rate per animal per year on
Interior Department lands was 44¢ per month; on the
forest lands (where forage is better) the fee was a bit
higher, 60¢ per month. Today the fee (cattle) is $1.51 per
animal per month, and for horses $3.02 per unit per
month. Despite the fact that ranchers graze a cow and a
calf on government lands for a year at much less than it
takes an urban family to feed a small pet dog, they are
complaining about the high fees. It is true that for a
decade or so, up until the first great increase in meat
prices that brought on the meat boycotts, ranchers found
it most difficult to make much money raising beef, the
growers' percentage of the meat dollar being somewhere
in the neighborhood of only 35¢. Continued inflation will
decrease the growers' share.

Q. *Who was the Western character called "Billy the Bear"?*

A. His real name was L.J.F. Yeager (sometimes spelled
Iaeger). He earned this name playing the role of a comic
bear in Buffalo Bill's Wild West Show. Billy was a cowboy
and a plainsman. Once, lost during a roundup and found
crazed in the Nebraska Sand Hills, Billy had to be tied
down in a wagon until he had regained his senses, according to John Bratt, a Nebraska cattleman of the day. Billy
lost both of his feet and some fingers in a bad blizzard in
the hills. He later learned to use a typewriter and was
clerk of the District Court at Chadron, Nebraska, for
several years; later he served as secretary-treasurer for the
Old Time Cowboys Association of Nebraska.

Q. *What is known about Colorado Charley Utter, Wild Bill
Hickok's friend?*

A. Colorado Charley Utter was a miner in the early days of
Colorado gold-silver and was known to residents of many
of the old mining towns, Middle Park, Georgetown, and
Central City. Utter, in 1876, was freighting and running a

stage line from Cheyenne to the Black Hills. Utter was born in New York state, near Niagara Falls, in 1838, according to his biographer, Agnes Wright Spring, in her work *Colorado Charley: Wild Bill's Pard*. His parents moved to Illinois, where Charley grew to young manhood. Charley came west to hunt and trap, and later went into mining and transportation. Utter could have met Wild Bill either in Kansas, when both lived there, or later in Colorado. It is well-known that Utter took care of the burial of Wild Bill and left the famous inscription over the grave, "Wild Bill, J.B. Hickok, killed by assassin Jack McCall in Deadwood, Black Hills, August 2nd, 1876. Pard, we will meet again in the happy hunting ground, to part no more. Goodbye. Colorado Charlie, C.H. Utter."

Q. *To what does the cowboy term "nose paint" refer?*

A. Whiskey.

Q. *What was a McCarty?*

A. A twisted horsehair rope on a hackamore. The rope was about fifteen feet in length and three-eighths of an inch in diameter.

Q. *In an old photo of a cow camp, I saw three iron kettles above the fire with horseshoes hanging on the edges of them. Why the horseshoes?*

A. These were probably used to handle the hot pots while pouring from them, or to hang the pots on a rod over the fire.

Q. *Where was the* first *cattle drive in North America?*

A. One source gives that honor to John Pynchon, a butcher, who drove a herd from Springfield to Boston in 1655. But actually Coronado, the Spaniard, drove a beef herd on his long trek in the search for the Seven Cities of Cibola in 1541! He was first!

Q. *What were the peak trail-driving years, and how many cattle moved up the trails from Texas?*

A. Joseph Nimmo's estimates show the drives starting in 1866 with 260,000 head. (Nimmo was chief of the U.S. Bureau of Statistics and compiler of the *Nimmo Report*, 1885, one of the foremost cattle books.) The years 1867–68 were light years. In 1869 major droving commenced and lasted for the following seventeen years, with 150,000 to 200,000 head and more coming north each year. The heaviest years were 1871, with 600,000 head; and 1873 with 405,000. The drives of the 1880s were averaging 260,000 head per year, ending about 1886. According to Nimmo, 6,000,000 Texas cattle came north from 1866 to 1885. But Nimmo's estimate is smaller than that prepared by George W. Saunders, famous trail driver, and Charles Goodnight. Frank Dobie once described to me how he had heard Saunders and Goodnight deliberate at great length before setting their estimate; to the year 1895, they set the number of cattle coming up the trail as 9,800,000. (As Dobie points out in his *The Longhorns*, these figures on trail cattle were badly garbled by atrocious printing in the famous book *Trail Drivers of Texas*, copyrighted by Saunders in 1924.)

Q. *Were many sheep trailed, as were cattle, from the Pacific states to the Western plains after the Civil War?*

A. Approximately 15,000,000 sheep were trailed out of the Pacific states in the thirty years following the Civil War. Records of these drives are scarce, since photographers and artists were almost nonexistent in that vast region at that early time. (See *Cattle and Men* by C.W. Towne and Edward N. Wentworth, 1955, University of Oklahoma Press.)

Q. *What was the meaning of the term "grubline gossip?"*

A. In the early ranching days, cowboys were laid off during winter months. Since they had no homes of their own, they rode from ranch to ranch, spending a few days or a week here, then a week or so there. This was called "riding the grubline," for the ranch cooks always gave the grubline riders a few free meals. In exchange, the grubline riders reported what news they had heard on their travels, —"grubline gossip". Since there were no newspapers, radio, or TV, "news" of the outside world and of the other ranches was a worthwhile exchange for meals.

Q. *Were such terms as "roundup" and "maverick" applied all over the Western states?*

A. Yes, with variations. A letter, written by a Wyoming cowboy then working the range in Nevada in 1884, and published in the *Caldwell Standard* (Kansas) noted some of these exceptions: "We have no general roundups, but instead of roundups they are called Rot here; and what are called mavericks in Wyoming are [here] called oreannas. Everything goes by a different name out here from what it does in any other country." In the Southwest, the

Spanish terms lent themselves to the usage of the cowboys, a buckeroo being a *vaquero,* and the "doughgie"
calves being *leppies.*

Q. *Where did Col. W.F. Cody (Buffalo Bill) die?*

A. In Denver, at the home of a relative at 2932 Lafayette
Street. His remains were interred on nearby Lookout
Mountain.

Q. *How did the cattle business, such as that on the great
Parker Ranch on Hawaii, get started?*

A. Capt. George Vancouver, English explorer, shipped cattle,
sheep, and other animals from Monterey, Mexico, to the
islands in 1792 and put King Kamehameha into the livestock business.

Q. *What was a "hold up" as applied to the cattle business?*

A. In Arizona the term was used synonymously with roundup. They would find a salt lick where gentle cattle hung
out, then drive the wild cattle to them, making the herd
easy to handle.

Q. *How did cowboys use lampblack to blacken their boots?*

A. They made a thick cream of saddle soap and lampblack
(from sooty lanterns and lamps) with a dash of whiskey
in it to make it smell better. After applying the mixture,
they let it dry, then polished it. At least that's what an
old Open Box A, Montana, cowboy told me.

Q. *My grandfather related an experience on a roundup
where one young cowboy shot another to death for looking in his bedroll for some cartridges without permission.
Why would one man kill another for such a small offence?*

A. In the West "a man's home is his castle." And on the
range, the bedroll was a man's *home,* his only privacy.
Likewise, no man ever "borrowed" another man's horse
when he was absent unless he had a desperate need for it.
Like a foot-soldier's locker or barrack bag, the cowboy's
bedroll was held inviolate. Normally, a man would be
warned first not to do such a thing. There was undoubtedly already bad blood between the two young men your
grandfather mentioned. The shooting was probably the
culmination of other troubles.

Q. *When cowboys spoke of "getting a good draw" in horses,
what was the meaning?*

A. Cowboys usually drew a string of six to eight horses for
their work. If they got good saddle horses, it was a "good
draw." At rodeos, the meaning is quite opposite: the

rodeo rider, to win, must put on a good show, which
means on a horse that really bucks!

Q. *Has any cattleman today attempted to raise cattle in the
old-fashioned manner, without the refinements of scientific land-use, breeding, modern medical care, etc.?*

A. What is certainly an approximation of the old-time
methods of *letting nature do the work* is being attempted
with success by Tom Lasater, a former Texan, ranching
near Matheson in east-central Colorado. He calls his privately developed breed of cattle Beefmaster. Lasater
apparently shares the Darwinian belief of the law of survival of the fittest. He permits his animals the luxury of
"being born, bred, and performance-tested under the
conditions under which they are to be used." His animals
are big, rugged, and fine-tasting beef. He permits his lands
to remain open to all sorts of wildlife—birds, snakes,
prairie dogs and coyotes. Poisons are not used, and his
forage appears particularly flourishing compared with
some other properties in the area.

Q. *Where did the name "cowboy" originate?*

A. The name can be traced back to Ireland as early as 1000
A.D., when the term was used in minstrel songs to describe
mounted cowmen, or herdsmen. The name was in use in
America before the American Revolution, being used as
early as 1655 to identify the herdsmen of John Pynchon,
a meat packer, who had stall-fattened Devon and Durham
cattle trailed over the Old Bay Path from Springfield to
Boston Common, Massachusetts. Among Pynchon's cow
hands were Peter Swink, a giant Negro from Jamaica;
John Stewart, an indentured Scot who also served as the
blacksmith; and John Daley, one of the trail drivers who
may have been imported from Ireland. The name cowboy
came west with the tide of immigration and found its
full usage in the bosques and thickets of Texas and on
the Great Plains.

Q. *Who doctored the men when they fell sick or were injured
on the long Texas trail drives?*

A. I once asked Oliver M. Nelson, then ninety-four and a
former camp cook and cowboy on the old T5 Ranch in
the Cherokee Strip, this identical question. "Oh, they'd
ride in the wagon a few days," Oliver said. "Some were
buried along the trail." With the few simple remedies car-

ried by the camp cook and administered by him, under
the eyes of the trail boss, most of the healthy young men
survived. But it was a very risky place for a truly sick or
badly injured man.

Q. *How long would it take to cut a steer from the herd? Are
rodeo cowboys faster today?*

A. Speed was not the criterion for such work in open range
days. Cowboys had ample time for roundup work, and
top cowboys were trained to never chouse up a herd.
Each man worked the animals away from the herd into
the individual ranch cuts as quietly and quickly as possible. In a Miles City, Montana Territory contest in early
days, each cowboy entrant cut ten head of big steers
from a gathered herd. The best time was four-and-a-half
minutes. The slowest, five minutes, ten seconds. However
time was only one factor in the judging. The smoothest
cutting, the least running, and the easiest manner of the
cutting horse were all considered. Each steer was put at
least twenty feet from the herd. This is good, clean work
on full-grown, range-bred steers. Contesting time is faster
today because the men work on small, quick calves and
cutting for fast time is the essence of the sport.

Q. *What was the name of the doctor who accompanied the
cattlemen when they set out against the "rustlers" in the
Johnson County (Wyoming) Cattle War?*

A. He was Dr. Charles Penrose. He later wrote up his experience of that event in a manuscript called *The Rustler
Business.* The manuscript lay in the archives of the Wyoming Stock Growers Association for many years, was
discovered and published by the late Keith Rider, publisher of the *Douglas Budget* (Wyoming) in 1956.

Q. *I once heard an old cattleman say "the worst horses were
ridden on the circle." What did he mean?*

A. "The circle" was when the cowhands rode out in a big
circling movement on roundups to gather the cattle. This
work required the biggest, toughest, and strongest animals,
those with good wind and staying qualities, for they
worked rough country and were required to do much
running over long periods of time. So the cowmen used
their roughest stock, not wanting to run down the cutting
and roping horses. This expression didn't mean these
horses were no good, for they were generally fine saddle

horses. But they had to be tough to stand the work. It was a job that "took the buck out of the buckers."

Q. *Did cowboys actually ride into towns and "take them over" when they got to drinking?*

A. No, the visitations were usually just the results of cowboy exuberance. Spiced with whiskey, the cowboys usually fired a few shots into the air, not into people. But these crazy pranks did result sometimes in the wounding or killing of innocent citizens. This is not to say that some actual gun battles did not also take place between cowboys and lawmen.

Q. *Why did cowboys sometimes wear those leather cuffs?*

A. They were protection for the wrists, particularly when roping.

Q. *Is there still much cattle rustling in today's West?*

A. *The Cattleman* magazine a few years back reported 113 cases of theft. Of these, 63 cases were tried, bringing about 53 convictions. This type of rustling, usually of young cattle, with a handy pickup truck or horse trailer, is said to be growing, possibly because of the rise in beef prices.

Q. *What are cowboys on the island of Hawaii called?*

A. *Panioles* (pronounced păne͞e-ō-lāys).

Q. *Why and how did Pierre Wibaux, Montana-Dakota cowman, succeed when others failed after the great blizzards of 1886-87?*

A. Wibaux had faith in the cattle business. He was also a widely experienced man. He had refinanced himself in 1886, so was prepared to buy cheap cattle when the other cattlemen wanted out. The staggering losses suffered in the West made this a splendid opportunity under the law of supply and demand. Wibaux, French-born and only in the cattle country three years, had money and savvy. He picked up the remnants of herds for a song.

Q. *Where did the term "Waddie," for cowboy, originate?*

A. From the Spanish-Mexican *Canaderos*, the early cowboys who used *picas*, or pikes, and pushed their herds north of the Rio Grande.

Q. *What single factor, in your judgment, gave to the cowboy the flair that has brought him immortality in Western literature?*

A. His horse—the fact that he was mounted, was mobile.

Q. *When was the largest roundup of cattle in the Dakotas?*

A. Probably the roundup of May-June, 1897. About 50,000 head were said to have been gathered on the Lake and Peno flats, on the north side of the Belle Fourche River. About six square miles of area were used to hold and work the herds. Twenty-eight ranches' chuckwagons were in attendance. This roundup followed one of the really bad winters, so drift cattle from several states were involved. Ed Lemmon and John Anderson led the work.

Q. *Why did cowboys wear their big bandana handkerchief around their necks? Why not carry them in their hip pockets as men do today?*

A. Ever sit on a big, soggy lump of a handkerchief all day in a saddle? That was one of the primary reasons for wearing it around the neck. In hot weather the bandana, or scarf, was used to soak up perspiration on face and neck, and leaving it out in the wind helped it to dry out fast. In cold weather it added warmth. On dusty trail drives it was pulled over nose and mouth to protect the throat. Around the neck it was mighty handy for its first purpose, *nose-wiping!* (Nose *blowing* by most cowboys was done on the ground, the index finger and thumb cutting off the flow). These were reasons my father cited when asked the question many years ago.

Q. *When Buffalo Bill Cody withdrew from his ranching operations on the Dismal River in Nebraska, who bought the Cody-North interests?*

A. John Bratt, of North Platte, Nebraska, later purchased the stock interests and ranch for $75,000, according to Bratt in his book, *Trails of Yesterday.*

Q. *When did the Dakota ranchers first begin to improve their cattle, switching from the longhorn breed?*

A. The change was underway as early as June 1885 when Joe Reynolds, ranching in the Black Hills, disposed of his shorthorn bull calves to neighboring ranchers who wanted to upgrade their herds. George McPherson at that time brought in about 100 Hereford bulls and quickly disposed of them to the ranchers wanting better beef.

Q. *Was Frederick Remington, the Western artist, ever a cattleman? Did Charles Russell, the Western artist, own a ranch?*

A. Remington once owned a sheep ranch in Kansas, but was

never a cattleman. He operated the sheep ranch south of Peabody in 1883–84. Russell worked for several cow outfits in Montana but never bought a ranch or operated one. Both men, however, were respected by ranchers and cowhands alike, for their great art perpetuated the fast-dying memories of the range cattle industry in North America. The art of each has its own great strength and beauty.

Q. *What became of Ed Wright, world's champion cowboy at Cheyenne and my favorite cowboy clown?*

A. "Old Cowboy" Ed Wright died a few years ago at his home in Valley Center, California. Ed was well up in his eighties and had written a book about his life titled *The Representative Old Cowboy– Ed Wright.* His wife, Virginia, survives him.

Q. *Who was the cowboy who was bound naked, like Mazeppa, to the back of a wild mustang and turned out in the plains to die?*

A. I believed this story to be an old folk tale until some research turned up a report printed in the *Democrat-Leader,* Cheyenne, Wyoming, July 18, 1884. The young man's name, according to the news story, was Henry Burbank. He was an Englishman, in partnership with a man named Thomas Wilson. In Wilson's absence, Burbank was playing around with Wilson's pretty wife, was discovered and given this treatment by Wilson and other cowboys. The incident probably occurred in the Nebraska Panhandle, near present Mitchell, Nebraska, not far from the headquarters of the old Ogallala Land and Cattle Company. The mustang was said to have traveled nearly 200 miles in seven days to the Boussaud Ranch, where Burbank was taken off, unconscious. He recovered from this terrible experience, but was not heard from again.

Q. *In any mixed crowd, the term "mountain oysters" brings chuckles from the men and a mystified look on the faces of the ladies. What are mountain oysters?*

A. At roundup time the cowboys often cast the calves' severed testicles into the branding fire, roast them, then peel and eat them. They are, in fact, fine tasting. Testicles of the sheep are called the same.

Q. *What is the name for the fancy Mexican sombrero, their dress hat?*

A. It is referred to as the *Sombrero ala Cravado.*

Q. *When did Nelson Story take his trail herd to Montana from Texas?*

A. Story reached Montana in 1866, in December. He is reported to have constructed corrals and windbreaks near Livingston, where he wintered.

Q. *Can you supply me with a list of cowboys who worked on the Spur Ranch in Texas?*

A. Unfortunately there are too many names to list. Refer to William C. Holden's work *The Spur Ranch,* published in 1934. In the Appendix, Holden lists 900 cowboys who at one time or another rode for the big Spur between 1885 and 1909.

Q. *Are there ranches where cattle are still worked as in the old time roundups?*

A. The genuine old-time "free range" roundup is a thing of the past. However, many ranches still retain many of the practices of gathering cattle, roping calves, and branding them as previously done.

Q. *I have heard that the cattle business gave to Georgians the name of "Crackers." True?*

A. Yes, true. Herdsmen of cattle in Georgia in the early seventeenth century used the long leather poppers on their whips. According to *A History of the Unites States* (Volume 1, p. 78) published by McGraw-Hill, the cracking of these poppers gave the herdsmen, and later all Georgians, this appelation.

Q. *From what open range practice did the "wild cow milking," an event we see in modern rodeos, originate?*

A. The event is actually a gag event, for cowboys seldom milked wild cows on the open range. Instead they used canned milk called "Iron Cow." On rare occasions, under blizzard conditions where the fate of a newborn calf might depend on its mother's milk, a cow is occasionally thrown and force-milked or held to permit the calf to nurse. Rodeo promoters make it even more difficult for the contestants milking a wild cow by making them milk into a beer bottle. The milker must show a recognizable amount of milk to the judges to qualify. The first to show milk wins. Usually, the cowhands get much more milk on themselves than they get into the bottle, and their struggle makes the event a barrel of fun to watch.

Q. *What is your judgment of the character of Nathan (Nate) Champion, the cowboy who was killed at the time of the Johnson County War in Wyoming?*

A. Champion came from a hard-working, honest Williamson County, Texas, family. He trailed cattle north and stayed in Wyoming. There, at that time, the large cattle interests claimed all the range and all wild game and livestock on it, even though it was free U.S. government range. Like many young cowboys, Nate Champion sought to get into the cattle business for himself. So, like others, he branded up a few head of "mavericks," not being too particular whose cows the calves were following. This made him technically a "rustler." But he was also then technically a "cattleman," for that is how many of the old cowmen first got their start in Texas: branding mavericks and driving them north to free range. One thing is certain: Nathan Champion was a brave man who went to his death fighting against great odds. His diary, found on his dead body, proved that. None of the gang who killed him were half the man Champion proved himself to be that day.

Q. *Why did they call the original Rodeo Cowboys Association the "Cowboy Turtles Association?"*

A. The group was at that time breaking away from the idea of a "management" philosophy to that of a "cowboy contestant" organization, peopled by active rodeo contestants. To the more reluctant members who feared the change, the members wanting change said, "A turtle can't get anywhere until it sticks its neck out." This, and perhaps the knowledge that old-time cowhands called their saddles "turtles," helped them make the needed changes.

Q. *The Humane Society of the United States declares that rodeo is a cruel and inhumane sport. What do you think?*

A. Some aspects of rodeo do appear most violent and cruel to the animals, in the eyes of some spectators. For example anyone who has watched calf roping cannot but have some pity for the calf. It is matched against a 1000 to 1200 pound horse with a skilled 150 to 200 pound man riding it, the roper using a hard-twist manila rope. The calf is not *physically* capable of outrunning the swift horse. The roper is so adept with the rope that he rarely misses catching the calf by the neck. When the horse sets down, the rope snaps taut and the calf is jerked to the ground in a sudden stop, after traveling as fast as its legs can travel. *Now, this is not an example of the actual calf roping practiced on the roundup.* There, the calf is usually caught by the hind legs and dragged as gently as possible to the branding fire, every care being taken to handle him as kindly and quietly as possible. So anyone *defending* calf roping as a gentle or humane sport should readily submit himself to the test of putting a rope around his own neck, tying the other end to a post, then running as swiftly as possible to the end of the rope. After the test is made, he may then offer his judgment whether it hurts or threatens to break one's own neck. Like many sports events where an animal cannot speak for itself in its suffering, humans should speak up for them. Wise old Oliver M. Nelson, age ninety-four, who had cowboyed on the old T5 in the Cherokee Strip as a boy, once told me: "Animals have feelings, too. They suffer pain. But they can't speak, or tell us. So we should not inflict needless pain on any animal."

Q. *In what year was the first official record kept of a rodeo? Who was the first bronc riding champion?*

A. Rodeo Association of America, the "management" association, started keeping records in 1929. Winners were named, based on several different rodeos held. Earl Thode, "a good bronc rider and out of a job," as he expressed it, was the first saddle bronc champion, winning that year and again in 1931. Earl had won the existing title also in 1927. In 1936 the rodeo *cowboys* at Boston founded the Turtle Association, predecessor of the present Rodeo Cowboys Association (RCA), organized in 1945 and now the official organization.

Q. *When did rodeos first start?*

A. Rodeos go back many years. As far back as 1874, one is mentioned in a letter from a Santa Fe man, Capt. Mayne Reid, in which he reported "roping and throwing, horse races and whiskey and wine...." Cheyenne had steer riding shows as early as 1872, and later saddle bronc riding. On the earliest cow hunts in Texas in the 1830s and 1840s, men made wagers and had horse races, rode broncs, roped for money prizes, and generally had their contesting skills viewed by others. Today's modern rodeos are in the old Western tradition, with modern gimmicks, clowning, Brahma bull riding, and wild-cow milking thrown in.

Q. *Who was the first president of the cowboys' rodeo group?*

A. The first president of the original Cowboys Turtle Association was Everett Bowman. The group then had sixty-one performer-members. Bowman, a great showman, died in a plane crash in October 1971.

Q. *What did the expression "pulling leather" mean?*

A. This meant holding on to any part of the saddle—strings, horn, or cantle—with the hands. A bronc rider was held in disfavor when he couldn't ride with both hands free, one hand grasping only the reins or hackamore rope. Pulling leather in a contest disqualifies the rider.

Q. *What would it cost to attend a school for rodeo training?*

A. Some instructions are provided through the RCA. There are also college rodeo teams over the country that offer instructions at about $150 a week. Rodeo is now said to be paying out more cash money than golf, and the sport draws truly talented and professional young sportsmen who are willing to lay their lives on the line for the top prize. No other American sport, with the exception of professional boxing, does this.

Q. *What is considered by the professional rodeo cowboys as the most hazardous and toughest event?*

A. Brahma bull riding. Bulldogging, no doubt, is next. Yet each classification has its perils and difficulties. A cowboy who easily sets the worst bronc may find calf-roping entirely out of his area of competency. But generally all cowboys fear the big bulls, for the Brahmas are big, strong, tough, and ofttimes mean. They buck crooked, and their skin is so loose the rider is often riding the skin, not the real bull inside of it.

Q. *I heard a rider say he "drew a blank" at a rodeo. What did that mean?*

A. Probably that the horse he drew to ride was known as a poor or nonbucker and would make him put on a poor show. A rodeo rider doesn't necessarily want to draw the worst of the bucking horses, yet he must draw one that will help him put on a good show for the judges.

Q. *I have seen the expression "seeing daylight." What does it mean?*

A. The expression was used in the Old West to describe a bronc rider when he is shaken loose and about to be thrown. Then you can "see daylight" between his seat and the saddle.

Q. *What, in rodeo, are "cruppers"?*

A. Most tricks that are performed by riders from the hips or rear end of a horse are called "cruppers." There are a wide variety of them.

Q. *What was "hoolihaning"?*

A. The now outlawed practice of falling forward on a steer's horns while bulldogging in such a manner as to throw the animal off balance and knock him down. The practice injured so many animals it was barred from rodeo. The rider must now grasp the animal by his horns, slow him down, and *twist him down* to the earth.

Q. *What is "team roping"?*

A. A steer is roped by two men, one roping the head, the second the rear legs (the heeler). The steer is thrown after both have caught him. He may be stretched, tripped, or tailed down. This is another rodeo event that can be extremely cruel to the animal if great care is not taken by the ropers in "stretching" the animal.

Q. *What is an "association saddle"? What are its dimensions?*

A. This saddle is used for bronc riding and is a saddle that is fair to both man and animal. It has a fourteen-inch fork and the cantle (back) must be no higher than five inches. The seat length is determined by individual choice, each rider selecting what fits him best. The only modification that is permitted is sawing off the horn as a safety factor if one wishes. The saddle is three-quarter double-rigged, with the rear cinch set far back, holding the saddle close to the horse's back. The only adhesive used or permitted is a little resin applied to the underside of the saddle's swells.

Q. *When was the first Frontier Days celebration held at Cheyenne, Wyoming?*

A. 1897.

Q. *What is a "hooey" when cowboys speak of tying a calf?*

A. It's the half-hitch the cowboy uses to secure the rope, or "piggin' string" (as it is called), after it has made its first two turns around the calf's foreleg and two hind legs.

Q. *Name the three greatest ropers of rodeo fame.*

A. Impossible! There have been too many great ones. But for a starter try Everett Bowman, or Toots Mansfield, Andy Jauregui, Troy Fort, Ike Rude, Don McLaughlin, Dean Oliver, Shoat Webster.... Even this list leaves out many of the greatest.

Q. *What do cowboys mean when they say "He scalded his calf?"*

A. Most ropers use the term to mean a calf is thrown too hard when roped and stopped (and most are!). It is really not the desire of the roper to injure the calf, just stop him so he can be thrown quickly by the roper and tied. Of course, a calf half knocked out, or with the wind knocked out of him, doesn't struggle or fight back, so the tendency is to let the calf down *much harder* than ordinary range or roundup-branding-roping would permit. In my judgment, *time* gets too much attention and importance in this event: skill, style, neatness, deserve equal attention to the rough, knock-em-dead type of calf and steer roping often seen at rodeos.

Q. *What is the meaning of the word* rodeo?

A. It is a Spanish term for gathering cattle and horses. The word, and the English "roundup," came to be used synonymously.

Q. *What was the recipe for SOB stew? This was the stew made by roundup cooks.*

A. Range cook Oliver Nelson once told me that when a calf was butchered the cook would toss the tongue, liver, kidneys, sweetbreads, heart and brains into a pot, after chopping them to small bits. Then he added what canned or fresh vegetables he might have at hand—potatoes, tomatoes, onions, etc.—and stew them slowly together most of the night in an iron kettle or dutch oven. "I'd soak a few thin slices of potato for each rider in vinegar and salt overnight; then tell him he was having fresh cucumber at breakfast," Oliver added, grinning.

Q. *What can you tell me about Dan Riordan, Petaluma, California, who was a famous horse breaker?*

A. Dan was a former Canadian Mountie and a Boer War veteran. He trained horses from youth, had been a jockey in Ireland, a British cavalryman, and was a noted trick rider. He continued to train horses on his ranch north of San Francisco, broke a leg at age seventy-eight, and at

eighty-eight "enjoyed a fall from the saddle" when a runaway horse struck the animal he was riding! His life
proved that life didn't begin at forty. His began at seventy!

Q. *What Western book contains the saddest story you have
heard?*

A. It lies between the fictional story of the hanging of "Steve"
in *The Virginian*, and the true story of the shooting death
of Bob Olive which I recounted in the book, *The Ladder
of Rivers*. Both young cowboys were brave, adventurous,
wrong-headed, kindly to friends, and foolish so far as
making enemies was concerned. Both paid with their lives.

Q. *Can you tell me something about the old cowboy, Jack
Potter?*

A. Jack M. Potter was a well-known cowpuncher in the
Texas-Oklahoma-New Mexico area. He was born in Caldwell County, Texas, and made several trips as a trail
driver, beginning in 1880. He was ranch foreman for the
New England Livestock Company at their ranch near
Fort Sumner, New Mexico. Potter is best-remembered for
his humor, much of which he wrote into his booklet,
Cattle Trails of the Old West. His reminiscences of a
return trip, after a northern herd was delivered and he returned "on the cars" to his Texas home, is a one-of-a-kind
story. Jack, with the help of A.C. Loveless of Clayton,
New Mexico, drew an excellent map of the old trails out
of Texas, 1866-95. Potter's story of "Buckshot Roberts,"
the mean steer that flattened him on the prairie and later
arrived on the cars "at Orin Junction, Wyoming, with the
seat of a pair of overalls on his horns," is a classic. On the
freight billing was a notation, "Beware! Vicious steer in
this shipment." Potter's story will match the best stories
of Charles Russell for down-to-earth humor. Crompton
Tate, who lived near Potter for years at Kenton, Oklahoma, said of Potter, "Jack Potter could laugh the maddest
man out of his ugliest mood. And he was one of the finest cowmen, and good sports, I ever knew."

Q. *Billy McGinty, in his book* The Old West, *claimed he saw
500 head of cattle die in a few hours, "dropping in great
bunches, trembling and dying in great numbers." Could
this be true?*

A. It does sound odd, but Dr. W.H. (Soda) Bray, Fowler,
Colorado, old cowboy and veterinarian, said he had seen
cattle die fast from anthrax and pulmonary edema, much

like that but not in such great numbers. Clara Blasingame, author of several books, including *Dakota Cowboy*, once told me she had seen 300 head die quickly after eating a fungus that came up fresh in the spring among the new grass.

Dr. Georgia Arbuckle Fix. Photo courtesy of Estelle C. Laughlin.

Q. *Were there many women doctors in the frontier days in the West?*

A. No, not many. In fact there were too few male doctors. But some women like Dr. Georgia Arbuckle Fix (1852-1918) came west to homestead and practice medicine among their neighbors. Dr. Fix lived near Minatare, later Gering, Nebraska. She played an important role in the cultural development of her region as well as fearlessly accepting the role of Country Doctor for more than 30 years.

4 CULTURE in the FRONTIER WEST

In 1862, in the middle of a great Civil War that had divided the nation and completely upset the social system, Congress enacted into law one of the most important bills that had ever come before it, The Homestead Act. This statute granted 160 acres of free land to every person in the U.S. able to qualify. Though the great flood of pioneers who took advantage of this law did not surge West until the war was over, many who were free to do so took advantage of it at once. By 1870, however, the second tier of states west of the Mississippi River was being rapidly settled. In a twenty-year period, 1870 to 1890, the populations of the Dakotas, Nebraska, Kansas, and Texas had increased ten-, twenty-, and thirty-fold!

The following decades were taken up in the settlement of the lands, the development of the towns and the railroads and the country roads systems, the building of schools and churches, and the increased socialization of the pioneer peoples.

There has been much written of the pioneer, his labors, trials, and difficulties. But little has been said of the cultural accomplishments that accompanied the plow onto the Plains and the pick and shovel into the mining areas of the mountains. Because little timber was available for home building on the Great Plains, the pioneer used the sod of the prairie and the logs from the timbered canyons. Dwelling in these humble quarters and wearing homespun clothes, the pioneer was thought to be "without culture" by his more effete Eastern neighbors. In a society based first and foremost upon survival, there wasn't much emphasis on the more refined aspects of life in the earliest years of the pioneers. As the day-to-day struggle became less exhausting, the pioneer had more time and energy for other pursuits.

With the development of schools, churches, better roads, the pioneers attended dances, socials, literaries, and, in general, enjoyed the culture they had known in their previous homes in Boston, Albany, Cleveland, Philadelphia, and New York. This culture was as normal to them, and as necessary, as the hardwood furniture, the Esty organs and huge walnut and oak pianos, the chinaware and family heirlooms which they had brought with them to the new land.

At first the pioneer depended on subsistence farming. Later small mills sprang up to do grain grinding, and sorghum was made at another mill. Much bartering was done because of the shortage of money for exchange. Under such a regime social contacts became more numerous, new friends were made, new policies that met the exigencies of the new environment were adopted. With these economic and social changes came the gradual evolution of the pioneers' previous culture.

In the new life the pioneer lived, one's word became as law. There were no facilities for drawing up legal contracts every time two or more men "struck a bargain." Not even a handshake was demanded to affirm an agreement. One's word was enough. In a land where everyone worked in sun and dust, the land being the productive machine which all attended, little attention was paid to dress or fashion. Where doctors were "as scarce as hen's teeth," the mother of the household became the prescribing physician. If a family had a small "doctor book" in the home, that family was lucky. Otherwise only home remedies, camphor, castor oil, turpentine, kerosene, and various poultices and plasters made from nature's supply served the sick. Where transportation was slow and irregular, families became self-sufficient, helped only by neighbors. The townsmen of a somewhat distant market center, the lawyers, dentists, musicians, saloonkeepers, teachers, and realtors, were viewed with suspicion by the homesteader, since the pioneer farmer always needed money to trade in those places of business.

But as the towns built up, as commercial trade expanded, and as the subsistence farming changed to a market-crop economy, the suspicion regarding urban people began to disappear, only cropping up on political occasions in mild disputes.

With all these changes came a cultural enrichment of the Western people. For example, when we speak of the ballads set to music, known as "Westerns," these were simple songs developed on the Great Plains and in the mountainous regions of the West. In verse and poetry there is a great mass of material devoted to the West or inspired by those writers who visited the region. On the Plains the square dance and other expressions of terpsichorean art were developed to their highest point;

these same dances have not lost their appeal, some even being recreated in a great musical like *Oklahoma!* In less than a hundred years, the West has contributed lavishly of its proud culture to the nation and its people.

Q. *Has a Pulitzer Prize ever been awarded to an author of a book dealing with American history of the West?*

A. Yes. Frederick Paxson, in 1925, received the award for his *History of the American Frontier.* Bernard DeVoto, in 1948, received the award for his *Across the Wide Missouri.* Paul Horgan has twice received the Pulitzer award: first for his 1955 book, *Great River: The Rio Grande,* and in 1976 for his *Lamy of Santa Fe.* In 1967, William H. Goetzman was awarded the Pulitzer for his *Exploration & Empire: The Explorer and Scientist in the Winning of the American West.* That is five (5) Pulitzer awards for Western history in the past sixty-three years, certainly small recognition for authors of "Western Americana." There have, of course, been many awards for journalists, some of whose work has doubtlessly been concerned with Western history in some aspects.

The biographies of famous men of the West have fared little better, for Western people seem unable to attract their Boswells to their cause. Had men like Buffalo Bill Cody and Charles Goodnight been born in the East, their biographers, J. Evatts Haley and Don Russell, would undoubtedly have been tapped for Pulitzers.

Despite the many magnificent film "Westerns," only a few have received Pulitzer recognition, though the New York Film Critics Award has been issued to films such as *Grapes of Wrath, High Noon,* and the Western-oriented *Around the World in Eighty Days.* But the Western Renaissance still remains undetected by the insular literary and art circles.

The film industry in its fifty-two years of picking prizes for top "Western films" has yet to recognize one of its best moneymakers. Only four actors have won Oscars: 1928-29, Warner Baxter, in *Old Arizona*; 1952, Gary Cooper, in *High Noon*; 1965, Lee Marvin, in *Cat Ballou*; and in 1969, John Wayne, in *True Grit.* This appears a mighty poor reflection upon the critics whose judgments—and biases—make these national selections of cinematic art.

Q. *Can you tell me something of how the old-time literaries were organized and what they produced in entertainment and education for the frontier people?*

A. The pioneer people were a sociable people, and when their sod homes and dugouts were established, their wells dug and their crops planted, they naturally turned toward others for social intercourse. One medium for this was the "literary," generally organized through school-church resources and designed to both entertain and educate. The school teacher, as the educational leader of the community, was usually in the forefront. A constitution and bylaws were framed, a program committee set up, and a name, such as Dry Creek Literary Society, adopted. Programs were based on the theory that "talent is where you find it," and all children and adults were given the opportunity to sing, play a favorite instrument, recite poems, or give "readings" of a literary nature. It was not unusual to hear a cultured young woman recite "Spartacus at the Bridge," followed by one of the burliest and roughest of the farmers who would give "The Curfew Must Not Ring Tonight." Plays were performed, Shakespeare's works being favorites. Debates were encouraged, and particularly in the Populist years they found great favor when regional politics emerged among the "sod busters." Humorous debates, such as "Resolved: That all lawyers are a public nuisance," were enjoyed, particularly if a young lawyer in the community could be enlisted to take the affirmative side of the issue. The literaries brought people together socially and intellectually, and played an important part in the development of a more cultured society.

Q. *Many years ago (1891) my mother recited a verse at a literary, which contained these words: "I have seen her rub and scrub / On the washboard in the tub / While the baby sopped in suds / Rolled and tumbled in the duds / Or was paddling in the pools / With old scissors stuck in spools / etc., etc." What was the name of the poem?*

A. The poem, with many more verses, was Ironquill's "The Washerwoman's Song." Ironquill was the pen name of Capt. Eugene F. Ware, soldier, newspaperman, author.

The poem first appeared in the *Fort Scott Daily Monitor* (Kansas), Jan. 9, 1876. It met with immediate public acceptance in the West and was widely reprinted in other papers. It told the story of a woman, a widow, who "had a friend (Jesus) who would keep her to the end," and whom she sang about as she did her daily work. Ware also wrote the book *The Indian War of 1864*, a quite comprehensive volume of the circumstances and battles of U.S. cavalrymen against the Indians on the Plains, a war in which he personally engaged.

Q. *Can you tell me what poem starts with "On the deck of my bronco / I skim over the prairie?"*

A. This is "Day of the Cowboy," first published in the *Prescott Journal-Miner* (Arizona), 1888. The first stanza reads: "Oh, I am a cowboy of legend and story / Whom the back-East youngsters so admire / The laughter of pilgrims is ever my glory / And few have escaped when they drew my fire."

Q. *Who wrote the verses to "The Cowboy's Shirttail"? Where may I obtain the complete poem?*

A. Bruce Kiskaddon was its author. One of the stanzas goes: "So I've had to explain to folks time and again / Their shirtttails come out 'cause they cain't keep 'em in." Try your public library to get the rest.

Q. *Who was the best-known photographer of cowboys in the West?*

A. The late Erwin E. Smith of Texas left hundreds of fine photos of working cowboys and is possibly the "best-known." Charles Belden of Pitchfork Ranch in Wyoming left scores of accurate photos depicting his own cowboys at work and play. There was the earlier work of such men as R.W. Day and F.M. Steele, who followed the roundups in Kansas and Oklahoma respectively and did beautiful work showing the Great Plains cowboys and their herds. Although both were skilled craftsmen, only remnants of the work of these two seem to have survived. The work of M.C. Ragsdale, of Texas, is also worthy of praise, and of course L.A. Huffman's work has been published in the book *Before Barbed Wire*. There are no doubt many more, such as Solomon D. Butcher's work in Nebraska, but Erwin Smith's work is no doubt the "best-known" of all.

Q. *Where is Solomon D. Butcher, the famous sod house photographer, buried?*

A. His remains rest beside those of his wife in the little Gates, Nebraska, cemetery. His son, Lynn, retired captain of the U.S. Army, who worked with his father for years, lived in Santa Ana, California. Lynn, a few years ago, placed a fine marker on his parents' grave, noting his father's great historical work in pioneer photography. S.D. Butcher's work has gained him recent national recognition.

Q. *Do you have an example of a comic poem about the West that I might use in a term paper?*

A. Here's a brief one, the author George Kress, published in the *Denver Post*:

> We found him on the trail,
> As skinny as a rail,
> And crazy in the head,
> By morning he was dead.
> There wasn't any clue,
> His name nobody knew.
> He's laid by Sue McCann,
> Who never had a man.

Q. *Where can I find a book on the Wild Bunch, Wyoming outlaws?*

A. Several good books on the Cassidy outfit have been published: *Desperate Men*, by J.D. Horan; *The Outlaw Trail*, by Charles Kelly; *The Wild Bunch*, edited by the late Dr. Alan Swallow. Your local library or a book-searching company will find copies for you.

Q. *Joel Moody, Kansas politician-philosopher, in his paper titled "The Science of Evil," states: "The early mind, struggling for truth, seized a fact of nature and dressing it in mythical garb passed it down in song to the world. Yet every explanation has some truth in it. Myths are by no means devoid of truth. They are the harbingers of science; the nursery songs of the world's infancy." How do you relate this statement to Western historical research? Do you agree with Moody?*

A. I note the questioner is a Kansas professor of philosophy at Kansas University. You have given me a tough philosophical nut, but I'll try to crack it for you. Myths, I believe, are like folklore. The myth, or the folklore, is *the husk* that protects the germ or seed of truth as it comes down to us through the centuries. Like a coconut, the great husk carries the seed thousands of miles over troubled waters and through long periods of time until the sea deposits it in its proper seeding ground. There the seed takes root and grows; and a fine tree appears, its roots striking into the earth, but its topmost branches reaching for the heavens. Yes, I agree with Moody. Myths, folklore, old wives' tales, adages, and old sayings often provide historical clues that lead us to rich discoveries. I myself, in research, have used this source of information.

Q. *What was the correct name of Bill Barlow, publisher of* The Douglas Budget, *Douglas, Wyoming, in the 1890s?*

A. He was Merris C. Barrow, throughout the '90s and until his death.

Q. *Why doesn't some Western writer tell about our grand woman clown of North Texas, Mildred Beeson?*

A. Mildred *deserves* a book. Harold Preece was once thinking of doing a book about her. For the fun of it, and without receiving pay, Mildred has made many performances at rodeos that have pleased adults and kids alike for many years. We doff our hats to you, Mildred!

Q. *Who was the artist that painted the picture of the Indian listening to the wires singing on the telephone pole.*

A. Henry F. Farney. The picture's title is *Song of the Talking Wire.* Farney also painted the touching picture of the cavalryman, staked out on the prairie, an Indian guard sitting nearby, while his fate is being determined in the council lodges in the background.

Q. *Has Montana produced any other great painters like Charles M. Russell?*

A. A current favorite is J.K. Ralston of Billings. His eighteen-foot canvas, *After the Battle of the Little Bighorn* is a splendid work, accurately reflecting the great Indian victory over Col. George A. Custer. This is the first work of its kind. Ralston has been a prolific painter for years.

Q. *When did Charles Russell achieve fame as a painter?*

A. His success didn't come quickly. In the 1880s he was just another cowhand, interested in drawing and dabbling with paints. A look at his early water colors fails to reveal the genius he was to become. Through the long, hard process called "doing," Russell eventually perfected his art and his colors. In the 1890s he was doing some of his greatest works. The decade marking the turn of the century caught him at his peak, a recognized master of Western art. His life work consists of more than a thousand paintings.

Q.   *Why didn't Charles M. Russell paint the great historical event to take place in Montana, the Custer Massacre?*

A.   Russell's masterpiece, *Lewis and Clark meeting the Mandan Indians is* the greatest historical event to take place in Montana, and he got it! But in regard to the Battle of the Little Big Horn, it is my personal belief that Russell, loving the Indians, yet sympathizing with the tragedy that befell Custer, never wished to portray the white man against the Indians. Also, Russell seemed to have little interest in the cavalry. His métier was the cowboy. Russell did, however, do one water color that might have portrayed the Custer battle, though it was done from the point of view of the Indians surrounding Custer's men. Another water color of Russell's depicted Curly (White Swan), the Crow scout, "reporting the Custer Massacre." Russell's pen-and-ink *Annihilation of the Fetterman Command* is often mistaken for being a depiction of the demise of the Custer command.

Q.   *In an early reproduction of Charles Russell's* The Wagon Boss, *an empty quart bottle appears near the front feet of the saddle horse. In my large reproduction, purchased fifteen years ago, the bottle does not appear. What happened to it?*

A.   After the painting was completed by Russell and delivered to its purchaser, the purchaser's wife asked that the artist paint out the bottle. This was done to humor her. However, the painting had been reproduced *before* the bottle was painted out. So repros of both kinds are in existence, with and without the offending bottle. It seems insulting to have a great artist's work "censored" in this manner. Yet Russell no doubt needed the money in 1909 more than he did that empty bottle. Fortunately, the purchaser's wife did not see the rattlesnake under the sagebrush nearby, or it, too, might have met the fate of the bottle.

Q.   *Is Fred Harman, who drew Red Ryder, still active in art circles? I know he was born February 9, 1902.*

A.   Fred was doing outstanding oil paintings of Western scenes after he withdrew from the comic strip business.

He was so busy, he wrote that "my paintings are all sold while the paint is wet." With the late George Phippen, Joe Beeler, John Hampton, the late Charlie Dye, and others, Fred helped organize the Cowboy Artists of America. The group is dedicated to preservation of the memory and culture of the Old West. Fred died January 2, 1982.

Q. *Is J.R. Williams, the cartoonist who drew Western characters, still living? Was he ever a rancher?*

A. Mr. Williams died several years ago. He had worked on the McMurray Ranch in the White Sands country of New Mexico as a boy. Later, he developed a fine 4500-acre ranch, the K4, in northern Arizona, on Walnut Creek. Williams was a modest man, likening himself more to his character Soda, than to that of Curly, the more heroic top hand who rode through his cartoon strips for years. Men who knew him well spoke of him as a good cowman and a warm and friendly person. Williams had also served with the U.S. cavalry, and many of his cartoons and paintings reflected this life in the Southwest, as well as his machine shop experiences.

Q. *We are planning on buying a good oil painting for the mantel in our ranch home. Whose work would you favor of contemporary Western artists?*

A. If I were you, I would contact the Cowboy Artists of America and get some of those fine artists to submit photos of the new work they may have available. You will be able to own fine art at a lower cost this way, for if you buy from those who already own the older work, they will charge you higher for it. During these inflationary times, fine art is about the best investment you can make. For example a George Phippen that cost less than $1,000 twenty years ago would sell for twenty times that amount today.

Q. *How may one gain membership in the famous "Westerners" organizations of Kansas City, New York, Denver, Chicago, Los Angeles, etc.?*

A. These *Posses*, or *Corrals*, of Westerners, usually acquire new members through invitations. However, I believe all are open to men of good character who have an interest in the old American West. Such memberships are called "Corresponding Members" and all groups are looking for

new blood. You may write to The Denver Westerners,
attn: R.A. Ronzio, P.O. Box 344, Golden, Colo. 80401
for information.

Q. *Did Mrs. Lew Wallace, the wife of the author of* Ben Hur,
do any writing?

A. Yes, Susan (Elston) Wallace shared her husband's love of
literature, history, and adventure. Her book *The Land of
the Pueblos* was published in 1888. It was a compilation
of articles she had written for *Atlantic Monthly*, after she
had joined her husband in Santa Fe. Wallace had previously published *The Fair God*, 1873, a study of the
Aztecs. Encouraged by its sale, he began *Ben Hur*, a portion of which was written at the Governor's Palace at
Santa Fe. Wallace once described his wife as "a composite
of genius, common-sense and all the best womanly
qualities."

Q. *Has a biography ever been written about Walter Walker,
former publisher of the* Grand Junction Sentinel *(Colorado)?*

A. Alan Pritchard did a piece about Walker in the Denver
Westerners' *Brand Book* of 1961 titled "The Walkers of
Grand Junction." Walter Walker came in for his share of
praise for his far-sighted views, his forty-five-year steward-
ship over the newspaper, *The Sentinel*, and for his courag-
eous stand against the Ku Klux Klan in 1927. "He was a
publisher to emulate," one of his former reporters said
of him. Walker's sister, Estelle Walker Reese, stood beside him in everything he did and urged him always to
take his progressive stands on political and economic
affairs. She was perhaps the biggest influence, next to
Walker himself, on the editorial policies of the newspaper, having taken over and written its editorials from
the time of the death of their father, for the following
thirty-five years, until her retirement in 1957. The
newspaper was then in the hands of Walker's son, the late
Preston Walker, and suffered from an attack of conserva-
tism, though it won many prizes for technical excellency.
The death of Preston, who left no progeny, left the
Sentinel without a Walker at its head. The Walkers are
most deserving of a book, yet none has been written
about them.

Q. *Is it true that Minnehaha, Longfellow's heroine, was a* western *Indian maid?*

A. The name comes from the Teton-Sioux dialect and means Laughing Water, or cascade. The name was first used by Mary H. Eastman in her book *Life and Legends of the Sioux*, published about 1849. Longfellow took the charming name from that work.

Q. *Why have some Western writers failed (like Andy Adams and Gene Rhodes) to capture the imagination of readers while others of much lesser competence (I am thinking of Owen Wister who wrote* The Virginian *and Stuart Lake who wrote* Wyatt Earp*) have met with such great success with their novels?*

A. Walter Prescott Webb, the historian, believed that Adams and Rhodes failed at popularity because of their dedication to truth. They wrote what they knew to be true, not what the Eastern notions about Western ranch life happened to call for. But Rhodes's plots were intricate, and his style hard to follow. Frank Dobie once pointed out that Rhodes "had but one string to his fiddle," which he nevertheless played with great variations. But that string may have gotten out of tune occasionally. Why Adams failed is another thing. His straightforward style, his simplicity, are qualities that Hemingway and Steinbeck struggled to gain for many years and sometimes failed to achieve. Yet Andy Adams's works are almost unknown today. When one re-reads his *Log of a Cowboy*, the reader is *with* the trail herd, living *with* the cowboys, not just reading *about* their life on the Texas trail.

Q. *Where may I find a work about frontier days in the West, published in the French language?*

A. *Histoire du Far West*, by Jean-Louis Rieupeyrout, with Claude Tchou as editor, published in Paris in 1967, may be available at your library. It shows the great interest in our Old West that currently prevails in Europe.

Q. *What is the verse called "The Horse's Petition?"*

A. "Going up hills, whip me not, / Coming down hills, hurry me not, / Of clean, clear water, stint me not, / With bit and rein, jerk me not."

Q. *Were hangings in the Old West actually excuses for a general holiday?*

A. One photo shows Durango, Colorado, where a dual hanging was taking place. Durango, that year, had a population of but a few hundred; yet in the photo you see what appears to be a crowd of thousands. So hangings *did* attract crowds, even if not with a complete holiday spirit. I believe that people wanted to be able to say, "I saw so-and-so hung." At Broken Bow, Nebraska, in the 1890s, when the hanging of Albert Haunstine took place, the crowd tore down the high board fence that had been erected around the scaffold to keep the gruesome scene from the public eyes. There is something sordid in human nature, and it may come to the surface at such times.

Q. *What became of Jack Hoxie, the Western movie star?*

A. Jack died March 27, 1965, at age eighty, following surgery at Elkhart, Kansas. Jack had married Bonnie Showalter of Boise City, Oklahoma, and he passed his later years with her at their ranch in the Oklahoma Panhandle, at Keyes. Hoxie once portrayed Buffalo Bill in *The Last Frontier*.

Q. *What happened to Bronco Billy Anderson, the old film star who played in* The Great Train Robbery?

A. Gilbert A. Anderson died in Hollywood aged eighty-eight, in January, 1971. His widow Molly and a daughter, Maxine, survive him. Born Max Aronson, in Little Rock, Arkansas, he came to fame as an actor and studio owner. In 1958 he was presented with an Honorary Oscar for his early achievements in films. Though the *Great Train Robbery* was filmed in New Jersey, Anderson later went to Colorado and then with the Essanay Company in Chicago. His favorite actor? Gary Cooper.

Q. *What did you think of the film* A Man Called Horse?

A. This historical drama of an English nobleman captured by the Sioux Indians in 1824 and compelled to show himself as good a man by brave deeds as the Sioux warriors themselves will appeal to all Indian buffs. The picture is a bloody one, but it is not a sadistic or brutalizing film. The film appeared well researched and as authentic as we are likely to get until the American Indian Movement films their side of the Second Wounded Knee struggle. Richard Harris, Dame Judith Anderson, Manu Tupou and many genuine Sioux tribesmen turn in an exciting performance.

Q. *Where is Tom Mix, the famous actor, buried?*
A. In Forest Lawn Memorial Park, Glendale, California.
Q. *In the film* Butch Cassidy and the Sundance Kid *it states among prologue credits that "most" of the film is true. What parts weren't so?*
A. Many parts, I would say, though one might still enjoy this humorous Western film. I balked at the picture's presentation of the girl (Etta Place, Laura Bullion, Annie Rogers, whichever she was supposed to be) as a rather demure schoolteacher. The really *true* story of the Hole-in-the-Wall gang is much more fantastic than any screen writers could persuade a producer to set down on film. Perhaps the *truest* part of the film was the old sheriff's remark to the two principals, "You are just two-bit thieves."
Q. *Was John Wayne, the actor, raised on a ranch?*
A. No, the late Mr. Wayne was born at Winterset, Iowa, an agricultural community, in 1907. His many Western films have led to the erroneous conclusion that he was a cowboy. Later, however, as a wealthy man, he owned ranch properties.
Q. *When did Dan Duryea, film actor who did so many good Western characters, die?*
A. Dan died in 1968. He was indeed a fine actor.
Q. *Where was the final show of the Tom Mix Circus held before it went bankrupt?*
A. Pecos, Texas.
Q. *Is George D. (Pete) Morrison, the old-time cowboy actor, still living?*
A. He was living on his ranch west of Denver, near Morrison, until his death. Pete spent thirty years doubling for Western stars who couldn't ride well, playing in more than 200 films. When he became a star, he drew as much as $500 a week (in tax-free times). Pete and his wife Lillian moved back to Colorado in 1936. She died in 1969, and they had been married fifty-seven years. Their sons Clifford and Douglas are still living.
Q. *Is it true that Maurice Barrymore, the actor, was once engaged in a Texas shoot-out?*
A. It was no shoot-out. In 1878 Barrymore and his troupe played a theatrical engagement at Marshall, Texas. After a performance one day, Barrymore was having a snack at the depot cafe with other members of the troupe, May

Cummings and Ben Porter. A townsman, drunk and insulting, came to the doorway and made snide remarks about Miss Cummings. Porter, though unarmed, arose to defend her, and was killed instantly by the intruder. Barrymore placed himself between Miss Cummings and the gunman and was wounded. The murderer, James Currie, was apprehended, tried, and freed by a Texas jury, apparently under the philosophy that "show people" needed shooting. Later Currie served a year or two for murder in New Mexico.

Q. *Who wrote the book* Saga of the Sawlog, *and where may I get in touch with the author?*

A. Kate Krumrey is the author. Write her at Offerle, Kansas.

Q. *Who composed the "Ballad of Sam Bass"?*

A. John Denton of Gainesville, Texas, is generally credited, yet some believe the entire ballad is the work of many persons who have added verses.

Q. *Why did folks in the West erect such pretentious show palaces as the Teller Opera House in Central City, Colorado, and the Tabor Theater in Denver? Surely there were not enough people caring for opera to patronize such places.*

A. The men who financed the enterprises were men of no great cultural background, but just lucky miners or mine owners, as was H.A.W. Tabor. This leads a few critics to say that these playhouses were constructed to bolster the ego of Westerners who yearned for the culture of their Eastern kinfolk. But remember, many of those who settled the West brought with them a taste for fine arts they had known in the more settled Eastern states.

Q. *Who are the members of the 300 Club in Texas?*

A. Originally they were the members of the 300 families the Mexican government permitted Stephen Austin to bring, as colonists, to Texas. They were called "The Old 300 Families." Now descendants to the tune of tens of thousands claim this distinctive title.

Q. *Was the Charles E. Dallin who created the statue of the Indian Medicine Man in Fairmont Park, Philadelphia, Pennsylvania, an American?*

A. Yes. He was born in Utah, in 1861, modeled in clay at age seventeen, and studied in Europe. He died in 1944. His Indian statues stand today in Boston, Kansas City,

Chicago, and Philadelphia, and his statue of his pioneer mother is at Springerville, Utah.

Q. *Can you give me some idea of the dimensions of the immense carving being made on the South Dakota mountain by sculptor Korczak Ziolkowski?*

A. The figure being sculpted is that of the great Chief Crazy Horse, mounted on a fine horse. The overall height will be greater than the Washington Monument, or 563 feet tall. The chief's head is 87½ feet tall; the outstretched arm of the chief is 263 feet; the head of the horse will be 219 feet in length. When completed the mass will dwarf the Great Pyramid of Gizeh (481 feet) and make puny, in comparison, the great heads of the four Presidents that Gutzon Borglum carved on the face of Mount Rushmore, which are 285 feet in height. The carving is being done on a mountain top, five miles north of Custer, South Dakota, and visitors may come and see the work any time in the summer months, or weather permitting.

Q. *What was the last state in the Union to abolish slavery?*

A. Colorado. Well after the Civil War, Indian men and women and children in that state were held as slaves. An order from Washington, D.C., to make a census of such persons resulted in a tabulation of some 200 slaves. The survey also determined that, out of that number, only six persons desired, after gaining their freedom, to return to their tribes! Most were permitted to remain with the same families that held them in bondage, if they so desired, but with a small monthly wage.

Q. *I am a librarian, selecting books on Buffalo Bill for our use. Where may I find a list of such works?*

A. Write Don Russell, Chicago Westerners, 191 Clinton Avenue, Elmhurst, Illinois. He has a comprehensive index of most everything written about the old scout. You'll also want Nellie Yost's new book, *Buffalo Bill*, published by Swallow Press, Chicago, 1979.

Q. *I visited Buffalo Bill's grave near Denver last summer. Now a friend tells me his grave is at Cody, Wyoming. What gives?*

A. You were right; Cody is buried on Lookout Mountain. However, the large monument with his statue on it at the Buffalo Bill Museum, Cody, Wyo., misleads some folks.

Q. *I have heard that Buffalo Bill's remains will be disinterred from the grave on Lookout Mountain near Denver, and removed to Cody, Wyoming. Is this true?*

A. The folks at Cody, planning a great celebration, did once (1926) talk of such a symbolic transfer of the old scout's remains. Many others felt the idea to be in poor taste. There has been a long-standing dispute between Cody folks and the people of Denver about where Cody *preferred* to be buried. An early Park County, Wyoming will filed by Cody selected a burial spot on Cedar Mountain, near his TE ranch on South Fork, near Cody. But the fact remains that the old scout and his wife rest in tombs of solid concrete within burglar proof grave vaults built by the Champion Chemical Company of Springfield, Ohio, atop Lookout Mountain. They will no doubt rest there till Gabriel blows his horn, summoning them.

Q. *I am a Buffalo Bill fan. Where may I see artifacts and relics pertaining to him when I visit the Western states next summer?*

A. There are three places devoted to memorabilia of Cody: First, his grave on Lookout Mountain near Denver and the Museum at that point; second, the Buffalo Bill Museum and the Whitney Gallery at Cody, Wyoming; third, his old Scout's Rest Ranch, North Platte, Nebraska, which is now a state historical museum. Other places may have some Cody mementoes, but these are major spots for Cody buffs to visit.

Q. *Was Buffalo Bill ever in politics?*

A. Yes, he was elected to the Nebraska Legislature on the Democratic Party ticket in 1872 at age twenty-six.

Q. *Who, or what group, directs the work of the National Cowboy Hall of Fame at Oklahoma City?*

A. Dean Krakel, formerly of Denver, is the director. He works under the direction of its president and other officers of the organization. The trustees of the organization include the governors of seventeen Western states, together with many other Western ranchers and businessmen.

Q. *How many books did Andy Adams write, and what are they?*

A. This may not be a complete listing but it names some of his best: *Cattle Brands; Log of a Cowboy; Texas Match-*

maker; The Outlet; Reed Anthony, Cowman; and the
two juveniles *The Young Cattle Kings* and *The Ranch on
the Beaver.*

Q. *What was the main source of the many old cowboy songs
that were popular in the 1870s and 1880s?*

A. They sprang from diverse sources. For example, "Streets
of Laredo" came from an old Irish song, "The Unfortunate Rake." That one was about 200 years old then! It
is said that this tune is the grandfather of "St. James
Infirmary." One of the early Negro blues songs, "The
Dying Cowboy" ("Oh bury me not on the lone prairie")
came from an English sailor's ballad, "Oh Bury Me Not
in the Deep, Dark Sea." Even the "Buffalo Skinners'
Song" came from a Maine logging-camp ditty called
"Canada-I-Oh." "Little Joe the Wrangler" is a take-off
from a Kentucky hoe-down song, "The Little Old Log
Cabin in the Lane," and I believe the later "My Little
Old Sod Shanty on the Plains" is from the same origin.

Q. *Name a few of the most popular songs played and sung
at dances in the 1870s and 1880s.*

A. "Fischer's Hornpipe"; "Irish Washerwoman"; "Devil's
Dream"; "Little Brown Jug"; "Pop Goes the Weasel";
"Captain Jinks of the Horse Marines"; "The Arkansas
Traveler"; "Old Zip Coon"; "Barney McCoy"; "Buffalo
Girls"; "Darling Nelly Gray"; "Old Dan Tucker"; "Listen
To The Mockingbird"; and "White Wings" are a few. My
father's favorite was a song called "Marguerite," though.
I have never been able to find the music for it or hear it
played.

Q. *Didn't the early pioneers add many new lines and stanzas
and parodies to the old songs they brought West with
them?*

A. Yes, cowboys and frontier editors added verses pertinent
to their own areas and their work, and so were born the
many so-called Western ballads. A very few songs, like
"The Old Chisholm Trail," had a true Western birthright.
"I'm up in the mornin' afore daylight / before I sleep the
moon shines bright / cum a ty yi yuppy, come a ti yi yay /
cum a ty yi yuppa yuppa yay." This, and other stories,
told the actual life story of the cowboys, how they fared,
what they thought, and the sad truth about their hard
lives. Such songs lent themselves to settling the cattle

down on the bedground at night and also expressed the loneliness felt by the cowboy as he worked at his task.

Q. *Who composed the song, "Home on the Range," which was said to be Franklin D. Roosevelt's favorite song?*

A. Dr. Brewster Higley, pioneer of Smith County, Kansas, wrote the lyrics, and a neighbor and friend, Dan Kelly, composed the music. The song was first published in one of the county newspapers. There was a legal contest in the 1930s to settle the matter of authorship, and Higley and Kelly were proved to be the two authors. The song was carried up and down the Texas trail by the trail-drivers of the 70s and 80s and became a Western favorite.

Q. *What was the Order of the E. Clampus Vitas of California?*

A. It was an historical group founded in the gold rush days to care for the widows and orphans of prospectors and miners. The Billy Holcomb Chapter, for example, was named after the discoverer of gold in the Holcomb Valley, in the San Bernardino Mountains, in the 1860s. This group exists today and has camp-outs, dedicates historical markers, and is a generally useful, as well as fraternal, group.

Q. *What President of the United States did the Dodge City Cowboy Band entertain?*

A. The band played at the inauguration of Benjamin Harrison.

Q. *Why, on so many covers of Western magazines, do they feature horses?*

A. The horse is the symbol of freedom and mobility in the West. The combinations that make up the symbols of adventure are Horse-Cowboy, Horse-Indian, Horse-Cavalryman, Horse-Pioneer, Horse-Buffalo Hunt, Horse-Railroad (robberies, mounting trains from a horse, etc.), Horse-Prospector, Horse-Sheriff, Horse-Hunter and Bear, and so forth. The horse symbolizes and represents the Old West and its people probably better than any other animal or object. Only the horse supersedes the gun as a Western symbol. The horse was transportation and power, as the locomotive, the auto, and aeroplane are today. Indian, settler, cowboy, miner, everyone depended on him. He drew the stages and the freight wagons, plowed the new sod, pulled up the earth when the wells were dug. He expresses action, and wise editors learned years ago to use his image on the colored covers of their magazines and books.

Q. *Was the writer who signed himself Captain William F. Drannan, and claimed to be a pal of Kit Carson, for certain?*

A. Drannan's books were actually written by his wife. The couple sold them to make a living. They are highly inaccurate historically, filled to overflowing with historical impossibilities. See the book *Dear Old Kit: The Historical Christopher Carson*, by Harvey L. Carter, 1968, for a complete exposure of Drannan as well as another imposter, O.P. Wiggins.

Q. *Who was the most prolific writer of Western fiction?*

A. You would have to check with Western Writers of America, Inc., for the correct answer to this. One of their members, though not a straight "Western" writer wrote 500 books. He was the late John Creasey, an Englishman. Scores of others such as Luke Short, Louis L'Amour, Ernest Haycox, have written enough books to fill a small-town library. Many of these prolific writers write under several names, turning out a book approximately every six weeks. Louis L'Amour probably leads the pack.

Q. *After whom did the late Milburn Stone, in "Gunsmoke" on TV, pattern his character of "Doc" Adams?*

A. Stone was a great admirer of Dr. Arthur E. Hertzler, M.D., author of *The Horse and Buggy Doctor*. Stone, as a young man, knew Hertzler, who lived about ten miles from Stone's home at Halstead, Kansas. Yet in his Introduction to Hertzler's book, Stone denies the credit for his characterization to this old horse and buggy doctor. He suggested that his own grandfather had given him the basic character which he depicted as "Doc" Adams in the "Gunsmoke" program. Whoever suggested to Stone the convincing role he played, it is one to which almost every older American can relate.

Q. *Where did author Zane Grey come from? Why did his stories take such a hold on readers?*

A. He was born Pearl Zane Grey, in 1872, at Zanesville, Ohio. In 1903 he was an undistinguished New York dentist, writing fiction between patients in a dingy room near his 47th Street office. After many rejections, his books started selling. By 1924 they were among the top

Western literature. Grey's wife acted as his editor, encouraged him, and was undoubtedly responsible for the financial success he enjoyed. Grey's stories, overloaded with adjectives and long descriptions, would probably never have found favor with American readers had he not skillfully woven into each work a beautiful, if not entirely credible, love story. Placing charming women in all his works, where other Western writers were permitting only males to ride horses and conquer the West, Grey eventually broke into the film industry. An ardent fisherman and hunter, Grey took to the West like a duck to water, once he was financially independent. His books have sold in the millions, intriguing several generations of youthful Americans. While working on a ranch haying one summer in 1918, I rode more with Zane Grey and his *Riders of the Purple Sage* than on the mowers, sweeps, and rakes with my boyhood companions and ranch hands.

Q. *When did E.F. Beadle begin his publishing career?*

A. He started publishing *Dime Song Books* in the late 1840s or early 1850s. In 1852 he turned to game books, and youth literature. In 1860 he brought forth the famous *Beadle's Dime Novels*. The war demand for "escape literature" soon made Beadle a millionaire.

Q. *In your judgment, who was the greatest literary portrayer of the real American cowboy, working longhorn cattle?*

A. J. Frank Dobie's works are classics of the range cattle industry of the early Texas years. Two of his books, *The Longhorns* and *The Mustangs*, are enough to have earned him his title, had he written nothing else. His work in folklore of the Southwest is a mammoth contribution to the literature. Among the actual old-time cowboys, writing of their personal experiences, I think Oliver M. Nelson's *The Cowman's Southwest*, Andy Adams's *The Log of a Cowboy*, Billy McGinty's *The Old West*, E.C. Abbott's, *We Pointed Them North*, John Bratt's *Trails of Yesterday*, and of course *Trail Drivers of Texas* (a compilation of old cowboys' stories edited by J.M. Hunter in 1925), have contributed their immense knowledge to the subject of range cattle work, each writer in his own specific way and style. But for literary style, plus substance, Dobie ranks first.

Q. *Was there an actual character upon whom "The Virginian" was modeled by Owen Wister?*

A. The author's character is no doubt a composite of what he believed all manly virtues would be if wrapped up in a single man. The Virginian is the Hero. But what woman could live with such a man? And if he existed today, other men would no doubt gang up and lynch *him*, instead of his pal, Steve!

Q. *I had heard so much about* The Virginian *that I bought a copy and tried to read it. To me it seemed dull and dated. Why?*

A. Because it *is* dull and dated. So many Western writers have lifted scenes and conversation from that work that every line of it now seems a cliché. As modern humans have read their daily newspapers, their tastes have changed and reading styles have changed. Today they prefer a terse, journalistic style rather than the long-winded, descriptive passages of Zane Grey, Owen Wister, and other writers of the early twentieth century.

Q. *Are the Western books written by Joseph G. Rosa accurate and responsible accounts of the pioneer West?*

A. Yes, as nearly so as one may write about the Old West with no actual experience living there. Many such writers miss the small, seemingly unimportant details. For example a young Frederic Remington could draw "Bronco Busters" and have the latigo strap running the wrong direction through the cinch ring! Real cowboys and horsemen notice such things. This kind of error is not found in the work of a genuine Westerner such as Charles M. Russell, for example. And so in "Western" books written by Easterners and Englishmen, there are often those slight giveaways. The late John Creasey, an Englishman and a splendid writer, is the only author I've heard of who admits he featured a "flying coyote" in his Western writing! Rosa has not yet done this badly.

Q. *Do you agree that current "Indian" films show better taste than in the past?*

A. Yes, they could do worse. We are past the "duck shoot" Indian battles, at least. Yet even today's films are basically a glorification of the white man's culture and his philosophy. Today's films are telling how the white man survives and becomes the best Indian of the tribe, little else. When an Indian director films Eve Ball's *In the Days of Victorio*, we will have a genuine "Indian" film.

Q. *What are the words to the verse, "The Burial of Wild Bill Hickok," by an unknown Deadwood poet, presumably spoken over Hickok's grave at the burial?*

A. A Deadwood newspaper once printed it this way: "Under the sod in the prairie land / We have laid him to rest / With many a tear from the sad, rough throng / And the friends he loved the best; / And many a heart-felt sigh was heard / As over the earth we trod. / And many an eye was filled with tears / As we covered him o'er with sod. / Under the sod of the prairie land / We have laid the good and the true / An honest heart, a noble scout / A friend who was tried and true."

Q. *When Washington Irving took his trip to the West, after which he wrote* A Tour of the Prairies, *how far west did he travel?*

A. Irving and his party left St. Louis in September 1832, traveled in a general westerly direction (up the Missouri River) to Independence, Missouri, reaching there September 24. On the 27 they started south to Harmony Mission, on the Osage River, and from there turned southwest to the Osage Agency. On October 4 they continued south to Fort Gibson, arriving there October 8. The party then turned northwest to the Cimarron River, which is today the state of Oklahoma, made a west by south trip to the Canadian River and followed it back east a few miles, then, turning northeast on October 31, headed back to Fort Gibson, arriving there November 9. From this you will see that while the party covered many miles, their travels were mostly confined to the southeast portion of Kansas and northeast Oklahoma, hardly a great "prairie" trip.

Q. *How could a cultured people be found who dressed in worn and ragged clothes, such as we see pictured in the photos of the sod house pioneers? Didn't they have any pride?*

A. When the drought of the 1890s caused pioneer people to attire themselves from the barrels of old clothes sent to them by sympathetic Easterners, relatives, and friends, they were a funny-appearing sight, even to themselves. For a man might plow his field with a silk dress hat on his head. A fiddler playing a dance, once remarked about a well-dressed couple on the floor, "That's the best-dressed, starving couple I've seen in a long time." He was being facetious, of course, for the couple were his friends, but dressed from the "relief barrel."

Q. *Did churches in the Old West have much trouble with ruffians?*

A. No. Most Western men respected the religious rights of others as they expected their own rights to be respected. Once, in the Nebraska sandhills, a circuit rider, preaching in the saloon on a Sunday morning, failed to gain the men's attention. "Doc" Middleton, a notorious horsethief and outlaw, drew his .45 sixshooter and laid it on the counter. "The preacher would like your attention," he told the woollies in the audience. There was silence, and the minister delivered his sermon.

Q. *Has a book of the late George Phippen's fine western paintings ever been published?*

A. Yes, *The Life of a Cowboy* with forty-three of George's drawings and paintings was published posthumously by the University of Arizona Press. Louise Phippen, George's widow, is now working up an even more comprehensive book of his greatest works.

Photo courtesy Western History Department, Denver Public Library.

Q. *In Wyoming last summer I heard some tall tales about Jackalopes. Is there such an animal?*

A. Most old-timers in Wyoming can recall seeing one, but the writer never did until he was shown this photo of a *dehorned* Jackalope throwing Don (Reckless Red) Bell, a bronc rider from Byron, Wyoming. This photo convinced me.

5 FOLKLORE

Lacking outside entertainment, the pioneer in his soddy or log cabin turned this "lack" into an opportunity for jawboning and creative story-telling. There was no dearth of materials and no dearth of imagination in reshaping them. The geography, the climate, the flora, the fauna all offered inspiration. Soon these tall tales became numerous enough to begin supplying magazines and newspapers of the East for many years to come.

One of the earliest tall stories I can recall was that of the skunks during the drought of the '90s. So dehydrated had the poor creatures become that they expelled not a liquid but an odorless dusting powder. To us range- and ranch-bred children, animals had thoughts and could perform all number of deeds. A bullfrog, for example, "could swaller things twicet his size." One incident in our family's history had happened "the night the frogs fell." Geese could navigate with precision from Canada to Texas, resting overnight on the Middle Loup River at exactly the same time, year after year. For hadn't an elderly trapper told my father, "I've seed that same greenhead mallard, with an Indian arrer through him, rest there in '79, in '80 and agin in '82."

Mother's Esty organ had developed a squeal in the bellows that father couldn't fix. But that brought on the discovery of a singing mouse inside the organ who accompanied the bellows when anyone worked the foot pedals fast. This anecdote came up in family conversations for the next forty years.

Such an incident often provided the seed for an ensuing legend or folktale. I was at one time inclined to lump all these tall stories in the category of plain superstition. My mother had been told by several of the older women she knew that small chickens could be retrieved even after being swallowed by a bullsnake. One day mother heard fussing in the henhouse, and she soon found a large bullsnake near its door, with seven noticeable lumps in it, making it difficult for the reptile to move. I quickly brought the spade to my mother. She chopped off the

117

snake's head, then with a sharp skinning knife neatly slit the snake open and laid the seven tiny chicks out on the ground in a row to dry, and come to life. But all were dead, crushed by the snake's powerful jaws as it swallowed them. The good advice mother had taken from the other women had proved to be just a folk tale, no doubt started by someone who had never taken dead chicks from a snake's belly. As an impressionable seven-year-old, I noted this.

But even as folk tales age and ripen, I, too, matured. In that process of becoming a little wiser, I began to see some of these old tales in a different light. Some folk tales lead to facts, and facts point the way to truth, or parts of the truth. Perhaps one day we shall be better able to analyze the stories and their origins. We know that they pass along from generation to generation, always changing, always being tested for their truths. We know that with each retelling, the most interesting materials in the story are adapted, the less compelling details dropped. But as the tale develops, it carries the true seed from which it was born. For that is its reason-for-being, to carry that seed to its proper planting ground, as the prairie wind transplants the grass seed.

There was an infinite variety of expressions, adages, and folk tales to fit every occasion in the pioneer West. A number of these grew from the old roots, transplanted and slightly transformed to a new land. Some bear a deep philosophical significance; many are just chaff, tossed up merely to drift away in the wind.

We can do little more here than skim the surface of the rich lode of folklore from the pioneer days. However, each western state now has its own society for the study of folklore, all of which publish books and periodicals on the subject. Readers who wish to explore in greater depth the many fables, tall tales, and legends of the American West will find excellent materials through their local library and folklore society.

Q. *What is the origin of the word "blizzard," used to describe bad weather conditions in winter?*

A. The actual origin is unknown. According to Webster's *Third International Dictionary*, the word comes from an archaic term used to describe "a volley of shots," after the invention of the harquebus and serpentine lock, when a rank of soldiers could simultaneously fire their pieces at an enemy before them. The German word *blitz* for *blitzkrieg* may have a common root. Many people of the Nebraska and Iowa frontier states thought the word had originated in Iowa during a particularly fierce winter storm of the 1870s, for German settlers there were heard to use it.

Q. *What name did the Spaniards give to the South Platte River?*

A. The expedition of Pedro de Villasur, shortly after 1719, called the south fork the *Rio Jesús María*.

Q. *Where did the river Pecos get its name?*

A. Mariano Velasquez de la Cadena, Spanish scholar, said it came from the word *pecoso*, meaning "freckled." The word *pecado*, coming from the same root for peccadillo, means "sin." Old natives of the Pecos region thought the river was named The River of Sin because of the vice and murder along its banks. The longhorn (speckled) cattle may have had some part in its naming. The word *pecus*, from the Latin, meaning "cattle," helps bear this out.

Q. *Where did the stream called Stinking Water, in western Nebraska, derive its name?*

A. During the hide-hunting period, it is said hunters killed so many buffalo near the headwaters of the stream, where the land was boggy, that the rotten cadavers scented the air downstream for many miles. Early cattlemen named it the Stinking Water.

Q. *Where did the epithets Lop Ears for Oregonians and Tarheads for Californians originate?*

A. Californians in earliest times confused the word Oregon with the Spanish *orejon*, the latter meaning "long" ear, or "lap" ear. Oregonians retaliated using the fact that the Indians of northern California placed tar on their heads (as a symbol of mourning) as their favorite epithet.

Q. *Where did the name Ozarks come from?*

A. From the French *Aux Arcs*, literally meaning "with bows." The term was applied by French trappers to a band of Quapaw Indians who inhabited the mountain region of Missouri and Arkansas. The term meant "bow carriers." A French trading post stood near the present village of Arkansas Post, Arkansas.

Q. *What county in the U.S. is bordered by four states?*

A. Cimarron County, Oklahoma, is bordered by New Mexico, Colorado, Kansas, and Texas.

Q. *What does the word Saguache (the Colorado town) mean?*

A. It's an Indian word meaning "blue earth."

Q. *What is the origin of the name of the Frying Pan River, in Pitkin County, Colorado?*

A. The river gets its name after the shape of the basin which, topographically, resembles a frying pan.

Q. *What was the source of the name* Llano Estacado *(Staked Plains) for the north Texas Panhandle country?*

A. W.L. Ormsby, *New York Herald* writer, who crossed those plains on the Butterfield Overland Mail Stage in 1858 wrote: "It derives its name from a tradition that many years ago the Spaniards had a road staked upon it from San Antonio, Texas to Santa Fe, New Mexico." The plain was so flat and so lacking in physical characteristics to guide travelers that it was necessary to so mark it, particularly across the waterless areas.

Q. *Where did the term "augurin'" come from?*

A. In the cowboy days one puncher would say to another about a third party, "Don't let him get his augur into you." This meant the third man was a great talker, was "windy," and would "bore" you with his conversation. To "augur" could mean to have an argument; but generally it was an expression that simply implied talking.

Q. *What does a man have to do to be called a "sourdough"?*

A. An old sourdough of gold rush days told the author that you had to see the Yukon River freeze over, then thaw the following spring. Until then, he said, you were a *Chee-chawker*, an Indian term for intruder, or tenderfoot.

Q. *What did the term "being on a high lonesome" mean?*

A. When a man went on a spree all by himself, he was said to be on a "high lonesome."

Q. *What did the term "salty" imply in the Old West?*

A. It could refer to a mean horse; or it could describe a man of vim and vigor, who was not always pleasant.

Q. *What was a "tinhorn"? How did the term originate?*

A. The name was given in gold rush days to gamblers operating the chuck-a-luck game. Dice were cast from a small tin container resembling a horn. "Tinhorn gambler" was almost an epithet, widely used by disgruntled chuck-a-luck losers.

Q. *How did the name "tenderfoot" originate?*

A. Originally, cowboys gave this name to the cattle and horses that came from the plains country into the rockier mountain areas. The immigrant cattle soon became sore-footed in the mountains and on the rocky lands, hence the name, tenderfoot. Later the name was applied to newcomers from the East, particularly young men who wanted to become cowhands. The term was never used, however, with the derision the Westerners reserved for the term "dudes." A dude rarely shaped up and became a cowboy; a tenderfoot often made the grade. Hence the term, "Dude Ranch."

Q. *I have heard actors in Western films speak of some men as "yah-hoos." My grandfather, a Western sheriff for years called them "yay-hoos." Which is right?*

A. Many words had different pronunciations in different parts of the West. Like your estimable grandfather, we (Nebraskans) always spoke of stupid or thoughtless men or fools as yay-hoos. I never heard a woman spoken of as such. But it bothers me even to this day to hear it pronounced "yah-hoos" by actors.

Q. *What does the Mexican word "gringo" mean?*

A. Most agree it comes from a Spanish slang word for foreigner, *griego*, or Greek. Some Texans still defend the story that it comes from the old song *Green Grows the Rashes*, by Robert Burns, published in 1787 and sung by General Taylor's troops as they marched on Mexico City during the Mexican War. All agree it is used to insult Yankees.

Q. *I am puzzled by a Western expression I heard last summer while on a trip. When I would say something and folks agreed with it, they would say, "You bet!" What does that mean?*

A. It's an old Plains expression, a kind of shorthand for "I'll bet money you're right." There was much gambling in the West, and no doubt the expression came straight off the poker tables.

Q. *What did the term "old woolly" mean?*

A. Old-timers spoke of their old-time friends as "old wool-lies," but it was a term of affection. Sheep, of course, are also called woollies, but the two expressions are different.

Q. *Where does the word "Chicano," for Mexican, come from?*

A. It comes, I am told by Marcella Trujillo, M.A., from the

word *Mexicano* as pronounced by the Aztecs, *Meshicano*. Since the *sh* sound does not exist in Spanish, the conquistadores wrote it with an *x* (as they did where all unfamiliar sounds were concerned, therefore Me*x*icano!). From the ending of the word *Mexicano* comes *xicano*, which was pronounced *shicano*. The sound *sh* passed to Chicano, since the *sh* and the *ch* share the same palatal feature. The word has recently come into popular usage among this minority group to indicate solidarity and unity, even as many Negroes now prefer the term Black.

Q. *So many Western people say "Howdy" when meeting you on the street that I wonder where the saying originated?*

A. It is a short cut for saying "How do you do?" It is always meant in a friendly way, and you do not have to tell the inquirer how you feel, for he doesn't care anyway! A cowboy once advised a friend to never say "Howdy" to a very glib and talkative Easterner whom both knew. "Why not?" the second cowboy asked him. "Because *he'll tell you!*" came the answer.

Q. *Was the term "graze" used as a noun, as we now hear it on the screen and on TV?*

A. Old cowmen used the term "to graze in good grass." Though I have lived in the West all my life, I have never heard an older cattleman use the term "good graze" for "good grass." This new use of the word may have sprung up, as did the term "cowpoke," from modern journalese. However, language is a changing thing, and younger cattlemen may have adopted this term. I did once hear a Texas cattleman refer to grass, in his southern dialect, as "graise." Maybe that's how it started?

Q. *I spent several months in Texas on business for my firm, and those cussed people talked so slow I thought I would never be able to wait and hear the ends of their sentences. Why, or where, does that style come from?*

A. "Texan" is a language all its own. My old friend, the late Fred Gipson, once told me, "Texans speak slow, easy goin', sort of soft-like. The Texas talk isn't as flowery as Spanish, maybe, but we're sure comfortable with it." I agree with Fred, and I always like to hear Texans, like my friends Elmer Kelton, Ben Capps, or Carl Lawrence, sit and give out with it. It makes the world seem less hurried, friendlier, more worthwhile.

Q. *I heard an expression in Montana last year that has stuck
with me. It was "a whale of a good time." Then one boy
threatened to "whale the daylights out of another."
Where did such expressions come from?*

A. Many terms such as "whale of a good time" were actually
brought West by ex-whalers who settled down on the
frontier when their seagoing days were over. Frontier life
itself inspired just as many colorful expressions as well.
"Clean your plow" is a threatening one, offering bodily
harm and in no way volunteering to shine a plowshare for
a friend. One also must watch out, or someone is apt to
"climb your frame."

Q. *What was meant by the line "Pop goes the weasel," from
the old song sung so much in the West?*

A. The "weasel" of that rollicking song, which incidentally
was originally an old English folk song, was not the
animal we know. The old song gave a ribald account of
the manner in which a workingman's money goes during
a Saturday night carousing. One verse said:

> Up and down the City Road,
>   in and out of The Eagle,
> That's the way the money goes—
> Pop goes the weasel.

Bartlett's Familiar Quotations explains that, "The Eagle
was a music hall in which drinks were sold on the City
Road, London. The 'weasel' was a tool used by hatters,
often pawned on Saturday night, 'pop' being the English
equivalent of our 'hock.'" The Western verse of the
above went:

> All around the hominy pot,
>   The monkey chased the weasel,
> And that's the way the money goes,
>   Pop! Goes the weasel.

Why the words changed, I do not know. Western
weasels popped in and out of the henhouses, but had
they made the noise attributed to them in the song it
would have brought forth the farmer with his shotgun.
But the tune was a lively one, well-adapted to frontier
dancing, and many a fiddler has plucked the strings,
making the familiar "Pop," rather than using the bow
at that point.

Q. *Who was the trapper who fooled the Indians by turning
one foot backward while he walked until they thought*

*they had two, one-legged men going in opposite direc-
tions?*

A. This was Charley Russell's story of "The Trail of Reel
Foot." Reel Foot was deformed in such a manner. When
the Oglala Sioux came on to him, asleep, they saw the
deformed foot and never disturbed him.

Q. *I have heard that the American Indians had a prophetic
insight that the horse would be given to them by the
Great Spirit. Where did this belief originate?*

A. One document, according to the American Museum of
Natural History, indicates that picture writing of the
early tribes shows that one of their calendar years is that
of the arrival of the Buffalo Calf Maiden. Among other
of her predictions was one that the horse would be given
to the Sioux People. Strangely enough, the Year of the
Buffalo Calf Maiden was the year 1540 A.D., as we call
it, and that year Coronado and his conquistadores brought
the first horses to the Great Plains area.

Q. *What is the Texas fable of the roadrunner saving the
rabbit from the snake?*

A. The story relates how the roadrunner (paisano) found a
wee rabbit being charmed by a wicked rattler until it
couldn't move. Paisano grabs a thorn, sticks it into the
snake's mouth, propping it open. The rabbit is saved and
becomes the lifelong friend of the roadrunner.

Q. *Can you tell the joke Charles Russell told about Simpson's cow?*

A. Russell told this old, old cow-country story on a man
named Simpson. According to Russell's version, Tommy
Simpson's cow always had six or seven calves annually.
Said Simpson, "Cows of this breed ain't uncommon in
the Scotch Highlands. They're built somewhat along the
lines of a lady bug." The center udder, said Simpson,
"gave pure cream; the rear udder gave buttermilk; the
forward udder gave only skim milk." Many settlers over
the cattle range "had a cow that annually produced twins
or more," was the way the cowboys put it. The calves,
of course, had been rustled.

Q. *Can you give the story of the "Death Waltz," said to have
taken place at Fort Union, New Mexico, about 1860-61?
Who was the woman who reportedly died?*

A. This fable (or folk tale, whichever it is) tells of a soldier who went to battle against the Apache, and whose sweetheart married another after he was killed. The soldier, a "Lieutenant Osgood," returned to the fort during a celebration. He appeared on the dance floor (his body in an advanced stage of decay) and swept his erstwhile sweetheart, a former "Miss Collins," into his arms and did a dazzlingly strange and macabre "death waltz" for the celebrants, who stepped aside and permitted the couple the total use of the floor! As the dance concluded, the lovely charmer died right there in the arms of her former suitor. Then the apparition fled. Soldiers were dispatched the following day to the location where Lt. Osgood was supposed to have been killed in battle, in Mora Canyon. They found the body in its shallow grave, exactly as it had appeared on the floor during the Death Waltz, decayed and with socketless eyes staring out of the skull. The two lovers were then buried, so the story goes, side-by-side in Fort Union Cemetery.

Q. *What is the fable of the subscriber who found a spider in his newspaper, published by Mark Twain?*

A. The story is perhaps allegorical. Here it is: A superstitious subscriber found the spider in his weekly paper. He wrote Twain, asking if it was a lucky omen. Twain replied: "The finding of this spider is neither lucky nor unlucky. The spider was merely looking over our pages to find out what merchant was not advertising so it could spin a web across his door and lead a free and undisturbed existence forevermore."

Q. *Is there any truth in the tale that James A. McFaddin of Victoria, Texas, imported monkeys from Africa and trained them to pick cotton?*

A. No. This was an extremely bad attempt at a racial joke, perpetrated by Jeff McLemore, the editor of the *Victoria Advocate*, toward the turn of the century. The story was reproduced in the *Texas Siftings*, published in Austin by Knox & Sweet. McFaddin, a prominent ranchman, immediately rejected the joke, stating that it was in such poor taste that it should hardly be dignified by a denial.

Q. *I have read a chronological biography of Buffalo Bill Cody that states he was herding cattle for Russell, Major, and*

Waddell at the age of nine years *(1854). It also says he
was assistant wagon master on a bull train at* age twelve.
*He must have been a real he-man boss-genius to be placed
over grown men at such a tender age. Could you comment
on this? Or are these just fabrications?*

A. Cody, like many "heroes," has been placed in positions
    that he would hardly place himself in were he alive today.
    Cody was, according to Don Russell in his authoritative
    biography of Buffalo Bill, "fighting skunks and going to
    school" like most any other frontier lad at age nine. But
    at age twelve, Cody was probably herding cattle (work
    oxen) that were pastured near his home, but under the
    watchful eyes of John Willis, a wagon boss who worked
    for Russell, Major, and Waddell. Cody, the young man
    and man, was a great buffalo hunter, army scout, and
    Indian fighter. He needs no such fabrications to enhance
    his career. Even as a boy he had fine qualities developing
    within him, which made him a man of good character,
    well-respected by all who worked for him.

Q. *What is the fable about the miners who "cured the scurvy
    but lost their patients"?*

A. An old story in *Frank Leslie's Illustrated Newspaper*,
    September 16, 1871, relates the tale of six miners who, in
    1850, "in the El Dorado Mountains," fell desperately ill
    from scurvy. To cure them, the other miners buried them
    in the earth up to their necks. "The result of this earth
    cure," said the story, "might have been happy but for the
    fact that in the night coyotes came along and ate off their
    six heads." The tale is, of course, only another of the
    many "Western windies."

Q. *I read where there was a fifteen- to twenty-foot rattle-
    snake skin in a Sterling, Colorado, museum? Is that true?*

A. This is another windy. A museum there did have at one
    time the skin of a boa constrictor of approximately those
    dimensions. No doubt someone was "stuffing" a tender-
    foot to get such a story in print. Rattlesnakes (prairie)
    rarely exceed five feet.

Q. *Is there a fly plant that grows on the desert in Arizona
    or California that can swallow a horse?*

A. I have crossed the Mohave on snowshoes, swum across
    every lake in Death Valley, soared like an eagle with
    only attached bird wings over the Superstition Moun-
    tains, but never, I repeat, never, have I seen or heard of

this fly plant that swallows cows and horses like ants. There are, of course, small plants that attract and trap small insects with their sticky fluids.

Q. *A half century ago or more, in the Nebraska Sandhills, we boys had a chant about "Old Jim Fye." Can you recall it?*

A. The chant went like this: "Old Jim Fye came ridin' by / Says I Old Man, your horse will die / Says he, If he does, I'll tan his skin / And iff'n he don't, I'll ride him again!" The little verse was composed by Bernice (Hunter) Chrisman, pioneer and writer, who knew Fye, an old Union Cavalryman. Fye rode a horse named Peanuts, and later presented the horse to Mrs. Chrisman for her personal saddle horse. Bernice H. Chrisman authored the book *When You and I Were Young, Nebraska!* It was her pioneer autobiography, 1877–1900.

Q. *What effort has ever been made on the part of the U.S. government to preserve and collect the folk music and tales of frontier times?*

A. In the 1930s, the New Deal set up the Federal Writer's Project, under the WPA. The work produced tens of thousands of pages of valuable books, pamphlets, and documents from the actual words of the pioneers still living at that time. Nevertheless, the work, while commendable, was thirty years too late to get the best from surviving pioneer people. Also, some of the poorly trained collectors missed much that had value.

Q. *Can you give me the chorus to the drought song of the 1890s that was sung to the tune of "Beulah Land"?*

A. The chorus went: "We have no wheat, we have no oats / We have no corn to feed our shoats / Our chickens are too poor to eat / And pigs go squealing through the street."

Q. *What was the fable of the hired man who plowed such a crooked furrow?*

A. The farmer told the hired man to go plow a straight furrow for a change, since all he plowed were crooked. The hired man asked, "About how long a one?" "Oh," the farmer answered, facetiously, "about to that chicken," pointing to a hen in the yard. The hired man set out, whenever the chicken moved he plowed after her, when she turned he turned, when she stopped to scratch, he stopped and scratched. Then the farmer came out of the house and gazed at the torn up yard. "That yahoo ain't got sense enough to pour water out of a boot with the directions on the heel!" he told his wife.

Q. *Why was there so much joking, tall-tale spinning, and fun-making among the pioneers?*

A. Theirs was a society without radio, TV, automobiles, motion picture theaters and with few newspapers, magazines and books. So it was only natural for them to entertain themselves, each person contributing what he could to the amusement and enjoyment of others.

Q. *I have heard that a suit for divorce was filed in poetry in a Western court. True? Was it granted?*

A. Yes, true and granted. The petition was filed in the State of Oklahoma, Texas County by Hughes and Dickson, attorneys for the plaintiff. The petition began: "Now come the plaintiff herein named / And for cause of action she's not ashamed / In Texas County she's lived for years / Where joy and happiness has mingled with tears." Manda Walters was granted the divorce from J.A. Walters. The judge of the court, F. Hiner Dale, not to be outdone by the rhyming attorneys set forth in his *Journal Entry, Case No. 5060,* in his fifth stanza granting the divorce: "Wherefore it is ordered adjudged and decreed / From her bonds of matrimony, this plaintiff is freed / A divorce is granted, but the costs she must pay / The same to become final six months from today."

Q. *Was ever a woman in the old hellhole of the Yuma, Arizona, prison?*

A. The woman was Pearl Hart, a twenty-one year-old who had the reputation of being a hard case. She had helped rob a stage and was sentenced to serve five years time. She was number 1559. Joe Boot, her companion, drew seven years. They were sentenced in 1899, and she served out her term. After a brief "theatrical" career in which she exploited her life as a prisoner at Yuma; and tried to have the place improved, she drifted to wild west shows, once appearing with Buffalo Bill's show at Yuma. After this period she dropped from public view. Many fables and folk tales are told of Pearl Hart, yet little is actually known of her, with the exception of her prison years at Yuma.

Photo from the collection of Harry E. Chrisman.

Q. *How did the Plains Indians preserve meat for winter use?*

A. The buffalo meat—and small game—was cut in strips (with the grain of the meat) and hung to dry on drying racks as shown in this old stereopticon view of a Cheyenne Village on the Yellowstone River. The meat was sometimes then pounded into a powder and seasoned with dried fruit such as wild plum or berries. This was called pemmican.

6 INDIANS

Having been born in Nebraska, and having worked as a youth on ranches and with telephone line gangs throughout that state, as well as in Wyoming and Montana, I was early made aware of the American Indian and his ancient culture. Once, when I was fifteen, riding across the great grass range at the head of Little Otter Creek, about fifty miles northeast of Sheridan, Wyoming, I came across an area on a creek bottom where a score or more of rock circles appeared in a line along the creek bank. Thirsty, I dismounted and watered my saddle horse, and while there I examined the curious rock circles. I soon realized these circles had been fashioned by men, but to what purpose?

Near each circle, I found another gathering of stones and recognized these latter stone groupings to be the remains of what had been campfire placements. Digging in the ashes of each, I began to exhume small bones, as of chickens, and a few stone relics, broken arrow points, and one piece of a beaded moccasin. Quickly the realization came to me that here had been an Indian encampment! From that moment forward, wherever I have been on this continent, I have been keenly aware of this ancient human presence.

From Point Barrow, the furthermost point in Alaska, southward through Canada and the Northwest Territories, across the U.S.-Canadian border, down through the western coastal areas and along the continental divide, and eastward across the continent, the white man always found the Indian there long before him. To Mexico, and through central America, down across the entire span of South America to Tierra del Fuego, there the Indian, as we call him, has made his home and has left his cultural mark upon the land.

Today, we continually uncover new aspects of that culture. The Indian's artifacts, while revealing little of their religious beliefs, do show a love for the artistic and the beautiful, qualities that have always accompanied, if not exceeded, the spiritual values. Along with their artistic accomplishments, we realize that on this continent once existed humans who, against great odds, survived for many thousands of years an Ice Age, predatory beasts, and other mammals as huge as the mammoth and the prehistoric bison. The tools and the implements which made this survival possible were fashioned from stone and wood, bone and ivory, the skins and sinew of animals. Clearly, the feat of survival on this continent marks the Native American as a superlative being.

But survival, though the mark of the Indian's physical toughness and tenacity, has not been the greatest part of his superior qualities. His natural instinct for the land as Mother, and for all creatures which shared the land with him as brothers, marks an extremely high point in a philosophical understanding of the elemental forces upon which humankind is utterly dependent for life itself. Only today, under the banner of conservation and ecological protection, has the white man begun to comprehend what the red man took for granted, that man and nature are one.

Q. *What happened to the Indians who survived the Chivington Massacre of 1864? Where did they go from Sand Creek?*

A. The remnants, including Chief Black Kettle, dug pits into the hillsides and along the bed of the creek and stood off the soldiers until they withdrew, about sundown. Some Indians who had escaped into the hills recaptured some of their horses and then returned to the battle site, putting their wounded on the horses. They took them up the creek about ten miles that night, covered the wounded with grass so they would not freeze, and built a large fire to keep them warmer. The following morning they proceeded to the Smoky Hill camp of their tribesmen. Though Black Kettle's wife was wounded, she survived. Both were later killed by Custer's 7th Cavalry on the Washita, in 1868.

Q. *Approximately how many settlers were killed in the great Sioux uprising?*

A. Most historians set the figure near 700 settlers and 100 soldiers killed in that fracas in 1862.

Q. *What was the principle reason for the Sioux Wars, 1865–76?*

A.   Basically it was the white man's conquest of the Indians' lands. The summary punishment meted out by generals Sibley and Sully in 1862-63 consolidated the Sioux bands and aligned the northern Arapahoes and Cheyennes behind them.

Q.   *What was the basic cause of the second occupation of Wounded Knee, South Dakota, in 1973, by the Indians?*

A.   The fundamental cause was the expropriation of the Indians' lands and the many broken treaties. The white man would like for all to forget, if not forgive. The Indians still remember how their ancestors were forced to sign contracts and treaties under duress. Now the Indian asks for his day in court. And he deserves it. But the white man cannot yield to these demands, for it would immediately raise a hue and cry from all *black* men, whose ancestors were worked, beaten, and exploited as slaves, and who would demand a monetary reconsideration over *labor*, the same as the Indians are asking over *land*. So the situation is terribly elemental, and dangerous, and cannot under our laws of today possibly be resolved to the satisfaction of all concerned. For just as the Israelites of today cannot seize other peoples' lands and hold them without risk of continuous war, neither can the American Indian revert back to the conditions of one hundred years ago. Any peaceful solution to either problem must be resolved with a change in men's hearts, and with some just redistribution of the stolen lands and adjudication of broken treaties.

Q.   *What Indian leader was responsible for the Pueblo uprisings in 1680-82?*

A.   The Tewa medicine man, Pope, was perhaps the most active. He led the revolt that drove the Spaniards from New Mexico and killed his own son-in-law to prevent his plans from being revealed to the padres. After losing the seige of Santa Fe, the Spaniards regrouped under Governor Antonio de Otermin, near El Paso. Beaten a second time, the Spanish finally sent the big expedition under Don Diego de Vargas, which ruthlessly crushed the Indian revolts. The Pueblo revolt represented the passion of a whole people for freedom.

Q.   *Is there or has there been any good work by the Indians whose people fought Custer at the Little Bighorn depict-*

ing the battle from the Indian's point of view? Since none of Custer's men survived, perhaps this would be a good source to actually determine what happened on that battlefield at that time.

A. There is, indeed. A fine picture-history of the Custer battle was drawn by Amos Bad Heart Bull, an Oglala Sioux of the Pine Ridge Reservation. This artist drew the pictures, with something of a running commentary in many of them, between the years 1890 and 1913, the latter the year of his death. The work passed into the possession of his sister, Dolly Pretty Cloud. In 1926, Helen Blish learned of the pictures, most of them drawn in a large business-office ledger. With the cooperation of Mrs. Pretty Cloud, who loaned her the pictures on a year-to-year basis, Helen Blish, with the aid of other Pine Ridge Indians, He Dog and Short Bull in particular, analyzed and interpreted the many pictures. The subject matter was broad and dealt with the many aspects of Indian life as well as the battles against the white man's encroachment of their lands. For Bad Heart Bull, though born in 1869 and too young to participate in those great events he depicted with his pencils and paints, foresaw the great need for a faithful Indian pictographic history. This splendid work was published under the title *A Pictographic History of the Oglala Sioux*, by University of Nebraska Press in 1967. It contains the Notes and Interpretive Sections by Helen Blish, together with many pages in color and in black and white by the artist, Amos Bad Heart Bull.

Q. *What induced Sitting Bull and his band of Sioux to return from Canada to the United States, following Custer's defeat?*

A. The U.S. government offered the starving Sioux a reservation, cattle, food, blankets, and horses, and this finally convinced them to return. There were approximately 5,000 Sioux led by Sitting Bull, Sweet Bird, and Spotted Eagle in Canada at that time. The Canadian officials feared the presence of so many Sioux after the Custer battle, and therefore gave them encouragement to return to their old homeland, although they did not mistreat the Sioux while across the border.

Q. *Prior to the Chivington Massacre of Black Kettle's people at Sand Creek, had not those Indians been attacking ranches and wagon trains of settlers?*

A. Small bands of braves from various tribes had been caus-ing depredations, killing ranchers and their families, cowboys and travelers. However, the Indians who had assembled under Left Hand and Black Kettle at Sand Creek were peaceful and had voluntarily placed them-selves under the protection of the Colorado officials. They exercised no control over the young warriors who were out raiding, for it was customary for chiefs not to attempt to control those who had left their camps and set out on their own.

Q. *Who or what was responsible for the uprisings of the Comanches, Kiowas, and other tribes of the Southwest in 1874?*

A. The loss of their lands to the white man was primarily on their minds. The buffalo hunters, horse thieves, and whiskey peddlers—together with the Indian Agents— were corrupting the Indian men and girls, much as our GIs in Vietnam were corrupted by the Vietnamese War, dope and whiskey and prostitutes. Confinement on the reservations irked the free spirit of the red men and ignited resentment of the white man.

Q. *Did the Chippewa consider joining with their hereditary enemy, the Sioux, in the 1862 uprising?*

A. No, there is no evidence to support such a belief.

Q. *I once heard a story about a chief who went to a U.S. general and asked for the loan of a cannon. The general refused, asking the Indian why he wanted the cannon— "to shoot his soldiers?" The chief replied scornfully, "No need cannon to kill soldiers. Can kill soldiers with sticks. Need cannon to kill cowboys." Where did this tale originate?*

A. Comic or apocryphal, the story was told on Gen. William T. Sherman during an inspection tour of forts in New Mexico. It appeared in the *Las Vegas Daily Optic* (New Mexico), December 17, 1883.

Q. *Where may I find information given by the Arickara Indian scouts who survived the Custer disaster at the Little Bighorn?*

A. One O.G. Libby interviewed several of the scouts in 1912 and published the results under the title *The Arickara Narrative*, Vol. 6, North Dakota Historical Society *Collections*. These stories are said to be incredible for detail and accuracy. They are still available but only in rare book stores, libraries, and museums.

Q. *What was the average age of the Indian scouts who accompanied troops into the Indian wars of the 1860s and 1870s?*

A. Of forty-five scouts at Ft. Lincoln, Dakota Territory, in 1874–76, from the Arickara (Ree), Sioux, and Blackfoot tribes, the average age was twenty-eight and one-half years. The oldest was forty-five; the youngest, eighteen.

Q. *How many Indian battles were there during the settlement of the U.S.?*

A. It has been estimated that if you listed the names of the many Indian battles, it would require 100 typed pages.

Q. *Was there ever an Indian chief who never lost a battle to the white man? This is assuming he fought white men, of course.*

A. Little Turtle, a Miami (Indiana) chief has this distinction, according to the *Amerindian and Western Historical Review*, May–June, 1969, Denver, Colorado. In 1780 a small band under Little Turtle destroyed a party of French cavalry under Col. Auguste de la Balme. Thereafter, Little Turtle fought the white man wherever he appeared, culminating in the destruction of a 1,500-man army that Gen. George Washington sent out under Gen. Arthur St. Clair to break the Indian power north of the Ohio River. This is reported to be the greatest victory American Indians ever had over the white man. When Gen. Anthony (Mad Anthony) Wayne was sent against the Indians with a huge force, Little Turtle then advised prudence and told his people to make peace with the white man, whose power was so great that, in his judgment, it could not be resisted longer. His people failed to take his advice and he withdrew as their leader. Other chiefs then led their tribes to the defeat at Fort Recovery, June 30, 1794. But Little Turtle had fought and won for thirteen years!

Q. *What brought about the Meeker Massacre at White River, Colorado, in 1879, by the Utes?*

A. Nute Craig, telegrapher at Rawlins, Wyoming, at the time,
    in his book, *Thrills, 1861 to 1887*, attributed the Utes'
    anger to the slowness of the federal government to pro-
    vide needed supplies when the Indians were hungry, as
    well as to their dislike of Nathan Meeker, Indian Agent,
    who sought to teach them how to farm. Farming, they
    knew, ruined the ground for hunting. Craig sent many
    messages from Colorow Ute war chief and his friend,
    Chief Douglas, civil chief of the Utes, asking that the
    Great White Father in Washington speed supplies to the
    hungry Indians. Craig conveyed over the telegraph wires
    Colorow's threats, and the many pleas of Douglas.

Q. *What was Gen. U.S. Grant's attitude toward the Indians
    on the frontier in 1864-65?*

A. Grant realized that the emigrants were showing little
    concern for the lives of the Indians they encountered on
    the Great Plains as they moved westward, and that the
    treaties meant nothing to land-hungry and gold-hungry
    white men. "It may be," he wrote to Gen. John Pope,
    commander of the Department of the Missouri, on
    May 18, 1865, "the Indians require as much protection
    from the whites as the whites do from the Indians. My
    own experience has been that but little trouble would
    have been had from them but for the encroachment and
    influence of the whites."

    Pope, in his *Report on the West*, 1866, fully recog-
    nized the lack of morality on the parts of the whites who
    encroached on the Indians' domain without permission or
    right to do so, and he set it down in his *Report*: "How
    can we expect the Indian to observe a Treaty which he
    sees us violate every day to his injury?"

Q. *Has there ever been a treaty made between the U.S.
    government and the American Indian that has never
    been broken?*

A. Until *all* the U.S. Indian treaties are studied, we still
    can't be certain. The only one of which I know was
    actually made between *two tribes* for themselves. When
    Buffalo Bill's great show played Ashland, Wisconsin, he
    learned there had been trouble between the Wisconsin
    Chippewas and the Sioux, dating back to 1862. Though
    the two tribes were technically at war, no fighting had
    taken place for twenty years. As a promotional stunt,

Cody's advance men proposed that a peace council and a treaty of friendship be signed between the two tribes. Chief Flat Iron headed the Sioux; chiefs Cloud, Blackbird, and Buffalo agreed for the Chippewas. Though Cody's publicity department wanted the council to be a part of the big show, in the big tent, the colonel refused to commercialize the solemn event, and the signing of the treaty was done in the circus "back yard." That treaty has never been broken.

Q. *Just how did the U.S. government manage to break the treaty that had given the Sioux Indians the Black Hills area in perpetuity?*

A. When the Custer expedition and a second one, under Prof. W.P. Jenny, New York School of Mines, had made certain there was gold in the Black Hills, the government called a delegation of Sioux leaders and attempted to persuade them to withdraw from the hills. When the government failed in this attempt, it also failed to keep the prospectors and miners out. The Indians began to fight back for their lands, and Congress passed a law stipulating that no annuities would thereafter be paid to Indians *until the Black Hills had been ceded to the whites.* A U.S. government commission visited the Sioux and induced them to submit to the will of the white man and abrogated the original treaty. A new "agreement" was signed February 28, 1877, with the usual results. Miners rushed in on the Sioux lands and then succeeded in getting the U.S. government to support their appropriation of the Black Hills land by sending in troops to keep the Indians at bay.

Q. *Were there any revolts by the Pueblos after Petriz de Cruzate reduced the Pueblo of Zia in 1688 and reestablished Spanish authority?*

A. Yes, there was an uprising at La Cañada, north of Santa Fe, New Mexico, in 1837. However, this revolt was put down in blood by Governor Manuel Armijo, who sent Colonel Justiniana, with 400 dragoons, and Captain Munoz, with the Vera Cruz dragoons, against the Indians. A treaty was signed at Jemez on July 15, 1839, following which the Pueblos entreated the Spaniards to return all captives in return for Spanish soldiers captured by the Indians during the fight.

Q. *How were Indian children treated in the Indian schools set up for them on the agencies and elsewhere by the government?*

A. Mrs. Zuzie Yellowtail ("Mrs. Indian America"), recalled that when she attended a "boarding school" as a young girl, "I often had my mouth washed out with soap for speaking my native [Crow] language. We were punished for speaking, or even thinking, 'Indian.' People my age still carry scars from white matrons who whipped them with rubber hoses." It is a fact that the old Indian schools did everything possible to "Americanize" the Indian children, to make them talk and think like white children of Anglo descent. "When we tried to dress in our Indian clothing," Mrs. Yellowtail said, "they refused to serve us in the stores in Sheridan, Wyoming. They had signs that read: "No dogs, no Mexicans, no Indians allowed.""

Q. *Was there ever an Indian slave trade in the Southwest in the nineteenth and twentieth centuries?*

A. Indeed there was, and long before that. From the time of the "discovery" of the new world by European Christians, slavery was practiced in America. The practice was carried into the Southwestern regions, and Spanish traders sought and captured Indians, selling them into the gold mines and cotton fields of Española. The first labor force marshalled for the New World came through the *encomienda* and *repartimiento* systems. The former was a system of allocating so many Indians to each settler who abided by Spanish law and custom. The second form, *repartimiento*, provided a weekly allotment of Indians who worked twenty weeks each year in the gold and silver mines. The latter came from and were returned to the Indian villages. Nearly 1,000 Apaches were enslaved between 1700 and 1760. The Church avoided use of the word *esclava* and preferred the term menials or servants, for the slaves. United States military leaders perpetuated the practice until and through the Civil War.

Q. *How many Indians served in the American Civil War?*

A. More than 10,000 served and on both sides of the issue. About 5,500 cavalrymen were recruited by the Confederacy. Though Secretary of War Stanton declared the Union would have no need of Indian soldiers, about 4,000 are known to have served in various Union units.

The Confederacy promised the Indians an "Indian State."
It was to be approximately where Oklahoma is today.
This inspired more Indians to enlist in the Confederate
cause than for the Union. Many Indians who already
lived in the Confederate states (the Cherokees, Creeks,
Choctaws, Chickasaws, and the Seminoles) owned slaves
and regarded the practice without scruples. Albert Pike,
a Boston man who lived at that time in Arkansas, became
the chief recruiter for the Confederacy. Pike was the
lyricist who wrote the words for the immortal song
"Dixie's Land." An Indian, Ely Parker, rode with Gen.
Grant at the Wilderness and is credited with saving
Grant's life at Spotsylvania, when the Union general
inadvertently rode into the Confederate lines. One early
group, a company of Tuscarora Indians, volunteered and
served with the 53rd New York Infantry. There were
many other company-strength groups that served the
Union. Nono Minor, curator of Plains Indians, the Kansas
City Museum of History, can supply the reader with
much more information concerning the Indians who
served in the Civil War.

Q. *Some authorities claim that the Indian practice of scalping an enemy indicates that Indians were originally of
Arab stock, or one of the "lost tribes" of Israel. Any
comment?*

A. These people quote the book of Maccabees where it
refers to torture of Jews by Syrians, tearing the skin from
the head. Actually, the American Indian copied the practice from the earliest whites who came to America, and
who used the scalp lock as proof of slaying an Indian
when bounty was paid for him.

Q. *Can you give me an idea of what constituted the several
"culture areas" of the North American Indians in the
United States? How many general culture areas were
there?*

A. The Indian Arts and Crafts Board shows seven such
general areas: (1) the *Northern Fisherman*, in Washington
and Oregon; (2) the *Seed Gatherers*, in California, southern
Oregon, Nevada, and northwestern Arizona; (3) the
Desert Dwellers, in southern Arizona, New Mexico, and
the Great Bend area of Texas; (4) the *Navaho Shepherds*,
approximately where their reservation is today in New
Mexico and Arizona; (5) the *Pueblo Farmers*, in central

New Mexico; (6) the *Hunters of the Plains*, in the massive remaining portion west of the Mississippi, Missouri, and Brazos rivers; and (7) the *Woodsmen of the Eastern Forests*, in the immense area lying east of those rivers.

Q. *Why doesn't the American Indian have hair on his body like the white man?*

A. Harry E. Chatfield, president of the Amerindian and Western Historical Research Association, puts it this way: "This is a popular misconception. Being of Mongoloid stock, the Indian lacks the *abundance* of hair of the white man. But most Indians can, and some do, grow beards or mustaches. This is particularly true among the Northwest Coast tribes. Chiefs like Tiscohan, a Delaware; Barboncito, a Navaho, and the Apache, Eskiminzen, had beards or mustaches. Most Indians of the past considered body hair unsightly and pulled hairs out by the root, thus appearing hairless—or clean-shaven, to our white ancestors."

Q. *What was the name for the Apaches who hunted buffalo on the Plains of the North Texas Panhandle country and in eastern New Mexico?*

A. Coronado's men first met these Indians in 1541, when his men trekked across that country, searching for the Seven Cities of Cíbola. These hunters were composed of bands from the Jicarillas, Faraones, and the Mescaleros. Their name has been set down as "Querecho Apache," a name probably given them by the Indians of Pecos Pueblo, which at the time was the funnel mouth for the Southwestern Plains Indians who rode after the buffalo on the Plains.

Q. *Where did the Kiowa Indians originate?*

A. The Kiowas were once located around the head of the Missouri River in Montana, but by the time the Spaniards arrived in 1732 they had migrated south. Lewis and Clark reported they had found them along the North Platte River. In their wars with the whites, they were driven south and had come as far south as the Durango River in Texas. By 1837 they made their first treaty with the white man—but as usual the treaty was broken by the whites.

Q. *Who were the Tenewa Indians?*

A. A small warlike tribe, the Tenewa Indians were the downstream division of the Comanches. They became extinct as a tribal unit by 1845 because of the wars with their enemies to the south of them. The remaining Tenewas were eventually absorbed into the Comanche tribes.

Q. *Who were the Minesetperi Indians?*

A. They were a division of the Crows and lived on the Plains while the other Crows lived in the mountains. The Plains Crows were called the River Crows.

Q. *Where was the Whetstone Indian Agency?*

A. In 1868 the government established this agency for the Brulé and Oglala Sioux about twelve miles north and east of present Bonesteel, South Dakota, where Whetstone Creek empties into the Missouri River.

Q. *What was a "mission" Indian?*

A. This was a tribe of California Indians who were so called because they were under the control of the Spanish missions between 1769 and 1823. The first mission was established at San Diego. The mission Indians worked in the fields, and though the sheep and cattle actually belonged to the Indians, the herds were held for them "in trust" by the Franciscan fathers. Many such arrangements made by the Church were a polite way of avoiding the term "slavery." It also provided the control needed by the Church.

Q. *Where did the Blackfoot tribe originate?*

A. The Blackfoot of Montana came from the region between the North and South Saskatchewan rivers, during the years between 1720 and 1800. They were an aggressive people, and no doubt came southwest to the higher plains, where the buffalo grazed.

Q. *Is there any basis for the belief that the Mandans were descendants of white peoples?*

A. The Mandans were a Siouan tribe, living in what is today North Dakota, when the first white man, Sieur de la Verendrye, a Frenchman, visited them in 1738. He described them as "white beards," for some did have blond hair and blue eyes. This factor gave rise to the belief that they had descended from some white stock. With today's knowledge of the early explorations of Norsemen into North America, and the fact the Mandans used a log-earthen technique for homes and were possessed of a semi-civilized culture, there may be a basis in fact for the belief. Wars and smallpox decimated the Mandans.

Q. *How early was trade opened with the Mandans of North Dakota by the white men?*

A. Jacques d'Eglise, ascending the Missouri River in 1790, met the Mandans and traded with them. The previous year, Juan Munier had made a treaty with the Poncas on the Niobrara River in northern Nebraska for their exclusive trade. The d'Eglise party was turned back by warlike Sioux and Aricaras, but by 1794 the Missouri Company was formed and dealt with the Aricaras. By 1831 the American Fur Company was using steamers on the Missouri River and the fur trade had begun in earnest. It flourished for more than thirty years.

Q. *What became of the Clovis people of the Southwest, the ones who depended upon the Columbian mammoth for food?*

A. Their culture (dated circa 9,500 B.C. by carbon dating), in Arizona, New Mexico, Colorado, and Wyoming, either progressed into the Folsom culture or was replaced by it at about 8,500 B.C. The extinction of the mammoth may have been the cause, for Folsom man is associated with the prehistoric bison, and his arrow and spear points are found with the bison's bones in these Western states.

Q. *Have the Washoe Indians ever been compensated for the lands they lost to the palefaces in California and Nevada?*

A. Yes, to an extent. The Indian Claims Commission ruled in their favor in the case of 1,555,000 acres of land lost to them when the whites expropriated it in 1853 and in 1862. The monetary consideration cannot, of course, compensate for the loss of their lands for the past one hundred years and more, nor will it reflect the actual value of the land at today's prices. However, it is a token of the white man's admission of wrongdoing, committed by him upon the American Indian.

Q. *Tell me something of Sabeata, chief of the Jumano tribe.*

A. He was a Christianized Indian who led Domingo de Mendoza's exploration into Texas in 1663-84. Later, after a disagreement with the Spaniards, Sabeata returned to his tribe. He was later seen, in 1691, leading a buffalo hunt for his people.

Q. *What became of the Karankawa Indians of coastal Texas?*

A. There were initially five principal tribes of the Karankawa stock: (1) the Kaopite; (2) the Coaque, or Coca, on Galveston Island; (3) the Karankawa, at Matagorda Bay; (4) the Kohani, north of the Colorado River; (5) the Kopano, on Kopano Bay. There were also Tiopane and Tups, Pataquilla and Quilotes, as mentioned by Cabeza de Vaca. These tribes never yielded to Spanish conquest and colonization. After American settlement began, the coastal tribes were decimated by reprisals, principally by other tribes. The last of the Karankawas are thought to have perished shortly before the Civil War. James Mooney's 1928 estimate was 2,800 Karankawas in the above tribes in 1690. (Mooney authored *The Aboriginal Population of America, North of Mexico*, published in 1928 as Vol. 80, No. 7, Smithsonian Miscellaneous Collection.) John R. Swanson, *The Indian Tribes of North America*, U.S. Government Printing Office, 1953, feels Mooney's estimate may be too high.

Q. *Why were so many powwows held by early-day travelers with the Plains Indians?*

A. The hunters and trappers, who were first to meet the Indians, claimed they were obliged to make a "treaty" of sorts with almost every tribe they met, in order to trap and hunt. This called for a powwow, or "big medicine talk." Only by holding such council, stating their business and agreeing to certain trade policies, could they maintain rapport with the Indians. But even a powwow was no assurance of complete safety and peace, for as soon as the presents were given, many Indians forgot the promises, as did the whites.

Q. *Why didn't the Indians of the West make use of pigs as they did the Spanish mustang? De Soto, I understand, introduced them to both.*

A. It is reported that Indians did love the taste of pork, and the pig, in the wild state, did remain along the bayous of the Mississippi River long after De Soto was buried. However, the arid Plains offered no food, no shelter, no safety, and little water for the sedentary animal. These conditions worked against his survival, and the Indians on the Plains depended on a much bigger and a much more productive food source, the Buffalo, a migrating grazer.

Q. *Why have some historians (the late Dr. E.E. Dale, of Oklahoma, for example) claimed it was an injustice to the Indians to force the cattlemen out of the Cherokee Strip in 1890?*

A. Professor Dale stated it well when he wrote: "...the forced removal of the ranchmen from the Cherokee Outlet, in order to deprive the Cherokees of further revenue and so force the sale of these lands at a price representing only a fraction of their value, presents one of the latest and most glaring examples of injustice done the Indian by the Government of the United States."

Q. *Were the Cherokee Indians permitted to make the "run" into the Cherokee Strip when it was opened for settlement in 1893?*

A. No. The Indians had ceded their rights to the nearly seven million acres of land to the U.S. government for $8,595,736.12, or about $1.40 an acre! This, together with the fact they were not considered to be "citizens," prevented Cherokee resettlement on those lands.

Q. *Why was the Spokane, Washington, area so important to the Indians?*

A. The falls of the Spokane River halted the salmon and made them readily available to the fishing Indians.

Q. *What brought about the physical decline of the Southwestern Indians and the collapse of their entire economy after Spanish rule had been established?*

A. Many factors may be responsible, but I believe that the saddling of the Indian's primitive desert farming-hunting economy, a marginal one at best, with the great mission-building craze of the Spanish conqueror, brought about the total collapse of the economy and the physical decline of the people. It was possible for the Indians to feed, clothe, and shelter themselves by dint of great enterprise on their part. But it was an impossible task to build all the rock temples dreamed up by the Spanish churchmen. These great ruins today cover New Mexico— Santo Domingo, Gran Quivira, Pecos Mission, Quarai, Abo, and many others.

Q. *What is the real mystery behind the supposed Cliff Dwellers? Why did they live in the cliff houses? How did they find food? What happened to them?*

A. The Cliff Dwellers, those who inhabited the now-abandoned cliff homes at Mesa Verde National Park, in southwest Colorado, were a primitive people descended from the Basketmakers, an even earlier culture that inhabited the area, but whose people lived in small cave homes, dug into the earth. Though they did hunt small game, and some deer and other larger game, their economy was basically a farming culture. They practiced a primitive form of irrigation, raised turkeys domestically, and grew corn and maize. In the years approximately 1,000–1,300 A.D., a slow, progressive drying up of that region caused a gradual exodus to take place, a twenty-four-year drought being the final cause for the people to depart. They left behind them the artifacts of ages—bones, feathers, woven garments and mats, and broken pottery, together with many burials in the dirt floors of the cliff dwellings. It is believed that the cliff people migrated into the Rio Grande Valley, and other less arid places. It is thought that their cliff dwellings earlier afforded a secure home for them, hence their reason for locating them under the sheltering canyon walls.

Q. *How did Indian women bear up under the pains of child-birth?*

A. Primitive women were physically quite able to cope with natural childbirth. I have been told by Indian men that both Sioux and Shoshone women practiced deep-breathing for relief of severe pains, using a squatting position, on knees and elbows when the baby was born. Some modern doctors today advocate these techniques rather than the use of pain-killing drugs.

Q. *Where, in the central-western states, may we see the Pawnee earth lodges as inhabited by primitive Indians?*

A. The Kansas Historical Society has built, upon a six-acre tract in Republican County, Kansas, an exact reproduction of the Pawnee lodge that once stood there. The exhibit contains both historical and archeological items of interest. There were formerly twenty-three such lodges on the spot. The location is fifteen miles west of Belleville, Kansas.

Q. *How many Indians were there estimated to be in the continental U.S. (excluding Alaska) when the white man arrived?*

A. An educated estimate was once made by Henry R. Schoolcraft in his seven-volume work on that subject (*Historical and Statistical Information Respecting the History, Condition, and Prospects of the Indian Tribes of the United States*, published in the 1850s). He came up with the estimate of 240,000 Indians, based upon his belief that it would require 40,000 acres to support a family of five persons living by the chase. Today, his estimate appears very conservative, for many families practiced agriculture and could produce enough food on ten acres for a survival diet, which was about all any Indian family expected. *The Columbia Encyclopedia* estimates there were 900,000 Indians north of Mexico in 1492.

Q. *Have the Seminoles ever been awarded damages for their loss of lands to the white man?*

A. In the late 1960s the Indian Claims Commission awarded them $12,347,500, less offsets for their Florida lands. The award covered some 29.7 million acres, or most of Florida taken after the treaties of 1823 and 1832, when Gen. Jackson marched on the Seminoles to punish them for aiding escaped black slaves. This lawsuit was in the courts twenty years before the Indians received a settlement.

Q. *On a trip east, we visited an Indian mound near Miamisburg, Ohio. We were told the Indians who built these mounds antedated the Plains Indians. The rock carvings were fine sculptures. What were these Indians called and how long did they live there?*

A. The Adena Indians appeared in the Ohio Valley about 2,000 years ago—at the very least. Some 5,000 of their mounds have been located; many have been dug up and artifacts found in them. One mound, the Great Serpent Mound, is nearly a quarter-mile in length. The Adena people were followed by an advanced people whom archeologists called the Hopewell, and whose wanderings took them as far west as Kansas, as far east as New York. Their great mounds may be seen near St. Louis, Missouri, Chillicothe, Ohio, and Seip Mound State Park, near Bainbridge, Ohio. These Indians were skilled in wood, stone, and bone-carving, and were fine craftsmen in copper and pottery. These great works of our earliest citizens are priceless, and every effort should be made by society to preserve them.

Q. *Why was it so difficult to settle the Plains Indians down on farm lands? What answer did they give when offered free housing, free hospitalization, etc.?*

A. Chief Ten Bears of the Comanches gave a good answer at the Medicine Lodge Treaty in 1867. He said: "You say you want to put us on a reservation, to build us houses, to make us medicine lodges. We do not want them. I was born upon the prairie where the wind blew free and there was nothing to break the light of the sun. I want to die there, and not within walls. I know every stream and wood between the Rio Grande and the Arkansas River. I have hunted and lived over the country, like my fathers before me, and like them I have lived happily. ...I want no blood upon my land to stain the grass."

Q. *By what* legal *or* moral *justification or right did the white man take away the lands of the Indians?*

A. A knotty question, never satisfactorily answered by white men. A leading legal case under Chief Justice John Marshal, *Johnson and Graham's Lessee* vs. *William M' Intosh* was tried in 1823. A grant by two chiefs was being questioned. Could the title be recognized in U.S. courts? It was argued this way: On discovery of the New World, nations of the Old World were eager to appropriate the land and the people to their domains. The potentates of the Old World found no difficulty in convincing themselves that they had made ample compensation to the inhabitants of the New World by bestowing on them civilization and Christianity, in exchange for unlimited independence. Discovery, it was said, *gave title to the government that could enforce its laws upon any other government with which it competed for the new lands.* The natives (Indians) were denied the power to dispose of their lands to any other nations. So the land, though occupied by the Indians, was appropriated by "the Discoverer." The title was acquired and maintained by force. Since the Indians did not lie down and submit, but fought back, it was then natural to impose the will of the conquerer upon them. So the court stated: "However extravagant the pretensions of converting the discovery of an uninhabited country into conquest may appear, if the principle has been asserted in the first instance, and afterward sustained; if a country has been acquired and held under it; if the property of the great mass of the community originates in it; it becomes The Law of the Land, and cannot be questioned."

Judge Roger B. Taney in 1842 summarized: "...the ...tribes...were regarded as mere temporary occupants of the soil, and the absolute rights of Property and Dominion were held to belong to the European nation [that made the discovery]." In other words, "might made it right." We conquered; we appropriated the lands; the title has now passed to us.

Q. *Why was the yucca plant so important to the South-western Indians?*

A. There were more than thirty varieties of the plant yucca, or soap weed, as it is called by many in the West. The Indians used every part, from the creamy blossoms to the root. The flowers were cooked and eaten; the yucca "bananas" were cooked, stored, and eaten; the seeds were ground into flour; the leaf was shredded and used for fibers; the narrow leaves were used for needles, and the roots were made into a soap.

Q. *What is the Indian name for the cradleboard used by many of them?*

A. When I went into this question, I was most hopeful of an answer. But, as tribe after tribe were examined, I learned that there were approximately 750 Indian dialects that were spoken at one time. Almost every tribe had its own particular name for the cradleboard. The Ute word, for example, was *Ah-ca-con.*

Q. *What does "pueblo" mean?*

A. There are two general meanings. The first refers to a group of homes or apartments, built into one larger home. Second, the tribal group who inhabit the South-west, and who live in these pueblo structures, are called the Pueblos.

Q. *Is it true that Indians got their greeting, "How," from the cowboys?*

A. No, this greeting "Hou," was used before the cowboys appeared on the Western scene. It was a word of peace, with the right hand raised, palm to the front, showing that it concealed no weapon.

Q. *What are the little shelters used by the Navaho called?*

A. Their summer shelters, over which they have a shade fixed so they can do their housework and weaving in comfort, are called *ramadas.* Their regular homes, logs and brush covered over with earth, are called *hogans.*

Q. *What is the source of the Indian word, "Mohave?"*

A. One source says it is derived from two Yuma words, *hamook*, meaning three, and *habi*, meaning mountains— or "the third mountain range from Yuma villages." It was originally Hamockhalves, Yamahabs, or Armochaves.

Q. *What is the meaning of the word* "piskun?"

A. The word *piskun* is from the Blackfoot, meaning cliff or rocky height. Early Montana tribes drove the buffalo over these cliffs on their hunts. The piskun usually has a long, gradual approach, where stone mounds can conceal the Indians "guiding" the animals along the run. As the herds ran by, the Indians would dash out, wave blankets and torches to scare the animals into a frenzied gallop as they approached the top of the cliff, where they could not turn back. In 1972, two helpful Tongue Indian Reservation families from Lame Deer showed me one of the most successful of the piskuns, where the buffalo, grazing along the Tongue River, could be started up the grade to the piskun in bunches of one to three hundred. They pointed out old rock cairns along the way that had been used by their ancestors to conceal themselves as they hurried the animals along, then told how frenzied the animals would become as their ranks became more crowded until, at the top, with a burst of energy to free themselves from the ranks, animals would plunge headlong over the 150-foot cliffs to their destruction. At the bottom of the cliff can still be unearthed bones from the animals that perished. Near this point, on the Tongue River, my hosts explained, was the point where the hundreds of buffalo tongues the Indians were drying in the sun had caused the early trappers and plainsmen to name the river "tongue" river.

Q. *Is the term "muskeg" from the Indian? What did it mean?*

A. Along the Canadian border, the Chippewa and the Kickapoo both used the word to mean grassy bog.

Q. *What word did the Plains Indians use for beef?*

A. Frank Dobie said they called it *wăhēē*. The animals, on the hoof, they called *wō-hă*. Jim Herron and other cowmen also said they used the term *wō-hă* when asking for steers from trail herds.

Q. *When asking for cattle from trail herds, how did the Indians ask in the Plains-country sign language?*

A. They used their sign for "buffalo" and "spotted," as much as to say "your spotted buffalo." The hands were placed, half-closed, palms forward, wrists at the sides of the head to indicate buffalo. Then they placed the left hand forward, palm down, touching the left hand between wrist and elbow lightly with fingers of the right hand to indicate "spotted." Try it. You'll get the *feeling* of Indian sign language.

Q. *What was a "potlach?"*

A. It was a form of party, given by one tribe or individual to others. There was always the propsect that the recipient would reciprocate; that is, a potlach would be *returned*. Among the Nootka Indians (Vancouver Island) this was a form of "redistribution of wealth," where the owner of goods or services divided with the others, or favored them in some way. This event seemed tied in with births, deaths, marriages, puberty, or other such fundamental occasions to the people of the tribes. But a potlach could be given for no reason at all. Basically, the potlach might be described as an expression of esteem and good will, offered to guests who would subtly witness the giver's claim to hereditary honors.

Q. *Could you give me the names, and meanings of those names, of some of the best-known Indian tribes?*

A. Tribes, it should be realized, were named sometimes by the white men, sometimes by other tribes. The Adirondack who lived north of the St. Lawrence River were named by the Mohawks, who called them "Tree Eaters." In hard winters, when food was scarce, the Adirondack Indians did eat bark from trees. The Sioux (Teton) called the Cheyennes *Shahiyena*, meaning "people who speak another language than ours." Many Indian tribes, the Eskimo, for example, called themselves "The People," and in their language this was *Inuit*. The name Apache means "enemy" in the Zuni language, and this Zuni name stuck *(Apachu)*. The Crow received that name from the Cheyennes, though exactly why is unclear. The Delaware, following usual custom, spoke of themselves as *Lenni Lenape*, or The Real People. The Diggers were so called by white men who first found them digging for roots, a staple portion of their diet. The Navaho was the name for the land of the Southwest, bestowed by the Spanish on land and people alike. The name Gros Ventre means "big stomach," and the name was given to the Indians by the French. The French named the Illinois Indians from the name of their language, *illini*, meaning sun. The French named the Sioux, using an Ojibwa word, *Nadowessi*, meaning enemy, and which, translated from French-Canadian, came out *Nadowessioux*. The Sioux tribes provided the names Dakota, Lakota, and Nakota, which meant "friends" or "friendly," to distinguish them from warring Sioux. There is skepticism among scholars about the many Indian names and how they came by them. Thus, the above is subject to doubt and scholarly criticism.

Q. *The early Europeans who came to this continent spoke of the "Indian nations" or the "Indian kingdoms." Why do we now call them "tribes"?*

A. The word "tribe" is incorrect when referring to the various Indian nations. It was the earliest recognition by European explorers that the Indians were organized into "nations" just as their peoples were. Later, the derogatory term "tribe" came into being when the white man began to regard the Indian nations as barbarian.

Q. *Did Geronimo, the Apache, ever run cattle or own horses?*

A. According to Jason Betsinez, an Apache aide to Geronimo, and also the blacksmith charged with making branding irons according to U.S. government specifications, Geronimo did own both cattle and horses of his own. His brand was recorded as the figure "18," below the letters US. The numerals were two inches high, one and one-half inches wide. The numeral "18" represented Geronimo's registration number as a prisoner of war. Every Indian had a registration number.

Q. *How did Geronimo die?*

A. The old warrior died February 17, 1909, when he was intoxicated and fell out of a wagon in which he had been sleeping. The driver, not knowing the old Indian was there, never missed him. It was cold and a rain fell, and Geronimo contracted pneumonia. Taken to the reservation at Fort Sill, he died shortly thereafter. The town of Geronimo, south of the Military Reservation, bears his name.

Q. *Was Crow Dog ever punished for the murder of Spotted Tail in 1881?*

A. No. The Supreme Court ruled, after Crow Dog was sentenced to hang, that the Court had no jurisdiction over the crimes committed on the reservations, and Crow Dog was released.

Q. *Who killed Nokoni, the Comanche chief who fathered Quanah Parker?*

A. Nokoni, who took Cynthia Ann Parker to wife and fathered two sons, Quanah and a brother, and one daughter, Prairie Flower, died a natural death while picking wild fruit on the Canadian River. He was a middle-aged man then. It had been the story in Texas for many years that Governor Ross had slain Nokoni, but J. Evetts Haley, Texas historian, had determined through Charles Goodnight, pioneer cowman, that Ross had been mistaken.

Q. *What is the story of Quanah Parker, Comanche chief, when he stayed overnight at a Fort Worth hotel?*

A. The story goes that Quanah and Yellow Bear, son of Red Cloud, stopped overnight at the old Pickwick Hotel. Came bedtime, they simply *blew out* the gas lights and turned in. In the morning Yellow Bear had passed on to the happy hunting ground. It took several hours to restore Quanah Parker, so the story goes. The Indians, like many whites of that same era, knew little about the hazards of gas poisoning. From the many deaths in homes and trailer camps today, we have not fully learned the lesson. This story may be true only in part, for Yellow Bear, son of Red Cloud, was gored to death by a steer, not gassed, according to Yellow Bear's daughter.

Q. *When was the Cheyenne chief, Two Moons, born?*

A. He was born in April 1847; died October 21, 1932. His place of death is not known for sure, though some say he died on the Tongue River Reservation in Montana. Two Moons is buried at Lame Deer, Montana, where a small marker shows his grave.

Q. *Why is Captain Jack, the Modoc leader, remembered so much for treachery? He was a great fighter, right?*

A. Captain Jack was, indeed, a fighter for his land and its people. He was certainly not a "white man's Indian," and was therefore always spoken of as "treacherous," even as we today call anyone opposing us "terrorists."

However, this term was well-earned by him. After arranging a meeting with Edward S. Canby, an army officer, and several other members, Captain Jack and his men opened fire in the large tent in which they were assembled, the morning of April 11, 1873, and killed one or two of the peace party, wounding others. This brought army troops into the lava beds where the Modocs were holed up, and the following month Col. J.C. Davis, commander of the Department of the Columbia, blockaded the lava beds. After several hard skirmishes, in which many soldiers were killed and wounded, the Indians surrendered. Along with his warriors, "Boston Charley," Schonchin John, and Black Jim, Captain Jack was hanged October 3, 1873. The Modoc dead were listed at fourteen; but eighty-three soldiers had been killed in the War of the Lava Beds!

Q. *Who were the Indians killed in the Battle of Adobe Walls, in the spring of 1874?*

A. White men's stories claim many more Indian deaths than the monument at that place shows. The monument gives the names of the Indian dead as Wild Horse, So-Ta-Do, Best-Son-in-Law, Wolf Tongue, Slue-Foot, and Cheyenne of the Comanche tribes; and Chief Stone-Cay-Son, Serpent Scales, Spotted Feather, Horse Chief, Coyote, Stone-Teeth and Soft Foot of the Cheyennes. The inscription over the battle site states: "They died for that which makes life worth living—Indian's Liberty—Freedom—Peace—on the plains which they enjoyed for generations."

Q. *Can you give me a thumbnail sketch of Cochise, the great Chiricahua Apache chief?*

A. Cochise needs and deserves more, but here's a try: Cochise became chief when Mangus Colorado was assasinated in 1863. He became incensed when Lt. George Bascom falsely accused his people of committing certain crimes. In a seizure of hostages, Cochise asked for an exchange. Bascom refused and Cochise tortured his white prisoners to death and Bascom hanged his. As is usual, such a "get tough policy" on the part of both led to more and more fighting and deaths. Through the mediation of Capt. Thomas Jeffords, a New Yorker whom Cochise learned to respect, negotiations were eventually fruitful in allaying fears and halting reprisals. When U.S. Grant was president, a peace agreement was negotiated and the Chiricahuas were given a reservation at Ojo Caliente, in western New Mexico. But Cochise was not designed to be a "reservation Indian" and returned to the Dragoon Mountains in Arizona with some of his people. His friend Jeffords became Indian agent of the Apache Reservation. Cochise died about 1874. Cochise's sense of honor is remembered to this day and several towns and places bear this honored name. Cochise's Fortress in the Dragoons is today a well-known park and recreation area.

Q. *Was Chief Joseph of the Nez Perce as great a leader and warrior as some have proclaimed him to be? I refer to the younger man.*

A. Actually, the Nez Perce had several leaders, or "chiefs," to whom the leadership fell. When the new treaty of 1863 was made, ordering the tribe from their Wallowa Valley in Oregon on to another reservation in Idaho which none wanted, Chief Joseph, his son Joseph, and several other leaders refused to sign. This, of course, led to war and to the attempt of the tribe to reach Canada, which Gen. Miles prevented. By October of 1877 the Nez Perce were exhausted and sent to Fort Leavenworth, then to Indian Territory. Old Chief Joseph died in 1872, but his son, young Chief Joseph, had rallied the tribe and carried it through perilous times. His leadership ranked with the best, although he personally was opposed to war. He died in 1904, after making peace with the white man and visiting the Great White Father Teddy Roosevelt in Washington in 1903.

Q. *Why do even white men speak so respectfully of Red Cloud, the old chief of the Oglala Teton Sioux?*

A. Red Cloud earned respect as a warrior and a leader of men. He led the Indian warfare against the establishment of the Bozeman Trail, the army freight-wagon road from Fort Laramie on the North Platte River to the Montana gold fields. He fought and won fights against this encroachment on Sioux lands, culminating in the Fetterman Massacre of 1866. In 1868 Red Cloud's military skill forced the government to abandon the trail and its major forts completely. After this he kept the peace and did not participate in the Sioux uprisings of

1876, or again at Wounded Knee. After losing his chief-
tainship in 1881, he lived till his death December 10,
1909 on the Pine Ridge Reservation in South Dakota.

Q. *Why is Chief Red Cloud spoken of as one of the greatest
Plains Indians' generals?*

A. Red Cloud proved the efficacy of Indian cavalry, forcing
the U.S. government to abandon the Bozeman Trail as a
military road. His tactics were new to U.S. cavalry and
infantry outfits of the Plains, forcing them to make a
continuous campaign. These tactics were similar to what
might be called guerrilla warfare today: cleverly concealed
ambush, hit and run attacks, drawing smaller groups of
cavalry into difficult terrain using an even smaller band
of Indians as bait, attacking inadquately guarded supply
trains, etc. Further, Red Cloud exercised control over his
forces, rather than permitting them the personal styles of
combat which were common to the Plains Indian custom
of "counting coup." The U.S. generals finally learned
that the only hope of defeating the Plains Indians was to
carry on a winter campaign. With this, they eventually
brought the power of the Red Man to an end.

Q. *What was Red Cloud's Sioux name? When did he die?*

A. He was called *Maq-pelu-ta*, which is said to mean "flying
red cloud." His name, originally, was Scarlet Blanket,
later changed to Red Cloud. His birth date is given as
1818, also as 1822; and his birthplace as somewhere
along the North Platte River. Red Cloud has been reported to have participated in two hundred pitched
battles and skirmishes. He was said to have claimed
eighty coups, more than any other Indian warrior or
chief. He fought against such outstanding U.S. generals
as Miles, Sheridan, Crook, Terry, and others.

Q. *For what was Black Beaver, the Kiowa, famed?*

A. He was one of the greatest Indian scouts. He was guide
for Captain French, for Marcy, and other explorers. His
greatest bid for recognition, if not fame, comes from the
fact that he mapped out the trail that later came to be
known as the Chisholm Trail. This trail existed many
years before cattle from Texas and Jesse Chisholm,
trader, caused it to be famous in song and story. Black
Beaver died in 1880 at Anadarko, Oklahoma.

Q. *Were there* two *Indian chiefs called Sitting Bull? I have heard that one was a Hunkpapah, the other an Oglala.*

A. William J. Bordeaux in his work, *Sitting Bull, Ta Tanka-Iyotaka*, brings out that on the document of the historic treaty at Fort Laramie, dated 25 May 1868, the name Ta Tanka-Iyotaka appears as an *Oglala* Sioux. Further, says Bordeaux, Sitting Bull's name *does not appear* on the document executed with the Hunkpapah band in that same year. So it seems Sitting Bull *was*, in that era, affiliated with the Oglala band. John Stoutenburgh, Jr., places Sitting Bull (early name Jumping Badger) with the Hunkpapah Sioux.

Q. *Is the story that Chief Washakie, of the Shoshones, ordered his son into battle to be killed a true one?*

A. It has been said that Chief Washakie's son did not show the bravado and courage his father liked to see in a son. When the chief verbally chastised his son for not displaying bravery, the boy rushed into the lines of white soldiers and was, of course, slain. Chief Washakie never forgave himself for playing even this small part in his son's death, an old Shoshone squaw at Riverton, Wyoming once told my father.

Q. *Are the many stories about the Cherokee, Sequoyah, true?*

A. In recent days, *Tell Them They Lie*, the book by Traveler Bird, a descendant of this great man, casts many doubts upon what the white man has written of Sequoyah. He was, as most will recall, a fighting revolutionary whose Indian name was Sogwili. The missionaries knew him as George Guess. According to Traveler Bird, he never *invented* the Cherokee alphabet, for the Indians were using it decades before Sequoyah was born. But he was abused and branded by a council of mixed-blood judges for even proposing that his people flee west. Traveler Bird's book attempts to set straight the many myths and outright falsehoods gathered about the Indians and their people.

Q. *How did Sitting Bear, the Kiowa chief, come to his death?*

A. This famous medicine man, who had lost a son in battle, came to his death while attempting to escape confinement at Fort Sill, in 1871. Sitting Bear deliberately invited his own death and chanted his death song as he was killed. He tried to bring peace between his people and the whites both in 1840 and at the Medicine Lodge Treaty in 1867. Disillusioned by the "credibility gap" he found between spoken words and acts on the part of white men, he had broken his confinement.

Q. *What was the name of the Indian whose image appears on the buffalo nickel?*

A. The likeness, according to the sculptor James Earl Fraser, is a composite of three Indians. He remembered the names of but two: Iron Tail, a Sioux, and Two Moons, a hereditary chief of the Montana Cheyennes. Several other Indians have laid claim to being the third model used. John Big Trees, a Seneca, has set forth a claim, as has George Squires, a Sioux, and others.

Q. *Tell me something about Peter Pitchlynn, the Choctaw chief. For what is he best remembered?*

A. According to his biographer, W. David Baird, Pitchlynn guided the Choctaw nation through the nineteenth century, participating in its constitutional convention and aiding substantially in its negotiations for treaties with the whites. Pitchlynn, it appears, while aiding the Choctaws in several of their economic ventures, was not entirely motivated by philanthropic purposes. Like many entrepreneurs of both white and Indian groups, he felt that what served his own purpose served his people best. Unfortunately many of his economic ventures came to naught and he failed to win the popularity many Indian leaders won from their people. Yet he bore up with fortitude and dignity, and will be remembered for his mediation between the white people and his own kind, whom he apparently served fairly well.

Q. *Who was the Indian shot to death in cold blood by Marshal Henry Brown in Caldwell, Kansas?*

A. The Indian was Spotted Horse, a procurer for his two wives. While begging for food on the streets, May 16, 1883, the two women and Spotted Horse were making a general nuisance of themselves. A complaint brought Brown, who asked Spotted Horse to accompany him to the store of a Mr. Covington, who could act as interpreter. When Brown took the Indian's arm, Spotted Horse drew a pistol. Brown fired four times at point-blank range, hitting the Indian but once! Though not "cold-blooded murder," it was a mighty poor performance by a town marshal. But Brown was capable of giving such performances. And the Indian may not have understood a word Brown said to him.

Q. *Where did the term "wampum," used for money, come from?*

A. It is believed to spring from the Naragansett word *wampompeag* which was used to indicate the less valuable white shell beads, to distinguish them from the dark purple or black shell beads. Beads were cut from the valves of quahog and other shells. The wampum belts were used ceremonially by the Indians and in the ratification of treaties. When the pioneer Massachusetts officials ordered the first metallic currency in 1637, it was specified that "... wampamege (wampum) should pass at a 6-a-penny for any sume (sic) under 12 d."

Q. *Why did the Apaches call the white man "white eyes"?*

A. The Indians' eyes have a Mongoloid appearance because of the heavy epicanthic folds of their upper eyelids, which cover the angles of the eyes and obscure the white sclera to a large degree. This is an inheritance from their Asian ancestry. The "white men," Caucasians, do not have this skin fold, so the "whites of the eyes" appear plainly. (Remember the military command of the Revolutionary War: "Don't fire until you see the whites of their eyes.") The term "white eyes" was a term of disparagement, not one of admiration on the part of the Apache, for white men looked strange—even funny—to them.

Q. *Were the Comanches of west Texas the cruelest of all Indians?*

A. The Comanche, fighting against their fiercest enemy, the white man, learned many of the white man's cruel traits and used them against him. In Coronado's *Journal*, 1540, he stated, "They [the Comanche] are very intelligent, which is evident... that they made themselves understood by means of signs. They are a kind people, and not cruel; they are faithful...." Perhaps we make people cruel by attempting to impose our own will upon them.

Q. *Did any of the American Indians (U.S.A.) use blowguns?*

A. Yes, the Choctaws and the Cherokees both used them, as well as other tribes of the southern Mississippi waters. However, they used them against small game, as hunting weapons. Quite to the contrary of white men's claims, there is no evidence to support the belief that any Indians of the continental U.S. used "poison-tipped" arrows. The Indians of Central and South America did, and still do, use poison darts and arrows, as did the Seris of Mexico.

Q. *In New Mexico I bought a small stone animal, shaped like a wolf or dog, and bound with rawhide, an arrowhead lashed with rawhide to its back. The Indian I bought it from said it was a "fetish." What is it good for?*

A. Indians believed that all objects were animate, incarnate. The little fetish the Indian sold you is to help secure the aid of these many spirits. Too bad he didn't tell you the secret of its construction—and use. These fetishes are kept private, and their powers revealed only to those who inherit the fetish. I own one, a lovely Little Bear given to me by an old Indian friend and trader, Rex Arrowsmith. It is exceptionally old, he says, and works hard on anything dealing with communication, such as mail, letters, and helping to bring favors to one from a long distance away. I use it to hustle business through the mail, keeping book orders coming in, and, of course, when I mail a manuscript to the publisher, the Little Bear fetish is turned in that direction, a Power no ordinary publisher can resist!

Q. *I have read where mummified Indian bodies have been found. Did the Indians have a way of embalming the body?*

A. No, Indians did not embalm. But many mummified bodies have been found in the drier climate of the Western states. I once saw the mummified body of a male, perhaps fifty years of age, and of a stature that would be twenty-four inches in height! The body was found in a cave on Casper Mountain, Wyoming, by Civilian Conservation Corps workers who were blasting ground to build a road. The tiny body was perfect in every respect, with no clothing or ornamentation of any sort on it. The tiny hairs of the body were in perfect detail. The hair of the head was four inches in length at the back. The figure was sitting, legs crossed, arms and hands at rest, folded across the stomach. An X-ray, taken by an Eastern university-museum, showed a fracture of the clavicle bone, left side. Otherwise, the bone structure was perfect. This small mummy has since disappeared, I have heard, after having been sent to a museum in the East. I have offered $500 for its recovery, for it is clearly one of a kind. The paleontologists who examined it first in the East could offer no explanation other than it was "a prehistoric Man of some sort." If anyone has seen it in the past ten years, I would like to hear. One anthropologist thought the mummy could possibly be one of the early Wyoming tribe of sheep-eaters.

Q. *Did the American Indian understand the value of quinine?*

A. Yes, South American Indians of Peru used it to halt fevers. The Jesuits took the cure to Europe as a "secret remedy" in 1632. Later, Juan del Vego used it to treat the Count of Chinchon, and the drug was given the name *Chinchona*. The countess, too, was treated with the drug.

Q. *What was the Indian custom of "mouth fishing"?*

A. Oliver M. Nelson, author of *The Cowboy's Southwest*, tells of this rather unhygienic practice which occurred when white men and Indian women attended the same dances. The man would place a small coin in his mouth, then offer the coin to the woman who fished it out with her tongue! The manner in which it was done was this: the Indian woman would place a shawl over the heads of both the man and herself, then he would put the coin in his mouth and she would fish it out.

Q. *What were the "breath feathers" of an eagle? How were they used by Indians?*

A. Breath feathers are those so light and fluffy they may be stirred by the breath of a person. They were used for the tufted base of the large tail and wing feathers around the forehead band of the war bonnet, and to tip the large feathers.

Q. *How were the Paiute biscuits made?*

A. They were made from squawberries, bullberries, sand-grass seed, some coarse corn meal, and yellow seeds from the blueweed, ground with *mano* and *metate*. All were ground and mixed together, and nothing added to make the dough rise. Placed in a stone oven for two hours, they emerged hard and small, capable of being carried around in a leather pouch for several months, much as hardtack was carried by troops. The Paiute biscuit was a staple food and was said to be very nutritious when amplified with meat from small game.

Q. *Did the American Indian show the same proficiency with the lariat as the American cowboy?*

A. Without the stout Western stock saddles, stirrups, and a saddle tree for holding the caught animals, the Indians were handicapped. But Catlin, the artist, shows them tying up wild stallions and holding them with ropes. Their ability to catch with the loop was very good.

Q. *How did the Plains Indians prevent their tepees from blowing away in the strong Kansas-Nebraska-Oklahoma sandstorms?*

A. Their lodgepoles at the top were crossed and bound together with rawhide strips. A stout rawhide strip was dropped from the center top to the ground, and there anchored to a heavy rock or to a substantial peg in the ground, in the center of the tepee. The edges of the tepee were anchored with pegs or with stones. Old camping grounds show these many "circles of stones" that indicate the location of the tepees.

Q. *Where did the Indian corn (maize) of the Southwestern Indians come from?*

A. It is believed that this staple of the Indian diet originated in southern Mexico where it had once grown as a wild grass, then been "tamed" and brought north by pre-Columbian Indians. Along with *frijoles* (beans) and squash, maize sustained generations of tribes. I once found small ears of corn in the kivas of the Cliff Dwellers, and one small ear, three inches long, in the Great Kiva at Pueblo Bonito, in Chaco Canyon, New Mexico. These ruins date back to 1200–1300 A.D.

Q. *Did Indians actually eat dogs?*

A. Yes, young dog meat was a tender delicacy to them, just as it was to the early Hawaiians. Those who have tasted dog meat pronounce it edible and nourishing. The prairie dog (actually a squirrel) was also eaten by the Indians and by pioneer settlers. In an age of high beef prices, in which horse meat is becoming a butcher-shop commodity, it is possible that Americans may again turn to dog meat for sustenance.

Q. *What did the Indians use for needles with which to sew their tough leather clothing?*

A. Many used bone points, fashioned into needles. Wood was also used at times. Spines from cactus were used, as were various thorns from bushes such as Osage orange. Human hair, horse hair, and certain woven fibers, as from the yucca plant, constituted their thread, together with animals' tendons and strips of finely cut rawhide.

Q. *What were the Indian bows made from, and how long were they?*

A. A pliable wood was used, as was elk horn. The bows were from four to five feet in length.

Q. *Was the spear used to a great extent by Plains Indians?*

A. Yes, the lance, as it is generally referred to, was carried by all war parties and by all hunting parties. The lance was also a ceremonial object and used for signaling. Along with the horse, the lance made buffalo-killing faster and much easier than had the old-time stalking practices. A lance was about eight feet in length, with a steel point often ten inches in length. Earlier, long stone points were lashed to the spear and were practical weapons for war or the hunt.

Q. *It is said that Pima Indians could be brothers-in-law without marrying one another's sisters. How is this possible?*

A. An early custom of the Pimas was to trade wives (as some of our white people do today). They felt the resulting relationship made the males brothers-in-law, and they accepted one another as such.

Q. *Without surgical instruments, how would an Indian extract a foreign object from the eye of another?*

A. Indians, particularly the far northern tribes and the Eskimos (whose hands are rough and lack agility because of subjection to great cold or due to work such as weaving, pottery-making, and jewelry-making), use man's oldest and most sensitive tool to do the extracting—the human tongue. Yes, they hold the patient firmly with their hands, thrust the tip of the tongue over the eyeball and literally lick the object out. Objects so small that they remain undetected by the eye of an observer may be extracted in this way.

Q. *How could an Indian distinguish between a real owl hooting and the voice of another, imitating an owl?*

A. The human voice casts an echo. An owl's hoot does not.

Q. *Did the Apaches wear feathers in their hair, like the Sioux?*

A. Yes, but the Sioux headdress was formed with the great eagle feathers; the Apache land offered only small birds from which their adornment could come. One observer said that the Apache adornment on the head "...looked like someone had thrown the small feathers atop a buckskin war hat."

Q. *Where did the term "Indian giver" originate?*

A. The epithet came from the first dealings the white man had with the Indian. But it arose because of a misconception about the Indian and his customs. Indians *never gave away* or "sold" land to the white man. The land was, to them, like a mother, giving them shelter, food, a home. They never thought of "owning" land, as we do, only using it. However, when the white man made gifts to the Indians, and went through *his own* legal processes and *his own* white man's conceptions of "buying the land," he expected to "own" it. This "owner" felt he was entitled to expel all others from it, post it against trespassers, and receive rental payments for its use. To the Indians this was simply beyond comprehension. They meant only to let the white man *use the land temporarily, to live off it*. So when they asked for the land back, the white man called them "Indian givers." Indians had a custom of believing that the most honored person in the tribe should be he who *lent or gave away the most to his people*. Many of his gifts were later returned by his fellow Indians who had become more affluent or fortunate. It is a white man's *misconception* of Indian custom to say that "Manhattan was *bought* for twenty-four dollars and a gallon of whisky." Manhattan was only *loaned*, and has never been returned.

Q. *Why don't the Navaho Indians shake hands?*

A. They do, in their own way, which is merely to touch the hand of a stranger.

Q. *What were the earliest known methods of preserving meat among the Indians?*

A. The most primitive men used freezing, salting, and drying as basic methods of preserving meats. Among the Western Indians "jerking" meat was the most practical, that is, sun-drying it. This method lightened the meat in weight, so it could be carried with ease. Freezing could only be useful to the far northern tribes. Salting was not used to any great extent, for the lack of salt prevented it. Actually, most tribes feasted when near abundant meat supplies, then fasted when without. This is a common practice among primitive people as well as predatory animals. The first record of "jerked" meat is reported to have come from Castenada, who prepared records of the Coronado Expedition (1540–42). He wrote: "They dry flesh of the bison in the sun, cutting it thin, like a leaf, and when dry they grind it like a meal to keep it, and make a seasoup of it to eat. A handful thrown into the pot swells up so as to increase very much. They season it with fat, which they always try to secure when they kill a cow."

Q. *What was Indian "bread"? I understand it came from the buffalo.*

A. It did. It is the strip of fatty tissue running from the shoulder blade backward along the backbone. However, the Southwestern Indians made theirs from cornmeal, just as most peoples have made their bread from grains.

Q. *What, among Indian hunting tools, was a stunner?*

A. A stunner was a blunt arrowhead, used to stun small game rather than risk the loss of an arrowpoint. Also, on hunts that extended two or three days away from camp, live game of the smaller sort would keep better and be fresh to kill when back at camp. Stunners made from large, broken-point spearheads have been found. The finely worked, sharp arrowheads were often as valuable to the hunter as the game shot with them. Undoubtedly, the primitive Indian prized the beautifully made points as we prize beautifully made guns today. If struck with a small arrowpoint, a wounded rabbit or badger could carry the point back deep into the ground, where it could not be recovered. A stunned animal could be quickly dispatched with a club, or knife.

Q. *Why didn't Indians use tobacco as the white man eventually learned to use it—that is, in snuff, and in cigarettes and cigars?*

A. The white man *learned* to smoke a pipe *from the Indians*. However, Indians did not inhale the smoke, which is the addictive factor in tobacco usage. Further, the Indian pipe was used ceremonially, and for sealing agreements and treaties, being passed among the officials of each tribe. The ceremony called for each official to blow a puff of smoke into each Wind (direction). The use of the peace pipe is known to all.

Q. *Did all Indians bury their dead on poles, or platforms?*

A. No, some placed the bodies in trees. Others heaped stones over the body, or secreted it in a cave or crevice in the rocks. Lacking digging tools, the tree or pole burial can be understood. Prairie earth is tight, heavy, sometimes rocky, difficult to penetrate. Modern Indian burials are like those of the white men.

Q. *Did Indians, in battle, lose as many braves against the white man as our Western literature and films depict?*

A. No. If we may believe eyewitnesses, such as Col. James Smith, a Pennsylvania native taken captive at age eighteen, and who lived with the Indians five years during Braddock's War, the Indians actually had the best of it. His eyewitness accounts from Catawba and Delaware warriors, 1755 to 1758, indicate that the Indians took from fifty whites (including women and children) to the grave for every warrior and squaw killed. However, once the guerrilla type of warfare conducted by the Indians was understood by the white men, it is possible that these odds were lessened.

Q. *Did Col. George A. Custer once have a demented Indian executed?*

A. This story originates from an episode reported in the Civil War, when Custer, finding a white man, David Getz, thirty, hunting near Woodstock, Virginia, thought him a southern spy or deserter. Though the townspeople vouched for the man, telling the Union officers the man was half-witted, Custer had him taken to a hill above Dayton, Virginia, where he was forced to dig his own grave and there executed. Adolph Heller of Woodstock told Custer at the time, "You will also sleep in a bloody grave for this merciless act."

Q. *Where in the Southwest may we see real Indians doing their old dances?*

A. In July, the White Buffalo Council of American Indians holds its annual Pow Wow at Denver, Colorado. The Pow Wow is held at the Jefferson County Fairgrounds, west of

Denver (in Lakewood). The general public is welcomed. At Gallup, New Mexico, the Inter-Tribal Indian Ceremonial is held annually. An inquiry to the Gallup Chamber of Commerce will get you the dates, which have been changed recently. Indian Pow Wows are held at many places throughout the West, including an excellent attraction at Sheridan, Wyoming.

Q. *Who was the first Indian female airline hostess?*

A. A Crow maiden of eighteen years, Bethaneth Pease (Princess Goes-to-the-Right), took off from the Billings, Montana, airport in April 1937, to be assigned to the Northwest Airlines after an appearance in New York, at the National Airlines Association dinner. Her father was Ben Pease of Lodgegrass, Montana.

Q. *Has there ever been a* professional *football team composed of Indians?*

A. Yes, the Hominy Indians were a tristate club (Kansas-Oklahoma-Missouri) organized by Ira Hamilton, an Osage, in the early 1920s. Players consisted of Osage, Creek, Sac and Fox, Cheyennes, Senecas, Pottawatomie, Sioux, and others. For their story, see the article by Art Shoemaker, *Oklahoma Today* magazine, August 1967.

Q. *What happened to all the medals Jim Thorpe, the great Carlisle Indian athlete, won in Olympic competition at Stockholm in 1912?*

A. Thorpe, winner of both Pentathlon and Decathlon, was later that year charged with having played semi-pro baseball in 1908–10. Though many claimed that all this great athlete received from baseball (which was not an Olympic sport anyway) was his bare expenses, Thorpe was stripped of all his medals. The medals are, today, on display in Lucerne, Switzerland. A movement has been launched in the U.S. to recover Thorpe's medals and bring them back to his home state, Oklahoma. The movement also demands to have Thorpe's amateur status reinstated, and to have his good name reinserted in the Olympic records. His daughter, Grace Thorpe of Phoenix, Arizona, supports the move. There are two groups to which you may write if interested: Project Jim Thorpe, Box 126, Carlisle, Pennsylvania; or, Jim Thorpe Memorial, Oklahoma Athletic Hall of Fame Commission, Harold V. Brown, Chairman, Box 246, Yale, Oklahoma 74085. Thorpe was a pure-blood Sac and Fox Indian from Oklahoma, one of the greatest all-around athletes the world has ever known.

Q. *I have heard that the first Congressional Medal of Honor winner was an Indian fighter. Who was he?*

A. Bvt. Lt. Col. Bernard John Dowling of the Army Medical Department won this medal in action against Chiricahua Indians when he took medical relief to Bascom's command, surrounded by Apache on the night of February 14, 1861. The medal was awarded to him on January 21, 1894, for it had not been in existence in 1861.

Q. *Whatever happened to those three California judges who were proved to have defrauded the Aqua Caliente Indians while serving in the legal role as their guardians?*

A. Actually, none were punished. The Interior Department wrote a caustic criticism of these "conservators" for their action of relieving the Indians of up to forty-four percent of their income as "business managers" and for "legal fees" for their crooked services. The three resigned from the bench (under pressure of course). Acts such as these have inspired the American Indian to demand that they, rather than the Bureau of Indian Affairs, administer their own affairs.

Q. *Where is the largest Indian reservation today?*

A. The Navaho tribe inhabits the sixteen-million-acre reservation in New Mexico and Arizona. Apaches and Utes occupy other reservations in those states, as do the Hopi, Papago, Zuni, Pueblos, Hualpai, and others.

Q. *Where do the Wyandotte (Wyandot) Indians live today?*

A. In northeast Oklahoma. They settled there in 1867. They were originally of the four tribes that spoke the Wyandot language and called themselves Wendat. Early in the seventeenth century they warred with the Iroquois and were driven out of their homelands. Formerly numbering 20,000, they now number perhaps 1,000.

Q. *How many Indians served in the armed forces in World War I?*

A. Six thousand volunteered; two thousand were drafted. This set an example for patriotism which helped bring about Indian citizenship legislation, or the Act of June 2, 1924. This act, and prior legislation, gave to the American Indian full citizenship in the United States of America.

Q. *How many Indians are on the Crow Reservation in south-central Montana?*

A.   Approximately 5,000. About 1,500 Crow Indians live away from the reservation. The Crow Reserve covers two-and-a-quarter million acres.

Q.   *Do any Indians who live off of the reservations have clubs or groups, similar to the old tribal societies?*

A.   There are urban groups like the White Buffalo Council in Denver, which was established in 1954 and which represents several hundreds of Indian families of all tribes. The group is nonpolitical, and it was organized to retain social aspects of early Indian life on the continent and to preserve their cultural heritage.

Q.   *When we think of Indians, and reservations, we usually turn our eyes westward, across the Mississippi. Are there modern Indians, on reservations, in the East?*

A.   Yes, there are a few small reservations. For example, there is the Allegany Indian Reservation, at Salamanca, New York, bordering the Allegany State Park. These Indians today produce and sell a fine—perhaps the finest I have ever used—pen and pencil set. As I write this, they sell this combination pen and pencil set for less than two dollars. Inflation will undoubtedly raise this price, but if you want the best, write them. They are called Indian Made Products Company.

  As the white man conquered the Indian lands, the Indians moved west. Those who remained stayed in the small reserves allotted them, and not a few were assimilated into the white race.

Q.   *Why have Indians become so militant in late years, seizing property, such as Alcatraz and at Wounded Knee, carrying guns and threatening law and order?*

A.   Indians have many unsettled grievances against the U.S. government, which took their lands by force and violence from them, then lied to them, failed to carry out the treaty promises and eventually packed them in on reservations, the poorest lands that could be found. The Bureau of Indian Affairs (BIA) budget is $500 million. This budget must cover the salaries of an army of white people, 50,000 of them, who "administer" the Indians' affairs for the 500,000 reservation Indians. Indian income is the lowest in the nation and unemployment among Indians is ten times the national average.

Q.   *Why don't the American Indian organizations form a press association to aid them in their struggle for equality?*

A. They do have one now. In San Francisco, at the organizational meeting of the American Indian Historical Society, Jim Jefferson, editor of the *Southern Ute Drum*, Ignacio, Colorado, was named board chairman of the Indian Press Association. There are a score of more active Indian publications in the Western states, most of which use this service, I am told.

Q. *Why are there no Indian clubs or organizations established by Indians themselves designed to help urbanized Indians to find jobs?*

A. There are a few, and more are continually being organized by urban Indian groups. These groups are also working to give information to young urban Indians about the dangers to them from alcohol and drugs. The Indian youth's traditional disregard of *time* and *money* also stands in the way of individual and group improvement, and these cultural characteristics are being explained and discouraged by some of these groups.

Q. *Where may I find literature on the American Indians of the Central Plains and the Gulf Coast areas?*

A. The Department of the Interior, Bureau of Indian Affairs, Washington, D.C., has an abundance of such literature available. Address Superintendent of Documents, Government Printing Office, Washington, D.C., and ask for the six brochures dealing with Indians of the Great Plains, California, Montana, and Wyoming. Also ask for the brochure, *Famous Indians*, Catalog No. 120.2:In. 2/26.

Q. *I am going to purchase three good Navaho rugs for my home. Price is not necessarily an objective with me, but how may I tell a good rug from one not as good?*

A. You had better hire an expert, one who knows Navaho weaving, and pay him five or ten percent to select for you. Navaho weaving is based on the quality of the wool carded and used, the quality of the weaving, the beauty and color of the pattern and, for many collectors, the antiquity of the piece. The most sought-after pieces are woven by the Two Gray Hills people, the Tees-Nos-Pos, the Wide Ruins, and the Crystal. This does not mean there are not others just as beautiful. Better consult a reputable Navaho rug dealer.

Q. *How long have the natives of Arizona and New Mexico been weaving their beautiful blankets?*

A. When the Espejo Expedition of Spaniards came to Arizona and New Mexico to trade with the Indians in 1582, they obtained 4,000 blankets woven from cotton by the Moqui of Arizona. It was not until 200 years later that the Navaho began weaving their beautiful blankets of wool for which they are so famous today. The earliest dated piece of Navaho woolen weaving comes to us from Massacre Cave in the Cañon del Muerte, dated at 1804-05 by experts. In 1883 merino sheep were introduced into the Navajo lands to replace the *churro*, the poor-wool sheep brought in by the Spaniards. Later, in 1903, the Rambouillet was brought in, and this remains the principal source of wool used by the Navajo to obtain their beautiful blankets and rugs.

Q. *A few years ago, U.S. government labor statistics showed that the Navajo women who weave their lovely rugs and blankets received only six cents per hour for their work. Surely this must be the lowest wages paid anyone in the U.S.?*

A. Yes, this wage was so low that welfare became a better proposition for many of the Navajo weavers. In the meantime, Navajo rugs and blankets have soared in price. For example, a Navajo tapestry that I bought for $100 twenty years ago from Harry Ohmstead at the Aztec Trading Post in New Mexico today brings nearly $3,000. Gilbert S. Maxwell, in his book *Navajo Rugs, Past-Present-Future*, wrote that a weaver who had shorn, washed, carded, spun, and dyed her own wool and woven it into two pieces, a thirty-by-sixty-inch saddle blanket, and a three-by-five-foot quality rug, would spend 628 hours on the project. That would mean approximately 104 six-hour days of continuous weaving—nearly four months time! In the 1950s she would have received about $50 for the saddle blanket, and $100 for the rug, or about twenty-four cents an hour. That's $150 for nearly four months' labor! Not to count the cost of wool, dyes, and materials used. Today, she might get (from the dealer) five times that amount, or $750. That would pay her about $1.20 per hour, still much less than the minimum hourly wages today. Is it any wonder that these women quit weaving, and that their skill and craft will soon be lost to posterity. Lee Anderson of the Anasazi Gallery of Art at Flagstaff, Arizona, has written, "No other cultural group in the world weaves as does the Navajo. Their finished work is a beautiful expression of the pride that lies deeply within these remarkable people."

Q. *Where may I buy* authentic *Indian artifacts?*

A. There are many dealers in authentic Indian artifacts, though they are sometimes hard to locate. Personally, I have made many purchases through my friend Rex Arrowsmith, Indian Trader, Santa Fe, New Mexico 87501. If he does not have what you want, I can promise you that he will tell you the name of the person or group that can find it for you. Further, what you buy from him will be exactly as he describes it to you. He buys from many Southwestern Indians and from others all over the United States, Mexico, and South America.

Q. *I am looking for authentic Indian war bonnets of the Sioux manufacture. Where may I find them?*

A. They are as rare as hen's teeth, and costly. Try the Sioux Reservation, or try dealers. But first check the federal laws on the purchase of eagle feathers. It is illegal to buy or sell them today.

Q. *What do you think of the exhumation of Indian graves for artifacts?*

A. Grave-robbing is done only by ghouls. I believe in letting the remains of anyone's dead remain there in peace. No artifacts are worth the price of a person's soul or his conscience. Leave the graves of the dead, black, white, yellow, or red men, alone.

Q. *I have heard that the Indian ceremonials at Gallup, New Mexico, were set back on the calendar one week because the Hopis in their Snake Dances produced too much rain. Correct?*

A. Yes, the annual Hopi Ceremonial, which includes the Rain Dance, started in the last week of August back in 1922, when the Celebration first began. But the heavy rains discouraged attendance. Officials tried to change the date of the rain dances, but the people would not accept the change. So the entire ceremonial program was set up for a week earlier. Now everyone enjoys the great ceremonial, then returns home to watch it rain over the lovely desert vistas.

Q. *Will you name a few of the most easily identified Indian petroglyphs to be found in the West?*

A. A few of the most easily identified are: tepee, means temporary home; horse, means journey; mountain, indicates abundance; arrowhead, says "Be alert!"; a man's figure, means that human habitations are nearby; a bird, signifies a carefree life. Figures of a bear, an antelope, or a deer sometimes indicates only the hunter's desire to project his successes, or perhaps a plea to the gods to help locate the animals for his arrows. These symbols are also applied to many tribal groups within a nation. But all the many Indian petroglyphs should not be confused with modern treasure hunters' signs, which supposedly point or lead to buried or concealed treasure, and must be studied for meanings in relationship to the treasure hunt. For example: An arrow, to a treasure hunter, is a sign to be followed to the treasure, but to an Indian, the arrow sign may only denote the "hunt" for meat, not abstract treasure.

Q. *Is it true that Adolph Hitler was influenced by Bavarian author Karl May's writings about the American West?*

A. Yes, some Germans have stated that Hitler, in youth, was greatly interested in May's writings, as were many other young Germans and Austrians. May's genocidal hero was called Old Shatterhand, and this personage was marked by many of the ideas we would today call "racist." He was intent on the genocide of the "Ogalla" Indians. May's Indian hero was named Winnetou, "noble chief of the Apaches." May's "model" was probably Cochise, who died in the same year as May, in 1874. May had never been to the American West, and knew little or nothing about the Indians. However, like Edgar Rice Burroughs and H. Rider Haggard, he concealed this lack of knowledge underneath skill as a writer. Three of his lengthy, rambling, unauthentic novels are today being republished by Bantam Books.

Q. *Was the swastika, as designed and used by the Nazis and Hitler, an Indian symbol originally?*

A. Yes, Der Fuhrer couldn't even design his own flag or party symbol, but stole it from the Indians. The swastika was an Indian symbol of "good luck." I first saw it as a cattle brand in the Nebraska Sandhills in 1917. As it was used on the ranch of B.F. Craig, Dickens, Texas, the points turned to the left, counterclockwise. Another Texan, M.D. Abernathy of Lubbock, Texas, used it with the points turned clockwise. It is regrettable that the German dictator made a "Mark of Horror" of the lovely Indian symbol. But today no man wants the mark on his animals or his place. Too much terror and suffering and death have gone on under the sign.

Q. *Is there a good book from which I may study the Dakota language?*

A. *The English-Dakota Dictionary* was compiled by John Poage Williamson (1835-1917), New York, for the American Tract Society. There is also the Dakota language glossary, *Language des Naoudoonessis*, by Louis Narciss, in his *Voyage à la Louisiana* (1802). These may be found in any good city library having a Western collection department. Paul Warcloud Grant, Sisseton, South Dakota, has recently compiled a *Sioux Dictionary*. Since the Dakotas are a member of the Sioux language stock, this work would have great interest for you. You may write Mr. Grant at Sisseton.

Q. *I would like to learn to speak the Cherokee language. Where may I find a teacher, or the books to study?*

A. You might ask your local librarian, if you live in a large city. Most smaller public libraries will make arrangements for persons interested in languages to borrow from larger city libraries. Also, your local schools will aid you if interested in learning languages.

Q. *I would like to get a better understanding of the various American Indian languages. Is there any book available that might help me?*

A. The University of Nebraska Press published, several years ago, a small volume containing the excellent works of Franz Boas and J.W. Powell. The work is titled *Introduction to Handbook of American Indian Languages*. For information, write them at Lincoln, Nebraska.

Q. *Is there a book that gives the sign language of the Western Plains Indians?*

A. I have in my library *Universal American Sign Language*, a book by William Tomkins, a man who lived near the

Sioux Reservation in Dakota Territory, near Fort Scully, Cheyenne Agency, Pierre, South Dakota, for many years, and who rode after cattle in the Dakotas. This book went through many printings. To find out if it is still available, write Indian Sign Language, 3044 Lawrence Street, San Diego, California. Check too with Indian traders or rare book dealers.

Q. *In the Plains Indians' sign language, what are the most-used signs given with the hands?*

A. A few of the well-known and most common signs stand for: Yes, No, Good, Bad, Come, Go, Water, Eat, Drink, See, Up, Down, High, Low, Me, You, Him, Me-all (meaning us or we), You-all (meaning ye), Him-all (meaning they), Walk, Run, Sleep, Small, Few, Big, Buy or Sell, Exchange, Trade, Stop, Wait, House, Tepee, and Question (Ask).

Q. *Why was the sign language of the Plains Indians so widely used?*

A. Following the buffalo herds for their existence, these Indians eventually had to find some method of communication with other tribes they encountered on the hunting grounds. So the "universal sign language" developed through necessity, much as did the Pidgin English in the China trade. As sign language developed among the tribes, grace in movement and expression increased, and a tribesman who could readily develop understanding with others became a "spokesman" for his chief and group.

Q. *Is it possible that Indians from all parts of the U.S. could understand one another through "sign" language?*

A. This is true in the same sense that you, though unable to speak or understand a word of Russian, could make yourself understood if you were in Moscow. Many signs of the "sign" language have universal meaning and are understood by all people. For example, the index finger over the lips will tell any human not to speak, to be quiet; the finger, feeding the lips, and the jaws chewing will indicate one's desire to be fed. A smile and rubbing the belly with the hand will indicate you have had a good meal. As in Hawaiian songs, water falls from the sky when the fingers of the hand indicate a falling, dripping motion; the moon is round, as shown by the two hands forming a circle; a parallel wavelike motion with one hand shows the fish swimming, and so forth.

Q. *When Indians made council with the white men and agreed to "peace forever," what sign was used for such an abstraction as "infinity"?*

A. The Indian speaker would pass his right hand, palm toward the head, around the front and back of his head, twice. This indicated a circle around, or encompassing, his head, his mind. (Similarly, the mathematical symbol of infinity is imaged as a circle bending back upon itself.)

Q. *Did the Indian worship many gods?*

A. Col. Richard I. Dodge, who served many years on the Western frontier, thought the Indian had at least two gods. Maj. R.S. Neighbors, Indian agent for the Republic of Texas in 1847, contended that the Comanches believed in only one supreme being. Dodge said that the Indian had the "good god" and the "bad god." Whenever things went well, the good god got the credit. If things went awry, the bad god received the blame. Generally, it is believed that the Indian's belief in the Great Spirit is parallel to the Judeo-Christian view of one god. While the Indians may have seen gods in the winds and in the rocks and trees, they seemed to believe that the one Great Spirit ruled supreme over these lesser manifestations. It is doubtful, though, whether any white person is able to state with accuracy much about the religion of Indians. Religion takes many forms.

Photo by McClure. *Courtesy Western History Department, Denver Public Library.*

Q. *What can cattle live on in those barren, grassless hills of Socorro County, New Mexico?*

A. In early spring, on that range, the earth produces a thistle that is both succulent and nourishing for cattle. By summer, if there has been normal rain, the grass is up. If not overgrazed, the range will support a minimum of cattle through fall. There are grasses like Curleymesquite, hardly known to humans, that hungry cattle soon turn into beef. Other forbs, legumes and grasses, well-known to Nature, and hungry animals, escape human eyes and lead us to believe food does not exist because it fails to fit our preconceptions.

7

GEOGRAPHICAL LOCATIONS and GEOLOGICAL FORMATIONS

The American West was always full of surprises; surprises such as the geological formations of the Grand Canyon, the geysers and mud pots of Yellowstone Park; the grandeur of Yosemite; the giant sequoias of California's Sierra Nevada Range. Stupendous as these sights, and many more, are to travelers today, think of how awesome they must have been to the early trappers, hunters, or gold seekers who viewed these scenes in all their pristine majesty.

Coming from the Eastern plains country into the mountainous areas has always constituted an adventure for men and women. The crossing of mountains, once such an arduous feat, has now become a matter of three hours of luxurious plane travel, or a day's drive in a car. Yet, however we traverse the nation today, we miss much that was once the great joy of pioneer travel—the sense of pride and accomplishment. In addition, a great deal of the pleasure of travelling came from the small discoveries made from day to day, the sighting of an extraordinary butte or mountain, the vision of a blue lake set in a mountain valley. Or the discovery may have been that of watching the mating dance of the prairie chickens as the covered wagons moved slowly through the sandhill rookeries.

Though we no longer travel so slowly as to savor these little miracles day by day over a period of months, yet we can read of them still. We may visualize for ourselves how interesting and new seemed the grasses, flowers, and forbs the pioneers encountered for the first time; or their reaction to the animals they had heard so much about, the buffalo, deer, and antelope. And those mysterious "cities in the sky," which they had seen with their own eyes (mirages), we may now also see in the comfort of our reading room or library, from the pages of a book.

Q. *When one speaks of "the West," what area or states does that encompass?*

A. The descriptive term "the West" is a relative one. In 1775, everything west of the Appalachian Mountains would have been called "the West." As the course of empire moved westward, the trans-Mississippi area was called "the West." In the middle and late 1880s, the Rocky Mountain region was included in the term, as was the West Coast area. Today, most of us think of "the West" as the area extending west of the 100th meridian to the Continental Divide. That region extending west of the Rocky Mountains is now the "Far West," or the "West Coast."

Though New Yorkers must laugh at the very thought of it, most folks west of the 100th meridian, and who are direct descendants of the pioneers, think of "the East" as being everything east of Des Moines, Iowa! (The author, as a fifteen-year-old horse wrangler, on being asked by a CY foreman at Careyhurst, Wyoming, where he came from, replied, without attempting to be facetious, "From the East," meaning from Scottsbluff, *in the Nebraska Panhandle!*)

Q. *Where are the Mule Mountains in Arizona?*

A. In southern Cochise County, in the southeastern part of the state. They lie between the Huachuca Mountains to the west and the southern extreme of the Chiricahuas to the northeast. Enormous copper strikes were made there in the past, and the silver and gold of Tombstone, to the north, made the area a fabulous mining area. The older maps show the mountain range as the *Puerto de los Mulos.*

Q. *When did the meteor that made Meteor Crater, in Arizona, fall there? Has the body of the meteor ever been uncovered?*

A. Geologists estimate that the meteor fell about 25,000 years ago. Daniel M. Barringer, a Philadelphia mining engineer, spent thousands of dollars over a twenty-five-year period attempting to locate the meteor's mass. He struck its debris at 1,376 feet, jamming his drill. As his funds were exhausted, the project was abandoned in 1929, as were many other economic activities in the nation. Later efforts also failed to locate the meteor. Some scientists believe the impact was so great that, like an atomic explosion, the true mass of the meteor was converted into a gaseous state.

Q. *Who discovered South Pass, on the California road?*

A. That is a disputed question. South Pass is not a "pass" in the normal sense of the word but actually a high mountain plain on the Continental Divide area, twenty-five miles wide, and people may walk over it without suspecting they are going through a "mountain pass." Robert Stuart is generally believed to have been the first white man to cross the mountains at that point, in 1812, on his eastward trip from Fort Astoria. Indians, of course, have been traveling the pass for centuries prior to this.

Q. *I have heard of a "walking hill" near McGrew, Nebraska. Why and how does it walk?*

A. This hill, actually blow-sand, is two-and-a-half miles west of McGrew. In the past fifty years, the hill has moved nearly a mile in a southeasterly direction, because of the predominantly northwest winds. The hill is about a quarter of a mile in length and about a hundred yards in width. It is composed of sand that is not fine enough to be carried off by the winds, but is fine enough to be wind-driven on the earth. Such "walking" hills are not unusual in the West and Southwest. In western Kansas and the Oklahoma Panhandle there are many such moving hills. They are a bane to irrigators whose ditches they fill, and they may obliterate buildings in dry and windy years. The late Burris Wright, Liberal, Kansas, an old-time cowboy, once told me of an Indian burial he and friends had come across on the spring roundup. The bones of the feet of several Indians were protruding from the north edge of one of these smaller walking hills, which was about 100 yards in length. That fall, when they returned for the roundup, the skulls were showing, but the feet and rest of the bodies had been obliterated by the drifting sand of the hill. The sand, he estimated, had moved, in a body, at least its length, 100 yards, in six to seven months, driven by the predominant south winds.

Q. *Who is credited with the discovery of San Francisco Bay?*

A. Ortego, a scout for Gaspar de Portola, governor of California, made the discovery in the summer of 1769, but from the land side, not the ocean. The party was attempting the colonization of Alto California and the occupation of Monterey. Father Crespi wrote in his expedition *Journal,* "It is a very large and fine harbor, such that not only the navy of our most Catholic Majesty but those of all Europe could take shelter in."

Q. *Is there any factual record of what the first white man who viewed the Grand Canyon thought of its vast size?*

A. Garcia Lopez de Cardenas, a member of the 1540 Coronado expedition in the Southwest, was selected to lead a party in search of a certain river mentioned by the Hopis. After twenty days march, Cardenas and his party came upon the Grand Canyon of the Colorado, and are believed to be the first white men to view it. Cardenas, fluent chronicler of the expedition, recorded the impressions of the three Spaniards who went down a third of the way into the Canyon's depths: "Those who stayed above had estimated that some huge rocks on the sides of the cliffs were about as tall as a man. But those who went down swore that when they reached those rocks they were bigger than the Tower of Seville." The Tower of Seville was, to those men, something of the very "biggest." So one may imagine the tremendous impression made upon those naive Spaniards, the first white men to attempt to describe the indescribable!

Q. *Many have now boated through the Grand Canyon, we know. But has anyone ever attempted to* walk *through its length?*

A. Yes. Starting at Hualpai Hilltop, west of Havasu Creek Canyon, Colin Fletcher, a Welshman and a veteran of World War II, in 1963 walked the Esplanade, nearly 2,000 feet above the Colorado River on the wall of the canyon, and along the Tonto Platform, emerging two months later at Point Imperial, on the Kaibab Plateau. His food supply came from caches previously made and from air drops. For the final two weeks of his hike, he kept his path quite close to the river below and on its banks. Fletcher is a professional hiker, and whoever duplicates his feat will need the stamina and courage of a soldier. His book *The Man Who Walked Through Time* tells of his experiences, both mental and physical, as he performed this fantastic feat.

Q. *Did Jim Bridger, the mountain man, actually relate all the tall tales about the Yellowstone Park area that have been attributed to him?*

A. No, Bridger reported only what he had actually seen. The newspapermen of his day seized upon Bridger's fantastic truths and distorted them into the "windies." It was many years before artists, photographers, and scientists documented Bridger's "tall tales" of geysers wafting their waters into the air a hundred and more feet, of boiling mud pots, roaring mountains, and the other natural phenomena that still distinguish Yellowstone Park and make it one of the truly wonderful recreation spots of our nation.

Q. *Where, in Wyoming, are the Spanish Diggin's, or are they another figment of the imagination?*

A. The Spanish Diggin's are real enough and lie near the junction of the county lines of Niobrara, Goshen, and Platte, north of Guernsey, Wyoming. They are actually primitive stone quarries in quartzite, where Indians dug out materials for stone axes and tools. The brittle upper layers of purple and golden-hued rocks were discarded, and the Indians went down twenty to thirty feet deep to gain the better rock. The early cowboys on the range thought the hole was a Spanish mine and referred to it as the "Spanish Diggin's." Until a few years ago, many half-finished tools and weapons could be picked up there. It appeared that the Indians "roughed out" tools for trade and exchange, for these same rock tools and spearpoints are found all over the West. One Nebraska rancher, Lee Cashler, took a half-ton truck filled with the rocks to his home and used them to cover the grave of his favorite saddle horse.

Q. *Is it possible to visit the place called the "Seven Cities of Cíbola"? I mean the place that Fray Marcos sought that had "streets paved with gold"?*

A. Yes, and quite easily. The ruins, for that is all that is there now, are called Hawikuh Ruins and are located seventeen miles southwest of present Zuni, New Mexico, almost on the New Mexico-Arizona state line. This is the village where the black slave, Estavanico, guide to Fray Marcos, was slain by Indian villagers. Fray Marcos's report, incidentally, was what we would call hogwash, for the villages were composed of stone and earth, the people were without great wealth, even lacking in the world's goods of that time. A fair gravel road leads from

Zuni to Hawikuh, and some excavations done in 1917 reveal earlier pueblos beneath those that were visitied by the Spaniards. Estavanico was reported to have been killed because of his lust for the native Indian women and his excessive demands for their turquoise and other treasures. Ninety miles to the northeast of Zuni is probably what Estavanico sought, the great villages of Chaco Canyon.

Q. *Are there many wilderness areas in Wyoming? Where are they?*

A. Yes, Wyoming has some of the most beautiful wilderness areas in the nation. They are in the Bighorn, Bridger, Shoshone, and Teton national forests. Ask the secretary of state, Cheyenne, Wyoming, to send you information on the Bridger, Cloud Peak, Glacier, North Absaroka, Popo Agie (pronounced Poposha), South Absaroka, Stratified, and Teton wilderness areas.

Q. *How long can one survive if lost in the mountains?*

A. It has been said on good authority that there are no wilderness areas in the U.S. or North America where a man or woman cannot survive by living off the land. To do so requires intelligence, the capacity to live from the food the land affords and the waters it provides. The land provides fowl, fish, insects and animals. Reptiles, plants, bulbs, and nuts are also good foods.

Q. *We plan a trip and wish to see the largest of the national parks. Which will it be?*

A. If it's just size you wish, the big Yellowstone Park will do, with its nearby Teton Park, to the south. Their combined area is greater than 2.5 million acres. The next largest, Mount McKinley in Alaska, is 1,939,492 acres. Either will keep you busy looking!

Q. *My buddy and I plan a horseback trip through the Rockies in August. Where is the best place to start, and what route could we follow?*

A. I would suggest a start at Billings, Montana, or maybe Lander, Wyoming. Cross the Red Desert into Colorado's western slope areas. Then follow south across the Colorado River, by Grand Mesa, to Mesa Verde and south through Indian country to Luna Valley, in New Mexico. Then take the crookedest road on the mountains south to Clifton, Arizona, and on to Old Mexico via Cochise

County, Arizona, through Tombstone and Naco, Arizona, to Naco, Sonora, Mexico, just across the border. Stop there at a cantina and have a drink of tequila.

Q. *What place was known as the Canyon of Bones along the Santa Fe Trail?*

A. This was a canyon at Diamond Springs, fifteen miles from Council Grove, the last trading post out of Westport, Missouri, 150 miles away. The springs had a gushing flow of water, and wagon trains stopped there to replenish supplies. A deep canyon nearly was filled with the bones of buffalo, probably winter-killed in a particularly bad blizzard when the animals bunched in the canyon for protection and smothered to death.

Q. *Where is the Register Rock in Idaho?*

A. This rock is one of the many found in Idaho's "Silent City of Rocks." This twenty-five-square-mile area lies between Almo and Oakley, about thirty miles south of Burley, in southern Idaho. The Old Immigrant Trail, or the Salt Lake Cut-Off, made a junction with the California Cut-Off Trail of '49 at nearby Almo. In this wide area are many formations such as Camp Rock, Signature Rock, Bath Tub Rock, and Turtles Rock; many of which bear thousands of names, dates, and messages left there by the pioneers. The area is state-owned and a lovely place to visit. An effort is being made to save the inscriptions from vandals by making this a national park area.

Q. *Where is the largest hand-dug well in the West?*

A. At Greensburg, Kansas. The well is about 150 feet deep, and is 35-feet in diameter! It was dug to supply water for the railroad at this point. It is a tourist attraction today, and you may walk a stairway to the bottom.

Q. *Can you tell me something about the "Maze Stone," west of Hemet, California?*

A. This stone has a most intricate maze carved into it which authorities claim is unlike any Indian carvings in North America. Some who have studied the maze believe it to be a Chinese pattern, and they estimate its age to be pre-Columbian. Some scholars have cited a seventeenth-century Chinese historian, Li Yan Tcheon, who wrote that in 1598 five Buddhist missionaries sailed to a far-off land to the east, 7,000 miles from the Chinese mainland. But, because Hemet is approximately forty miles from the California coastline, critics have wondered how sailors would have been able to carve the maze at that distance from the sea. Some defenders of the Chinese thesis fall back upon the possibility that these missionaries sailed in on the old sea that purportedly covered the Salton Sea-Imperial Valley region at that time. There are doubts that such a sea existed. Whatever its origin and history, the Maze Stone is certainly a curiosity. Recent discovery of stone ship anchors in a West Coast harbor indicate that Chinese may have landed in America as early as 3019 B.C. The stones match those of a Chinese geological formation, it has been determined.

Q. *When was gold first discovered in the Black Hills?*

A. In August, 1874, scout Charley Reynolds brought news to Cheyenne, Wyoming, of the discovery of gold in the Black Hills. However, new information has set the discovery date much earlier, if it can be relied upon. The finding of the *Thoen Stone*, by Louis Thoen, near Spearfish, South Dakota in 1887, indicates that gold was taken in the hills as early as 1834. The story of the discovery of gold by Ezra Kind, one of a party of eight men, was carved on this piece of sandstone. A book, *The Thoen Stone*, by Frank Thomson, Harlo Press, Detroit, Michigan, details the strange and amazing story of these ill-fated men who found gold in quantity, then were slain by hostile Indians. Kind, in his carvings, relates the story.

Q. *What happened to the twenty-one million "4 x 6 inch" deeds of land in the Yukon that the Quaker Oats Company gave away in 1955 to promote its products? Are any of them in the oil or gold country there? What are they worth today?*

A. Vern Thomas of the legal department of the company says that the promotion has returned to haunt them. The deeds never did give rights to any minerals, so they're worthless in that sense. Besides, their minuscule size makes it unrealistic to consider them for commercial purposes. The deeds were unnumbered, so they are impossible to locate. One man collected 10,880 of the deeds (about seventy-five square feet of space) then asked the company if they would "consolidate" his purchase! So if you come across one of the "deeds" (or one of the diminutive deeds to the Buffalo Bill Ranch at North

Platte, Nebraska, which are being used for promotional purposes), just keep them as a curiosity. Don't write the Quaker Oats Company. They're fed up!

Q. *Where are the Shining Mountains, spoken of by the early Spaniards in the West?*

A. That is the name they gave to the great cordillera, the Rocky Mountains.

Q. *Where are the* Gloss *Mountains in Oklahoma?*

A. Many Western writers, following a typographical error, have been calling the Glass Mountains the Gloss Mountains. These hills—what they really are—lie about forty miles west of Enid and are on the south side of the Cimarron River. They were named because of the gypsum-covered buttes and scarps which reflect the sun's rays, giving the appearance of broken glass shining in the sun. They are a part of the old Greever & Houghton and Quinlan cattle ranges in the Cherokee Strip.

Q. *Do spelunkers—cave explorers—ever find anything of historical value? Or do they just look for treasures?*

A. They search for and find both. A few years ago, in Feather Cave, near Capitan, New Mexico, spelunkers took hundreds of Indian artifacts from a cave; many of the objects were ceremonial articles that command high prices among collectors and are valued treasures to art and archeological museums in the West. Rich treasures of saleable artifacts are frequently taken from cave floors which are dug away to a depth of several feet at times. Archeologists and paleontologists prize these rich finds.

Q. *What is the difference between a mountain and a mesa?*

A. The mesa is a flat-topped mountain. For example, Grand Mesa, in western Colorado, though a 10,000 foot mountain in its own right, is spoken of by the natives as "The Mesa." Some small hills, with flat tops, are also called mesas.

Q. *Where is Dead Man's Canyon?*

A. There are no doubt many "Dead Man's Canyons" in the West. One with which the author is most familiar lies north of Broken Bow, Nebraska, about five miles. Today no one knows who the young man was from whom the canyon took its name. He was about twenty-five, six feet tall, well built, and spoken of as a "half-breed," which in pioneer times meant half-Indian, or half-Mexican, and half-white. Inside his shirt, covered with blood, was the badge of a Cincinnati detective agency. The young man was shot to death by a Custer County sheriff's posse in 1887. He, and another man who escaped, had been committing a series of petty robberies over the county.

Q. *What caused the Great Salt Lake in Utah?*

A. A large, prehistoric lake, Lake Bonneville, which was then nearly as large as Lake Michigan, lay over that region with glaciers feeding it from the Wasatch Mountains. When the lake waters were high, the lake's drainage was north, to the Snake River. As the water lowered, this outlet was higher than the remaining waters of the lake. Evaporation, over a great geological age, reduced the remaining waters of the lake, causing its high saline content. This is now Great Salt Lake, in Utah.

Q. *Has anything ever been done to prevent the Great Salt Lake from completely drying up from evaporation, and to stop people from polluting it?*

A. Yes, a Great Salt Lake Authority has been organized for this purpose and a long-range program for reducing the lake's salinity and for maintaining the south half of the lake at a 4,200-foot level using a dike is underway. Bathing beaches, parks, roads, housing, and recreational facilities will be improved, so it is hoped. Although the plan will be costly, conservative figures estimate that the lake's greater use will pay the entire bill for improvements in a few years.

Q. *What is meant by "water tanks of the desert"?*

A. There are two objects bearing this distinction on the desert: (1) natural reservoirs in solid rock that hold rainwater and (2) the saguaro cactus, often called giant water tanks, which store enough water to bear their fruit and blossoms for a year or more without replenishment of moisture. A saguaro weighs as much as five tons. There are also, of course, artificial reservoirs and tanks of various sorts established by man, where he may impound spring water, or river water, or water pumped from underground sources, and even rain water—for it does rain occasionally on the deserts.

Q. *Were there any eastern land grants similar to the Maxwell land grant in New Mexico? If so, was Beal's or Deal's Island, Maryland, once such a grant?*

A. Yes, there were land grants under the king of England. For example, much of the Shenandoah Valley in Virginia was granted to Yost Hite, a German, and others. I have not heard of and cannot find a Deal's Island or Beal's Island grant.

Q. *What happened to the "petrified man" that was dug up near Creede, Colorado, in 1892?*

A. The fabricated figure, for that is what it was, was dug up by J.J. Dore, in April 1892. The piece of sculpture was given the name McGinty (probably after that popular figure, Billy McGinty, the bronc stomper) by the *Creede Candle*. McGinty the statue had been bought in Denver, and buried near Creede by Bob Fitzsimmons, a gambler. After some manipulation, he and Soapy Smith became its owners. It was eventually shipped east, where it disintegrated. There have been other such hoaxes in the past, such as the Cardiff Giant and the Solid Muldoon.

Q. *Do mirages such as those our pioneer ancestors witnessed still appear on the Great Plains?*

A. Yes. Mirages are an optical illusion, therefore not dependent upon time, but rather upon place. They still confuse folks, however. In southwest Kansas I have seen grain elevators ten to twenty miles distant appear in the sky like great cities. In eastern Colorado, I have seen the Rockies rise up 20,000 feet in the sky! It was my thought, when I first witnessed these almost unbelievable mirages, that Fray Marcos and other Spanairds who reported seeing the "Seven Cities of Cíbola" may have been the victims of this natural phenomena. Most tourists passing along the Southwest's highways have seen the wide lakes of blue water appear across the highway ahead of them, only to disappear as they drew nearer to them. The "cities in the sky" mirages are less common, but it is the same physical principle of nature that causes both.

Q. *Is it true that electric balls of flame sit on cattle's horns in an electrical storm, and that "balls of fire" roll over their backs? Couldn't this be an optical illusion the cowboys saw?*

A. No, it is a physical fact, though I cannot explain it. My mother's home was once struck by lightning, in 1888, at Anselmo, Nebraska, the bolt killing her younger sister and temporarily blinding her mother. She described the bolt that struck, as she recalled it, as a great round ball of fire that rolled into the room near the chimney, then exploded in a white sheet of flame. Old cowboys have described similar balls of fire rolling over the backs of cattle, and on down to the earth. They have said that the tips of the longhorn cattle's horns would display small flames of electricity that brightened their backs with its light. Understanding little of electricity, but knowing that metal objects drew the bolts of electricity to them, many cowboys threw away all the metal objects they carried—pistols and cartridges, knives and belt buckles. Trees also drew electricity, as did fence lines, and high points of the landscape. So the cowboys shied away from those places in storms. One old cowman, Bernard Lemert, of Liberal, Kansas, once told me, "The storm was so bad I carried my saddle and bridle, which had silver ornaments on them, back a way from the chuckwagon, left my gun and knife there, and picketed my horse with only the rope on him, and lay down in the rain." Lemert wouldn't even sleep near the wagon so fearful he was of its iron tires and other metals drawing a bolt down to it.

Q. *Has Shiprock, that tall, isolated rock sentinel in the desert in northwest New Mexico, ever been climbed?*

A. Shiprock, near the town of Shiprock, on the Navaho Reservation, was scaled as early as 1939 by a group of four mountain climbers. This outstanding formation, rising 2,000 feet above the desert floor, is called "the Rock With Wings" by the Navaho people. Its elevation above sea level is 7,178 feet.

Q. *What is a chinook wind?*

A. Chinook winds are warm winter winds that come in from the Pacific Northwest coast, bringing relief to the cold northern states like Montana, Wyoming, and the western Dakotas. The winds come quietly, almost unnoticed, thawing snow and ice in a matter of hours. One Montana freighter said his bobsled outfit once ran into one, near Havre, Montana. "My front sled-runners were in the snow; the back ones in the mud," he said. "My dog trailed along behind in the dust." The warm winds are believed to come from the Japanese current which has picked up the warmth from the southwest Pacific and brought it up the China coast and around and down from Alaska and the Canadian coastal areas.

Q. *Where was the largest prairie fire in the West, and when did it occur?*

A. That fact would be difficult to ascertain. John Bratt, Nebraska pioneer cattleman, told of one in 1874 that reached from old Plum Creek (Lexington, Nebraska) to Julesburg, Colorado, burning everything from the Platte River on the north to the Republican River on the south. Cowmen thought Indians had set the fire to drive the buffalo north of the Platte, where they could hunt them with greater ease and success. But Bratt thought it the work of a careless white man, hunting buffalo, which is more believable.

Q. *I made a bet that the Missouri River is longer than the Mississippi. Did I win?*

A. No, you lost. The Missouri extends more than 2,315 miles. But the Old Miss, arising near Bemiji, Minnesota, extends some 2,348 miles to the delta in the Gulf of Mexico. But it was a close race, wasn't it?

Q. *Do any forms of animal or vegetable life exist in their natural state in Death Valley, California?*

A. Yes, contrary to general opinion, many forms of vegetation—in fact 600 varieties of flowers and shrubs—exist there. Many animals, including rodents, coyotes, mountain lions, and wild burros, also live there. There are, as well, 240 kinds of birds. Though the ecology is finely balanced and could not undergo any great change, it does and will support these creatures for many more centuries if man does not disturb it too greatly.

Q. *A California friend tells me the temperature in Death Valley can range as high as 125° F. Can this be true?*

A. Yes, the highest recorded temperature in the United States was 134° F., reported July 10, 1913, in Death Valley.

Q. *Is Hoover (Boulder) Dam on the Colorado River the world's highest dam?*

A. No, it is 726 feet high, but topped by several others in India, Switzerland, and Russia. The 1,017-foot dam at Nurek, in the Soviet Union, is the world's tallest. Russia's two great dams, the Dnieprodzerzhinsk (Dnieper), crest length 118,090 feet, and her Kiev (Dnieper River), crest length 177,448 feet, dwarf anything the rest of the world has built. The Hoover Dam, for example, is only 1,244 feet crest length and the Fort Peck, 21,026 feet. For sheer bulk, these three are the world's largest dams, according to the *1981 World Almanac:* New Cornelia Tailings, (U.S.), 274,026,000 cubic yards; Tarbela (Pakistan), 158,268,000 cubic yards; Fort Peck, (U.S.), 126,612,000 cubic yards. These three were completed, respectively in 1973, 1975 and 1940.

Q. *Which three Western cities have the most abundant sunshine throughout the year?*

A. In this order: Sacramento, Cal., 322 days of sun per year; Phoenix, Arizona, 313 days per year; Albuquerque, N.M., 283 days per year. Miami, Florida has but 240 days of sun per year. So you see how sunny and bright it is in the Southwest!

Q. *What types of stone were used for tools in the West during prehistoric times?*

A. Eolithic man used only quartzite and flint, generally speaking. However, Neolithic man widened his base to include sandstone, basalt, hard shale, limestone, soapstone, volcanic glass (obsidian), jade, granite, and other hard substances. Obsidian from the Yellowstone has been found among Mound Builders' artifacts in Ohio, indicating that rocks were traded and traveled long distances in prehistoric commerce. Most prehistoric Indians, such as those of central Arkansas, made spear and arrow points from novaculite, a stone found in their vicinity. In hunting prehistoric relics, look also for stone that has been worked very little; that is, chipped and shaped very little, whatever its contents in minerals. These were trade stones.

Q. *Which is highest in elevation, Denver, Colorado, or Bisbee, Arizona?*

A. Denver, "the Mile High City," claims 5,280 feet. Bisbee claims 5,300 feet. Looks like Bisbee wins. However, Lakewood and other western suburbs of Denver claim 5,500 feet and more.

Q. *Where may be the transition from the northern and central grasslands of the Great Plains to the pine forests of the mountains be best seen along a good tourist route?*

A. I recommend a tour along the eastern slope of the Rocky Mountains. If you watch the transformation that goes on right before your eyes from Cheyenne, Wyoming, to Colorado Springs, Colorado, you will see this transition in one day's time. Another good plan would be to travel west from Oklahoma or Kansas, and drive to Trinidad, or Pueblo, Colorado, then strike north up Interstate 25 to Cheyenne, Casper, and Buffalo, Wyoming.

Q. *If a man was on the central prairieland for a year or two, how would he know when spring had come?*

A. Even if he were blind, he could tell by the croaking of frogs. If he had sight, the greening grass would tell him. If he looked inwardly, his own spirit, refreshed and eager to try again, would tell him "Spring is here!"

Q. *Why has it been considered impossible to grow trees in a national forest project in the central Dakotas, and south to the southwestern portions of Kansas and Oklahoma?*

A. A Kansas national forest was started in 1906 near Garden City but was eventually abandoned in 1915. But the Halsey National Forest in the Nebraska Sandhills, in central Western Nebraska, was a phenomenal success. Why? The amount of precipitation, while important, was not the final reason for the failure of the former. The hot climate of the southern plains, the greater evaporation, and the hot, dry winds that blow almost constantly, made the difference between failure and success. Later, in the 1930s, much success was made in this arid area or strip with "shelter belts." By drawing upon much that had been learned in the years from 1906 to 1930, such as preparation of the land, summer fallowing, chiseling, listing, etc., the young trees of the shelter belts were brought through their tenderest years and managed to survive the heat, evaporation, and winds.

Q. *What is wild hay?*

A. Just the natural grasses of the prairie lands and bottomlands that are cut, dried, and stacked or baled for winter feed. Good wild hay usually has some buffalo grass, gramma grass, bluestem, or such nutritious grasses in it, together with the usual wild forbs and other vegetation found on the prairie.

Q. *What is the agrita bush?*

A. A bush of the Southwest with spine-tipped leaves, a member of the barberry family. It is called wild currant, or chaparral berry.

Q. *What does the expression "grubbing loco" mean?*

A. Loco weed is a poisonous bush for livestock to eat, hence the ranchers try to rid their range of it. "Grubbing" it out with spade, hoe, or shovel is the hardest way to get rid of it, but the surest. Usually loco weed does not grow in such massive quantity that a few days' work by a half dozen men cannot eliminate it. The stalks are piled up, left to dry, and then burned.

Q. *What is a devil's claw?*

A. There is a rope knot called a devil's claw. There is also a weed whose pronged tentacles, when dry in the summer, form a veritable "claw" that fastens itself to the fetlock of horses or on to the cows' tails. This is the method nature has provided for distribution of the plant's seed. Clever craftsmen are now making decorative items, such as Christmas angels, from the devil's claw. It is not dangerous, just a pest to animals.

Q. *Is the thistle called buffalo burr poisonous? How may I keep it out of my corrals?*

A. It's actually more bothersome than dangerous or poisonous, though it is listed as such. Its drought-resistant qualities make it a real pest, particularly on over-grazed grassland or in cultivated areas. Chemical sprays will stop it. Keeping it mowed down so it will not seed will eventually kill it out.

Q. *What is pitch pine?*

A. Old dead pine stumps have pitch lumps within and make excellent fire-starting wood. The pitch in the wood has a flammable quality that makes it popular among woodsmen for fires.

Q. *Is the method of dating historical events by tree rings at all accurate?*

A. Yes, this process, called dendrochronology, has been most helpful in dating Indian archeological discoveries, such as the cliff dwellings and pueblos (Chaco Canyon) of the Southwest. The rings in the logs that support the old pueblo walls are matched with key logs to determine time, just as the hands of a clock are turned to certain places to make certain hours visible to us. See *Dendrochronology in Mexico*, by Stuart C. Scott, University of Arizona Press, for a fine exposition of the process and its phenomenal results. The newer process of carbon dating is also being used to implement dendrochronology in determining time elements in prehistorical research.

Q. *What is the scientific name for the soapweed? I mean the plant they call Spanish bayonet?*

A. The plant is known as *Yucca Glauca*, or just yucca. We find it from Montana to Texas. The flower is tasty to cattle. Indians valued the fleshy fruit. They gave it the name soapweed, for they took its roots for the manufacture of soap. The larger and more fibrous soapweed, such as found in southwest Colorado, was used for making a tough garment fabric and sandals by the Basketmakers and the Indians called Cliff Dwellers. Such fragments of their garments and shoes are found in burials today, preserved by the arid climate of the country.

Q. *What is saltbush?*

A. This plant exists from North Dakota to Mexico, and grows best in alkaline soils. Cattle, deer, and antelope feed on it in spring when it is green and its nutritive qualities are high. It is often wrongly called sagebrush, and shadscale. It is a relative of the Russian thistle.

Q. *Do cattails in the Western lake and river countries have any beneficial value in nature?*

A. You have no doubt heard the old fellow on TV who pulls a cattail stalk and tells you, "Cattails are edible." But did you ever see him *eat one?* I never heard of a pioneer who ate cattails. Yet they do serve a most useful purpose in nature, for they make wonderfully safe nesting and resting spots for migratory waterfowl. They also supply food for the insects that birds live on. And I suppose a human could eat one, though I'd prefer to eat a feather pillow!

Q. *What is the life span of Western grasses?*

A. If annuals, they reach maturity and seed within a few weeks to a few months. If perennials, full growth may not be reached until the plant is four or five years old. The plant itself may be bearing seed when it is ten, twenty, even fifty years of age, according to prominent experts in the field, such as David F. Costello, botanist for thirty years with the U.S. Forest Service.

Q. *Do Western grass seeds lose their viability after a few months in arid soil?*

A. Some do. Others can maintain their storage for several

years and still germinate. Most grass seeds must root in moist soil within a few days to get their proper growth cycle.

Q. *Do Russian thistles (tumbleweeds) have flowers?*

A. Yes, in season they have a tiny but beautiful flower. Very few people know this, for few look for it. The flower has three yellow-red stamins, with a tiny, hair-covered pistil which ultimately produces the seed when mature. The rolling of the weed, when dry and mature and uprooted by the wind from the soil, distributes the seeds everywhere. High winds even carry the tiny seeds when the weed remains rooted to the ground or hung up on a fence. When young, and green, Russian thistles provide nourishing food for cattle, particularly in drought years when grass fails to grow.

Q. *How many species of grasses, legumes, and forbs would one find on, say, an acre of Western range land? On a square mile?*

A. It would depend on where the land lay, in an arid or moist region. On a square mile of eastern Colorado plains, horticulturists once identified 143 species of forbs alone, 22 species of grasses, 10 kinds of shrubs and four kinds of trees. The earth is, as pioneers learned, truly an "ocean of grass."

Q. *Should yucca be grubbed out of pasture areas? We are now debating this matter among Cimarron ranchers.*

A. Yucca, if not growing too thickly, may well aid the grass areas. It holds the plains soil and therefore helps against erosion caused by the wind and water. It catches snowfall in winter and holds its run-off. Its tap roots go deep and open up the earth's subsoil to moisture. Unlike the spreading, shallow root systems of other shrubs and forbs, the deep tap root of the yucca does not steal from the grass roots. And the cattle love its blossom in the spring. Where yucca has "taken over" an area, it is good policy to thin it out, leaving a yucca stalk every twenty to thirty feet.

Q. *Where does one find the purple sage that Zane Grey wrote about in his many novels?*

A. Grey's purple sage is a plant found growing extravagantly in the region near Zion National Park, in southern Utah. The sage that is so well-known in the Western states is actually a silvery green when in bloom and loaded with seeds. It is often pictured in the paintings of Russell exactly as it appears on the land.

Q. *Is halogeton, the weed that has been blamed in the West for killing so many sheep, widely distributed over the country?*

A. Yes, since its original introduction into the U.S. about 1935, this forb has appeared over two million acres in Montana, Wyoming, Idaho, and Nevada. It is now no doubt in other Western states. It was originally brought to the U.S. from Russia, probably as a contaminant in agricultural seed, as was the Russian thistle. The weed contains salts of oxalic acid, which are poisonous to sheep and cattle. Animals do not usually graze it in the green stage, but will consume it in toxic quantities where range land is poor and little choice of grazing is offered the hungry animals. Keeping sheep out of halogeton areas is the best way to save them from death, for once this weed is in the stomach it is too late to aid the animal much.

Q. *Can you describe buffalo grass so I could identify it?*

A. Buffalo grass is a short, sod-forming, warm-season perennial that reproduces by seeds and vigorous surface runners which root at the joints. The seeds are reproduced in small, hard burs and are borne along elongated seed stems an inch to three inches above the base of the plant. Green in summer, in fall it turns into a curly reddish-brown as it cures, growing rarely higher than a horse's fetlock.

Photo from the collection of Harry E. Chrisman.

Q. *Where did the Plummer Gang, famous for their depredations around Virginia City, meet to plan their acts?*

A. One of their hangouts was said to be this old roadhouse
on the Vigilante Trail in Montana. It was called Robbers
Roost. Some of Plummer's men lived in and near Virginia
City. After death by hanging, five of them were buried
there on Boot Hill.

8 LAWMEN, OUTLAWS, GUNFIGHTERS

Readers of Western Americana have always been intrigued with the stories of badmen, gunfighters, and lawmen who could step back and forth between the roles of lawman and outlaw. It is a truism that in the Old West a man fleeing from the law in one place might readily establish himself as The Law in another Western town. In the Old West men were often accepted at face value. Someone like Wyatt Earp, a man recently charged with horse theft in the Indian Nations, might, within a few weeks or months, become a policeman at Wichita. A Jim Herron, convicted of the theft of a *trainload* of longhorn steers in Kansas, could easily escape and then settle down as a successful saloonkeeper and cattle buyer in Pearce, Arizona, or Tombstone. Billy Stiles and Burt Alvord did it; Bob and Grat Dalton did it; Joe Beckham, Henry Brown, Ben Thompson, John King Fisher, and many others did so as well. Two good books for further exploration of this phenomena might be Ed Bartholomew's two-volume *Wyatt Earp* and Jim Herron's true-life story *Fifty Years on the Owl Hoot Trail.*

It would be greatly satisfying to tell the reader that we speak herein of all the old outlaws and badmen and gunfighters the frontier West produced. Unfortunately not even a work twice this size, and devoted strictly to that subject, could do this. First, much information is simply lost in time. Second, outlaws were men who deliberately covered their trails, using false names and whatever physical disguises they could muster. Third, the Old West did not produce the scribes and journalists to record the many facets of those men's natures.

Writers usually sought out only the most sensational facts—perhaps an outrageous murder committed by a man—and then developed their subject's character around that one incident. Naturally, what resulted was a stereotype of the real person. Often, too, we only know the deeds performed by a man. In such cases we get only the dim outlines of real people, as with the Bender family of Kansas. Did they murder wholesale with knives and axes solely for money? Old John, Mrs. Bender, Katie, and her brother, Gieger, remain dim ghosts when evoked by latter-day writers.

In the Old West, when crime became a threat to the whole community, vigilante organizations were formed by the residents. Without proper law organizations and courts, there were no other means to put down the criminal element. At times some of these vigilante organizations became as much of a menace to the community as were the criminals they hanged. Eventually, the better citizens overcame both elements to establish courts and proper legal procedure for dealing with the badmen and the outlaws of the frontier.

Herewith we deal only with those questions that have been repeatedly asked about these characters of the Old West history who frequently found themselves at loggerheads with The Law, yet whom at one time may have served that very Law themselves as Peace Officers.

Q. *Was Bat Masterson's name William* Bartholomew *Masterson, or William* Barclay *Masterson?*

A. Bat Masterson apparently preferred "Barclay," for on August 3, 1907, he signed his will using that middle name. However, in recent years, several top researchers and Western writers have disputed this second name of the famous lawman-editor-Indian fighter. And, presumably, if their facts are straight, Masterson *preferred* the name Barclay to his given name, Bartholomew. Waldo Koop of Wichita, Kansas, writer and Western researcher, and Ed Bartholomew of Fort Davis, Texas, publisher and author, in the book *Wyatt Earp* brought the matter up, and throughout the two-volume work on Earp, call Masterson "Bart," for Bartholomew. Joseph G. Rosa, in his *The Gunfighters*, uses the name Bartholomew and offers the evidence unearthed by Chris Penn, a British writer, to show that Bat was born Bartholomew Masterson, Nov. 26, 1853, in St. George Parish, County Rouville, Quebec Province, Canada, and with only that one given name. Though the *Diary* of old buffalo hunter H.H. Raymond is cited as using the name "Bart," for "Bat," I have found both "Bat" and "Bart" in the copy of the *Diary* found in his library, a true copy of the original made by J. Evetts Haley, Texas historian, in 1935. (Haley's cover letter to Mr. Raymond, in this file, is dated April 29, 1936.) Most historians of the past have accepted *Barclay* as Bat's middle name. There is now, however, enough new evidence at hand to make the question debatable.

Q. *Is it true that Bat Masterson actually killed twenty-six men?*

A. No. There is no substance to this tale. Bat is recorded as having killed one or two men, that is all. But he did participate in the Battle of Adobe Walls, against a large number of Indians, so his record might include more killings. Bat was said to be a friendly and agreeable fellow most of his life, becoming a rough customer when caused to fight. He went along with the stories such as of his long record of shootings, didn't deny them and this probably accounts for his big name.

Q. *In what Western towns did Bat Masterson serve as lawman?*

A. He was sheriff of Ford County, at Dodge City, Kansas. He was later marshal at Trinidad, Colorado. At Tombstone, Arizona, for a brief time, he held no office. Later, at Denver, Colorado, he was reported to have been a deputy sheriff of Arapahoe County. He went to Creede, Colorado, afterward, and though holding no office as a lawman, he was reported to have worked closely with the law, through his employers, Watrous, Banniger & Company. Following the demise of Creede, after the Silver Act of 1893, Bat turned to the East and became a sports writer on the *New York Morning Telegraph*, having had much experience sponsoring and promoting sporting events in the West. He died at his desk October 25, 1921, of a heart attack.

Q. *How much can we believe that was told by the old-time lawmen of the West, or written by them, long after the events?*

A. These tales and writings should be subjected to critical analysis. Take this example of one of Bat Masterson's stories. Bat, probably as honest a scribbler as any of the old peace enforcement men, once wrote in *Human Life Magazine*, 1907, "Charley Harrison was the most expert man I ever saw with a pistol. . . ." But Harrison, the Con-

federate gunfighter and gambler, was killed in 1863 by
Osage Indians—when Bat was a small boy! Actually, Bat
remembered *another* Charley Harrison, who was killed
by Jim Levy in Cheyenne, in March 1877, and was
giving this latter, second-rate gunman, credit the first
should have gotten for his work. I doubt that Bat had
seen either man in action. In Bat's booklet *Famous
Gunfighters of the Western Frontier*, published in 1907
and republished in 1968 by Frontier Book Company,
Fort Davis, Texas, it is noticeable that while he praises
Wyatt Earp for his ability to fight *with fists*, he never
credits Earp with having any great capability *with the
six-shooter*. This remained for the post-Stuart-Lake-
Western-writers to build up, together with the TV series
on Earp which featured him as a peerless Western marshal
of the Bill Tilghman type. Masterson, a friend of the
Earps, accepted Wyatt Earp's stories uncritically, lock,
stock and barrel. What Bat wrote about the career of the
Earps at Tombstone undoubtedly came directly from
Wyatt's and his brother's mouths, not from any critical
research done by Bat on the subject. Yes, all stories
should be taken with a grain of salt, even those you read
in these pages!

Q. *What was the legend about Henry Brown, the marshal of
Caldwell, Kansas, who was either hanged or shot while
escaping from jail? Was his name Henry or Hendry?*

A. Henry Brown (with no "d" in his name) was marshal at
Caldwell and had performed competently as a lawman.
He married a young woman, and from all indications had
"settled down" to be a respectable lawman. Then the
bank of Medicine Lodge, Kansas, was held up and robbed,
and the bank's president and cashier killed in the holdup.
A town posse formed (Henry Brown, the Caldwell marshal
was away from his town that day) and soon had the
robbers cornered in a canyon. The robbers surrendered,
and lo! one of them was Henry Brown, the Caldwell
lawman! The four robbers were Brown, his assistant Ben
Wheeler, Billy Smith, the horse wrangler from the T5
Ranch, and another cowhand, John Wesley. The men
were put in the town jail, and that evening a lynch mob
sought them out. When the jail door was opened, Brown
made a dash for it and was riddled with buckshot. Wheeler,

Smith, and Wesley were taken to a large elm tree and lynched by the mob.

Q. *Who, besides Henry Brown and Ben Wheeler, were ever suspected of arranging the Medicine Lodge bank robbery?*

A. In addition to Smith and Wesley, who were also mentioned above, Oliver Nelson, a former T5 camp cook who authored the book *The Cowman's Southwest*, was privy to some of the earlier preparations of this robbery that ended in tragedy. In a conversation with him at age ninety-four, I was told that:

> There were strange goins on. Some evenings several strangers would drop in. One, a Mr. Johnson, said to them that they could get twenty-thousand at Medicine without any trouble. Now this Johnson was a lodge brother of Payne, the president of the bank, and George Geppert, the cashier. He helped set up the robbery, then warned Payne three times before the robbery came off. The third time, Brown and his men appeared. It was Johnson's plan to get possession of fifty head of stolen Indian ponies Billy Smith had been holding, hid out on the T5 range, just as soon as the robbers were apprehended and either shot or hung. The citizens were watching. Johnson and Cook [Johnson's confederate] traded Payne and Gephardt [*sic*] for the bunch of stolen ponies. Cook was a member of the "Wildcat Pool."

Billy Smith, a wrangler for the T5, was a conniving young man, and, though friendly to Oliver, was never trusted by the cook. Who the man "Johnson" was, Oliver never said. The Wildcat Pool was the group of horse thieves Smith dealt with. As Oliver put it, Johnson set up the robbery by these reckless men, then warned the bankers so he could get the ponies Smith had stolen and hidden out.

Q. *Who was J. McConnell, head of the Payette Valley, Idaho Vigilantes?*

A. McConnell, a rancher, became incensed when thieves stole his horses. He enlisted aid from neighbors and captured one of the thieves, who confessed. McConnell then organized the vigilantes and captured the rest of the outlaws and thieves.

Q. *Who was the greatest of all the Texas Rangers in your opinion?*

A. Such a judgment would be strictly in the area of pure speculation at this late date, and no informed person would attempt to name one above all others of the many great men who served the State of Texas. Where would you, in such a list, place Frank Hamer, who with his men killed Bonnie and Clyde; who had scores of gunfights; who was reported to have slain more than fifty men, and who was wounded, it is said, seventeen times?

Q. *What was Larry Deger's occupation before he became a Dodge City lawman?*

A. He had been foreman of Lee & Reynolds' freighting outfits. Deger became a key figure in the Dodge City War. He was later the mayor of the town.

Q. *Who was Colonel Kosterlitzky? For what was he noted?*

A. Col. Emilio Kosterlitzky, born Moscow, Russia, in 1853; died in 1928, was in charge of the rurales (police of the border) in northern Sonora, Mexico, from 1886 to 1913, when forces under General Obregon drove him out of Mexico. He was a hard-bitten soldier who dealt out justice with a free hand in a land infested with rustlers, outlaws, smugglers, and crooked politicians. Later, from 1913 to 1926, he worked for the U.S. Department of Justice and the FBI as a special agent. He has been painted as both military martinet and as an honest law officer, who did his duty as he saw it. He backed Porfirio Diaz, the Mexican dictator-president, in the early part of the Mexican Revolution. It is said his *cordada* (police unit) was the terror of border criminals for many years.

Q. *Name three old-time lawmen who managed to carry out their duties without having to kill their prisoners.*

A. Bill Tilghman, U.S. Marshal, Kansas-Oklahoma; Edgar Neal, Texas Rangers; and Ham Bell, Sheriff, Ford County, Kansas. There are many more old law enforcement officers who went into outlaw territory, such as the former No Man's Land, and brought back the worst desperadoes

in the West, alive and kicking. Jim Herron, the first
sheriff of No Man's Land, claimed he could go and talk
most outlaws into returning with him to take their
chances with the law. He saved many men's lives this
way, and some were perhaps rehabilitated. Unfortunately,
an escapade when he was twenty-eight years old put him
on the "Owl Hoot Trail" for more than fifty years, a
trail from which he could not find his way back to law
and order.

Q. *Who was Joe LeFors?*

A. LeFors was a Wyoming peace officer. He had some dealings with the Hole-in-the-Wall Gang and was familiar with
the activities of Tom Horn and Billy Nash, whom he
once trailed. LeFors wrote an interesting account of his
life, and it was published posthumously by his widow,
Mrs. Nettie LeFors, under the title *Wyoming Peace
Officer.*

Q. *What happened to William L. Brooks, who was a former
marshal at Newton, Kansas?*

A. Billy turned to stealing horses for a living, was caught
and lynched together with Hasbrouck and Smith at
Wellington, Kansas, according to news stories of that
time, 1874.

Q. *What years was Wyatt Earp marshal of Dodge City,
Kansas?*

A. Earp was never marshal there. He was a deputy, or
assistant marshal during the years 1876-79. He served
under Marshal Lawrence E. Deger (1876-77) and under
marshals Charles E. Bassett, a Mr. Clark, and James P.
Masterson (1878-79). His role as an assistant marshal
was actually that of a policeman.

Q. *Is there any documentation for the charge that Wyatt
Earp was a horse thief in Indian Territory, long before
he became famous as a lawman?*

A. Yes, there is. In Volume 1, *Wyatt Earp: The Untold
Story,* pages 33ff, Ed Bartholomew documents this
charge with the Records at the Federal Commissioner's
Files, Government Records Center, Fort Worth, Texas.
The records name Wyatt Earp, together with Edward
Kennedy, as horse thieves. A third man, John Shown
(Shaughn?) is named as an accomplice whom Kennedy
and Earp threatened with death, should he not collab-

orate with them in the theft. Shown's wife, Anna, appears to have been held hostage by Earp and Kennedy until he delivered the stolen animals at the Kansas border for them. This was dated 13 April 1871, Case No. 21.

Q. *What caused the initial hatred between Wyatt Earp and John Behan at Tombstone, Arizona, in the 1880s?*

A. One authority—Frank M. King—claims the feuding began when Gen. John C. Freemont (a Republican), appointed by President Rutherford B. Hayes as governor of the Territory of Arizona, selected Behan (a Democrat) as the first sheriff of the new Cochise County over Wyatt Earp, a Republican and an unannounced candidate for the office. Fremont, says King, scanned the records of both men and decided that Behan, who as sheriff of Yavapai County had cleaned up that county with a minimum of deaths and fuss, was to be preferred over Wyatt Earp. Earp found it difficult to accept a Democrat appointee over himself, so he and his followers did everything they could manage to obstruct and hamper Behan in his duties as sheriff at Tombstone.

Q. *How come a man like Ben Thompson, a known gunman and killer, let Wyatt Earp disarm him at Ellsworth, Kansas, after Thompson's murder of Sheriff Whitney?*

A. The facts of this affair are: Billy Thompson, Ben's brother, was in a saloon, Ben outside with a rifle. The two had been hurrahing the town. Ben raised his rifle and took a shot at Happy Jack Morco, nearly a block away, missing him. Billy hearing the shot and believing Ben to be having a shoot-out, rushed from the saloon, and seeing Sheriff Whitney standing there, shot him with the double-barreled shotgun he was carrying. After the killing, Ben met Billy in the saloon where he had gone, gave him a revolver and said, "For God's sake, leave town; you've shot Whitney, our best friend." Billy indicated he had misunderstood what had happened, and concluded before jumping on his horse, "I don't give a damn! I would have shot even it had been Jesus Christ [standing there]." Billy was drunk, as was Ben when this took place. But now about Wyatt Earp. Where was he? Well, there is no newspaper or court record that shows he was even in town that day! The story, made up of the whole cloth, seems to have first appeared in that fictionalized "biography" of Earp, written by the late Stuart Lake, titled *Wyatt Earp, Frontier Marshal.*

Q. *Was Wyatt Earp ever under arrest in Los Angeles?*

A. Yes, the records show he was arrested and charged with attempting to fleece a Mr. J.Y. Peterson, a Los Angeles realtor, in August 1911. The story was carried by the local newspapers. No money having changed hands, Earp was released.

Q. *Was Wyatt Earp as dishonest a policeman as some writers have stated lately?*

A. There is a difference of opinion about Earp. In Wichita, on December 15, 1875, the *Wichita Beacon* reported the news when policeman Earp found a drunken transient with $500 in his pockets. Earp took the man to jail. The next morning the man paid his fine, after his purse was returned to him. "The integrity of our police force has never been questioned," the *Beacon* proudly stated. This indicates that Earp was honest at that time, if the story is factual.

Q. *Was Wyatt Earp actually a procurer, as some have stated?*

A. Earp has been accused of about everything, and the trouble is that whenever we go into the story in any depth we find good reasons to believe it. For example, Earp was living in Wichita when the 1875 census was taken, having been appointed policeman April 25, 1875. Also recorded in that census was Bessie Earp, the "wife" of Earp's brother, James. Her occupation was set down by the enumerator as "Sporting," the census term for whoring. Bessie was then thirty-two, James thirty-four, and Wyatt S. twenty-six. Both Bessie (Betsey) and Sallie Earp, who ran the house at the rear of Black's Hotel, near the river bridge, are recorded regularly in the town court's list of prostitutes through February and March, 1875, and their arrests appear to not have continued after Wyatt was appointed policeman that year. Other Earps or Erbs, as the name is frequently spelled in old records, who were fined for prostitution were Eva Earp, Kate Earp, and Minnie Earp. The position Earp's family members placed him in indicate that, if not a procurer for the Earp women, the man's morals must have been those of an alley cat, for what self-respecting "lawman" would serve as The Law on the same streets where sisters-in-law and other female relatives were hustling?

Q. *What do the Dodge City and Wichita newspapers of the time have to say about Wyatt Earp's claims to having "tamed" those towns?*

A. The old newspapers—and the court records—of the time when Earp was in Wichita and in Dodge fail to substantiate hardly a word of Earp's claims to fame. Since the book *Wyatt Earp* by Stuart Lake appeared, and since the TV series on the man's supposed career were shown, American readers and film viewers have been treated to the most ghastly mountain of half-truth, hearsay, and downright lies that any people should have to endure. The reason for this appears to be the drive of writers and film producers to make sales to the commercial world. Caution was thrown to the wind, no attention was paid to fact. There is no legal penalty for "fictionalizing" history, so Western writers by the score, more interested in money than truth or relevance, are busy at their typewriters pounding out absolute nonsense about the Old West and its people. Unfortunately, the lies they concoct have wings to spread them (book publishers, TV, magazines, newspapers, and films). The facts of history, genuinely lean in drama, travel by dog-sled (word-of-mouth or in historical quarterlies). And so such false history plunges madly on.

Q. *Bat Masterson claimed Wyatt Earp served "in an Iowa Regiment the last three years of the Civil War, although he was only a boy at the time." True or false?*

A. False. James, Newton, and Virgil Earp served, but not Wyatt, Morgan, or Warren, who were all too young. Wyatt was only twelve in 1860, the other two younger. Another falsehood Bat heard from Wyatt Earp.

Q. *Can one place great stock in Wyatt Earp's story that Texas cattlemen had offered a large reward to anyone who would kill Earp?*

A. No. The actual records do not support such a charge. As a matter of fact, Earp was of little importance to the Texas cattlemen who put the large herds into Dodge City when he was an officer there. Ed Bartholomew repeats the answer of one Texas man who was told about Earp's

status as a Dodge lawman who had been threatened by
Texas drovers. "If this Arp, or whatever his name, needed
killing, someone would have done it for nothing." Wyatt
Earp, with an eighteen-inch revolver, would have been
looked upon in Dodge City in 1879 as odd as a two-headed
rooster.

Q. *How was Newton J. Earp related to the famous Earp
   family of gunfighters?*

A. He was a half-brother. Newton's father was Nicholas
   Porter Earp; his mother was Abigail (Storm) Earp. She
   died when Newton was two years old. Nicholas Earp then
   married Virginia Ann Cooksey, and to this latter union
   were born James C., Virgil W., Virginia Ann, Wyatt S.,
   Morgan, Baxter W., and Adelia Earp. Newton J. Earp
   was marshal at Garden City, Kansas, for some time. He
   also lived at Casper, Wyoming, and at Paradise, Nevada,
   finally moving to California. He died at age ninety-three
   in 1928, and was buried at Sacramento.

Q. *How was Virgil Earp killed at Tombstone?*

A. Virgil wasn't killed, just badly wounded. He was marshal
   at Tombstone and on his rounds was walking from the
   Oriental Saloon toward his room at the Cosmopolitan
   Hotel, at 11:30 P.M. At the crossing of Allen and Fifth
   streets, five shots were fired from the old Palace Saloon
   that then stood on the southwest corner of the intersec-
   tion. Earp's arm was shattered, and he was also wounded
   in the left side, but recovered. The assailant fled and was
   never positively identified.

Q. *What can you tell me about the character of Virgil Earp,
   brother to Wyatt?*

A. Virgil is said to have been a quiet and well-mannered
   man, not possessing many of his brother Wyatt's dis-
   agreeable traits. The familial feelings between Wyatt's
   and Virgil's families were not good, because of the bitter
   hatred Mrs. Virgil Earp held for her brother-in-law,
   Wyatt. But Virgil was a loyal brother to Wyatt and for
   this loyalty suffered the shoulder wound on the streets
   of Tombstone, following the fight near the O.K. Corral.
   Though his wound healed, his arm was crippled for life.

Q. *What are the facts of the Wild Bill Hickok-McCandless
   fight at the Rock Creek Station in Nebraska, July 12,
   1861?*

A. *The Nebraska History Quarterly*, No. 1, Vol. 49, Spring 1968, gave a factual report of those celebrated killings. It happened this way:

David C. McCanles (as he spelled his name), with his son Monroe, a boy of twelve years, appeared at the Stage Station to collect a bill owed him by the Overland Stage Company and its employee, Horace G. Wellman, the stage keeper. When McCanles knocked on the door, Wellman refused to go to the door and sent Mrs. Wellman instead. James Butler Hickok (named as Wm. B. Hickok in the court records) was inside the building with Wellman. When McCanles demanded that he talk with Wellman, Hickok took up Wellman's cause, and the two men exchanged bitter words. When their quarrel grew more bitter, Hickok, standing concealed behind a curtain, took up a rifle and taking a careful bead on McCanles, shot him through the heart. McCanles fell backward into the yard, dead.

Hearing the shot, Woods and Gordon, two of McCanles' men who had come with him ran to the doorway. Hickok, now standing in the doorway, took out his Colt revolver and shot both, wounding them. As the two men fled, Wellman dashed outside, seized a heavy iron hoe, and stalked the wounded Woods, felling and killing him. Wellman, then accompanied by Hickok and J.W. Brink, the stocktender at the Stage Station who had joined them, carrying a shotgun, searched out the wounded Gordon, who had taken refuge in some brush. He was killed with Brinks' shotgun.

Hickok and Wellman and Brinks, charged with murder, appeared in court before a Justice of the Peace, T.M. Coulter, of Gage County, Nebraska. The old records show that (their names being unknown at that time) "Duch Bill [sic], Dock and Wellman" were charged with murder. On appearance, their names are shown as "Wm. B. Hickok, J.W. Brink, and Horrace G. Wellman." The warrant for their arrest was served July 15, 1861. At this so-called hearing, Monroe McCanles, the boy, was *not* permitted to testify and Mrs. Wellman was obliged to testify "in favor of the Territory [Nebr. Terr.]." The old record states only that "...a charge of murder was not sustained." The three murderers were freed after this "examination of July 16-17 & 18, A.D. 1861."

Q. *Was Wild Bill Hickok actually an Army scout?*

A. Yes, history records him as a wagonmaster in 1861; as a special policeman in 1864; as a scout or spy for Brigadier General Sanborn in Missouri in 1865. The *Springfield Patriot*, January 31, 1867, in an editorial decrying the wild tales published about Hickok in *Harper's Monthly* (the story by "Col." G.W. Nichols that made Hickok nationally famous), recognized nevertheless Hickok's basic good qualities, and his war service, by stating: "The portrait of him on the first page is a striking likeness, features, shape, posture and dress. . . . No finer physique, no greater strength, no more personal courage, no steadier nerves, no superior skill with the pistol, no better horsemanship than his, could any man [of the Union army] boast of: and few did better or more loyal service as a soldier throughout the war." But Nichols cuts it very fat when he describes Bill's feats in arms. And the Springfield editor laughs at the claim that Hickok, according to his biographer, killed, of Confederate soldiers, ". . . several hundreds with his own hands." In 1867, Hickok was a scout with Maj. Gen. Winfield Scott Hancock on an expedition to Fort Larned. Lt. Col. George A. Custer was with this outfit. In 1868 Hickok was a deputy U.S. marshal. In the Winter Campaign against the Indians in Kansas and Oklahoma, when Custer routed Black Kettle's camp on the Washita, Wild Bill and Buffalo Bill were serving as scouts farther west up the Canadian River, with General Carr. In 1869 he was serving as a military policeman and scout with headquarters at Fort Hays, Kansas. In September, 1869, he had gotten away from the army and was sheriff of Ellis County, Kansas, apparently appointed, not elected. He was beaten the next election by his deputy Peter Lanihan. But, as one can see, Bill's *army service as a scout* was genuine.

Q. *What is "The Dead Man's Hand" in poker?*

A. When Hickok was murdered by McCall in Deadwood, he was holding a poker hand consisting of aces and eights, with a queen kicker. Thereafter, this hand has been called the Dead Man's Hand.

Q. *Did Wild Bill Hickok have a harelip, or deformed mouth?*

A. No. (See the glass-plate photo made of him at Fort
    Leavenworth by E.E. Henry.) Hickok was called "Dutch"
    Bill by the men at the Rock Creek Stage Station where he
    worked. Writers, attempting to provide a motive for
    Hickok's murder of McCanles, have jumped on this fact,
    switching the name to "Duck" Bill, and attempting to
    show that McCanles' men used the term *"Duck* Bill"
    derisively to describe a facial blemish of Hickok's. All
    who personally knew Hickok, and this includes Mrs.
    George A. (Elizabeth) Custer, wife of the famous army
    officer, described Hickok as "handsome." She called
    Wild Bill a man "with fine features and straight posture."
    The name "Duch Bill" (*sic*) appears on the legal papers
    made at the time of the hearing, after Hickok's murder
    of McCanles.

Q. *Why was Hickok discharged as marshal at Abilene?*

A. He was discharged when the cattle shipping season had
    ended, December 13, 1871, along with other deputies.
    James A. Gauthie was appointed in his place the follow-
    ing month. The reason for dismissal appears to be un-
    known.

Q. *Has any gunman killed, in a single shoot-out, as many
    men as Hickok killed in the Rock Creek Station fight?*

A. The murders of McCanles and his two men can hardly
    be called a shoot-out. However, Commodore Perry
    Owens, a Holbrook, Arizona Territory lawman, killed
    three men and wounded a fourth in a real five-minute
    shoot-out September 4, 1887. The dead: Andy Cooper,
    Houston Blevins, Mose B. Roberts. Wounded: Johnny
    Blevins.

Q. *Is it true that Wes Hardin once backed-down Wild Bill?*

A. Hardin told that story; it's as hard to swallow as those
    that Wild Bill told himself, or let others tell about him.
    The fact is both men liked to hear "brag" tales about
    themselves.

Q. *What brought about so much shooting and killing in the
    1870s?*

A. To answer that, we must look at the larger historical con-
    text. Much of the shooting was done by men fresh from
    the Civil War battlefields; they did not hold life in very
    high regard. A man you didn't like was "worth killin'"
    was the way they expressed it then. Hickok, owning up

to many murders, justified himself saying, "I never killed a man who didn't *deserve* it." When the ex-Confederate soldiers met the old Union men on the Great Plains, where the range cattle industry was burgeoning by 1870, the agreement Grant and Lee made at Appomattox meant little to them. The scene of battle had simply shifted from the cotton plantations of the South to the grasslands of the West. Men were re-establishing themselves in life after a bitter war, and they had learned to fight and kill for what they wanted.

Q. *Give me a few facts about Jesse James, the Missouri outlaw.*

A. Jesse Woodson James was born in Clay County, Missouri, September 5, 1847. From 1863 to early 1882 he and his gang of outlaws, train robbers and bank robbers, rampaged virtually with impunity throughout the Middle Border States. The outlaws, like guerrillas of today, lived among the people, sharing some of their spoils with the poor who hid and fed them. The Pinkertons, hearing that some of the gang were holed up at the log cabin of Jesse's stepfather, Dr. Reuben Samuel, the third husband of their mother, Zeralda, bombed the cabin. Killed was their eight-year-old son, Archie Samuel, and Mrs. Zeralda Samuel lost her arm. This foolish act turned many people toward the Jameses and caused the Pinkertons no end of trouble. The James gang, helped by the Youngers, raided a bank at Northfield, Minnesota, and lost their power, as well as several of their men. They were never able to mount a successful raid after that. Jesse, while hanging a picture in his home April 3, 1882, was shot in the back by Bob Ford, a hanger-on, while the brother Charles Ford looked on. The Fords were convicted of murder, sentenced to be hung, but granted a pardon by Gov. Thomas T. Crittenden of Missouri, who had offered a reward for Jesse's death. Bob Ford was later murdered at Creede, Colorado.

Q. *Where may I obtain the book* The Life and Daring Adventures of Jesse James and Frank James, *published in 1882?*

A. Only a well-stocked rare book outlet would have it, unless you find it in a library with a good collection of Western Americana titles. I recommend Carl Breihan's *Complete and Authentic Life of Jesse James* as well.

Q. *I have two books, one by Paul Wellman and one by J.D. Horan, each giving dates for Jesse James' robbery of the bank at Russellville, Kentucky. Wellman gives May 20, 1868; Horan gives the date of March 20, 1868. Which is correct?*

A. I believe March 20, 1868 is correct, as published in reports by the *St. Louis Republican* in their March 23, 1868 edition. This latter date is also quoted by William A. Settle in his work *Jesse James Was His Name*.

Q. *Did Jesse James engineer the robbery of the train at Rocky Cut, near Otterville, Missouri, on July 8, 1876?*

A. According to Carl Breihan's *Complete and Authentic Life of Jesse James* (1953), Jesse was not present at that robbery. Jesse had even taken the trouble to protest, in a letter to the *Kansas City Times*, against the charge that he was responsible for the crime. He denied knowing Hobbs Kerry, the man who informed the authorities that he was with Jesse and others in robbing the train. The express was rifled of more than $17,000.

Q. *Who killed Luke Short, the Dodge City gambler-gunman?*

A. Short died a natural death of dropsy, at Geuda Springs, Kansas, in August, 1893. He was buried at Fort Worth.

Q. *I have heard that one of the Dalton brothers was a lawman. Right?*

A. Yes, Frank Dalton was a U.S. marshal in Indian Territory, but he was never connected with the later "Dalton Gang" and was a good law officer. He was killed by a bootlegger and the felon's female companion, while in the line of duty. His brothers were Bob, Emmet and Grat. Bob and Grat were killed, together with Bill Powers (alias Tom Evans) and Dick Broadwell, during their raid on the Coffeyville, Kansas, banks in 1892. Emmet, after a prison term, survived to old age.

Q. *When Pat Garrett killed Billy the Kid, was there ever any doubt as to the way Garrett told about it afterward? I have heard, in Lincoln County, New Mexico, that not everyone believed what Garrett told, that he shot Billy as Billy entered the darkened room where Pat and Maxwell were visiting, Maxwell lying on the bed.*

A. Garrett's story has been generally accepted as the truth. There was, however, this story, told me by Clara Blasin-

game, the late author of *Dakota Cowboy* (her husband
Ike's biography) and other books. Clara said that a Mrs.
Valdez, of Casper, Wyoming, a relative of Pete Maxwell,
the man in the room with Billy the Kid the night he was
slain, told her that Maxwell had reported the killing this
way: Maxwell was sitting in the deep window, upstairs,
his knees up even with his chin, trying to get some cool
air. Billy the Kid was standing in the room behind him,
near the window, talking with him. When Garrett appeared
in the courtyard, Billy asked Maxwell, "Who is it?" Then
Billy spoke louder to the figure in the dusk below,
"¿Quién es?" Garrett, *from below*, fired his *rifle*, the
bullet passing under Maxwell's legs and into the youthful
outlaw, killing him instantly. Fear of Garrett, after he
had told his version of the killing to the Mexican people,
prompted Maxwell to remain silent and accept Garrett's
story, though Maxwell had repeated it a time or two to
relatives.

Q. *What town did Jim McIntyre serve as city marshal?*

A. McIntyre served at Mobeetie, Texas, in 1878 at the end
of the buffalo hide years, and when the cattle business
was burgeoning in the area. He was reported to have run
Mysterious Dave Mather and Wyatt Earp out of the
town when they attempted a "gold brick" swindle.

Q. *Were the murderers of George Brown, the Caldwell,
Kansas marshall, ever apprehended?*

A. Yes, but it was several months before the two brothers,
Edward and Jess Green (Canadians by birth, but who
were Texas cowboys) were tracked down and after two
shoot-outs were caught in a night camp and filled full of
lead. Ed died instantly under the posse's fusillade; Jess,
with many bullets in him, died a few days later. The
Green brothers had several other killings behind them
before they murdered Marshal Brown in a Caldwell red-
light, where he had gone to disarm them. The reward
monies on the pair totaled $1,400.

Q. *Was Wild Bill Hickok all they say he was as a lawman?*

A. James Butler (Wild Bill) Hickok does stand out as one of
the West's greatest characters. As a lawman, he was too
quick on the trigger, perhaps, but he outlived many who
failed to understand that criminals on the Western frontier

would kill an officer as quickly as they would a buffalo. Hickok left a long record of service as both a scout for the army and as a lawman who didn't bluff easily. The stories of his being "backed down" by Texas cowboys and other badmen, like Wes Hardin, fail to stand up when the facts are examined. Hickok had some good friends, like Buffalo Bill, and he was a friend to others, less wealthy, like Calamity Jane. Starting his career as a peace officer at age twenty, when he was elected constable in Monticello Township, Johnson County, Kansas, he served the law many years and appears to have been a trusted officer. The "windy" tale of his battle with the McCandless gang (which said he killed ten men with knives and guns in as many minutes) actually hurt Hickok's name. Hickok will rate with the good, if not the best, peace officers of the Old West. And his career was absolutely fantastic!

Q. *Were many men buried, literally, "with their boots on" in the frontier days of the West?*

A. Very few. Most men who died, even those who were shot to death by lawmen or were hanged legally by paid executioners, had a friend, or relative, who pulled off their boots—and sometimes tucked them under their heads for a pillow. Old-time burials have been found this way. Another factor was in the deceased favor: boots were rather scarce and could be used by friends or others who attended the burial. Of course, "wearing dead man's boots" was highly in disrepute, for there was a belief it was an unlucky omen. But many men would prefer to challenge the superstition, rather than walk over hot sands and through cactus in their bare feet, or with thin soles on their own boots. Some cowboys' boots were hung on the cross over their graves, but the usual practice was to save them, carry them along in the chuckwagon, or probably line the brake shoes of the wagon's brakes with them.

Q. *Did the superstition that it was unlucky to wear a "dead man's boots" apply to his clothing?*

A. No. The clothing of the deceased cowboy, for example, was divided among his best friends, his six-gun and holster to one, his hat to another, his saddle to another, his boots to one who wore the same size, and so forth. Of course, if the man's relatives were known and it was possible, the friends made up a kitty so that the widow, perhaps, could be paid for the articles. I have heard personal stories from old trailmen where a watch, or perhaps a valued gun, or even a horse, was taken back to Texas after a trail drive to the deceased's home.

Q. *Were there many outlaw women in the Old West?*

A. There were really very few women in the Old West who, with or without men, robbed stagecoaches, banks, stole money, lied, cheated and earned their bad names solely by their own actions. Oklahoma had Belle Starr, Little Britches, Cattle Annie, Rose of the Cimarron, and Pearl Black. Other women who were all on the "outlaw trail" were Bronco Moll of Ogallala, Nebraska; Doña Gertrudis of Sante Fe; and Virginia Slade (Mrs. Joe Slade) who started out in Colorado and ended up in Montana.

There were many more women who consorted with outlaws, changing their place of residence right along with their men when the pursuit grew too hot. But such women, even wives, could not be called "outlaw women," though their husbands and sweethearts were fleeing the law.

Further, when the land was becoming settled by big ranches and the mining industry was in full swing, there were many women who came West as prostitutes in order to profit from the new wealth. Many of these later married and settled down to a more conventional life. Some are still remembered, such as Calamity Jane Canary, a coarse and ignorant tart who roamed Wyoming, the Dakotas, and Montana. She eventually made friends among more respectable folk and never fell totally into disrepute. Except for Calamity and Big-Nosed Kate, Doc Holliday's paramour, and a few others, most of these women have been swallowed up into obscurity.

Q. *Where did Calamity Jane die?*

A. She died at Terry, South Dakota, but was buried in Deadwood, alongside Wild Bill Hickok, whom she knew well in life.

Q. *Was prostitution in the Old West practiced as widely as many Western writers tell?*

A. The world's oldest profession was popular in the Old West, just as it is today in the modern West—and in the East. The towns of Wichita, Dodge City, Caldwell,

Newton, Fort Worth, Mobeetie, North Platte, Cheyenne, Billings, Great Falls, Sante Fe, Creede, Dawson City, all were peopled by scores of whores. Gambling, drinking, and fornicating were all popular.

Q. *What was the usual bounty offered for an outlaw when the posters read "Wanted, Dead or Alive."*

A. About $500 would bring a man in, either dead or alive, for that was an immense amount of money in the 1870s and 1880s.

Q. *Who were the last felons hung in Arizona. For what crime?*

A. They were Francisco Rentezia, from Guanajato, Mexico, and Hilario Hidalgo, from Chihuahua. The pair had murdered Charles Goddard and Frank Cocke, February 1, 1903, at Stanton, Arizona. They swung July 30, 1903.

Q. *What was meant by a "bad actor"?*

A. An undependable person, who inclined to booze, fight, and make a general nuisance of himself. Gunmen like Wes Hardin, Rowdy Joe Lowe, Clay Allison, Billy Thompson, and Billy the Kid would have been given that appellation. It was a special one, and would not have applied to Hickok, Wyatt Earp, and others who were equally tough. A bad horse would sometimes earn that name among cowboys, "He's a bad actor!"

Q. *When was the last train robbery in the nation, and who robbed it?*

A. According to E.B. Block's *Great Train Robberies of the West*, published in 1959, the last one was the attempted holdup of the Southern Pacific's Sunset Limited on February 15, 1933. Conductor J.G. Caster borrowed a .38 revolver from a passenger and shot to death George Clinton Powers, a steamshovel operator who had been long out of work and was actually not an outlaw at all. The attempted holdup took place near Ontario, California, east of Los Angeles. Ed Mahoney, Arvada, Colorado, believes this is the last recorded holdup attempt. Ed was former rate chief clerk in the San Francisco division of the Southern Pacific and Sante Fe.

Q. *Were not most of the Western outlaws paranoiacs and kill-crazy madmen?*

A. No, that seems to be a stereotype that emerged with the influence of psychology and psychiatry on popular thinking. Amateur head shrinkers have tried to stick these labels on every man who fell afoul of the law and never could reestablish himself in polite society. The old outlaws were *individuals*. They were all different, as unpredictable as a Kansas wind. That is why our bag of motives, crimes, criminals, and such is so big, and such a mixed assortment, when you deal with outlaws of the Old West. There is no pattern, just individuals like Tom Horn, Sam Bass, Jesse James, Luke Short, and others, living out their particular life in the unusual pattern it followed from birth to death.

Q. *Can you provide me with some information on the Sherburne, Minnesota, bank holdup in 1896?*

A. On October 7, 1896, two young brothers by the name of Kellihan from Rock Rapids, Iowa, held up the Sherburne bank, killing O.J. Oestern of Luverne, Minnesota, and the cashier, George Thorborn. They took about $1,000 cash. A posse headed by Marshal Gallion of Bancroft, Iowa, surrounded a house near Elmore, where the brothers had hid out. Gallion was killed by the two boys, and they fled, strange as it seems, *on bicycles!* Hans, the younger of the two brothers, shot himself when the pressure on them got high. The older brother was arrested and taken to jail at Fairmont, Minnesota. The two boys were rank amateurs, neither having a bad record before this instance. They had been influenced by the tales of bank robberies by such as the James Gang.

Q. *Was the man who attempted to rob the Canadian Bank of Commerce at Skagway, Alaska, in September 1902 ever identified?*

A. No. In his holdup attempt, while holding a stick of dynamite in his hand and threatening the bank officers with his revolver, the pistol went off, discharging the dynamite and shredding his head and body. He had been in the town only a few days, playing cards at the local saloon, and he was not really known to anyone there.

Q. *What was "leg bail"?*

A. That was what flight from the law was called, especially when a man was marked for arrest and learned about it before the law had him collared.

Q. *What is meant by the expression "seeing the elephant"?*

A. The phrase apparently originated along the Oregon Trail, or when the gold seekers traveled that route to California.

"The elephant," to them, was a symbol of adventure, trouble on the trail, the shattering experiences they often passed through. A man who had passed through a particularly trying experience, a breakdown of his wagon, or the loss of his ox teams, and had somehow survived the experience, might say to another, "I didn't see the elephant, but did catch a glimpse of his tail as he barged through the camp that night." Later, the Texas trail drivers who had witnessed stampedes and slept out on the prairie for several months might say, "I saw the elephant, and heard the owl holler." Ham Bell's big barn at Dodge City where the trail men put up had a huge running elephant painted on the front of the building. Many "Elephant Stables" sprang up in the West in the 1860s and 1870s. There was an Elephant Saloon at old Beer City, in the Neutral Strip in the 1880s.

Q. *Where may I find a good and accurate book on the outlaws and lawmen of Dodge City, Kansas?*

A. I recommend *Why The West Was Wild* by Nyle H. Miller and Joseph W. Snell of the Kansas Historical Society. It draws on many old newspaper stories of the 1870–80 era.

Q. *Will you list the twenty gunfighters in the Old West who received the most publicity? List them in order of their notoriety, if you can.*

A. This question could never be answered to satisfy every Western or badman buff, for their reputations were a relative matter and depended upon who read about them, who knew them personally, and how much publicity they received in the uncritical pulp and dime magazines of another age. However, I believe they would run something like this, in the order of *their publicity* or *notoriety:* (1) Jesse James (2) Billy the Kid (3) Wild Bill Hickok (4) Wyatt Earp (5) Frank James (6) Doc Holliday (7) Ben Thompson (8) Bat Masterson (9) Luke Short (10) John Wesley Hardin (11) Black John Ketchum (12) Burt Alvord (13) Ike Clanton (14) Tom McLowery (15) Clay Allison (16) Rowdy Joe Lowe (17) Print Olive (18) Ed Masterson (19) John Ringo (20) Bill Longley. It will be obvious that some of the worst killers of the time are not on the list, for the obvious reasons (a) they may have been lawmen, not just gunfighters, e.g., Commodore

Perry Owens; (b) they may have been well-known and publicized "outlaws," such as the Daltons, but they were *not* actually "gunfighters"; (c) like Henry Plummer, they may have been the worst of the man-killers, but didn't get quite enough publicity to outrank some of the above. Others in this category include Joe Slade, William Clarke Quantrill and several of his men, Tom Horn, Boone Helm, John King Fisher, Jim Courtright, Curley Bill Brocius, and Billy Stiles fail for one reason or another, in my judgment, to rank over any of the twenty names on my list. Looking over the list, one may understand the perils of the frontier lawmen in maintaining law and order in the cow towns, mining camps, and cotton towns.

Q. *Where were the worst of the outlaw gangs in Texas located in the early days?*

A. Williamson County, and south to the Knobbs area, had its full share following the Civil War. But perhaps the biggest concentrations were in east Texas and in the border area from Langtry around the Big Bend country. In Reconstruction days, when cattle became gold, outlawry spread all over the state. As in the Prohibition days of 1919-35, the Big Money boys followed the crowd. There were reputed to be upward of 200 outlaws, scalawags, and bummers from both of the old armies in the Austin section of the country. Murders and lynchings of blacks, whites, and Mexicans were a common, almost daily, occurrence there. *The Austin Statesman* reported editorially in 1876: "There have been more men killed in Williamson County this year than were lost [from Williamson County] in the Civil War."

Q. *Why was Billy the Kid known as Billy Bonney, Henry McCarty, and as William Antrim? Who was he, actually?*

A. One authority says this: His mother, Kathleen McCarty, married Wm. Harrison *Bonney* and had two sons, Billy and Joe. When Billy's father died, Billy's mom anglicized her name and used the name Catherine *McCarty*. She then married William Henry Harrison *Antrim*. Thus, Billy was often referred to as Billy *Antrim* and as Henry *McCarty*. But his *real name* (his father's) remained *Bonney*.

Q. *Has there ever been a documented case where two men met on the street for a gunfight and shot it out as shown in scores of movies and TV films?*

A. At least one is known and so reported. At Cheyenne, Wyoming, Charlie Harrison and Jim Levy met and exchanged shots on the street. Harrison died two weeks later of his wound. However, most old-time so-called gunfights were actually bushwhackings, or cases where one man "got the drop" on the other, aiming his gun at the other's back, and then calling out his name and shooting him down when the other attempted to draw his own revolver. An example of such cold-blooded murder which was later reported by Western authors as a "gunfight" (see Marie Sandoz' *The Cattlemen*, pages 288-92) was the shooting of I.P. (Print) Olive at Trail City, Colorado, by Joe Sparrow. The court records show Olive was unarmed, in his shirtsleeves, entering his own saloon, when he was shot several times, the last time as he lay on the floor, helpless and dying.

Q. *What is the Hole-in-the-Wall, where the Wild Bunch, Butch Cassidy and Sundance Kid, held out?*

A. It is not actually a *hole*, but a trail through and over the 600-foot high red sandstone bluff that bisects central Wyoming for a distance of about fifty miles. The pass through the bluff is about fifteen miles southwest of Kaycee, Wyoming, in southwest Johnson County. In 1902 county officers blasted the narrowest portion of the trail so livestock and a wagon road could pass through "the hole."

Q. *Did Butch Cassidy die in South America, fighting a group of* rurales, *or soldiers, as the film* Butch Cassidy and the Sundance Kid *shows?*

A. Some books and stories have him die this way. One account has Butch shoot Harry Longabaugh (the Sundance Kid) and then commit suicide. A Utah author writes me that he is working on a book manuscript that will prove, with adequate documentation, that neither Butch Cassidy nor Longabaugh died in South America. That story, says my friend, was started by the Pinkerton Agency to cover up their own inability to catch the pair of robbers. The sister of Butch Cassidy, Mrs. Lulu Parker Betensen, eighty-eight, who lives in a small town in Utah, says Butch died a natural death at age sixty-nine in the

United States. But even her statement is disputed. Most members of the Wild Bunch, though popularized in film and story, were mediocre roustabouts, who chose a few brief years of crime over the fulfillments of a more ordinary existence.

Q. *Is it true that Ben Thompson served several years in prison for shooting his own brother-in-law?*

A. Yes, Thompson served two years of a four-year sentence at the Huntsville, Texas, prison for shooting his brother-in-law, James Moore, in the leg. It was a flesh wound, and Ben said he did it to teach Moore a lesson. Whatever the lesson was, it was not well learned, for Moore had him arrested and prosecuted. Ben might have been freed, but his bad temper asserted itself and he threatened to kill the judge, W.D. Scott. Scott gave him a tongue-lashing and a sentence at hard labor for four years.

Q. *Why wasn't Curly Bill Brocius (or Rosciotis, as the* Tombstone Epitaph *printed it) charged and sentenced for the murder of Marshal Fred White at Tombstone in 1880?*

A. White's deathbed statement was that Curly Bill had not intended to shoot him, but that the gun was discharged accidentally when White attempted to jerk it from the outlaw's hands. Curly Bill and other cowboys were "firing their pistols at the moon" when the accident occurred. Had White died instantly, and made no statement, Curly Bill probably would have been hanged.

Q. *Was Doc Holliday as dangerous a man as he has been shown to be in movies and on TV?*

A. Yes. He was a sick man (tuberculosis), in addition to being a heavy drinker. Bat Masterson said that Holliday couldn't have whipped a fifteen-year-old boy with his fists. And he intimated that Doc's physical weakness inclined him to use "equalizers," that is, six-shooters or shotguns. Like many weak men, Doc paired up with the one man he regarded as "strong," Wyatt Earp. The two, both being weak in character, needed each other.

Q. *Why did Luke Short, the gambler, gun down Long-haired Jim Courtright? Was it over a woman?*

A. Reliable Western researchers claim that Courtright was operating a detective agency which attempted to shake down the local gamblers for "protection" from the Fort Worth ordinance against open gambling. No mention of a woman is made in their accounts. Luke's first bullet fortunately tore away Courtright's right thumb, rendering him almost helpless against Short's final attack.

Q. *Was Ben Thompson actually able to terrorize the entire city of Austin, Texas, as has been told of him? Why didn't the police lock him up?*

A. Thompson, before his election as city marshal of Austin, visited the editor of the *Austin Statesman*, a newspaper that opposed him. He overturned the editor's desk and jumbled the type cases in an effort to change the viewpoint expressed by the paper. Neither editor nor staff fought Thompson physically, but they did give him reason to believe he could not change their opinion of him, so he left. The next morning the *Statesman*'s editor wrote: "The state cannot afford to be dominated by desperadoes. The only way to stop such careers is for the papers and the people to denounce such men and their acts." This was good advice then, and still is.

Q. *Curly Bill Brocius was said to have shot his own horse. Why?*

A. Billy Breakenridge told how Curly Bill was lying on a card table that day in Tombstone, recovering from a previous night's drinking. A friend was drinking from a tin cup. (A galvanized tin cup then caused whiskey to make a man deathly sick, even if he drank little from it.) Curly Bill roused himself, said "Don't drink that, Shorty, it's p'ison!" Shorty still held to the cup, and Curly Bill shot his revolver at it. The shot went through the clapboard building, killing his fine saddle horse that had been tied outside all night, waiting for Curly Bill to sober up and feed and water him.

Q. *What happened to Ben Kilpatrick, one of the last of the Hole-in-the-Wall Gang?*

A. He and a confederate were killed between Anderson and Dryden, Texas, while attempting a train robbery. The express messenger killed both. He got Kilpatrick with a hammer, when he wasn't paying close enough attention, and the other robber, variously identified under the names of Ole Holbeck, Ed Welch, or H.O. Beck, with the dead Kilpatrick's rifle.

Q. *Who killed Bob Ford, the man who murdered Jesse James?*

A. He was Ed O. Kelly. The name, when set down on the police blotter, was written with an apostrophe, causing many writers to put it as Ed O'Kelly. Kelly blasted Ford with a shotgun as Ford came into a saloon.

Q. *Did anyone who saw him ever describe Kid Wade, the outlaw who was lynched by a mob at Bassett, Nebraska, February 8, 1884?*

A. Yes, Judge Lewis Cananburg described Albert (Kid) Wade as "...about 25, medium height, shambling gait, low forehead, massive jaws, face angular, sharp features, thin blond beard." The judge also expressed the opinion that some of the "Regulators" in the mob were afraid the Kid would squeal on them for being horsethieves themselves! This causes the thought to arise that probably many outlaws and thieves were hung by their comrades who placed themselves temporarily above suspicion by associating with the lynch mobs.

Q. *Can you provide a description of Clay Allison?*

A. One authority has described him as six-foot two-inches in height, black hair, weight 175, blue eyes, handsome; high forehead with heavy black eyebrows and usually wearing a mustache. He walked with a limp in the right foot which showed plainly if he had been on horseback for a while.

Q. *Where was Billy Claiborne born? When did he join up with Johnny Ringo, and who killed Billy?*

A. My sources fail to reveal Billy's birthplace. He probably joined Ringo in Arizona, about 1878–80, for his name is not connected with Ringo's Texas activities. Buckskin Frank Leslie shot Billy down after calling pleasantly to him, "Hello, Billy!" Leslie claimed he thought Billy was gunning for him, for Billy, he had said, was blaming him (Leslie) for Ringo's death, which was declared a suicide. Claiborne and Ringo were reputed to be close friends. Leslie, later in prison, falsely boasted that he *had* killed Ringo. But the freighters who found Ringo's body sitting in the fork of the bush or tree had looked the body over carefully, according to Frank King, whose friend Robert M. Boller had written him, "I called it suicide fifty-two years ago and am still calling it suicide. I guess I am the last of that coroner's jury."

Q. *Was the mystery of Johnny Ringo's death ever solved?*

A. As mentioned above, Ringo's body was found propped up against a tree on July 4, 1882, in West Turkey Creek Canyon, near the old town of Shakespeare. Death had been caused by a bullet wound in the head. The coroner's jury gave the cause of death as suicide, after a careful examination of the body and Ringo's gear. The news of Ringo's death immediately brought claims from Wyatt Earp, Frank Leslie, and John O'Rourke that each of them, and alone, had killed Ringo. Their claims were not substantiated by the evidence at hand. The real mystery, why he shot himself, remains. All suicides leave a trail of question marks after them. Ringo had been as dangerous as they come.

Q. *Who was Club Foot George?*

A. He was George Lane, a shoe cobbler, who drifted into Alder Gulch, Montana Territory, in the early 1860s. He was on the lookout for the Plummer Gang and had his shop in Walter Dance's Store, where he could watch all stages come and go at the livery stable across the street, where they loaded up with gold bullion. Alder Gulch became Virginia City (Montana Territory). Lane was hanged with three other members of the Plummer Gang. His club foot is reportedly on view at a museum there, but his body rests on Boot Hill.

Q. *Who killed Wild Bill Longley, Texas badman?*

A. Longley was hanged for a murder at Giddings, Texas, October 11, 1877. From the scaffold Wild Bill apologized for his bad actions and asked forgiveness from the people he had wronged.

Q. *Why is there such a diversity of opinion about John King Fisher of Texas fame? Some say he was all bad, others say all good.*

A. No man can be all good or all bad. Probably two factors contributed to this diversity of opinion: hero worship and misunderstanding. Although few western "badmen" could easily be *understood*, there was a bit of both good and bad, and much ordinary human-being in all of them. Many were mean, kind, loveable, despicable, surly, cruel, strong, weak, and every other human attribute you can apply. King Fisher was no doubt like that. He had been a lawless man; he had been a lawman. He was in bad company the night he and Ben Thompson entrained from

Austin to San Antonio, and whether his motives were good or bad, as a result he died with Thompson.

Q. *Was Black Bart, California stage robber, ever captured and put in jail?*

A. It has been written that after many successful stage robberies, Black Bart left a laundered handkerchief at the scene of one of these crimes. Following an examination of ninety-one laundries in the area, he was apprehended and gave his name as Charles E. Bolton, an elderly man from Boston, Massachusetts. He served a short term at San Quentin, then disappeared.

Q. *Who was Mabry Gray of Texas fame and what was he known for?*

A. Gray was a dissolute outlaw upon whom the fictitious character "Mustang Gray" was fashioned by Jere Clements, an Alabama writer. Gray was active around Victoria, Texas, from 1838 to 1842. He once tied a party of seven innocent Mexican peons together and then shot them for their meager belongings. One of them, Manuel Escobar, survived his wounds and lived to tell who committed the atrocity. Mabry Gray died on the Rio Grande from acute alcoholism, according to John J. Linn, Texas historian and scribe. There was, as is the fact with most criminal types, nothing noble or fine about Gray. He was just a degenerate murderer.

Q. *Why were so many black men and Mexicans killed by the early-day Texans?*

A. There had been bad feelings between Mexicans and whites since the Mexican War, when the United States seized so much territory and wealth from Mexico. So Texans understandably disliked Mexicans, but this still didn't excuse the murdering of innocent people. In the case of the Texas whites murdering black men, that was common throughout the South, where black men tried to establish their rights to freedom. Even after the Civil War, white, bed-sheeted figures rode at night attempting to cow the freed Negroes. Gradually, the better elements of white society reacted against such hooliganism and night-riding, and murder became less acceptable.

Q. *Where was Black Jack (Tom) Ketchum buried after his hanging?*

A. He was first buried at Clayton, New Mexico, in the old

Boot Hill Cemetery. In 1933 public interest on the part of Clayton citizens caused the remains to be removed from that grave and reinterred in the new Clayton Cemetery. The casket was opened so all could see that it was actually the body of the outlaw. A man who witnessed the opening of the casket described it this way: "The coat-sleeve was folded back over the stump of the right arm and was pinned down with a safety pin. However, the black mustache and the black hair had turned a reddish shade, a maroon red, in the intervening years since April 26, 1901, when I first saw him buried. But it was Black Jack, alright."

Q. *Why did Billy Stiles, who helped rob the train at Cochise Station, Arizona, later surrender?*

A. Stiles was, at the very best, difficult to understand. He had implicated his friends in that robbery, and all had been jailed for it. Then he successfully held up the jailor, Deputy Bravin, and permitted all who wished to go to escape. Like many criminals, Stiles was an enigmatic character, both to the lawmen and to fellow outlaws. Actually, no one could trust him, for he was continuously back and forth, on both sides of the law. Stiles helped convict three of the men who robbed the Fairbank Station. His price, like that of most felons, whether involved in a Watergate break-in or a common train robbery, was immunity. He would always "sing" on fellow bandits for his own freedom. That is what happened to him when he came back from Mexico with a trail herd of Jim Herron's to see his wife; one of the hands with Herron's trail herd informed the authorities and Billy was caught, though Herron knew nothing of Billy's impending arrest.

Q. *When Dora Hand, the dancer and singer, was shot to death at Dodge City, how did they capture James Kennedy, her murderer?*

A. On October 4, 1878, following her murder (her real name was Fannie Keenan), a coroner's inquest was held. They named Kennedy as the assassin, for they knew he was at loggerheads with the mayor, Dog Kelley, in whose room the woman was sleeping, when Kennedy, shooting through a window at the figure on the bed, killed Dora instead of the absent Kelly. When the posse returned

Kennedy to Dodge, his arm had been shattered by a bullet. At the hearing Kennedy was acquitted! The fact that he was from a prominent Texas family, and was badly wounded, losing the use of one arm, no doubt influenced the judge, R.G. Cook, who was also justice of the peace and acting coroner. Kennedy's father, Miflin Kennedy, had been contacted and returned to get his son, so Kennedy was released into his father's custody. One of Kennedy's previous feats of gun play was in shooting Print Olive while the latter sat at a poker table in Ellsworth, in July 1872. Kennedy was not apprehended or punished for this, though Olive nearly died from bad wounds in the groin and shoulder.

Q. *When the final evidence was in, was the shooting of Sheriff Whitney at Ellsworth by Billy Thompson accidental or not?*

A. At his trial, Billy was found "not guilty." But the verdict came long after the shooting, and the residents of Ellsworth at the time were shocked by the verdict. The *Ellsworth Reporter* summed it up: "The clerk commenced reading [the verdict] and just as we expected to hear the word 'guilty,' he read 'not guilty.' This was a great surprise to most of our citizens, especially those living in the country at that time. Thompson shot Whitney. They expected nothing less than twenty years in the penitentiary for him, as, *until this court met, the shooting had not been called accidental.*"

Q. *Was Alfred Packer, called "the Man Eater," actually guilty of cannibalism?*

A. Yes, it is generally believed that after a terrible winter ordeal crossing the Rockies, Packer saved his own life by eating the flesh of at least some of his five companions—Bell, Humphrey, Miller, Noon, and Swan. However, Packer's own story of the event has never been disproved. Returning to camp, after a reconnaissance and search for food, Packer said he found Bell had gone berserk, slain the others with a hatchet, and was roasting human flesh on the campfire. When Bell attacked him, Packer said he had to kill Bell in self-defense. The roasted meat sizzling where Bell had dropped it into the fire suggested to the starving Packer, who had not eaten for several days, that he might yet survive.

Packer was a Union War veteran of Company F, 16th
U.S. Infantry in the Civil War and a man of otherwise
good repute. Local quidnuncs of Colorado have attempted
to make Packer's and his companions' tragedy into a
comedy by organizing "Alfred Packer" clubs and restau-
rants at colleges. This lack of understanding of the
tragedy of this poor man and his companions seems
beyond reason.

Q. *Was Tom Horn actually guilty of shooting the boy,
Willie Nickell, the crime for which Horn was hanged?*

A. Horn denied the killing, of course, and charged LeFors,
Stoll, Snow, and other officials and clerks with alter-
ing and editing his original confession. Since then, a considerable body of literature has thrown doubt on Horn's
guilt. Yet Horn was known to be a mercilous killer, a
"blood killer," as bounty hunters are called. He had a fair
trial, was convicted, and was hanged November 1903 at
Cheyenne, Wyoming.

Q. *Who was North America's greatest guerrilla leader, red or
white?*

A. In my opinion, Pancho Villa, the Mexican revolutionary
leader. His great fighting army, once numbered at 50,000
men and women, grew from the grass roots under his
indomitable leadership. He was defeated ultimately by
friends who betrayed him and treason in the government.

Villa was assassinated at Hidalgo de Parral, July 23,
1923, by eight men. He died with twelve bullets in his
body, two in his head. Before he died of these wounds,
Villa managed to shoot Ramon Guerra, one of the
assassins, through the heart.

Q. *Is Pancho Villa's widow still living? Did he leave her
wealthy?*

A. In 1971 she was living in Mexico in a Victorian mansion
with nine other families who paid her no rent because of
their poverty. Luz Corral de Villa, then seventy-seven
years of age, maintained many of her husband's relics of
his Revolutionary War life, among them being the bullet-
riddled limousine in which he was assassinated. She receives no aid from the Republic of Mexico, but tourists
contribute more than $500 monthly to her to see the
fifty-room mansion and Villa's collections. Villa, she
stoutly maintains, was at heart a kindly man who fought

against the tyranny of the rich Mexican families who kept the peons in abject slavery under Diaz' rule. "He wanted to end poverty and the accumulation of riches in the hands of a few," she says. "He was rough, because he was without education. The rich ones wished to keep all the workers ignorant and illiterate. He learned to read and write when he was an adult," she said proudly. "Unfortunately, these things have not been resolved fifty years after his death," Luz explains to tourists who are interested in their history.

Q. *Is the story true that Joe Mason, Dodge City policeman, once shot a man, then just took the body to Boot Hill, dug a grave, and buried it himself?*

A. No, only partly true. This happened in Sweetwater, Texas, after Joe had left Dodge City. There, in a saloon, another man by name of Edward Ryan, whom Mason had once arrested in Dodge City, began to curse Mason and threaten him with a whipping. Mason tried to stop the abuse and told the man he would shoot him if he didn't shut his mouth. Ryan continued to badger Mason, who pulled a revolver and killed his tormenter. The Dodge papers reported that Mason was running a free-and-easy house and had shot the man, then taken the corpse and buried it. Mason wrote the newspaper, "Your correspondent has misrepresented me. I was in no way connected with a 'free and easy' at Sweetwater. Nor did I dig a hole and place the victim therein."

Joe Mason was later a partner in the M Bar Ranch with "Toot" Over, in the Neutral Strip. He was highly regarded as a stockman. Mason, incidentally, was freed of the charge of murder by a U.S. military tribunal that met at Fort Elliott, January 5, 1878, and found him innocent of the charge, being "justifiable in the premises." The board was headed up by Cap. C. Mauck, 4th Cavalry, and Lt. Col. John P. Hatch, 4th Cavalry, commanding.

Q. *Can you relate something about the "Bloody Benders" of Kansas?*

A. The Bender family—the father, Old John, Old Mrs. Bender, the daughter Katie, and the son, Geiger—came to Labette County, Kansas, in 1871. They established a small grocery store in their farm home and put up travelers for the night, for it was along the main road crossing the county and many settlers and others used the road. Katie practiced spiritualism and attracted men with her good looks. Within a year, stories began to circulate of travelers who had turned up missing along this trail. The disappearance of Dr. William H. York of Independence, Kansas, brought his brother, Colonel York of Olathe, with a posse searching for him. Following Colonel York's visit and his interrogation of the Benders, the Bender family disappeared. About a week after their disappearance, Leroy F. Dick, the constable, visited the place and from the ugly smell determined that the odor came not entirely from the calves in the corral that had perished from lack of water, but from underneath the house—and the smell was that of decaying human flesh. An investigation by Dick and his neighbors brought forth a blood-pot from beneath the cabin floor. Searching the yard behind the house, the unmistakable cracks outlining graves appeared in what was intended to be an apple orchard. Digging, the neighbors unearthed the corpses of seven men and a child, all victims, murdered by the Benders with hammers and knives and buried by them in the night after taking all their money and possessions. A search determined the Benders had left the country, abandoning their team and wagon at the railroad station in Thayer, Kansas. One story tells how the posse found, captured, and exterminated the Benders. Other stories say they were never apprehended.

Q. *How much truth and fact can one find in the usual "Western" fiction story? Are the badmen in them typical of the early West?*

A. While each book of Western fiction may have some literary or historical merit, most are a mish-mash with stereotyped characters and well-rehearsed events. There are the Hero, the Villain, the Chase and Capture, the Gun, the Horse, Revenge, Violence, Death, and the Moral. There is little of real historical value contained in much of our "Western fiction."

Q. *What did the cryptic numerals 3-7-77, used by the Montana Vigilantes, mean?*

A. It is believed that figures were taken from the California Vigilantes movement and used in lieu of person's names, to prevent detection. Numbers 3, 7 and 77 all held executive positions in the Vigilantes in San Francisco, hence the three signed all orders. These three numerals became sinister, for the bylaws of the group read, "The only punishment that shall be inflicted by this Committee is death."

Q. *How did a vigilante organization hold a trial?*

A. Committees differed in their work. The better ones tried to maintain a semblance of recognized legal procedure, electing a president, and holding trials that were duly scheduled with all notified ahead of the trial date, and selecting a jury of the defendant's peers. Other committees simply took a man they believed needed it, held a brief "drumhead" trial, and hung him to the nearest tree, telephone pole, or wagon tongue. In some of these latter trials, it was generally a very crooked committee that attempted to serve The Law, with too frequently some criminal at its head.

Q. *Why is there so much dope traffic in the West today, when there was little of it in pioneer days?*

A. Although the crime and dope in the old days could not compare to the drug traffic today, there were drugs in the Old West, as witness this news story from the *Idaho Statesman*, Boise, Idaho, in 1876: "Our City is becoming rotten to the core... There are too many lecherous loafers who live on the earnings of fallen women; too many hop [dope] fiends; too many yegg men and fakirs; too many saloon bums, and men of the never-sweat stripe. Crime in every form, from murder down...."

Q. *Who, in your judgement, were the top ten gunfighters in the frontier West? Which one killed the most men?*

A. The question is impossible to answer. Misinformation over the past thirty to fifty years has tended to place men as "top" gunfighters when the cold record does not sustain them there. For example, one would consider Bat Masterson in that category, yet Bat actually killed only two men, not twenty or thirty, as has been recounted. And others, such as Billy the Kid, have been held in esteem as gunfighters when actually their half-dozen murders were more in the nature of bushwhackings— cold-blooded and premeditated murder—of clerks, barbers, and men who did not even wear guns! Still others known as "top" gunmen were those who penned autobiographies boasting of scores of killings in which they actually had no part. Wes Hardin was such a one. Wyatt Earp, if his biographer, Stuart Lake, quotes him fairly, can be considered only an outright fabricator of tall tales of his own deeds. And so it goes. Most of the men who have been glorified for many years as the West's "great gunfighters" have killed fewer men in face to face combat than the average combat soldier of any of the twentieth century's major wars. Many of the names which have become sanctified among Western badmen buffs were little more than riffraff of the times.

Q. *Why was there no dueling in the Old West? What ended the practice of the duel to settle grievances between men?*

A. The Anti-Dueling Act of 1839 penalized any man proposing a duel or carrying one out. Within the next twenty-five years the great Civil War was in progress, and all men began carrying arms for self-protection. This habit inaugurated the age of the "fast draw" and of "getting the drop" on the other man; that is, practically ambushing him on a city street, where you could approach from behind, call out his name or curse him, and when he attempted to draw his gun, kill him with your own drawn gun. On the great cattle range of Western America, the Range Law could be expressed as, "You treat me right or we'll have trouble." Then, if trouble came, it came fast, and certain death was almost unavoidable. For "The Peacemaker," or Uncle Sam Colt's "Equalizer," made all men the same size. The new custom of arms-bearing ended dueling.

Q. *In Western stories we hear the term "hide out" and "hideout." What do they mean, and how do they differ?*

A. To *hide out*, in the Old West, was to avoid the law. A *hideout* was *where* you hid out. Men also spoke of a hideout gun, a small concealed pistol which might be used if your regular six-shooter was taken from you.

Photo from the collection of Harry E. Chrisman.

Q. *What, if anything, remains at the site of old Fort Union, in Mora County, northeast New Mexico? Is it worth seeing?*

A. Fort Union is now a national monument, and there are many still-standing walls of adobe construction and the brick walls and chimneys of the old Officer's Row. The site is well worth a visit if you are in the neighborhood of Sante Fe, Las Vegas or Taos. Bring your cameras, for the areas has vast picture possibilities.

9 the MILITARY

As the European nations set up their flags on the perimeters of the continental United States of America, as it is now defined, their armies followed to keep order. It is noticeable that, as the various treaties between the contesting nations for new lands were drawn up, no mention was made of the Indians who, for centuries, had occupied those tracts as homeland. Eventually Chief Justice Marshall, in 1823, touched on this matter in the case titled *Johnson and Graham's Lessee* vs. *William M'Intosh*. (See Vol. 8, *Wheatland Reports of U.S. Supreme Court*, p. 543 ff.)

With the discovery of America, Marshall wrote, the great new land discovered by the white man "offered an ample field to the ambition and enterprise of all, and the character and religion of its inhabitants offered an apology for considering them a people over whom the superior genius of Europe might claim ascendency." Using the superior European jurisprudence, the white nations then ruled that possession of the new lands came under the laws and authority of that government whose title might be consumated by possession of the land. "This exclusion of the other European nations," wrote Marshall, "necessarily gave to the nation making the discovery the sole right of acquiring the soil from the natives...."

While the rights of the natives were not entirely disregarded, the Indians were, under this ruling, so impaired that they could not freely dispose of the soil to whomsoever they pleased, but must accept the white man's law as imported from abroad. This, coupled with the fact that by Indian custom they had no such concept of individual ownership, as did the Europeans, handicapped them terribly in dealing with the encroacher.

And so came Spain, under her grant of the Pope, to butt heads with Great Britain and France, whose claims also rested on "the right of discovery" and conquest of the native peoples. As the great Western empire, called the Louisiana Purchase, became appropriated under this law by the burgeoning United States of America, war against the rightful possessors of the lands became inevitable.

Much rationalization has been devoted to explanations of how the white man "legally" acquired the Indian lands over such vast areas. But as Erl H. Ellis, estimable Denver lawyer and historian, put it on page 9 of his monograph, *International Boundary Lines Across Colorado and Wyoming*, published by Johnson Publishing Company, Boulder, Colorado, in 1966:

> In simple words, the so-called civilized nations of the world have conquered the heathen Indians and have appropriated their lands and the Courts of the whites have of necessity and expedience said this passed good title from the Indians to the whites.

Today, with a more enlightened view of human rights, a whole spectrum of new legal issues confronts our nation. Indians are now, through the white man's own courts, bringing lawsuits to regain lands and to be recompensed for their losses. In some cases, courts are even allowing for interest on the money they deem has been owed on Indian lands for a century or more.

Our literature of the past reflects a long era of violence on the part of both white and red men. And so the questions arise, Are we western people, foaled in the western tradition, a new species of violent men? Do our six-shooter episodes on TV and in theaters contain the genesis of more violence to come? Will our descendants be even more violent than we are?

As Louis L'Amour, the dean of Western fiction writers and one of the nation's most disciplined Western researchers has put it: "Nonsense. The West didn't promote violence. Every great, creative period in history, whether medieval Europe or the age of the Samurai in Japan, has been violent." How true! All the proof one needs is to study the history of Egypt and see Thothmes III in his horse-drawn chariot dashing to the battle of Megiddo, or the young King Tutankh-Amon, lying in his tomb surrounded by his six war chariots! All ancient history—and modern—depicts the bestiality of man and his wars: the great feudal princes falling before the assaults of the serfs and peasants armed with scythes and bludgeons, the colonists wresting control from the British King, George III, and then throwing all their weight against the American Indians to take possession of his lands to the west of the Ohio River.

As we examine the military history of the discovery and settlement of The American West (1800-1900), it may appear as an especially violent age. Yet in our own day we have witnessed four devastating wars since 1917 alone—wars of mammoth weaponry and savage destruction the like of which could not even have been imagined in previous centuries.

As we have seen, land and the conquest of land is the basic contention between men and nations. There is only so much land surface on Earth. Logic demands that all men must share and share alike that soil. The choice is ours. We must not lay blame on the Military when it is our civilian prerogative to make the choice—war or peace. We have less than twenty years left in this century to make our decision about atomic warfare, a type of war that will make all former struggles seem harmless. Let us choose wisely.

Q. *Who was it that said, "The first brigade mobilized for any war is the Liars' Brigade"?*

A. Mark Twain (Samuel Clemens) gave us that gem of truth.

Q. *Where is the battle site of Val Verde, where Sibley's Confederates met and were defeated by Union forces in the Civil War?*

A. It is ten miles north, up the Rio Grande in New Mexico, from old Fort Craig, north of the *Mesa de la Contedena* (as shown on old maps), and near the present village of Valverde. This is about nineteen miles south of present San Antonio, New Mexico, but on the east side of the river. (The old fort was on the west side.) Many tourists today view the "battlefield" marker west of the river. However, since only a primitive road from San Pedro leads down to the actual battlefield site, few pass that way. The battle was fought in 1862. The Confederate failure to capture Fort Craig made it a danger point in their rear. When they were forced to retreat from the state, the presence of the fort compelled them to jettison most of their cannon and equipage and retreat down a corridor west of the Magdalena Mountains. The ragged and hungry remnants of Sibley's force eventually reached El Paso, the New Mexico campaign a failure.

Q. *I have heard that many Southerners fled to Mexico to avoid the Civil War. Is this true?*

A. Yes, particularly Texas men who were pro-union. Also many German immigrants who hated slavery and militarism fled Texas then.

Q. *Can you give me the casualties suffered by the 2nd Texas Infantry before and at Vicksburg, where they were compelled to surrender?*

A. Under command of Col. John C. Moore, the 2nd Texas arrived in Mississippi with 1,300 men. Casualties at Shiloh were 433 men. At Corinth, they lost another 430 men. The brigade numbered about 250 to 300 men when they retired toward Ripley, Tennessee. In March, 1863, 150 Texas recruits joined them. Their strength was about 450 men when they arrived at Vicksburg, where they lost 38 dead, 73 wounded, and 15 missing, a total of another 126 men. From these figures it will be seen that the Confederate losses totaled almost two-thirds of the total men engaged, or 989 dead, wounded, or missing. The 2nd Texas Infantry inflicted casualties upon Union forces of perhaps twice their own total, it being reported that in one day, May 22, 1862, the 2nd Texas Infantry lunette— east of Vicksburg on the Baldwin Ferry Road, where Grant's attack came heaviest—covered the field with more than 2,000 dead and wounded Union soldiers.

Q. *What happened to the railroad engine stolen by the Yankee soldiers in Georgia and used to burn bridges behind the enemy lines as they headed north with it?*

A. The engine was on display at Chattanooga for many years. A few years ago the Supreme Court ruled the engine was originally the property of the Georgia State Railroad and ordered it be returned to the private company now owning that railroad.

Q. *Was there great crime among the Negroes on the plantations of the South when their masters were away at war with the Confederacy?*

A. There were undoubtedly some incidents of violence, as would be natural in such a climate as existed there during the rebellion. Yet *Rose's History* praises the Negroes of Texas and declares: "What a volume is contained in the announcement that not a single outrage was attributed to the plantation Negroes during the entire course of the war...." It is doubtful if the white people could match that record made by the Texas blacks.

Q. *Where may I obtain records of my grandfather's service in the Civil War? He was a Southerner with the Confederate Army.*

A. For *both* Confederate and Union records, you may write to the General Services Administration, Washington, D.C., and ask for the blank forms to fill out to obtain these records. They will provide the forms, then you will know exactly where to send them. There is a nominal fee for copying the records, which you will be asked to pay. You will need to supply complete information as to when, and with what unit he served, and in which army. Since photography was in its infancy then, it is doubtful if you will be able to find photographs of your ancestors in uniform, unless they were high-ranking officers.

Q. *How many Negro troops served in the Union Army? Were any killed in battle?*

A. About 180,000 served, and more than 33,000 were killed in action or died in the service. After the war four infantry regiments and two cavalry units of Negro troops were organized. Of these the 9th and 10th Cavalries served on the Western frontier, and many died in the Indian Wars. They were called "Buffalo Soldiers" by the Indians.

Q. *In Civil War histories we often read of "lunettes." What were they?*

A. The lunette was a projecting protection of defensive lines and forts consisting of two faces and two flanks. For example, the 2nd Texas Infantry occupied the lunette east of Vicksburg, Mississippi, successfully defending it for forty days against massive attacks by tens of thousands of Grant's troops. This lunette extended eastward from the regular defense line, with rifle pits extending north and south from it. The lunette was constructed of high earthworks and heavy timbers, rock, and other materials. Cannon were mounted atop it. This lunette curtained the railroad that ran eastward to Jackson, the main supply route.

Q. *I have read that Quantrill's raid on Lawrence, Kansas, was both right and wrong, depending on who was writing it. What is the historian's view of this attack on a village, August 21, 1863?*

A. Most objective historians view the raid as "ruthlessly bloody, unprovoked and thoroughly devastating."

Q. *What was the actual human and monetary loss resulting from Quantrill's raid on Lawrence?*

A. Old Kansas histories estimate 150 dead; money loss and damage $1.5 million—a considerable sum in 1863.

Q. *Was there ever a firsthand account of the U.S. Army's camel corps and its trek from Camp Verde, Texas, to Arizona?*

A. Yes, Harvard University Press in 1929 published the diary of May H. Stacy, an officer in the Union Army, but commissioned by the U.S. Navy. He was nineteen when he made the trip with Leonard F. Beale's command. His writings were titled *The Journal of May Humphreys Stacy, Supplemented by the Report of Edward Fitsgerald Beale (1857-1858).*

Q. *How did the Negro soldiers fare in court-martial proceedings in frontier days?*

A. William H. Leckie, in *The Buffalo Soldiers*, stated that the Negro soldier could expect little mercy when he came up against the white officers who staffed the courts-martial boards. A dishonorable discharge and a year at hard labor was "virtually automatic for drunkenness while on duty," Lecke wrote. This sentence was given to two black privates who were caught in petty theft. It must be remembered, however, that hard sentences were almost the order of the day, for white men received them as well as blacks when charged with the same offenses. The old Army was rough on recalcitrants and order-breakers in the Indian war days.

Q. *What was the real cause for Pancho Villa to raid Columbus, New Mexico, and burn the town? What could he gain from it?*

A. When President Woodrow Wilson recognized Carranza's government in 1915, he also placed a strict embargo on arms and supplies crossing into Mexico. This hurt Villa, who was then planning an attack upon Gen. Plutarco Elias Callas, a Carranzista backer, who was then at Agua Preita, in northern Chihuahua. Worse yet, when Villa did meet Callas, his men were mowed down with machine guns. It seems that Wilson had permitted Callas to transport new troops over American soil on trains to beef up the forces, while Villa had fought his way to the battle site over rugged, snow-covered mountains. Villa is reported to have lost 2,000 men in that battle, the Callas forces being significantly aided by the Americans.

On March 9, 1916, Villistas raided Columbus, New Mexico. It has been said by old Villistas that this raid was revenge upon the Yankee president whom they felt had done them in.

Q. *What cavalry units composed of Negroes served on the frontier?*

A. The 9th Cavalry, organized July 29, 1866, at New Orleans, and the 10th Cavalry, organized under the same authorization at Fort Leavenworth, Kansas, and commanded by Col. Ben Grierson.

Q. *When were the slaves in Texas officially freed?*

A. On June 19, 1865. The date afterward became called "June Teenth" by most of the freed slaves and many of the Texas citizens.

Q. *Did frontier wars against Indians have any influence upon tactics adopted by the U.S. military?*

A. Definitely. The flag signal system originated after A.J. Myer, later chief signal officer, had it suggested to him by Comanche lance signals which he had observed on the Plains.

Q. *What is the story of the great massacre of the Cypress Hills?*

A. A band of American and Canadian wolf hunters had their horses stolen while on the Teton River, in Montana. Their search took them to Farewell's Post. There, after drinking a lot, another of their mounts was stolen and when Hammond, its owner, and a man named John Evans, the leader of the party, went to a nearby Assiniboine camp to recover the horse, the massacre began. The wolfers, hearing gunfire, hurried to back up their friends and, from a coulee, turned their Henry repeating rifles into the Indian camp, indiscriminately killing men, women, and children. Between eighty and two hundred (sources differ on the count) Indians of all ages were slain. One wolfer, Ed Grace, an American, was killed; he was buried under the floor of Solomon's Fort. The wolfers then burned the entire settlement and continued on to Fort Whoop-Up to see if it had been Blood

Indians who had taken their horses. This disgraceful massacre on the part of the wolfers helped bring about the Canadian legislation to established mounted police in that area.

Q. *What brought on the Texas war for independence from Mexico?*

A. The cultural differences between the two peoples (Mexicanos and Anglos) was the primary reason, of course. Second, the swelling tide of immigration into Texas alarmed the Mexican officials, for they viewed it for what it actually was, the imperialist expansion of the burgeoning United States of America, pressing westward and southwest. The sharp restrictions and regulations then imposed by the Mexican government angered all the new immigrants and the colonists who were already settled there, and they moved for independence from Mexico and for a Republic of Texas.

Q. *How many men actually defended the Alamo at San Antonio, Texas, when it was attacked by the Mexican army under Gen. Santa Anna?*

A. About 180 men.

Q. *I have read that the Mexican Army which attacked the Alamo had only eight or ten cannon. Could this be true?*

A. This is doubtful, for several Mexican cannon were resurrected in 1935 when the foundation of the San Antonio Post Office was excavated. Those cannon were placed on the walls of the Alamo at that time. The cannon were undoubtedly damaged or burned out, for no general, at least one short of cannon, would bury undamaged cannon with the remains of the dead. And many skeletons were unearthed with the cannons at the time.

Q. *How many forts or trading posts for defense against Indians have been officially recorded in old Washington Territory?*

A. Seventy-two old forts are indicated in one recently prepared map. There were perhaps others that were not entered in the records. The various forts appear to have encompassed every section of the territory. They dated from the 1700s to 1900.

Q. *Is there anything remaining of Old Fort Mitchell on the Oregon Trail?*

A. No. A modern highway cuts through the old location, and only a concrete memorial marker attests to its former being. The site is two miles directly west of Scottsbluff, Nebraska, at the west end of the old Mitchell Bridge (West Twentieth Street).

Q. *Where was the original Bent's Fort?*

A. The Bents, it appears, built several stockades at various points along the Arkansas River where they traded with Indians. One of the earliest, discussed by the late C.W. Hurd in his pamphlet, *Bent's Stockade, Hidden in the Hills,* was located at the head of Turkey Creek, on a mesa near Penrose, Colorado, halfway between Pueblo Creek and Canyon City. Another stockade was erected near present Pueblo, Colorado. Still another near present Fort Lyons. Perhaps the most famous and celebrated of all has been the one totally reconstructed near La Junta. Known as Bent's Old Fort, it is a national historical site. Parkman, in his *The California and Oregon Trail,* mentions visiting this old fort in August, 1846. Nothing remains of these old, original forts and stockades.

Q. *What was the reason for the reconstruction of old Fort St. Vrain?*

A. The original fort was constructed by Ceran St. Vrain, a French trader and trapper. The location is northwest of Platteville, Colorado. With collapse of the fur trade by 1844, the fort was abandoned, but reopened as a general store in 1846. The buildings served as the Weld County seat when Colorado Territory was formed. Today, Public Service Company of Colorado operates the 330,000-kilowatt nuclear generating station at this location. An information center is maintained there for the general public, and visitors are welcomed.

Q. *What was "Camp Fletcher," in Kansas, in early days?*

A. It was established near present Fort Hayes, and later the name was changed to Fort Hayes. The fort was built to guard the railroads going west, as well as to protect the pioneer trails. Fort Hayes was a well-known Plains installation, and many famous Army officers were stationed there at various times. Wild Bill Hickok was a scout there at one time.

Q. *Where was Fort Maginnis? When established?*

A. It was built and activated in 1880, northeast of present Lewistown, Montana, at the head of Boxelder Creek. It was active for ten years, until 1890.

Q. *Were there two Fort Mohaves in Arizona? What areas?*

A. *The Army Register* for 1883 lists only one, and as follows: "Fort Mohave, Ariz (Dept. Ariz), Post Office Mohave City, Ariz: Railroad and Telegraph Station, William's Station on A and P. R.R., distance 100 miles; steamer monthly from Yuma on Colorado River."

Q. *Was there ever a Fort Ellis in the old days in Kansas?*

A. Yes, it stood on the left bank of the Smoky Hill River in what is today Ellsworth County. The name of the fort was changed to Fort Harker, and under this name the fort became famous as a buttress against Indian attacks on settlers.

Q. *Was there ever a fort named "Jasper House" in the Northwest?*

A. Yes, it was an important trade outpost for Hudson's Bay Company on the east side of the Rocky Mountains between the eastern ends of the Athabasca and Yellow Head passes, at the outlet of Lake Jasper. It was named after Jasper Hawes, a clerk of the company. It was built in 1800 and for fifty years was a key to defense of the Hudson's Bay Company.

Q. *What was the purpose of Fort Steele, on the U.P. Railroad near Rawlins, Wyoming? When was it built?*

A. This old fort, now gone, was built in 1868 and named after Gen Frederick Steele, a West Point graduate, who had served in the Mexican and Civil wars. Its primary purpose was to protect the railroad, particularly the bridge over the North Platte River, as well as to guard the work crews along the line.

Q. *Where was Fort Cottonwood at the time of the Civil War?*

A. Fort Cottonwood (later Fort McPherson) was located at the site of the McDonald Ranch, at Cottonwood Springs, Nebraska Territory. The site is a few miles south and east of present North Platte, Nebraska, and now embraces a national cemetery.

Q. *Was there a Fort John in the Old West? Where was it?*

A. This was one of the several names for Fort Laramie in the earliest days. The fort started as a trading post, built by William Sublette and Robert Campbell and named Fort William in 1834. When the Sublettes sold the post to P. Fontenelle, the name was changed to

Fort John, in honor of John B. Sarpy. It remained Fort John until the American Fur Company moved the fort a few hundred yards up the Laramie River. Then it became Fort Laramie, after Jacques La Ramee, a French trapper who was killed about 1822 on the river that bears his name (Laramie).

Q. *Where was Fort Churchill located? Was it named after ancestors of Winston Churchill?*

A. It was located in Lyon County, Nevada, on the north bank of the Carson River, a mile west of Buckland's Bridge, opposite Samuel S. Buckland's trading post. This was on the old Overland Stage Road, running into Virginia City, twenty-five miles to the east. The fort was named after Gen. Sylvester Churchill, a Vermont native who had entered the army as a first lieutenant, March 12, 1812. He served in the Mexican War, died at Washington, D.C., 1862. He was not related to the family of Winston Churchill.

Q. *Are the present walls and buildings of Sutter's Fort at Sacramento, California, the original buildings?*

A. Only the central building is the original. Sutter left there shortly after the gold discovery. The property was subdivided and by the 1880s only the central building remained. Reconstruction was started in 1891. Eventually the area became a state historical monument. The walls, blockhouses, and other buildings have been reconstructed to match the old fort as it appears in woodcuts and drawings of the late 1840s and 1850s.

Q. *Where was Fort Totten located?*

A. Between the towns of present New Rockford and Devils Lake, North Dakota.

Q. *Who located Fort Concho, near present San Angelo, Texas?*

A. Capt. Edward J. Strang was assigned the task and was guided throughout that area by Capt. George Gibson Huntt, H Company, 4th U.S. Cavalry. The new fort was to replace Camp Chadbourne to the north. Fort Concho was named for the many concha shells found in the nearby river.

Q. *Where was Fort Rice?*

A. Fort Rice was established on the west bank of the Missouri River, now North Dakota, in 1864. The location is about halfway between Fort Yates and Fort A. Lincoln. It was abandoned in 1878.

Q. *After whom was Fort Robinson, in the Nebraska Panhandle, named?*

A. The fort was named in honor of First Lt. Levi H. Robinson, 14th U.S. Infantry, killed by Indians February 9, 1874, on Cottonwood Creek, about thirty miles from Fort Laramie, Wyoming. It is reported that Robinson never served in the vicinity of the fort named after him. He was from Vermont, commissioned August 11, 1865.

Q. *What, briefly, was the background history of old Fort Lyon, Colorado? Isn't it a hospital today?*

A. Yes, it is a neuropsychiatric institution today, and more than 12,000 patients have been treated there. It is beautifully located in a peaceful rural atmosphere on the Arkansas River. Originally, in 1860, the place was named Fort Wise when Maj. John Sedgwick was ordered to build a fort near Bent's Store, nineteen miles east of the present hospital complex. After the Civil War started, it became Fort Lyon, after Nathaniel Lyon, the first Union general killed in action. In 1876, floods washed away some of the buildings, and the decision was made to move the fort to the present hospital location. The army remained at the fort until 1888. In 1907, the navy used the post as a tubercular sanitarium, and in 1922 it was turned over to the Public Health Service.

Q. *Will you tell briefly of the Grattan Massacre?*

A. It's a sad tale. A Mormon's cow, lagging behind the wagons, was abandoned near the villages of Brule, Wazzazi, and Oglala bands of Sioux Indians, not far from Old Fort Bernard, on the North Platte River, east of Fort Laramie. A wandering Indian caught the cow and butchered her. At Fort Laramie, the Mormon filed a notice of theft of the cow, hoping the government would make restitution for her. Lieutenant Grattan, with twenty-nine men and an interpreter, was sent to the Indian village to get the cow back. Learning she had been butchered, the lieutenant, unaccustomed to Indian ways, threw his weight around and started firing his cannon into the tent where the Indian was living. In the foolish rifle and cannon fire that followed, Bear That Scatters, a chief of the Wazzazi, was wounded. At this, the Indians rushed the soldiers and killed all within a mile of the cannon. The Wazzizis then rushed Bordeaux's home, but the trader apparently talked them out of any mischief they might do to him. The chief, Bear That Scatters, died soon afterward, and the lieutenant's rash action set off a chain of events that eventually culminated in the Indian uprisings of 1864.

Q. *Why were Mexicans labeled as cowardly by many writers of Western military fiction?*

A. There is some evidence that the city-bred *caballeros* and some members of the wealthy families of northern Mexico were peace oriented and less inclined to belligerency. However, competent authorities of the old days state that the *rancheros* and their *vaqueros*, as well as the yeomanry (peons) of the country, as inured to hardships, fatigue, and danger as they were, possessed a high caliber of physical courage.

Q. *What did the Indians call Col. George A. Custer?*

A. One of the Sioux terms was "Yellow Hair," which Custer preferred to "Squaw Killer," which the Cheyennes named him, after the attack on the villages at Washita, in the winter of 1868.

Q. *Was Custer as careless and thoughtless of his men's lives as some charge?*

A. Custer's actual military record does support such a charge. In addition to the charge of abandonment of Major Elliott's small force at the Washita, in 1868, it was pointed out at Custer's court martial (earlier in his career) that he did knowingly leave two of his troopers to their fate after an Indian skirmish at the time of his controversial march from Fort Wallace to Fort Harker (Hayes), in 1867. Custer glossed over this matter (*Court-martial*, pp. 176-77). But Capt. A.B. Carpenter, 37th U.S. Infantry, reported: "As General Custer moved on without giving any directions concerning the bodies [*sic*] of these [wounded] men, I sent out a detail to find them. They found one man killed and one wounded. I had the body buried and the wounded man is at this Post under treatment." The wounded man, who had been shot in the leg, told Carpenter he would not have lived had not the captain rescued him. Custer was new in the West at this time. He had much to learn. But it *is* surprising that a West Point man, one who had been breveted a major general in the great Civil War, would be so insensitive to military customs—if not to common human decency and sympathy for the suffering. For no noncom or officer would abandon their wounded in the field.

Q. *Who first advanced the theory that Col. George A. Custer was contemplating the presidential nomination on the Democratic ticket when he left for the Little Bighorn fight? I read about it in a book by Mari Sandoz.*

A. The first time this writer saw it in print was in an article by Bill Judge, Casper, Wyoming, author and historian. There may have been other accounts before this one, I do not know. However, when Sandoz picked up the idea, it created a bit of a flurry among some historians.

Q. *Was Custer's defeat at the Little Bighorn the worst ever suffered by U.S. troops at the hands of American Indians?*

A. Many believe it to be, but on November 4, 1791, General St. Clair lost more than 600 men (three times Custer's loss) in a battle with Little Turtle's Miami Indians. At Fort Recovery, Ohio, stands a monument marking this battle site. St. Clair beat a hasty retreat with the remnants of his force to Fort Jefferson. This is the worst defeat that I have read of at the hands of Indians.

Q. *Why didn't the Indians scalp Custer after the Battle of the Little Bighorn? Had he committed suicide as some have written?*

A. One version has it that the Indians believed that if you scalped a great man, a hero, you lost his services as your valet and gun-bearer when you passed on to the Happy Hunting Ground. Another version has it that Indians didn't scalp great warriors whom they admired. (This latter seems incredible when so many Indians despised Custer for his attack on Washita.) Two Sioux Indians who survived the battle once told Capt. James H. Cook that a Sioux squaw killed Custer (finished him off, that is) with a skinning knife, and forgot to take his scalp lock. Whatever the reason, he wasn't scalped. There is no evidence whatever that he committed suicide.

Q. *Was Custer a crack shot, and what kind of guns did he carry and use?*

A. Custer carried a Remington sporting rifle with a rolling block, refusing the regulation Army Springfield. His revolvers were English, double-action with white grips. It has been said that he was a crack shot, yet old-timers who hunted with him laughed at this. He was no doubt as good with his guns as most regular army officers who had received West Point training. Yet he appeared to have little faith in the arms the service required his soldiers to carry.

Q. *Why was Custer court-martialed?*

A. He was court-martialed and "set down" in 1867 for leaving his command in the field while at Fort Wallace, Kansas, without orders. Many claimed his fast trip back to Fort Harker was to visit his wife. He was reinstated in September 1868 through the efforts of Gen. Phil Sheridan with whom he had been a favorite since Civil War days.

Q. *What was the secret of Maj. George A. Forsythe's successful defense at Beecher's Island, when attacked by Indians, Sept. 16, 1868?*

A. Weaponry, terrain, lack of complete surprise and experienced Indian fighters among his forces help account for Forsythe's splendid defense of a sandspit in the Arikaree fork, against what would seem was overwhelming Indian power, an estimated 750 Cheyennes and Sioux. Forsythe's fifty-two scouts, armed with Spencer repeating rifles and six-shot revolvers, were aided by a warning of trouble when a few Indians rode through their earlier camp, trying to stampede the horse herd. Forsythe's quick judgment that the sandbar offered the best hope of defense (as well as drinking water, if besieged) showed his skill at command. From then on it was raw courage until couriers, sent by him, brought help on the ninth day.

Q. *What were the greatest stands made by pioneer army men, or scouts, against fearful odds in Indian battles?*

A. One could add to the above defense of Beecher's Island, the Wagon Box Fight, the Buffalo Wallow Fight, the Battle at Adobe Walls, plus many others. There may also be some unrecorded battle in which white men and women defended their homes or camps against insurmountable odds which eventually brought them to defeat and death, leaving no one to relate their story. And it must be recounted that there were fights where the American Indians in a small band fought to the death when attacked by scouts and troopers in great numbers. Brave men were not the property of any one race.

Q. *What happened to Col. Charles Harrison, Confederate States of America (C.S.A.), who started for Colorado in 1863 to commandeer troops for the Confederate cause and to take over the gold supplies in that region?*

A. Harrison and all of his party, with the exception of two men, were killed by Osage Indians. Only Col. Warner Lewis survived the war; John Rafferty, the other man to escape, was killed shortly afterward.

Q. *Was Lt. Henry O. Flipper, the first Negro graduate of West Point, in the Indian Wars?*

A. Yes, Flipper spent five years on the frontier. He was with the 10th U.S. Cavalry and fought one engagement against the Apache. See *Negro Frontiersman*, by T.D. Harris, for his story.

Q. *What is the correct spelling of Bvt. Maj. Gen. Ronald (or is it Ranald) S. Mackenzie, the officer who distinguished himself in the Southwestern Indian wars in the 1870s?*

A. *The Official Army Register* for January 1883 gives the spelling as Ranald, with two *a*'s.

Q. *How did Capt. Samuel H. Walker meet his death. Was he shot or stabbed?*

A. He fell at Huamantla, Mexico, "pierced by two escopette balls," according to a contemporary soldier. Some old drawings show him being shot from a balcony, and also being stabbed with the lance of a Mexican soldier. The Walker Colt revolver bears his name.

Q. *Where was Quantrill killed? Who killed him? Where is he buried?*

A. Cornered by federal troops near what is today the town of Taylorsville, Kentucky, Quantrill was shot while making a dash for his horse from the barn in which he and friends had been sleeping. Captain Terril, in charge of the troops, had the body carried into the farmhouse, and a Dr. McClusky gave first aid. Quantrill was taken to the military hospital at Louisville, where he died of his wounds. He was buried in St. John's Cemetery, now called St. Cecelia's. The body was later exhumed and removed to Dover, Ohio.

Q. *I have read where Quantrill was called a "military genius." Is this factual, or nonsense?*

A. Neither. Quantrill did use exceptional skill in maneuvering with his guerrilla bands; however, he was aided by some of the best men in the business, namely "Bloody Bill" Anderson, George Todd, and Cole Younger. How he would have performed as a leader of a large military force is a question mark. He was a merciless killer and pillager, but he lived in an extremely rough period of American history and was opposed by men as ruthless as himself.

Q. *What fate did "Bloody Bill" Anderson meet?*

A. He was killed by Union soldiers in October 1864, near Orick, Missouri. One writer says Anderson's body was taken by wagon to Richmond, Missouri, where the head was severed from it and placed on a tall pole as a warning to the townsfolk to stop harboring guerrillas.

Q. *Who was Gen. Ulysses S. Grant's chief of staff after the Civil War was over?*

A. Bvt. Maj. Gen. John A. Rawlins, from Illinois, who had entered the service March 3, 1865. Rawlins was breveted a major general April 9, 1865, probably the fastest rank ever made by anyone in the army! He was not a West Point man, but was appointed from Illinois.

Q. *Can you give me a few facts about the life of Claris Talbot, a former sheriff of Custer County, Nebraska?*

A. Talbot was born in Sylvania, Indiana, November 13, 1869. He came with his family to Nebraska in 1878. He joined a volunteer group, Company M, National Guard (Holcomb Guards) for service in the Spanish-American War. He also served in the Philippines. Later he went into the cattle business with his father in Nebraska, marrying Eva Jewett in 1899. His children were John, Oren, Charlie, and Roberta. He was sheriff of Custer County, Nebraska, from 1918–30. Talbot lived to age ninety-seven, and is buried at Broken Bow, Nebraska.

Q. *Who was the ranking officer in the Lewis and Clark Expedition?*

A. President Jefferson intended that Lewis, who was an Army captain, be in charge. However, Lewis told Clark, who was a lieutenant: "Your situation will in all respects be precisely such as my own." The two did share in policymaking; however, military custom did prevail. Clark, eminently qualified for leadership, was four years Lewis's senior.

Q. *Was the Lewis and Clark Expedition an "army" expedition? What happened to Sacajawea's (the Bird Woman) baby whom she carried along on this long trek?*

A. Though not strictly an army expedition, many of the men on it were carried on army payrolls and no doubt they did draw supplies and some of their equipage from the army sources.

The baby son of Toussaint Charbonneau and Sacajawea, born February 11, 1805, somewhere in present day Montana while his parents were accompanying the expedition, was named Jean Baptiste Charbonneau. On the return trip, the baby and his parents dropped off at the native village where they lived, and the expedition returned to St. Louis. Upon his return, Capt. William Clark, who had formed a strong attachment to the baby, sent word back up the Missouri River to the baby's parents, asking if he might have the baby boy, Jean Baptiste, to rear as his own son. The parents agreed, it is said, though in my mind there lies great doubt whether Sacajawea approved such a transfer of her infant son. Anyway, the boy was sent to St. Louis, and his education began. When the lad was sixteen, and at a frontier village at the mouth of the Kansas River, he met a traveling German prince, Paul of Wurttemberg. Paul was impressed by this eighteen-year-old French-Indian who spoke French, English, and several of the Indian dialects. Paul took Jean Baptiste to Europe with him and the two hunted and visited all over the continent. In 1829, young Charbonneau returned to become a trapper and guide for John Jacob Astor's fur men, starting on a fifteen-year career that was to center mostly in the Rockies in Colorado. He met and was friends with most of the great mountain men of that era, including Bridger, Vasquez, and Sublette. He died in Montana in 1866.

Q. *How large a force did Gen. H.H. Sibley, C.S.A., take into New Mexico to attempt to conquer the region?*

A. In *Texas and the Confederacy*, author Col. H.M. Henderson gives the figure 3,500 as total strength.

Q. *Was there a captain or colonel S. Clayton, a former Confederate, with the Indians at Custer's last fight, who escaped from the Indians to warn Custer and who later joined up with Reno's command?*

A. There is no such man shown in the records of the Custer command, nor does Maj. Marcus A. Reno mention such a person in either his report from his camp on the Yellowstone, July 5, 1876, after the fight, or in his testimony at the Reno Court of Inquiry, January 13, 1979. It is most doubtful such a person existed.

Q. *What was Gen. George Crook's personal opinion about the Apache Indians?*

A. Strangely enough, Crook did not appear to hate the Apaches. Like most good soldiers, he regarded them as "enemy," and admired their fighting spirit. In 1884, in an address to cadets, he stated that though they had been taught "elements of war," he urged them to not forget "that your constant thought must be the preservation of peace." Said Crook: "Let the Indian see that you administer One Law for both the white-skinned and the red-skinned...."

Q. *Was Lt. Caspar Collins noted for anything other than having a town named after him—Casper, Wyoming?*

A. Yes, Collins gave his life to save one of his supply trains. This act was enough to honor his name. But he was something of a cartographer, we learn, and together with his father, Col. William O. Collins, responsible for some of the early maps made of eastern Wyoming and northern Colorado. One sketch of Fort Laramie made by the younger Collins in 1863 and sent to his mother at her Ohio home for preservation is a remarkably fine drawing, portraying the old fort in its latter years. The discrepancy in the spelling of the town's name and the man's name is said to have resulted from a clerical error in the post office department. The intent was to honor the young man's name in the naming of Caspar, Wyoming, but it turned out to be Casper, Wyoming.

Q. *Was the person who killed Capt. Emmet Crawford an Indian or a Mexican?*

A. Harry E. Chatfield, president of the Amerindian & Western Historical Research Association, Denver, calls this "a

complicated question deserving of an equally complicated answer." However, he simplifies the matter by
stating that Crawford was killed by "*Mexican* irregular
troops, who were Tarahumari *Indians*." The official records, he says, do not reveal any one person responsible
for Crawford's death.

Q. *What did the Pawnee Scouts under Maj. Frank North
call him? Why were they so fortunate in Indian battles
against the Cheyenne?*

A. Major North understood Indian fighting tactics. He
trained his scouts to never doubt his commands, to go
where he pointed, and to act fast in a charge. They called
him "White Chief" and felt they led a charmed life so
long as he was with them.

Q. *I read a criticism of William F. Cody, by George Bird
Grinnell, stating that Cody "was scarcely to be called
a scout" and stating that Cody "used his former position
at Ft. McPherson, his admirable physique, and the advertising given him by E.C. Judson, to announce himself as
scout and Indian fighter, but this was merely to promote
show business." What do you think of such low-grading
of Buffalo Bill Cody?*

A. You are using the word, "low-grading" in the right sense.
No one who knows the faintest thing about Cody's work
while with General Carr in the campaign of 1868—and
how he saved the command from starvation in No Man's
Land by his prowess at buffalo hunting and by knowing
how to live on the Great Plains in winter weather—can
"low-grade" the great scout and showman. Cody was
chief scout for General Carr, and that speaks for itself.
There was a tendency among writers to "low-grade" one
man, hoping to build up another. Grinnell's comments,
which appeared in *Man of the Plains: the Recollections of
Luther North*, no doubt were written to build up the
Norths. Certainly, with such a grand record as Maj. Frank
North and his Pawnee Scouts left behind, no latter-day
writers need to embellish it by devaluing the achievements of others.

Q. *I read a story, that was originally published in* McClure's,
*June 1889, titled "Midnight Call to Arms." It was so
agonizing, I wonder if it was true?*

A. I saw it in *The West*, Oct. 1971 issue. Checking out the

*Army Register*s for the period mentioned, no officers mentioned in the tale are shown, i.e., Captain Fox and Lieutenant Keene. And the only Colonel Kellogg shown was with the 1st Cavalry, not the 2nd, and he had *retired* February 6, 1865, before that alleged winter march took place. Many "windies" appeared in those old magazines, and some editors, it seems, never attempted to check out any story for facts back then.

Q. *Was Col. John M. Chivington, victor over the Cheyennes and Arapahoes at the Battle of Sand Creek, Colorado, actually a minister, as described in so many articles and books?*

A. Yes, he joined the Methodist Church, moved west from Ohio about 1850, and then entered the Ministry. He was transferred to the Missouri Conference. He was Presiding Elder near the beginning of the Civil War, in western Kansas and Colorado. He rejected a chaplaincy, and was commissioned a major by Governor Gilpin, because he wanted to fight in the war, instead of preach.

Q. *Is the site of the Sand Creek Battle (or massacre), in which Chivington played a major role, accessible to tourists today?*

A. Yes. The location is eight miles north and a mile east of Chivington, Colorado. Between Eads and Turner is a marker where you turn north from Highway 96, and drive up Big Sandy Creek. A second battleground marker is atop a sand hill, and below (north) is the creek and the site of the massacre. At that location on November 29-30, 1864, the command under Col. J.M. Chivington practically exterminated a peaceful village of Cheyenne and Arapahoe Indians, murdering anyone before them and taking no prisoners, scalping the dead and acting like a bunch of savages themselves, not soldiers. Ten soldiers were killed and thirty-eight wounded. This massacre of the innocent set the stage for the following Indian wars of the late 1860s, in which no quarter was given or taken by either side.

Q. *Was Chivington entirely responsible for the massacre at Sand Creek?*

A. No, add to the list of names for this disgraceful act those of Maj. Scott Anthony, commander at Fort Lyon; Governor John Evans of Colorado, who refused the Indians' peaceful entreaties prior to the massacre, and assorted others who wanted war more than peace.

Q. *Can you name a few of the great army scouts of the West?*

A. Almost any list will leave out many top scouts, but a few well-known ones were: Al Sieber, Kit Carson, William F. Cody, Wild Bill Hickok, Frank North, Jack Stillwell, Ben Clark, Billy Dixon, Mose Waters, George Oaks, Tom Donnell, Baptiste (Little Bat) Garnier, Baptiste (Big Bat) Pourier, James H. Cook, Luther North, and Theodore Baughman. There were, as well, many *Indians* who faithfully served in the army as scouts and whose names and deeds of valor are shown in the old records. Maj. Frank North lists seventy-seven Pawnee Scouts who served with him in 1864.

Q. *What is known of "Spotted Jack," one-time scout and guide for General Mackenzie in the Indian Wars?*

A. He was a tall, dark-skinned, black-eyed man of Indian-Negro-Caucasian parentage who had lived with the Comanches as a boy. He was rated a top scout and an excellent rifle marksman. He was killed while leading the Battle at Yellow House Draw, in the Texas Panhandle, when a group of drunken buffalo hunters attempted to raid an Indian camp there in March 1877. His body was hauled back and buried in the Lee & Reynolds and Charles Rath Trading Post near Fort Griffin (Old Mobeetie), Texas. One old frontiersman said that Spotted Jack received his name because of smallpox scars on his face and body.

Q. *Who was Micky Free?*

A. He was a white boy captured by Pinal Apaches when very young. He grew up with them and became one of the famous scouts for the army. His left eye had been gouged out in a hunting accident by a deer, but even with one eye he was a good marksman and one of the finest trailers among the scouts. Army scout Al Sieber described him as "half-Irish, half-Mexican and all son-of-a-bitch."

Q. *Why did Maj. William R. Price, late at the scene of the Buffalo Wallow Fight, fail to aid the scouts and soldiers who had fought there?*

A. Billy Dixon, Amos Chapman, sergeants Woodhall, Rath, and Harrington had been surrounded by Indians. They took refuge in a buffalo wallow and survived (Smith, a soldier with them, was killed) after a long, hard fight. The fight took place while the group of soldiers and scouts were, under Gen. Nelson A. Miles's orders, carrying dispatches to camp supply. When Major Price and his command came upon them, after the fight, his surgeon examined their wounds, the soldiers under Price gave them some of their water and hard tack, and then Price's command moved on. Price did send a courier to notify General Miles of the men's predicament. It must be assumed that Price considered what he did to be all that needed to be done for soldiers and scouts of some other command. Certainly, he prejudiced their position and endangered their lives by leaving the wounded men there. There seems to be no accounting for the actions of some army officers in times of danger. And not all serve their men well.

Q. *Was Kit Carson killed by Indians? Where and how?*

A. Kit died of what his doctor, Asst. U.S. Surgeon H.R. Tilden, described as an "aneurism of the aorta, a tumor pressing on the pneumo-gastric nerve and trachea, causing frequent spasms of the bronchial tubes." Carson's death came May 23, 1868, 4:25 P.M. He was in Tilden's quarters at Fort Lyon, Colorado. Carson was then fifty-nine.

Q. *Can you tell me anything about Col. Francis Deimling whose grave is on the mesa near Virginia City, Montana?*

A. Colonel Deimling commanded the 10th Missouri Volunteer Infantry in the campaigns of the West (Vicksburg, etc.) during the Civil War, under Gen. U.S. Grant. He was honorably discharged 24 August 1864, and went to Montana, settling at Virginia City, where he was the Postmaster for several years. He married Mary Lovell, and they had two sons, James Flintham and William. Deimling was from Philadelphia.

Q. *I have read that only one man in history, Ben Clarke, won the Congressional Medal of Honor twice, and also, that he was not a soldier but an Indian scout. Is this true?*

A. No, this is incorrect. Ben Clarke was a noted Indian scout, but his name does not even appear on the list of Medal of Honor winners. Actually 3,170 medals were awarded up to the time of the Vietnam War. There were five army double-medal winners; nine navy double-winners; five marines who won *both* army and navy medals. These double-winners were usually men who won, as did F.D. Baldwin, captain 19th Michigan Infantry, a medal each for Indian Wars and for the Civil War. Twelve Indian scouts won the medal during the Indian Wars in Arizona: Sergeant Co-Rux-Te-Chod-Ish, or Mad Bear; Nan-na-saddie; Nantaje; Sergeant Rowdy, and others. These scouts *did* have military status, however. Among the Clark's and Clarke's who won the medal are: Charles A.; Harrison; James G.; John W.; Wildred; William A.; Dayton P.; and Pohatan H. Clark(e).

Q. *How is it known that Jedediah Smith, guide, trapper, and explorer, was killed by Comanches?*

A. Smith's brother, Austin, who was on the same wagon train trip to Sante Fe, at the time of Smith's death, purchased Jed's rifle and pistol from Mexican (Comancheros) traders. They told Austin what the Comanches had told them about Smith's death and Austin wrote to his father: "Your son Jedediah was killed on the Semerone, the 27th of May on his way to Santa Fe, by the Comanche Indians. His party was in distress for water and he had gone in search for the above river when attacked by fifteen or twenty of them...." (When I prepared a paper on the subject of Smith's death for the *Denver Westerner 1962 Brand Book*, the thought kept repeating itself that the *Comancheros* might well have been responsible for the murder of Smith, for they had the guns. Austin had only *their word* for the fact that it had been *Indians* who slew Smith and took the guns.)

Q. *Did William F. Cody (Buffalo Bill) kill the Indian, Chief Yellow Hair (Yellow Hand) on July 17, 1876?*

A. There appear to be competent authorities on *both sides* of this argument. E.S. Sutton, historian and writer of the Nebraska State Historical Society, says that Cody told M.I. McCreight, a writer and friend, that he was not even in that fight. Luther North, brother of the famous scout and soldier, Maj. Frank North, said that Major North killed Yellow Hand. Don Russell, eminent biographer of Cody and a researcher in depth, presents almost irrefutable evidence in his *Lives and Legends of Buffalo Bill* that Cody, and no one else, shot and killed the Cheyenne Chief. Their meeting was accidental, and

Yellow Hand's death was fast and certain, the way death usually came on the Plains, without any of the dramatics usually added later to the story. Cody did not know at the moment who he had killed. Perhaps one piece of good evidence that it *was* Cody who killed Yellow Hand is the letter he wrote his wife immediately after the fight, in which he stated: "We have had a fight. I killed Yellow Hand, a Cheyenne Chief, in a single-handed fight. You will no doubt hear of it through the papers...." There were newspaper reporters on the scene. Cody thought nothing of immediately claiming the coup, and no one else claimed it at that time. So he undoubtedly shot the Indian. The young chief's father, Cut Nose, called "a leading spirit among the Cheyennes," offered Cody four mules if he would return the war bonnet and other items taken off his dead son. Cody declined to make the trade. This fight occurred in 1876 while Cody was serving as a scout under Col. Wesley Merritt, 5th U.S. Cavalry. The Regimental History of the 5th Cavalry credits Cody, "favorite scout of the regiment," with the shooting of Yellow Hand. Chris Madsen, a soldier at the scene, wrote later that it was Cody who killed the Indian.

Q. *Who was the best rifle shot of all time—Buffalo Bill, Annie Oakley, Johnny Baker, Dr. Carver, or Frank Butler?*

A. This is a good list, all "good shots," but there are others such as A.H. Bogardus and Ad Topperwein, and "Plinky" Topperwein, his wife, less known to the general public, who excelled with both revolvers and rifles. Ad Topperwein at San Antonio, Texas, December 13 to 22, 1907, fired at 72,500 two-and-one-half-inch wood blocks, tossed into the air. *He missed only nine!* He used a Winchester Model '03, .22 caliber automatic self-loading rifle for this feat, which has never been equalled. It took him ten days, 68½ hours shooting time, to complete the act. Plinky Topperwein, his wife, once acknowledged by Annie Oakley to be the greatest woman marksman of all time, fired 100 consecutive shots into a five-inch diameter spot target at 25 yards distance with a revolver. However, firing at a live, human, moving target is a different thing. Since the Topperweins were never forced to fire at human targets, or at running game, such as Cody had done all his life, I expect that Cody would be considered the best at that. But no such comparison is possible between *target marksmen* and *game hunters* or *man-killers*. Theodore Roosevelt is said to have been an excellent shot with a rifle, despite the fact he wore eyeglasses.

Q. *Following the Civil War, Amos Chapman, Indian scout, is said to have accompanied a wagon train West. Has anyone reported he was as good at guiding people West as at army scouting?*

A. Yes, he was even better than some people said of him. One lady who accompanied her husband on a wagon train across Kansas wrote about Chapman. She told of Chapman being attacked by a burly drunken man, and how Chapman was forced to "buffalo" the man; that is, strike him with his revolver barrel. The man died of the blow that night. Wagonmaster Biggers said of the event: "I am well aware of how you all feel. But Mr. Chapman did not intend to kill Smith, or he could have shot him. I hired Amos Chapman because he is one of the most able scouts on the frontier. He has a way with Indians, second only to Kit Carson." The members of the wagon train said no more about the accidental killing. Chapman was holder of the Congressional Medal of Honor.

Q. *Does the U.S. cavalry have any horses left in service?*

A. Chief, the last cavalry mount, died of old age at Fort Riley, Kansas, in 1968, where he was stabled at the Fort Riley Riding Club. Chief was then thirty-six. The news dispatch, apparently written by a cavalryman, mentioned: "Tanks are a great improvement, yes. But you can't love a tank the way you did a horse." To that, we all say, "Amen."

Q. *What was the U.S. cavalry record for high-jumping a horse?*

A. In 1912, the *Denver Republican* reported the breaking of a previous record of five-feet, one-inch with a jump of five-feet, three-inches by the mount of Lt. W.C.F. Nicholson of the 9th Cavalry, at the Denver National Western Livestock Show. Virginia Bonella, in her book manuscript titled "Hambone," tells of the army's jumping mule, Hambone, serial no. 9Y11, who put jumping horses to shame with his jumps of over six feet. Whether there is an "official" high-jump record, I do not know. But the jumps above, and the memory of Hambone's feats, indicate that horses and mules can, and probably have, cleared nearly six-feet.

Q. *Was the horse ridden by Captain Keogh the only animal that survived the Custer defeat?*

A. No, many of the cavalry's horses were captured by the Indians, during and after the battle. Capt. Myles W. Keogh's mount, Comanche, was the only survivor *on the field of battle.* The horse was badly wounded, but was recovered, its wounds treated, and he was pensioned for life by the U.S. government. Comanche was at Fort Riley, Kansas, for many years until death.

Q. *Who named the Colt revolver the "Peacemaker"?*

A. An ad writer is reported to have coined the name; where and when we have never learned.

Q. *Where are the Colt Walker revolvers owned by Capt. Samuel A. Walker?*

A. Until a few years ago, they were, and perhaps still are, in the possession of Walker family members. His were unmarked with army company initials, numerals, inspectors' initials. A captain of the Texas militia in the Mexican War, Walker suggested improvements which were incorporated into the Colt Army model of 1848. Thus the improved model bears his name, "The Colt Walker."

Q. *What other handguns besides Colts, Smith & Wesson, and Remington were popular on the frontier?*

A. Merwin Hulbert & Company (through Hopkins & Allen Mfg. Co.) made a 44-40 that enjoyed some popularity, though it lacked a proper extractor for the empty shells. Several English revolvers enjoyed popularity, both during and after the Civil War, such as the Adams and the Tranters. The L.W. Pond .44-caliber six-shooter was carried by many veterans. Sharps made a .30-caliber four-shot rimfire pepperbox. Merwin & Bray produced a single-shot, .38-caliber weapon. There were scores of gambler's specials and suicide specials, the smaller handguns carried by pimps, gamblers, and prostitutes. Winchester came along with a good revolver but never got it into large-scale production, preferring to make an arrangement with Colt to keep Colt out of the production of rifles, which Winchester felt was its own field. A few Starr revolvers found their way West after the Civil War, as did many other lesser-known brands.

Q. *I have a Winchester Model 73 with inscription: "Presented to W. Booker Kimbrough by the Citizens Committee of Denver, March, 1885." Who was this man? What is the gun's history?*

A. A search of the files of the March, 1885 *Denver Daily Times* and *Rocky Mountain News* reveals nothing on the rifle. No such name is in the *Denver City Directory* for 1885. There *was* a Citizens' Protective Organization in Denver at that time. Many questioners have had old guns, with inscriptions on them, and have asked for information on them. The best source is to photograph them and to have national gun magazines run the photos for leads.

Q. *Why was the S & W, single action .44-caliber revolver so popular in the West? How do I recognize one?*

A. The Smith & Wesson No. 3 had a simple ejector that tossed out all six shells at once after firing. It was a reliable weapon, well-constructed with an eight-inch barrel, weighed two and three-fourths pounds, and took a center-fire cartridge.

Q. *What do Westerners mean when they speak of a center-fire cinch?*

A. They're not speaking of guns, but of saddle girths. This was a cinch that fit well behind the animal's front legs, not close up on the animal's chest.

Q. *A friend has a .38-caliber Winchester rifle, Model '73. It has the initials JFK or JHK on the brass plate under the magazine. Do you know of any outlaw with such initials in the old days?*

A. Such inscriptions often represent ranch brands, as well as individual's initials. Since your address is in the Cimarron country in western Kansas, it may be that those initials represent the old ranch brand of Rowan Brothers, a 7JK connected. You may be reading the 7JK connected as a JHK. Bill Rowan was a "tough hombre," according to old-time cowhands who knew him. He was killed by a bushwhacker; Charlie, his brother, wounded. If the initials of this inscription represent the name of an outlaw, you have many to look for—Ketchums, Kellys, Kilpatricks, Kings, Kidds, and many others.

Q. *How may I recognize the early Hudson Bay and other Indian trade muskets?*

A. Look for the following manufacturer's names: P. Bond; W. Chance & Son; Henry E. Leman, Lancaster; Sargent Brothers; and J. Hollis & Son. Usually, a date will be on the weapon. These trade guns were usually .60-caliber flintlocks, later percussions. Most of them bear the figure of a serpent or a dragon on their lock plates. On some weapons the dragon figure is so stylized as to almost resemble a scroll or wavy lines. Many earlier guns manufactured in Europe prior to 1740 bear the dragon insignia, but following that period the emblem appears only on the Indian trade guns.

Q. *I have a 12-gauge, double-barrel shotgun, made by the Wilmot Company. There are no numbers or dates on it. It does have a horned animal on the stock, with red beads for eyes. About when was it made?*

A. Nathaniel N. Wilmot made guns in Boston, 1852-62. He migrated to St. Paul, Minnesota, and established a shop there from 1862 to 1867. The date depends on which period of his work the gun was made.

Q. *I have a J. Stevens A&T rifle, patent application 1874, manufactured in Chicopee Falls, Massachusetts. It is single action, lever, twenty-inch barrel, .22-caliber long rifle only. When were the last of these made. Are they valuable?*

A. They were made by the Stevens Arms & Tool Company, 1888-1904, under the early patent. Such rifles have no great value, but consult a reliable gun dealer before selling.

Q. *What is the smallest handgun you know of that actually fires?*

A. Gun dealers have from time to time shown me small guns, some specially manufactured. They get down to two inches in length (revolvers) and actually fire a small cartridge. But they are just for fun. The Smith & Wesson No. 1 is a small, seven-shot revolver that was carried in the West in the earlier days. Its manufacture began about 1858-59. The Blue Whistler, a 28-caliber revolver, five shot, is about the same size. These were the kind of little guns women might have carried in purses or been used as Hide-away weapons by gamblers and gun-fighters. Mark Twain, who owned a S & W #1 said about the little revolver: "It is a fine weapon; the only trouble is that you can't hit anything with it."

Q. *Who made the famous Henry repeating rifle?*

A. The New Haven Arms Company, from 1860-66. It was chambered for a .44-caliber bullet; weighed nine-and-one-quarter pounds, with a twenty-four inch barrel. Some had brass frames, others not.

Q. *What was the Calderwood pistol, made for the army in 1808?*

A. They were called Kentucky Pistols and were flintlocks with ten-inch barrels, made by William Calderwood on contract for the army. Only 120 of them were made. They bear the inscription, "Calderwood, Philadelphia," also "US 1808," and the letter "P" with an eagle's head. They are a valued collector's item, bringing from $500 to $1500, depending on condition—with current rates of inflation, perhaps more. Because of inflated prices, a seller of a rare handgun or rifle should consult several dealers and never sell at a price listed in an older gun catalog.

Q. *What was the Walch revolver like?*

A. Walch Fire Arms Company, in Brooklyn made it. It was an oddity among guns. Under a patent of February 1859, this ten- and twelve-shot percussion revolver was made. It had five chambered cylinders with ten and twelve percussion nipples and double hammers to fire two charges from each cylinder. Only a few were made under a U.S. government contract—the ten-shot for the army and the twelve-shot for the navy. It is a very rare gun today.

Q. *A friend claims his grandfather has a Springfield "cap and ball" rifle. Did Springfield make such a rifle?*

A. He no doubt has the old Springfield muzzle-loading rifle. This gun wasn't a success, for the ball kept sticking in the barrel. It was converted to the Springfield breech-loader .50-70 caliber. Actually, the conversion didn't improve the gun much.

Q. *I have a Flintlock pistol, about .60 caliber, with the legend "A. Waters, 1838. Millbury, Massachusetts" under the hammer. It is a bit rusty but all there and basically in fine condition, without having had any conversion work done on it. What is its present value? It has initials "MPL" in script, in a box, on the grip.*

A. You have a "collector's item" in handguns, for only about 4,000 of these were made under U.S. government contract for the army, and most of them were converted to percussion. A true flintlock, unconverted, with this marking is rare. If your piece can be cleaned—*cleaned*, NOT burned off or filed off—and given some bluing by a gun expert, you have about $500 in it. The initials on the wood grip are those of Maj. M.P. Lomax, U.S. Army inspector of ordnance.

Q. *I have a revolver with the name Joslyn on the stock, or grip. What kind is it? It is about .45 caliber.*

A. If it is a side-hammer, single-action, five-shot, solid frame .44-caliber percussion (cap and ball) type, you have an army revolver made by Joslyn Arms Company, Stoningham, Connecticut, patented by Benjamin Joslyn May 4, 1858. This gun was in use in the West, and many of them have turned up at gun shows in recent years.

Q. *What can you tell me about the Remington single-shot pistol, .50-caliber, breech-loader?*

A. I assume this piece is the navy .50 caliber with a stud trigger. The company sold 5,000 of these to the navy, but the revolver wasn't satisfactory. It was too heavy to wear with comfort, and the guardless trigger was not practical. So Remington made a second piece. This gun had a trigger guard and a seven-inch barrel with an overall length of under twelve inches. It weighed two pounds and used center fire cartridges. The second model is not rare, but the first model commands a good price if in good condition.

Q. *What can you tell me about the Moore Patent Firearms Company. Are their guns rare today?*

A. In 1862 they had shops in Brooklyn. They manufactured single-action revolvers patented by Daniel Moore. Smith & Wesson sued them for patent infringement and won. The Moore company turned to making derringers. In 1865 the company became the National Arms Company and in the 1870s was bought by the Colt Company. Some of the little derringers made by Moore are collector's items today.

Q. *Can you tell me what Bishop George Allen Beecher said of guns and the ministry?*

A. In his book *A Bishop of the Great Plains*, page 30, he related an experience in which his hunting rifle and shotgun were stolen from his buggy while he delivered a sermon in the Nebraska Panhandle country. He wrote: "I might say in passing, that to me the harmony between guns and preaching is as natural, in this particular period of my ministry, as the harmony between a game of golf and preaching is today. It means that legitimate recreation in the prosecution of any man's professional occupation is as important as a regular night's rest after a weary day of toil." It is doubtful the rabbits, the prairie chickens, and the antelope which the good bishop killed would agree with his lofty sentiments on getting rest from his "weary day of toil." But, perhaps the golf ball, had it a voice, would also protest the heavy blows it takes from the driver or midiron!

Q. *Is there any press publishing only frontier army material? Where is it located?*

A. The Old Army Press, 405 Link Lane, Fort Collins, Colorado.

Q. *Would you advise others to buy hunting weapons and other goods from today's army surplus stores?*

A. By all means. But be careful what you buy, for many such stores sell just ordinary merchandise, goods that were never made under the rigid U.S. military specifications, which is what gave them their fine quality. Any guns bought at army surplus outlets should be carefully tested and checked by an ordnance man or gunsmith.

Photo courtesy Southwest Daily Times, *Liberal, Kansas.*

Q. *Did pioneer women consider it a distasteful task to pick up the cow chips on the prairie to burn in their stoves?*

A. At first, yes. Soon, however, they accepted the task as we would getting a yule log for the fireplace at Christmas time. The lady at right is handling the chips with fingerless gloves, as you will note.

10 PIONEER LIFE

To be called a pioneer was a singular distinction. There were but two generations who settled the West that may properly wear that title: the fathers and mothers who came West and settled on the land, and their children who lived contemporaneously with them. All others are late-comers or descendants of the pioneers. Today only the pioneers' grandsons and granddaughters survive, and they wear crowns of frost in their hair. Soon they, too, will be gone. And the pioneer epic will truly be closed.

It is with this in mind that I have selected questions and answers for this section. The questions are generally concerned with the minutiae of pioneer life, for it is the small and ordinary details that are being forgotten and lost. For instance, many people can discuss Custer's defeat at the Battle of the Little Bighorn, citing casualty figures, relating the escape of Curly, the Crow Indian scout, or telling of Comanche, the horse who was the sole survivor on the battlefield when supporting forces arrived. This history still remains fresh. But how many remember the manufacturer's name on the old windmill that pumped water for the pioneer household, livestock, and garden crops, even though its creaking melody lulled the pioneer family to sleep every night? Or, today, who would know how to build a sod house? Well, read on.

Q. *Who was Ezra Meeker and for what was he best known?*
A. Meeker was an Ohio-born man who crossed the Great Plains with an ox team in 1852, to Oregon. There he prospered. In 1906, to perpetuate the memory of the pioneers who followed the Oregon Trail, Meeker set forth with another ox team and covered wagon and returned over the same route to Omaha, thence to Indianapolis and on to Washington, D.C. He was then seventy-seven years of age. Meeker's return journey via

ox team brought national attention to the Oregon Trail. Historical societies, under Meeker's encouragement, began to set up markers and monuments along the length of the trail from Independence, Missouri, to Puget Sound. Meeker's book *The Old Oregon Trail, 1852-1906* tells the story of his backward trek.

Q. *Was old John Brown of Kansas a "martyr," as some call him, or a "tyrant," as others review his life?*

A. John Brown was first of all an abolitionist, a man who utterly detested the institution of human slavery. Brown lived through a violent period of American history, and as an openly proclaimed abolitionist, he drew the attention of all slave holders and their supporters, many of whom were vengeful, imperious men. Brown, his sons, and supporters fought fire with fire, and that drew criticism on Brown's head. Perhaps the greatest monument erected to Brown was the song sung by men of the Union armies as a marching song, "John Brown's body lies a'mouldering in the grave, but his soul goes marching on." His stout spirit inspired them. If slavery was right, Brown was wrong. History has a special niche for him.

Q. *Did John Brown's family ever find peace and a place to live after his execution?*

A. Yes, following his death the family moved to Iowa, where they found it difficult to make a living. They then went on to California, and after a hazardous trip, with both Indians and Southern sympathizers threatening their lives, they were met and welcomed by the townfolk at Red Bluff, a small village in the nothern end of the Sacramento Valley. Salmon Brown, a son, and his family, along with Mary, John's widow, and her three daughters, Annie, 24, Sarah, 17, and Ellen, 9, made the long journey across the mountains and deserts in a covered wagon.

Q. *Who took out the first homestead under the Homestead Law?*

A. Daniel Freeman was one of the first. He took his claim at the land office at Brownville, Nebraska, and is generally credited as homesteader no. 1. He took out his papers a few minutes after the act became law. However, there were other land offices where simultaneous filings were made, e.g., Des Moines, Iowa, Palmyra, Nebraska, Vermillion, South Dakota, and so on. To pinpoint the matter, Freeman is generally given this honor.

Q. *Who was the biggest man (physically) to ever live in the West?*

A. If you mean physical weight, he was Robert E. Hughes, who died at Bremen, Iowa, July 10, 1958. At birth Hughes weighed eleven pounds. He grew to six feet in height and weighed 1,069 pounds. His girth was 124 inches. He was born, however, at Fish Hook, Illinois and was buried at Sterling, Illinois.

Q. *Why did the former governor of Texas, James S. Hogg, name his only daughter, "Ima?"*

A. Probably out of a distorted sense of humor. If not, we would like to hear why. Yet Ima Hogg went on to make a good life, despite the handicap of such a name laid upon her by her father.

Q. *What was Horace A.W. Tabor's first wife's name?*

A. Her name was Augusta. His second wife was Baby Doe, for whom he left Augusta. Tabor was one of the silver millionaires of the 1890s. Augusta did quite well without him, despite the stories that his divorce broke her heart. She was a practical person and understood that she had married a weakling.

Q. *Who was the first homesteader in the Dodge City area?*

A. Frederick C. Zimmerman appears to hold that claim. He came to Dodge the year the railroad reached there, 1872, and settled a mile west of the depot. Zimmerman lived at Dodge all his life, operating a store and working as a gunsmith. He became one of Dodge's prosperous and popular merchants, was a banker, school board member, county commissioner, and treasurer. He knew everyone worth knowing in western Kansas, and a few not-so-goods as well.

Q. *Where was Sam Houston, Texas statesman, born?*

A. Near Lexington, Virginia, in 1793. He died in 1863. His family moved from Virginia to Tennessee in 1806, to live among the Cherokee Indians. Later Houston moved to Oklahoma, and in 1833 moved on to Texas. Houston gave Texas brilliant leadership, both in Mexican War days and when the Civil War came. On the latter, he advised Texans to remain in the Union, but they failed to take his advice.

Q. *I know that Moses Austin, father of Stephen, came to Texas from Missouri to settle colonists. But since he was originally a Connecticut man, why was he in Missouri?*

A. Moses Austin was born in Connecticut in 1761. He had acquired lead mines in Virginia by the time he was thirty, and was exploring for lead in Missouri in 1796–97. Securing a grant of land, near what is now the Potosi area, he soon became Missouri's first industrialist in the *Mine 'a Breton* area. The collapse of the Bank of St. Louis bankrupted him, and that new "Star of the West," Texas, beckoned him. He went there to start his colony, but the trip was too much and he died on the return trip near Potosi, at the home of a son-in-law, James Bryan. He was buried there. His son Stephen went forward with his Texas colonization plans. (Texas has since sought Moses Austin's remains, but Missouri residents refuse to have them removed from the state.)

Q. *What type of home did Mark Twain live in as a boy in Hannibal, Missouri?*

A. The home was a rather small, two-story frame affair, with shuttered windows, yet a fine home for its time. Today it occupies a place beside the larger Mark Twain Museum and is a part of that museum. The board fence that Tom Sawyer persuaded his gang to whitewash for him, by a ruse, occupies the prominent lot next to the Clemens' home. The building is in downtown Hannibal, Missouri, not far from the Mississippi River. A large monument, depicting Tom and his friend, Huckleberry Finn, stands in the town in memory of the books Clemens wrote of his life as a boy there.

Q. *What happened to the Negro colony, Votaw, near Coffeyville, Kansas, established in the 1880s?*

A. The colony was disbanded about 1900. Though several colonies were formed in Kansas after the Civil War with the hope that they might offer the freed men opportunity to come north and get farm land, the colonies were not successful. It seemed that the freed Negroes preferred to go their own way and not be bound to any one particular place. Many Negro families did homestead lands in Kansas and Nebraska, apart from the colonies. Dr. George Washington Carver, who made a name for himself in Alabama educational circles, and who gave to the nation the many hundreds of uses for the lowly peanut, had homesteaded as a youth in western Kansas.

Q. *I have heard that people who went West in the early days and settled on remote farms were mentally affected by the loneliness they were forced to endure. Is this true?*

A. Yes, this was true in some instances. Women in particular suffered because they had to stay home with the children while men found ways to get away and meet others. One expression was sometimes used, "She's got the loneliness," or "She's got the lonelies." In my own family a child once expressed the desire to go back to Pennsylvania, where the family came from. "I want to see G'amma," the child said. The mother answered, "You can see me." The child retaliated, "I see you every day." It was the terrible sameness every day that preyed on peoples' minds, much as make men go "stir crazy" in prison.

Q. *What was the term used by fashionable women of the Old West when they saw others—ranch-bred women—riding astride instead of with sidesaddles?*

A. The more reserved women called it "riding clothespin style." Others called it "riding straddle."

Q. *Was marijuana used to any extent in the settlement of the West?*

A. Marijuana was not used as a drug. However, one Western expert has noted that even Bibles and covered-wagon sheets were often *made from* the Devil's Weed, in addition to some of the clothing the pioneers wore and the hemp rope they used.

Q. *Was marijuana smoked to any extent by the* vaqueros *(Mexicans) who tended cattle in the Southwest?*

A. Undoubtedly some use of the weed was made by the Mexican cowboys, yet it is an indisputable fact that the weed is not even mentioned by the trail drivers of Texas who rode with the thousands of Mexican trail drivers who came north with the herds of longhorn cattle. Nor, as a boy, working cattle with some of the older men, did I ever hear mention of it. In the early 1920s I recall the cowboys' disgust at an ancient Mexican beggar man who smoked the weed and lay alongside the corral at the stockyards in shipping season, dreaming his dreams as we loaded cattle on to the cars. Most of us had a pint of moonshine in our boots, but no "grass" in our pockets.

Q. *My grandfather homesteaded in Nebraska. He said he learned to tell temperature by counting the chirps of crickets. Was he joking me?*

A. No. A common method of performing this seeming magic art is to count the number of chirps per minute of a performing cricket, divide the number by four and add forty to the result. If the temperature is actually above 50° F., your results will be accurate in most cases.

Q. *Why is there so little love interest in Western stories?*

A. You must not have read Zane Grey! However, you are right when you consider most Western fiction and even nonfiction. For one thing, women were scarce on the frontier. However, it is generally understood that many Western writers exclude females from their stories to offer relief from the plethora of love stories on the market in almost every other publication. Serious Western *historians* are finally giving women greater attention and a larger role in the development of the Old West. Yet even the historians play down the "love" angle and try to develop the mother, the sister, the companion, the martyr, and the pioneer helpmeet role. With more and more women reading "Western stories," authors of Western works will probably change their plots to meet the changing times.

Q. *Which have killed the most people, prairie fires or forest fires?*

A. Though prairie fires were a great threat to the pioneer people and to their property, there are not many recorded deaths attributed to them. Forest fires, on the other hand, have a long record of bringing death to humans as well as animals and destruction to the trees and other vegetation. For example, a fire near Peshtigo, Wisconsin, in 1871, took the lives of 1,182 people. Nowhere in the pioneer West is there a record of anything similar due to prairie fire. Another forest fire, near Cloquet, Minnesota, on October 12, 1918, took 400 lives. Of course, since those times a better fire-warning system has been established by the Forest Service. Building fires continue to take many lives, many more than prairie fires ever took. The Chicago Iroquois Theater Fire in 1903 took 602 lives; the Ring Theater fire in Vienna, Austria, took 850 lives in 1881. The great Coconut Grove fire in Boston in 1942 or 1943 took nearly 400 lives. The most people killed in any prairie fire in my recollection was two or three persons. The prairie fire, while dangerous to life and property, did offer both humans and animals an opportunity to run from it, to get into streams, into sod houses and dugouts. Men could often backfire and burn off the prairie, so the fire ended when it came to the burned areas.

Q. *I am interested in the missionary history of the Pacific Northwest. Where may I find works dealing with this region?*

A. Get in touch with Dr. Clifford M. Drury, former minister of the Presbyterian faith, and a member of the Los Angeles Corral of the Westerners. He can be reached through the Arthur H. Clark Company, Publishers, Glendale, California. Dr. Drury has done much research on this subject.

Q. *I have heard that the Utah Mormons are moving back to Nauvoo, Illinois. Is this correct?*

A. Only partially. The Mormons are restoring several historical places at Nauvoo, such as the old home of Brigham Young. The hope appears to be to make Nauvoo the "Williamsburg of the West." Local merchants, non-Mormons, have approved the move, for it will undoubtably bring tens of thousands of tourists to the town, now a village of approximately 1,000 population. So far, the blacksmith shop of C.G. Webb has been restored, as well as the Brigham Young home. The temple lot is completed, showing where the temple stood before it burned down in 1848, its size, and a replica on a pedestal. The temple at Nauvoo, with its four-acre setting, at one time was the largest building north of St. Louis.

Q. *Is there a good book on the construction of sod dugouts and sod houses?*

A. Yes, Prof. Roger L. Welsch wrote, and had illustrated with many of the famous Solomon D. Butcher photos of soddies of the plains, a work titled *Sod Walls: The Story of the Nebraska Sod House*. It was published by Purcell's, Broken Bow, Nebraska.

Q. *What is a "jacal"?*

A. It is a small, sometimes grass-covered shelter built by the residents of the Southwest and Mexico.

Q. *What was the difference between a dugout and a soddy?*

A. The dugout was dug all or partially into the ground, usually on a side hill, and roofed over with logs, brush, and sod. The sod house (soddy) was laid up with sod strips above the ground, and usually had a log-brush-sod, and, later, shingle, roof.

Q. *Why do we sometimes see the word* adobe *written as* abode?

A. Probably because abode means a home, and the writer or editor or typesetter may not understand that the original writer meant the actual adobe home, one made from the earth. Or it could be a simple transposing of the letters "do" to "bo."

Q. *Were tin cans ever used as shingles on dugout homes?*

A. You bet! They made an excellent substitute for shingles when hammered flat. There were never people more capable of improvising than the pioneers. "Make do" were not just words to them; it was their way of life.

Q. *Were sod homes really habitable, or were they used in lieu of anything better?*

A. Many people today live in less comfort-providing homes than many sod homes were to the settlers—and I can say this from practical experience since I was born in a sod house. They were cool in summer, easily warmed in winter. With a good roof they were most comfortable, though lacking light within. One of the problems with the sod homes was the presence of snakes and mice if one failed to keep the exterior yard area clean of them. But this would be true of any home, even today. Fleas and lice, now controllable, were other pests.

Q. *What was a puncheon floor?*

A. When logs were split down the middle, and the flat side turned up, this was called a puncheon floor. The flat side was smoothed with a sharp axe or drawknife. Puncheon floors were common in the wooded areas from which many pioneers had originally come. There were no logs for such use on the Great Plains, so the floor was usually an earth floor, wet down to prevent dust, or covered with carpeting of whatever materials (hides of animals, carpets brought from eastern homes, grass) were available.

Q. *What was a sad iron?*

A. It was a flat iron, pointed at both ends and with a removable handle. Several of such irons could heat at one time on the stove, while the handle was used on the hottest one for ironing.

Q. *What was a "pitcher and catcher hotel" in the early West?*

A. The term was used to describe a hostelry that provided a pitcher and washbowl for washing, and a chamber (ofttimes called a thundermug) under the bed. The former was the pitcher, the latter the catcher.

Q. *What was a bitch light?*

A. A tin can filled with grease and a wick made from twisted rags.

Q. *What was an ash hopper?*

A. It was an inverted cone, made from wood, with stone containing-vessels at the bottom. Wood ashes were dumped into this cone to manufacture lye, which was then used in the making of homemade soap.

Q. *In an old manuscript, my grandfather told of working in a "stomping barn." What was that?*

A. In early days a stomping barn was a place in which horses or cattle tromped over bundles of grain scattered on the floor to separate the grain from the straw. The floor was usually a substantial puncheon floor. When the grain was separated, it was taken outdoors and "winnowed" by tossing it into the air when the wind was blowing. This permitted the wind to blow the chaff away and let the grain fall back on a blanket or canvas. The grain harvesters, binders, and other machinery outmoded this practice.

Q. *In 1900 my father found a bronze horseshoe in the Oil Trough Bottom in Arkansas. It had no holes for nails, but on its three cleats these words appeared: "TAKE IN TIME." What was its purpose, and who made it?*

A. These old horseshoes are quite rare. They were an advertising gimmick for *Simmons' Liver Regulator*, and possibly other patent medicines of that day.

Q. *A great controversy is raging here in southern California over the question of whether it is proper to hang a horseshoe over the door for good luck with the toe tip up, or the heels of the shoe up. What is correct?*

A. Among the ranchers of the Great Plains the shoe was hung with the *open end* up. One grandfather said, "It keeps the luck from running out." But other Westerners differ on this—for we differ on many little things of no great importance.

Q. *How did the label on a pound of Arbuckles' coffee read?*

A. It read: "One Pound ARBUCKLES' *Dich die andre Geite.* No Settling Required; ARIOSA COFFEE, New York, Pittsburgh." The manufacturer, Arbuckle Brothers, had a horse ranch on Pole Creek, twenty miles north of Cheyenne, Wyoming. They had pretentious ranch build-ings in the 1890s and branded their cattle L5 and their horses PO. Their coffee was sold by the tons to ranchers all over the West, and almost every camp cook preferred it to other brands.

Q. *What type of fish were found by pioneers in the waters of prairie streams? In mountain streams?*

A. In the cold waters of the higher levels were trout. Farther downstream were suckers, darters, and minnows; in the deeper river flows came the buffalo fish, catfish, crappies, bass, sturgeon, and gar pike. Although many of the species are still in the streams, those such as pike and sturgeon, once familiar in many Wyoming waters, no longer exist there unless stocked by the fish and game departments.

Q. *What food items were the most enjoyable because of their shortage in early days?*

A. Pickles were one; sugar another. The heavy meat diet caused a great longing for sour items, such as condi-ments. Coffee when in short supply was greatly yearned for, and cracked roasted corn kernels were a poor substi-tute. Salt was always much desired, if not available. Most fruits were, of course, great treats until orchards began producing. Wild fruits from the canyons, such as grapes and plums, served the earliest settlers.

Q. *What substitute for candy did pioneer mothers have for their children?*

A. A "sugar tit" was one substitute. A spoonful of sugar was placed on a clean piece of linen or muslin cloth. The cloth was then tied with string into a small teat which the children could suck.

Q. *How were eggs kept in storage in early days without refrigeration?*

A. A large ten- or fifteen-gallon crock was placed in a cool storage place, such as a cave or cellar, or in a well-house. Eggs were placed, layer upon layer, with an inch layer of salt between each layer of eggs. Another method was called Water Glass, in which plain old sodium silicate was placed over the eggs. Although eggs kept under these methods were not "fresh eggs," they did store well and tasted fine on cold winter mornings.

Q. *Why were there so many deaths from cholera along the Oregon Trail? At Scotts Bluff National Monument, I saw nearly forty skeletons of Indians dug out of one pit where they were digging a potato cellar. They were thought to have perished from cholera.*

A. Ezra Meeker, who had gone up the Oregon Trail as a youth with a covered wagon, thought that a poor diet of fat pork was the cause of so many deaths. He may be right, and if he was, the people were actually dying of *trichinosis*, not cholera. For as he pointed out, "when buffalo supplied a change," deaths diminished. However, it is doubtful if either cholera or trichinosis killed those Indians, who rarely ate fresh pork. Smallpox, perhaps?

Q. *How did pioneer women make a "cornstarch cake?"*

A. One hundred years ago in Texas, Mrs. Tom McKinney wrote this recipe: One package of cornstarch; eight eggs; one pound sugar; three-fourths pound of butter; lemon to flavor; bake in small pans. Her cookbook was published by *Pioneer News-Observer*, San Angelo, Texas, and is an excellent one.

Q. *How can I make a sourdough starter?*

A. Here is one way: Soak a cake of fresh yeast in water until dissolved. Add two tablespoons of sugar and enough flour to make a soft batter. Let stand two days if warm weather, longer if cold. To use it, add a tablespoon of sugar and a teaspoon of soda, stir, and it is ready to use. Save some of the starter by just adding flour and water. As you use from the starter, add a tablespoon of sugar and a teaspoon of soda for your biscuits. An egg will improve your biscuits if stirred into the dough. Keep your starter covered, and warm, so it will continue to "work."

Q. *What was the "mast crop?"*

A. Mast is the crop from nut trees, such as oak, pecans, etc. Hogs and wild javalinas used to get fat on the mast dropped annually from the trees.

Q. *What were the worst factors pioneers had to contend with?*

A. Probably a hundred drawbacks to pioneer life could be named, but here are some that have been long-remembered: blizzards, Indians, fleas, snakes, cholera, small-pox, diphtheria, lice, bedbugs, prairie fire, falls into deep wells, accidents from normal work life and working livestock, cyclones, runaway horses, stampeded cattle, heat, sunstroke, the silence of the Plains, and loneliness. Many women thought the latter two the worst.

Q. *Why did so many pioneer children die of diphtheria?*

A. Fifty percent of the children who had diphtheria died because a diphtheria anti-toxin had not yet been discovered. Pasteur made his discovery in 1895, and this knowledge did not reach the pioneer doctor level until later. Diphtheria strangled children, so the pioneer manner of combating it was to mix equal parts of tar and turpentine, hold the vessel over the stove until the room was filled with the fumes. This would make the children cough up membraneous matter, which the country doctors thought responsible for the disease.

Q. *Did whiskey actually help to prevent snakebite, as many Western men thought?*

A. Doctors will tell you that, to the contrary, any alcohol in the blood will help to spread the snake venom throughout the human system. Yet I heard a Texas woman who had been bitten by a rattlesnake proclaim that her husband saved her life by making her drink nearly a half-pint of whiskey within a half hour of the time the snake bit her! He contended that the whiskey relieved her of pain and anxiety, and that relaxed her. When a person relaxes, he said, there is far less possibility of the snake venom killing a human, though it will always make them deathly sick. My personal thought is that a small shot of liquor *might* help a person to relax and bear the pain, but I would go along with the doctor's advice.

Q. *I read that the chokecherry bush was used as a medicine for dysentery and other ills in the West. Was this an Indian medicine?*

A. It is possible that Indians did learn of the curative powers of leaves and twigs of the chokecherry bush, but it was Lewis and Clark whose use of it made it well known in the West. Stricken with dysentery, Lewis took the leaves and twigs of the bush and boiled them. He got a black liquid which he and his men drank. It apparently cured their dysentery. Blackberry cordial has the effect of stopping dysentery. But a warning should be given about eating or making a "tea" from chokecherry leaves or twigs: the common chokecherry (*Prunis virginiana*) is a *deadly poison to livestock* when they eat the green leaves or the brown leaves in hay. The poisonous principle, *hydrocyanic acid*, is found in toxic quantities in the leaves. So you better try a blackberry cordial, and leave Lewis and Clark out of it.

Q. *What were some of the pioneer folk remedies for the common cold?*

A. A few were: gargle salt and vinegar; rub goose grease on the chest; drink whiskey with rock candy or sugar on it (toddy); wear a clean silk stocking around the neck (where pioneers would find a silk stocking, clean or dirty, I wouldn't know); drink a tea of red seeds of the sumac bush. Others were: put honey on a sheet of brown paper over a lamp until the honey melts, then eat it; eat fried onions, and also wear a fresh one around your neck; turpentine and lard rubbed on the chest and throat is good, and add a little sulphur if you have the itch. A hot whiskey toddy and hot foot bath are a fine combination.

Q. *I have read where the powder from a dead horned toad was believed to be a cure for many diseases. Were people in the West that superstitious?*

A. This was also a Chinese superstition. It was believed that such a powder, used as a catalyst, gave other drugs or medicines a hundred times more power. There is a point where a person suffering great pain will try anything, even the most fantastic concoction—even as a person suffering an internal cancer for which modern medicine is unable to guarantee a cure, will try anything a doctor may have at hand to suggest, from cobalt, to X-rays, to great shots of medicine into the bloodstream, to eating a paste made from apricot seeds! Even a ground up horny toad, taken internally twice daily, helps a person to hold on to their hopes!

Q. *What were the ingredients of "hard soap" in pioneer days?*

A. One source told me the ingredients were "a can of potash, three pints of cold water, two heaping tablespoons of powdered borax, five pounds of grease, one half ounce of oil of sassafras." The salt is boiled out of the grease (fat) by covering over with water. The clean grease is skimmed off and mixed into the other ingredients and stirred until it hardens.

Q. *What did Westerners use for insect stings?*

A. Some would put raw onions over the sting or bite. Others used plain mud. Both were effective. Hornet and wasp stings are still treated with a plain mud and poultice. Some mix a little barnyard manure into the mud. Mud actually stops the pain in a few minutes. Alcohol applied after the sting will also relieve the pain.

Q. *How did a pioneer doctor remove an imbedded splinter from the body of man or animal?*

A. A shoemaker's wax poultice was effective but had to stay on the wound from two to four weeks. Although it carried the danger of blood poisoning, it would always bring out the splinter.

Q. *Can you list some of the pioneer's tools and their uses?*

A. Broadaxe, for hewing; auger, for boring; hatchet, for hewing and cutting; saw, for cutting; maul, for striking; hitting-beetle-and-wedge, for log-splitting; hitting mallet and cornering chisel, for squaring holes; reaping hooks, for harvesting; adze, for paring; prong-fork, for hay pitching; draw-knife, for planing; hollowing-gouge, for making holes in wood; sledge, or sleigh, for hauling; pounding-commander, for pounding; sledge-hammer, for pounding; felling-axe, for cutting down trees; cross-cut saw, for sawing. This is only a few of the total. Stonemasons, farmers, builders, metal workers, blacksmiths, and farriers all had specialized tools for their trade.

Q. *I am interested in pioneer farm machinery. Is there a museum for such I might visit?*

A. Yes, the University of California at Davis, California.

Q. *What type of fences were used in the West and Southwest before barbed wire?*

A. Where wood was available, the zigzag, or worm, fence; the Mexican picket fence; the straight rail fence. The Osage orange and other thorned bushes were employed as fences, including the *bois d'arc* and weesache. On the Great Plains sod was laid up.

Q. *Has stone ever been used for fence posts?*

A. Yes. Old limestone slabs quarried in western Kansas more than ninety years ago still hold up three to four strands of barbed wire on ranches in Hodgeman and Ness counties today. The "bell rock," so named because of the bell-like ring of stone when struck with a hammer, is from the Cretaceous formation. It is estimated that this rock once held up more than 50,000 miles of barbed wire. Great amounts of bell rock were also used in construction of ranch houses, barns, and other buildings in pioneer times. Old snubbing posts in corrals were often long slabs of this stone, sunk deeply in the ground, and still show the rope imprints from many struggles with wild horses in the 1880s.

Q. *We have all been told in school how inventive the pioneers were, how they improvised when they needed an article and didn't have it. Can you give me a specific example?*

A. Yes, I could give you many. For example, in 1906, in the Oklahoma Panhandle, a threshing engine broke a drive gear. Repairs were not available, so Jacob Berends made a turning lathe from a common grindstone, whittled the pattern of the broken drive gear from a cottonwood log to cast the gear. This improvised gear was used for many years in the machine. Necessity was truly the mother of invention. In a later example, a southwest Kansas pioneer, Charles E. Hancock, age eighty-nine, constructed three small horses from wood, carpentered them, didn't carve them. They were five-eighths of the normal horse size. He wanted to present them to the Seward County Historical Museum as a memento of the three horses his father drove into western Kansas in 1885. But he needed *ears* for the horses. So he sliced an angle across three cardboard toilet tissue cores and came up with the six ears!

Q. *What brought about the sudden wave of windmills built on the Great Plains in the 1880s?*

A. When the earlier homesteaders came, 1860-70, they took lands adjacent to streams. The later settlers, who arrived in the 1880s, had to occupy the high, hill lands set back from the streams. So the latter dug for water. The earliest wells were the rope and bucket sort, "The Old Oaken Bucket." Soon windmills were seen to offer many advantages, and the windy Plains were a perfect setting for them, for they lifted the water up 150 to 300 feet and supplied all the water the livestock needed—and with no cost for power! Soon the settlers irrigated their garden crops and other fields from windmills, the wells sunk with drilling rigs.

Q. *What was the most unusual type of windmill built in the West?*

A. Probably the "Merry-Go-Round," designed and built by S.S. Videtto, near Lincoln, Nebraska. Its wheel turned like an old-fashioned merry-go-round, parallel to the earth. The diameter of the wheel was forty feet. The mill was designed to produce almost unlimited power, depending on the size of the wheel.

Q. *Did the windmills originate on the Great Plains?*

A. No, windmills had been in use since antiquity. The great Dutch mills of Holland were pumping water and grinding grain before the New World was settled. The Industrial Revolution added new dimensions to water wells and use of manufactured (steel) windmills on the Plains. Well-drilling equipment soon made it possible to quickly put down a 300-foot well in the arid sections of the West. Today's great irrigation pumps on deep wells, 300 to 400 feet in depth, are only an extension of the windmill, now using fossil fuels for energy, instead of the ever-present wind.

Q. *How big was the largest windmill ever used on the Plains?*

A. The largest, in diameter of the wheel, that we know of is also the most unusual as stated above, and that is the mill built by S.S. Videtto, the "Merry-Go-Round." However, the largest wheel on an *upright mill* may well be one erected near Wayside, Texas, in 1921. Its wheel measured thirty-two feet in diameter, pumping sixty-five gallons of water per minute. This large wheel was supported on a platform only eighteen feet high!

Q. *We recently tore down an old windmill and I saved a cast-iron buffalo figure that was used as a weight on its fan. Do these have any value among collectors?*

A. Yes, they bring up to thirty-five dollars. Other figures, including horses and cattle, are also in demand.

Q. *Where may I find information on "homemade" windmills of the West?*

A. A very good article was published in the *American West* magazine, winter issue of 1966, Vol. III, No. 1, by Donald Danker.

Q. *What were some of the popular windmills?*

A. The brands called the Fairbury, the Challenge, the Halliday Standard, and the Holland were some. Many handmade mills were created by individuals on their farms, such as the Battleaxe, which a farmer built at a cost of eleven dollars. Another, Mock Turbine, lifted water forty-four feet into a storage reservoir at a low cost.

Q. *Were the Dutch windmills ever used in the West?*

A. Yes, both Henry Boarman, near Portal, Nebraska, and August Prinz, near Chalco, Nebraska, built and used the Dutch mills.

Q. *Were windmills ever used for any other power purpose than for lifting water from wells?*

A. Yes, the Giant Turbine, built by J.M. Warner, near Overton, Nebraska, cost but sixty dollars to construct, yet was used to operate a four-horsepower feed grinder as well as to irrigate ten acres of alfalfa and eight acres of corn.

Q. *What was the single most obvious and visible effect after the erection of a windmill on a claim?*

A. First, the tall mill changed the physical appearance of the place, making a veritable oasis of green where there had been little greenery before. Trees soon grew, fruit and berry bushes were started. The story of *Old Jules*, by Mari Sandoz, beautifully illustrates this point. It was not long until a fine garden flourished there in the Nebraska Sand Hills, and flowers graced the once arid and brown prairie scene, and melon vines were to be seen wherever the water could reach.

Q. *How much land could a pioneer family irrigate with only a windmill to provide water?*

A. Elmer Jasperson had a farm in Saunders County, Nebraska, where he built a retaining pond to hold the well's water. With this reservoir, and the well's daily pumping, he watered forty acres of land to produce abundant crops.

Q. *What did children find to play with on the Plains?*

A. Dolls were fashioned from clothespins, corncobs, and sticks of wood. The boys were given "string" lariats when small. Later, they used their father's old throw ropes and roped dogs and chickens. Tying a string to a tumbleweed and running alongside it provided action. And there were many farm dogs and horses and calves for pets.

Q. *What form of recreation did the men on a farm or ranch turn to when through with their work?*

A. Sitting on their hams visiting, just talking, was about the most popular diversion. But the men also engaged in many a horseshoe game when time permitted. On the CY Ranch, Wyoming (Pea Green Division), the spring of 1922, the ranch foreman, Nick, and his men enjoyed a diversion called "flippin' turds." It was a game much like tossing a Frisbee today, only they used dried cow chips, throwing in the same fashion, underhanded. Recently, this old ranch game has become a legitimate sport in Oklahoma, and at a contest held in Forgan, Oklahoma, Harold Smith, of that town, successfully defended his title as champion flipper, by tossing a cow chip 166.11 feet. I would judge that Nick, the old CY foreman, could have just about matched this toss. Most tosses were twenty feet short of this. Another sport was broad jumping and standing jumps for distance. Occasional boxing and wrestling were also enjoyed, particularly when threshing crews met, or when new hands came to work on a farm or ranch and cared to challenge the best wrestler or boxer there. Steer riding, with a rope girth for a handhold, was a popular sport for the men on the Bighorn Ranch in Banner County, Nebraska, as was bareback bronc riding. Saddle bronc riding was a part of their day's work, so not considered a recreation. But, occasionally, bets would be made and a ranch hand would attempt to ride a bad horse that had thrown several others. Of course fishing and hunting were year 'round attractions to almost every rancher and working cowboy, depending on the locale.

Photo from the collection of Harry E. Chrisman.

Q. *What process of harvesting wheat was used before the combine became popular in the West?*

A. First was the binder. Then came the header machine that clipped off the top of the wheat. The header then loaded the wheat heads on to the header barges (wagons used for hauling) and the wheat tops were taken and stacked in the field. Later, a steam threshing machine (with separator), came to thresh the grain from the stems. (In the photo at left, the header. A header barge stands at each side of the stack.)

11 TACK and EQUIPMENT

On the frontier, necessity was truly the "mother of invention." Thus, the frontier man or woman had to be an improviser, a "make-do" person. In my own family, I had an uncle, Randall (Ren) Sargent, a trained blacksmith and farrier who was also an inventor and a builder, principally of various labor-saving machines. He was also a well-driller and surveyor. Needless to say, this man was looked upon as a genius by his neighbors and friends. He was a fine example of the pioneer type, a man who could invent, improvise, repair. It was only natural that he *built* a horse-powered merry-go-round in the 1890s when such a device was truly a novelty. He took the machine to all the neighborhood gatherings and fairs.

When my own father, Henry E. (Gene) Chrisman, saw an opportunity to make money, he did so in this manner: a neighbor, Frank Carlin, had fallen into an abandoned well, but had managed to dig his way out with only a pocketknife as a tool. The well was one of the many abandoned deep wells of the region, this particular one 140 feet in depth. During the drought of the 1890s, these wells had been left behind by settlers who left the country. The state and local governments set up a fund for filling the old wells, and this fund gave employment to settlers who had had no income for a year or two. My father and his brothers started filling wells—by hand—using the sod from abandoned sod houses to fill the holes. Soon it became apparent that he could construct a type of fresno, built it wide so his team could straddle the well hole, and fill as many wells alone as he could with the help of two or three men. So he built the device and started filling wells on a wholesale basis. But, alas, the county commissioners ruled that all wells had to be filled by hand in order that the work could be spread around more widely. So father again took up his shovel with the others.

The building of the West is marked by thousands of instances of human improvisation. Though the tack and equipment of the pioneer was limited, he made his tools do ten times their regular duty. Many an old saddle skirt has been cut apart to make leather washers for a pump or soles for boots and shoes. In the same way the brass balls children found around the windmill after the men had repaired and adjusted the shutoff valve, were quickly appropriated for marbles. The mothers soon learned how to make dolls from clothespins, and every worn-out work shirt and piece of cloth on the place went into quilt pieces for crazy-quilt patterns.

The average member of a modern saddle club would hardly recognize what he calls the "tack room" of an old ranch establishment. The contemporary horseman would soon discover it to be as bare of martingales, breast harnesses, and fancy gear as Old Mother Hubbard's cupboard was of canned dog foods. He would find bridles with one rein made from a leather strap, the other from a piece of rope; he would find a harness with many straps missing, appropriated for use where they would hold something else together. He would notice the doorways hinged with pieces of leather backstraps, and he would observe that every piece of wire to come on to the place had been carefully coiled up, lariat-style, and hung up for future use.

Every article that appeared on the ranch or farm was used for its original purpose, then husbanded, when worn, for whatever use could be found for it later. A pioneer tack room was actually a very tacky room!

Q. *Could you tell me the various parts of a harness for a work team, starting at the front and working to the rear?*

A. The bridle, with lines attached to the bit for guiding the team. Over the neck, the collar, and buckled on to the collar, the hames, with breast straps that attach to the hames to hold up the neckyoke. The traces, or tugs, that attach to the hames and extend back and attach to the singletrees. The backstrap, with attached bellyband, which helps support the tugs and the quarterstraps. The breeching (or britchin'), with straps that attach to the backband, and the quarterstraps that extend forward from the breeching under the animals' bellies and are looped around the neckyoke. These quarterstraps serve the purpose of halting the forward progress of the wagon or vehicle, and enable the horses to sit back into the breeching to back up the wagon if needed, for the quarterstraps are the connection (via the neckyoke) to the wagon tongue. Describing without the help of an illustration almost equals in difficulty Mark Twain's description of "how to harness a horse." But these are the basic parts of a Western work harness.

Q. *How do the reins, or lines, work so that a driver when pulling on a left rein may turn the horse on the right side to left?*

A. The lines, as they are called on a driving team (reins on a saddle horse), are fashioned like a "Y," with the two short ends crossed over and attached to the bridle bits on the inside, the longer lines fastened to bits on the outside of the team. Consequently, a pull on the line on one side turns both horses' heads that direction.

Q. *What was the weight called that was attached to the rein of the bridle bit and dropped to the ground to hold the horse when the driver stepped away from the wagon or buggy?*

A. This weight had many names. Generally it was called a "hitching weight," and the old Sears-Roebuck catalogs list them in such weights as ten to fifteen pounds and twenty-five pounds. Some horsemen called them a headweight; others called them a tetherweight. Still others spoke of them as a hitching block, and they are so listed in an old hardware catalog of Hibbard, Spencer & Barlett Company. I have heard them called a tiedown by my mother, who was of Pennsylvania origin, yet she said her people called the weight a whiffenwoofle! A man told me his father called it a fetter, and his uncle spoke of it as a clog. Other names for the weight, according to *Collector's Weekly*, the Kermit, Texas, collectors' publication, are woofenwhiffle, trammel, tie weight, whipple bopper, dolly, divot, staub, hitching ball, frog, plug, snub block, hitching bob, buggy hitch, throwweight, tie pad, holdback, and standweight. An old Union veteran I knew called it a picket iron and a horse picket. A cowboy called it a ground tie, for cow horses were trained to stand where their reins were dropped.

Q. *What did they call the black objects on the bridle that kept a horse from looking backwards?*

A. Blinders.

Q. *On which side of the buggy did the driver sit?*

A. Either side—but the whip socket was on the right hand side, so he usually sat there.

Q. *How would people keep warm on a real cold day riding in a buggy or on a wagon seat?*

A. They dressed warmly. They also used laprobes, often made from buffalo or cowhide. Sometimes they would set a lighted lantern under the robe near their feet to keep them warm. On many trips the riders would get down and walk a mile or two to get their blood circulating better.

Q. *How fast could a driving team travel over long distances?*

A. A good, speedy team could easily travel twenty to forty miles in a day without hurting themselves. It was necessary to feed, water, and rest them, however, on the trip. Many a trip of fifty or sixty or more miles in the day has been made with a buggy team. However, they were not expected to do this daily.

Q. *Why do some men prefer mules to horses as a driving team?*

A. I have not seen many who did. However, mules are fine walkers; they stretch out and cover many miles in a long-walk. They require little attention, just ordinary feed, water, and rest.

Q. *What is a "reach" on a wagon?*

A. It's the two long wooden pieces, usually of 2" x 4" lumber, that connect the front and rear wheels, via the axles. As a coupling pole, one could extend or diminish distance between front and rear wheels with it.

Q. *What years did the Abbot-Downing Company of Concord, New Hampshire, make the Concord Stage Coaches?*

A. The beginning years of the company were between 1813 and 1828. By 1840 their Concord coach was perfected. They made 700 by 1847, and 3,000 were built altogether by successor firms by 1899.

Q. *Who used the Concord Coaches besides the Western stage lines?*

A. The famous Concord Coaches (in various designs and types) were used all over the world—Europe, Africa, South America. They were the choice for the hotel trade and served almost every large American city. They were expensive vehicles, a twelve-passenger mail coach of the 1870s costing $1,050. Many types of vehicles besides the stage coach were made by Abbott, Downing & Company, such as the Australian Passenger Wagon, the Large Overland Wagon, the Western Passenger Wagon, the California Passenger Wagon, the Hack Passenger Wagon, the Florida Passenger Wagon, the Powell Passenger Wagon and the Overland Mail Wagon. In addition to these strictly passenger vehicles, there were the One Horse Chaise (Shay); the Business Buggy (such as doctors liked); the Pleasure Wagon; a boatlike wagon called the Concord Buggy; an Omnibus, for hotels; a closed Two-wheel Delivery Wagon; a Pie Wagon; Ice Wagon, Warehouse Wagon, Dray Wagon, Closed Delivery Wagon, Standard Oil Wagon, the Monitor Street Sweeper vehicle, the Horse Wagon on four ski runners, the Monitor Street Sprinkler, the Ambulance Wagon, and many others. One body was designed and made for use on a truck chassis in the early twentieth century. All were beautifully and soundly constructed wagons, the best woods and finest art scenes used. The company ceased business in 1945 and Wells Fargo & Company purchased the use of the company name.

Q. *What was the Mother Hubbard, or Mother Machree saddle?*

A. In about 1890 F.A. Meanea, Cheyenne, Wyoming, saddlemaker, made a saddle with a *mochilla* (similar to that used by the Pony Express) built on to the saddle. It was quite ornate, with saddlebags. Because of its long skirts, the cowboys called it a Mother Machree.

Q. *I read where some men used gunny sacks for saddle blankets. Will you please comment?*

A. Although many poor farmers have done this, the practice injures the backs of the horses. No self-respecting horseman or cowhand would be caught dead with a gunny sack under his saddle (unless it were filled with ten dollar bills). The dust, grain residue, and dirt from old sacks work into the animal's fur and skin. A good saddle blanket, even the fine Navaho weavings, only cost five dollars or so in the old days.

Q. *I have bought two good Western saddle horses for my boys. What will good Western saddles cost?*

A. You can get fairly good saddles for just under $200. And you can find excellent ones at $250 and up. Get good bridles to match up, too! But don't permit your boys to use severe bits.

Q. *How many different brands of saddles were being manufactured in the 1880s and 1890s?*

A. That's a tough one to answer, since there is no record on hand to consult. There were Hyers, Gallups, Keystones, Clays, Houstons, Dooleys, Meaneas, Bacons, Collins, Manns, Kirkendalls, Porters, and I'll bet any old-timer can rattle off a dozen more.

Q. *What are the various parts of a Sinaloa saddle called?*

A. (1) The *Fuste*, or tree; (2) the leather *mochilla*, or wide skirts, similar to Pony Express, is called the *cognillo*; (3) the two huge sheets of leather that extend from the horn down to the horse's knees protect the rider's legs from the thorns on the thick brush and are called the *armas*.

Q. *Father had an old-style Texas saddle with a dish-pan shaped horn. On the back of the cantle was the inscription:* Los golpes hacen al jinete. *What does that mean?*

A. It is a Spanish phrase meaning that hard knocks make the rider better, that is, by experience, we learn.

Q. *About when did the steel fork replace the cast-iron fork on Western saddles?*

A. Probably about 1885, though many cast-iron and wooden forks were still in use. One cowman pulled the cast-iron fork out of a saddle as late as 1910. By then, saddle styles had changed, and the swell was becoming popular and the older fifty-pound rigs were giving way to the thirty-five pound saddles. Using soft woods permitted the swells to be fashioned in several patterns and styles from twelve- to twenty-four inch widths were in use. The fourteen-inch fork was popular with stockmen and even bronc riders. Lower forks are now popular, with aluminum and laminated woods being tried out.

Q. *What was the name Mexicans gave to the nosebag, or* morral, *for feeding a horse?*

A. They call it a *cebadera*, or fodder bag; their word *cebadero* means a place where game or fowls are fed. It also means "bell mule."

Q. *What is the leather strap, leading from the top of the bridle to the backband, called?*

A. It is the checkrein; its purpose is to keep the driving horse's head up, to "check" him.

Q. *What is the krooper, or crupper? I recall that as a child we always laughed when that part of a harness was mentioned.*

A. That is the loop that goes under the horse's tail and is fastened to the backband. It helps to hold the light harness on a driving animal, particularly when there is no breeching to the harness. It prevents the harness from sliding forward when the animal stops, for with the light buggy harness the vehicle is stopped only with the collar, or breast strap, and the leathers attached to the buggy shavs. The loop was sometimes called the "cooper." Old Dobbin's tail always drew a laugh for some reason or another.

Q. *What is a* correea?

A. It is a leather strap or thong used in early days of cow hunting in Texas to tie the feet of the wild cattle the cowboys roped and threw down. It is a Spanish word. Rodeo men today, using rope, speak of it as a "piggin' string."

Q. *What was a cowboy's terrapin?*

A. It was a slang word he used for his saddle. He also spoke of it as his "turtle."

Q. *What did old cowhands call the strap on the bridle that goes under the animal's throat?*

A. The throatlatch.

Q. *How long have men used spurs to rouse jaded horses?*

A. At least back to and before the Roman Empire, probably earlier, for it is almost certain that man designed a prick, a prod, a goad, or a sharp object attached to his heel almost as soon as he had a horse to ride and abuse. Roman prick-type spurs have been found in England. Early Greek, Byzantine, and Roman sculpture do not show them worn, however. The rowel for the spur is said to have originated in France, about 1300.

Q. *What type of a bridle bit is easiest on a horse's mouth?*

A. The straight bar bit is probably as easy as any. The snaffle bit, which is made in two parts, joined in the middle, is an old-time and well-known bit for soft-mouthed horses. The curb bits are more severe, and just a touch of the hand on the reins is enough to guide a horse with them. The saw bit, once designed for hard-mouthed mules is an extremely savage bit and a danger-ous one to use since it fails utterly in its purpose—to control an animal. The saw bit only tears at the flesh, and terrorizes and aggravates an animal, making him even more unmanageable. The early Spanish bits were about as bad as could have been made. They reflect *the fear of the rider* in wanting a bit that will totally immobilize the animal beneath him. Properly broken, a harness horse needs only a snaffle bit for control. The saddle horse needs a modified curb bit (no spades or rollers in the animal's mouth). Some may disagree with the foregoing, but the better horse trainers learned these facts from hard experience. The saddle horse can be best broken to neckrein by using a hackamore first, and crossing the bridle reins under his chin later when teaching him to turn with a bit in his mouth.

Q. *What is a* tapadero?

A. *Tapaderos* are leather covers for the stirrups, to keep the rider's feet from being punished in the thorny brush. The word actually means a pot cover, in Spanish, but is used by the *vaqueros* for "stirrup covers."

Q. *What causes the loud crack when a blacksnake whip is popped over the backs of oxen?*

A. The six- to eight-inch leather cracker at the end of the whip is suddenly reversed, traveling faster than sound. Like the modern, fast jet planes, the sound barrier is broken, and the loud crack results. It is odd to think of bullwhackers on the old Oregon Trail breaking the sound barrier before the Wright brothers first flew at Kitty Hawk, isn't it?

Q. *What is the best length for a blacksnake whip for a beginner to learn with?*

A. They can be purchased in six-foot to twelve-foot lengths, but the beginner, if an adult, should go ahead and learn with the regular long whip. A child might be started on a six-foot whip. Bear in mind, these whips are *not*, repeat, *not* to be used on animals, but only as a popper or "scarer." A first-class cowman can use one all day, as did many of the old-time bullwhackers, and never lay the lash on an animal. An old freighter, Squier Jones, Casper, Wyoming, once said: "The whip is a teacher, an organizer, not a punisher. A good man with a whip can get the work done without abusing his teams."

Q. *Did the Studebaker auto people ever make harness? I know of a set of harness with the name "Studebaker" in brass on the tug keepers.*

A. Perhaps the Studebaker company processed brass hardware, and this is how the name got on the harness. I have never heard of them in the harness business, but they may well have been.

Q. *Would a plastic or fiber glass saddle be as comfortable as a leather one?*

A. I have never set a plastic saddle, so would not be a fair judge. It would seem, however, that if a man were riding all day, the plastic or fiber glass would fail to take up the perspiration and dissipate it as do the leather saddles. Saddle corns come from friction and dampness. I have worn plastic shoes that were fine for fit, but too warm, and failed to dissipate the perspiration, making the feet sore. Plastic and fiber glass can be moulded for a fine fit, no doubt, if a saddle were being ordered "tailor made." But I would say leather is still best for saddles. I stand to be corrected, and will accept proof to the contrary.

Q. *Why did cowboys like such high heels on boots?*

A. One of the comforts of wearing Western boots is that when you are in the saddle all day, you sit back and let the *front* of the boot press back against the front of the leg, evenly, taking the strain off the leg muscles. In this position you can trust the high heel of the boot to prevent the foot from slipping through the stirrup, especially on fast turns and stops. The high heel also gives one better leverage on a roped horse or calf, when roping in the corral afoot.

Q. *What size lariat rope is preferred for horse roping?*

A. A 1/2 to 5/8-inch hard twist pure Manila in a 35 to 45-foot length is sufficient for any wrangler. Lariats were usually sold in 7/16-inch size at about a cent-and-a-half per foot of length.

Q. *Where was the Conestoga Wagon, famous for crossing the Plains, manufactured? What were its general dimensions?*

A. The big Conestogas that first crossed the Plains were made in Lancaster County, Pennsylvania, and had been manufactured from the early 1700s. The average wagon box was twenty-one feet long, eleven-feet high to the jet top, and four feet in width and depth. The actual bed of the wagon was a boat-shaped affair, fine for stream crossings, and was sixteen-feet in length. A hinged end-gate permitted easy loading and unloading. Eight to twelve wagon bows held up the heavy canvas which had puckering draw ropes to close each end. The wood was usually of oak, well-seasoned, and a wagon would weigh from 3,000 to 4,000 pounds. The front wheels were three-feet six-inches in diameter, the real wheels four-feet eight-inches in diameter. Where well-organized freighting systems functioned, and trains of several wagons were made up for the same route, an extra front wheel and an extra rear wheel would be carried on every fifth or sixth wagon. A large tool box and a water barrel were ironed to opposite sides of the wagons. It took six to eight big draft horses, or a dozen oxen to pull the wagons, loaded with two to four tons of freight.

Q. *What are the principal parts of a saddle?*

A. The Western stock saddle has the horn, the fork or tree, the seat, and the cantle, with which all riders are familiar. It has the skirts, with their sheepskin lining to soften the wear on the horse's back. It has the cinch, and the latigo strap, with which the saddle is "screwed down" on the horse. There are many additional parts, such as the gullet (the open front part of the fork), the fork covering of leather, the tie strings for tying parcels, raincoats, etc., on the saddle, the lariat strap, or keeper, to hold the rope, the cinch rings, stirrup leathers, fenders and stirrups.

Q. *On which side of the saddle was the rifle, in its scabbard or boot, carried?*

A. It depended on the rider. Guns were carried on either side. Some cowmen like the rifle, or carbine, on the left side, so it would not interfere with getting and using the lariat, which almost all carried on the right side. The gun scabbards were slung in various ways, so the rifle stock could be in a forward position, or to the rear. The U.S. cavalry usually carried the carbine on the right side, stock to the rear for easy access to right hand and shoulder.

Photo courtesy Union Pacific Railroad.

Q. *Was the first transcontinental railroad relatively free from maintenance and in a position to return profit on capital once it was completed?*

A. The completion of the railroad, and the driving of the Golden Spike at Promontory, Utah, marked the beginning of a long and costly period of up-grading and improving the right-of-way. An example is shown of the replacement of wooden pilings with heavy stone in this view along the Union Pacific. Also many new and improved sidings were called for.

12 TOWNS, TERRITORIES, TRANS-PORTATION and COMMUNICATION

The westward advance of the pioneer was not that of settlements which gradually extended further and further across the continent. For one thing, there was the "Great American Desert" to be hurdled. For many years after the discoveries of Jedediah Smith and the trips made by Army dragoons across this "wasteland," which is now a part of the productive Midwest, peoples from the eastern parts of the U.S. who might otherwise have been enticed into settling this broad region were scared away by the term *desert*. That the region was arid was true. But it was not desert. Still, the pioneers who settled Oregon, the miners who opened up California, and the many freighters who passed along the Sante Fe Trail never considered stopping to try out the lands over which they trod. Instead they hurdled it. Vast areas were merely outlined on maps and known as Territories.

This situation did provide the impetus for the development of one or two needed civilizing factors—transportation and communication. And so the great stage routes were developed to cross the Great American Desert as quickly as possible, and such names as the Butterfield Trail and Ben Holladay became famous. And when greater speed to deliver the U.S. mails became necessary, the Pony Express was born. Only a year's time later the new transcontinental railroad was built, and the telegraph lines spanned the Western lands. These latter two factors soon established the basis for the settlement of the Midwest and West, and began that long process of town building, statehood, and the settling of the vast lands that had been acquired by the railroads. A benevolent government had bestowed upon the railroads such land grants as had never been known since the Spanish kings. Every other section of land was donated to the railroad builders, in some instances as far as twenty miles back from the rail lines. So it was only natural that the railroads' sharp business managers soon were offering these lands at what seemed to be extremely attractive prices both here and abroad. Now the land boom grew. When the

303

lands alongside the railroads had been comfortably settled, pioneers searched for government homestead lands along the water courses. When those lands were settled, still later homesteaders took up claims in the hill lands, where water had to be pumped with windmills from wells nearly two hundred feet in depth.

With all this development, towns sprung up along the new railroad lines like morning-glories along a fence line; within a few years other inland villages set up a struggle for existence. County road lines were surveyed, and the farmers along them were permitted to work out their tax debts in constructing and maintaining these roads. Post offices were established, and the star mail routes provided services for all within the reach of a greatly expanded U.S. Post Office Service.

Thus was the barrier of the Great American Desert resolved, with rail lines, mail routes, county roads, productive farms, livestock ranches, and irrigation, where such was available from the water sources. The great revolution in labor-saving machinery that was in its infancy soon burgeoned into the Industrial Revolution.

Territories became states. The empty prairie lands became towns and cities and farmlands. The railroads and later the automotive industry, and still later the great air transportation services, resolved the problems of personal transportation and the carrying of heavy crops to market. The telephone and later the radio and the television resolved the problem of fast communication. The newspaper and all the printed forms permitted people to know what had happened in distant lands the day the events occurred.

But it had not always been like this. There were the years when a mother and father with a baby sick with diphtheria could do little but sit over its crib in their little sod home and watch their child die. They had no telephone, and there was not a doctor within thirty miles. Nor would that doctor have known what to do had they been able to ask him. Nor could they find transportation even had there been a hospital within thirty miles. Yet somehow they endured and solved their problems in their own way. This is what we now call a nation a'building.

Q. *Why did the pioneers speak of the Black Hills as being near Cheyenne, Wyoming? Are they not far to the north and east, in South Dakota?*

A. The Laramie Plains, in Wyoming, elevation about 7,000 feet, extend a hundred miles north and south from the Colorado line and are some fifty miles in width, from the crest of the Laramie Mountains, on the east, to Medicine Bow Mountains on the west. The Wyoming cattle industry originated in this region, and through here the Union Pacific Railroad first completed its transcontinental tracks. This area became well known as the "Black Hills" to trappers and explorers and mountain men before the now famous Black Hills of the Dakotas came into prominence during the later gold discoveries of 1874-76. This original Black Hills area, before the white man came, was highly prized by the Indians who fought over it, for the land produced much wild game, timber for fuel, and wonderful wood for bows, from whence the town of Medicine Bow received its name.

Q. *How did the Dakota Bad Lands get their name?*

A. From the Indians: *Mako*, land; *Sica*, bad. An early French-Canadian trapper made his literal translation, *Mauvaises Terres*, or "bad lands."

Q. *Who was the man who did the most to promote the state of Oregon when it was a frontier land, far from the population centers in the East?*

A. Hal J. Kelley is generally given this honor as Oregon's pioneer one-man chamber of commerce, when the region was a territory. In the 1820s, this Boston schoolteacher wrote pamphlets and letters and made speeches petitioning Congress for its aid to claim and settle Oregon. Not until 1833, however, did Kelley himself set out for this land, going by Mexico and overland to California and then helping to take a horse herd to Oregon. Though he was disappointed with his reception, he returned to Boston in 1835, still lauding the land; he was effective in promoting further American settlements there.

Q. *Where did the state of Arizona get its name?*

A. Arizona Territory was named after a place called Arizonac, in the Altar Valley of northern Arizona, where silver was found in 1736. A "silver rush" followed, but within five years the mines played out and the camp was abandoned. But the name stayed on.

Q. *When was Nevada Territory organized and when did that state enter the union?*

A.   The territory was organized March 2, 1861, out of western Utah. Nevada entered the union as a state (the thirty-sixth) October 31, 1864.

Q.   *When was Dakota Territory organized?*

A.   Three attempts were made, in September 1858, again in 1859, and in 1860, at Yankton, South Dakota, before Congress passed the Act of March 2, 1861, creating the territory out of the western remnant of old Minnesota Territory and the new Dakota lands.

Q.   *Has any history been written about southwestern Nebraska?*

A.   Yes, the comprehensive *Andreas' History of Nebraska* tells of every county in the state. A recent booklet, *Tepees to Soddies*, by Everett S. Sutton is a charming and interesting history of Dundy County and includes accounts of adjoining counties.

Q.   *When did Father Kino begin his explorations in southern Arizona?*

A.   Eusebio Francisco Kino, Italian-born and Bavarian-educated, became a Spanish missionary by consecration. He first visited the Pima Indian village on the Santa Cruz River in 1691.

Q.   *What does the word "Nebraska" mean? My home valley in Vermont has borne that name for 100 years.*

A.   The state's name came from an Indian word, which Indians along the Platte River pronounced *Nebrathka*. It means flat water. The Indians referred to the wide, slow-flowing Platte River. Gen. John C. Fremont, as a young lieutenant in 1842, exploring the plains and mountains, first used the word to refer to the region of the Platte's waters. William Wilkins, secretary of war, in his report of 1844 said, "The Platte, or Nebraska River, being the central stream, would very properly furnish a name to the [new] territory."

Q.   *What, in your opinion, is the prettiest-sounding name in the West?*

A.   There are so many lovely names that I find it hard to state a preference. For example, there are Uravan, Colorado and Coeur d'Alene, Idaho—and isn't Idaho itself a beautiful name? There is Capulin, in New Mexico, and Ovando, Montana. How about Sierre Madre? And Amarillo? Or Tonopah, in Nevada? Or Atascadero, California?

And Cheyenne is beautiful too. My old home towns of Broken Bow and Scottsbluff in Nebraska both have interesting names, though perhaps not as pretty to the ear as some others. I expect, had I to choose only one, I would take *Cimarron* for phonetic beauty; a Spanish word, it means "wild" or "pristine."

Q. *What happened to the old territorial prison at Yuma, Arizona?*

A. After the new prison was constructed at Florence (1912), the old prison was eventually turned into a state park (in the early 1960s). They have a museum there now, displaying many items associated with the vile old prison that once held the felons there on the Colorado River.

Q. *What happened to the old Ezra Meeker mansion at Puyallup, Washington?*

A. The Ezra Meeker Historical Society, Inc., was formed in 1970 and received a bank loan for the restoration and perpetuation of the fine old home, I am told by Hazel Hood, the chairman of the Meeker Family History organization. The loan is nearly repaid now, and with volunteer work by local people, the restoration is nearly complete. The mansion is on the National Historic Register and tourists are invited to tour the building. The Society has republished several books on Meeker, in addition to his own 1907 autobiography *The Ox Team, or the Old Oregon Trail, 1852-1906*. Meeker, who with his wife, Eliza Jane, in 1852 traveled the old Oregon Trail to Washington state, founded his landhold there and attained an enormous success as a farmer. In 1906, in a desperate attempt to interest the American people in marking the old Oregon Trail, he took an ox team and made the return trip to New York and Washington, D.C. A second trip was made in 1910, when Meeker was eighty years of age. At age ninety-four, Meeker flew over the old Oregon Trail in a plane. Though he was ruined financially in the 1890s, Ezra Meeker never wavered in his crusade to see the Oregon Trail included as a landmark in the heritage of this country.

Q. *When I read the autobiography of an old pioneer recently, I was amazed at the number of towns, trails, and other places named after the book's subject. Could all this be true?*

A. Yes and no. The earliest towns did receive names from pioneer mountain men (Bridger, Wyoming), cattlemen (Goodnight, Texas), soldiers (Casper, Wyoming), and animals (Wolf Point, Montana). Some old trails were named after ranchers and cowmen, like the famous Jones & Plummer Trail from Mobeetie, Texas, to Dodge City. And many towns drew names from geographical features, like old Indian names, from heroes of various sorts, and from businessmen and developers of the West. But there is a weakness in writers of autobiography for proclaiming themselves "the greatest," insisting that towns and rivers and places were named after them. This creates problems for the later historian trying to ferret out the real origin of the name.

Q. *A cowhand here on this ranch tells me there are fewer towns in Rhode Island (where I am from) than in this unpopulated state of Nevada. Tell him he's crazy.*

A. He's right. Rhode Island has approximately 91 towns, with Nevada having about 111. But Rhode Island's population has *dropped* to 945, 762. Nevada's population has *grown* to 663,000.

Q. *Where was the original Boot Hill Cemetery located?*

A. Many Western towns had one: Dodge City, Tascosa, Mobeetie, Tombstone, and others. Nearly all ghost towns have a nearby hill called "Boot Hill." These cemeteries served a need in pioneer times, receiving the remains of both respectable citizen and outlaw. It is impossible to say which was "first."

Q. *What is the name of the cemetery that replaced Boot Hill at Dodge City, Kansas?*

A. The bodies from old Boot Hill were removed to the newer Prairie Grove Cemetery. Later, when this cemetery was closed, the bodies were removed again to Maple Grove Cemetery, west of the town. Such famous Dodge citizens as Ham Bell, R.J. Hardesty, I.P. (Print) Olive, Ida Ellen Rath, Robert M. Wright, and the notorious Ben Hodges rest there today. The old Boot Hill Cemetery is now a part of the Front Street replica and enjoys a fine tourist business, with false graves of "bad men" and "bad women" of the early Dodge demi-monde.

Q. *Where did the stream called Weeping Water, in Nebraska, derive its name?*

A. As far back as 1755, as indicated on an old map, the French trappers and traders called it *L'eau qui pleure*, or "the river that cries." Possibly the sound from a cataract where a creek falls into the river suggested the name to the Frenchmen. There is also a tradition of a great battle between Indian tribes where many from both sides died in the struggle. The weeping of the survivors and the widows, so this old folk tale goes, suggested the name.

Q. *What is the story behind the ghost site of Kelso, Texas?*

A. When the great XIT Ranch of Texas was broken up and sold, land promoters acquired 80,000 acres around the area where Kelso was planned. The speculators surveyed the region, plotted a town, erected a nice hotel building and a large red barn and wagon yard. They then brought in special trainloads of prospects, wined them and dined them—and sold them land at inflated prices, as some developers do today. When the land was sold, the promoters dismantled hotel, barn, and wagon yard and moved. Kelso was no more.

Q. *Can you give me the exact geographical location of the Hole-in-the-Wall Gang's operation in Wyoming, the hide-out of those outlaws?*

A. *The Writer's Project Book on Wyoming* gives this location and description: "Take the dirt road from Kaycee, Wyoming, cross the Red Fork of Powder River to Red Canyon, or Hole-in-the-Wall, a gap washed through the Red Wall by the Middle Fork of Powder River. The Wall, a jutting fork 35 miles in length, runs straight south and then bends west. The region to the west is also known as Hole-in-the-Wall, but is not a basin or deep valley.... To the 35-mile length there was only one eastern entrance, which a few armed men could easily defend...." A practical way to reach Hole-in-the-Wall from Casper, Wyoming, is to take the highway US 26 to Powder River, go north past Dead Man's Butte and on to the Buffalo Creek Ranch, then follow Buffalo Creek north to the Hole-in-the-Wall.

Q. *What is the meaning of the word, "Uncompahgre," as used in western Colorado?*

A. There are two interpretations: (1) It is said to come from the Ute Indian word, *ancapogari*, meaning "red lake." (2) Others believe it is from the Ute words *unca,* or hot, *pah*, water, and *gre*, meaning spring, "hot water spring." There is a hot, red-water spring near the head-waters of this river, the Uncompahgre.

Q. *Was there ever a town called Beer City, Kansas?*

A. No, not in Kansas, but there was such a disreputable place two miles south of what is today Liberal, Kansas, and just across the Oklahoma panhandle line. The town originally was known as "Tent City," and "White City," for it was composed only of tent saloons and it came into being just as the railroad arrived in that section of the country. Beer City was a "bloody, boozy spot on the Plains, the Southwestern Sodom and Gomorrah," which appealed to the cowboy trade when the Rock Island Railroad started picking up the trainloads of longhorn cattle, from New Mexico, Texas, and the Indian Nations, which the state of Kansas had forbidden to cross its lands in 1885, because of the Texas ticks that killed settlers' cattle. The town's dissolute characters and their exploits are described in the book *Lost Trails of the Cimarron*, published by Swallow Press, Chicago.

Q. *How did Cripple Creek, Colorado, get its name?*

A. One source says a Levi Welty and family lived along its banks. Their cow stepped in a prairie dog hole and broke its leg. Welty's son cut his foot with an axe, causing his father to remark, "We better call this place Cripple Creek." Another source says the rocky nature of the creek bottom caused horses and cattle to become crippled. The last time I was there in 1978, the great, gaping holes along the sidewalk on the south side of its main street could have caused a man to become crippled. So the name is still applicable.

Q. *Why is the name Lead, South Dakota, though spelled like the metal "lead," pronounced "leed"?*

A. It is pronounced as it should be, for a miner's lead (leed), in a vein of ore, is responsible for its name.

Q. *Why was Council Grove, Kansas, such a discussed town and so highly rated as a stopping place on the Santa Fe Trail?*

A. Originally it was just a rendezvous point for traders and trappers. It had a fine spring, timber for fires, and became a place where the wagon trains stopped overnight and formed their trains to head west. The caravans dated their departures from that point. There, the Government Survey Commission made treaties with the Indians, obtaining safe passage across their lands. There was the Kaw Mission, the Council Oak Tree, the old post office oak (just a great hole in an old oak tree where mail was left for others to sort and carry either West or East). There was the Last Chance Store where those heading West could pick up some items, and also the Hays Tavern, where one might have a drink or two before passing on. Tourists still stop there to see its interesting features.

Q. *Can you tell me something of Winona, North Dakota, which was a gambling town back in the 1880s?*

A. Winona started up in 1884 and declined after nearby Fort Yates was abandoned in 1903. The town was said to have once had nine saloons and a race track. The soldiers went to Winona to visit the brothels and drink whiskey. The Indian agent at Standing Rock Agency made complaints because the "blind pigs" and the "hog ranches" in Winona sold whiskey to the Indians.

Q. *When Amarillo, Texas sprang up, Panhandle City, just thirteen miles distant, was already a good-sized town. What happened to make the former such a large city today, and the latter another small town?*

A. The late Laura V. Hamner, Texas historian, said it was because of the failure of the railroad to keep its commitment to build through Panhandle City. Though the Fort Worth & Denver City main line missed Panhandle City, the railroad did build a spur to the town. But Amarillo, on the mainline, grew apace and soon eclipsed Panhandle City, becoming a central shipping point for the great north Texas cattle industry. With the natural gas and oil booms of recent years, Amarillo has become the true "Queen City of the Texas Panhandle."

Q. *How did Show Low, Arizona come by such a name?*

A. Two partners on a large ranch near that place engaged in a card game of dealer's choice. They were Croyden E. Cooley, a famous Indian scout, and his friend Marion Clark, a cowman. Cooley, when challenged by Clark to "show low," that is show the lowest hand in a bet to win the ranch, did so with a deuce, trey, five, six and seven, in all suits. Clark, holding a pair of eights, dropped his cards and said, "The ranch is yours, take it and be damned."

They both went to the bar for a friendly drink, and the town became Show Low.

Q. *What was the "Drunk's Hole" in the Old West?*

A. Beaver, Oklahoma, when a young village in the 1880s, had no money for a jail. At first the villagers stretched a dried steer hide and pegged drunks under it. Later, they had a deep hole dug in the ground for a town well, not yet completed, and put them in it to cool off. This was soon called the "Drunk's Hole."

Q. *How long was the town of Border, on the old National Cattle Trail in Stanton County, Kansas, in existence?*

A. The first supply store was erected there in 1885. A post office was authorized August 12, 1887, and discontinued November 15, 1893. The end of the trail cattle business, in 1886–87, guaranteed the town's death. But homesteaders kept it alive for a few years into the '90s. Trail City, Colorado, its counterpart on the cattle trail, lasted from 1884 to 1887. The latter was three miles west of present Coolidge, Kansas, just across the Colorado state line.

Q. *Who was the first white child born in Dodge City?*

A. Robert M. Wright, a good authority, in his book *Dodge City, The Cowboy Capital*, relates how a young doctor came into the drug store early one morning and admitted he had delivered an illegitimate child from a notorious whore in the city. The child's name was never given out. "This was in the fall of 1872," Wright wrote. Soon afterward, Claude McCarty, son of Dr. and Mrs. T.L. (Sally) McCarty, was born, and just a bit later Jesse Rath, a son of Mr. and Mrs. Charles Rath was born, dying in infancy. So Claude McCarty is generally credited with being the "first honored child" born in Dodge City.

Q. *Who first owned the famous Longbranch Saloon in Dodge City?*

A. In 1877 Colley & Manion owned it. In 1878 Chalkley Beeson bought the building from Robert M. Wright and the name, Longbranch, stayed with the building. Colley & Manion moved into the Alamo, one door to the west.

Q. *I see so many wild stories on TV and in magazines about Dodge City, Kansas, I would like to get some factual books or papers about the place, 1872 to 1900. What do you recommend?*

A. *The Cowboy Capital*, by Robert M. Wright; *The Rath Trail*, by Ida Ellen Rath; *Early Ford County*, by I.E. Rath; *Annals of Kansas*, Vols. 1 and 2; *Why the West Was Wild*, by Miller & Snell; *Lost Trails of the Cimarron*, by H.E. Chrisman. All are books that deal honestly with this subject. Also the original Robert A. Eagan collection on Dodge City, at the Denver Public Library (Western Division) contains much factual material in photos and text on Dodge. Also ask at this Denver library for the Merritt Beeson card catalog of the Dodge City newspapers of that era.

Q. *Who organized Trail City, Colorado, on the old National Cattle Trail?*

A. A group of Dodge City men, among whom were H.M. Beverly, Martin Culver, and I.P. Olive, organized the town company about 1884-85. They hoped to make it another Dodge City, but the trail days came to an end shortly and the town died.

Q. *Was Mrs. Louisa Gore, who operated the Drover's Cottage at Abilene, the same woman who was in the hotel at Ellsworth?*

A. Yes. The Drover's Cottage itself was moved by rail to the new cow town, at Ellsworth, when the cattle shipping business tapered off (because of the settlement of the country) at Abilene. Mr. and Mrs. Gore simply had their business building moved.

Q. *I know that Joseph McCoy was largely responsible for getting Abilene started as a cattle shipping point. But how did he manage to get the Texas drovers to bring their herds there?*

A. McCoy, a shrewd businessman, was sustained and financed by Kansas City businessmen, who realized that if McCoy could wrangle lower freight rates over the Hannibal & St. Joseph Railroad from the Missouri River to Quincy, Illinois, and on to Chicago, then he would bring the Texas cattle into their area, and hence profit their railways, their packing houses, and their entire region. So when they backed him, making it easier for the Texas growers to get their beef to market, they won the Texas business. We must recall that in Reconstruction years, Texas was flat broke, as was the rest of the Southland, and the "Yankee Gold" that Texas drovers brought back with them appealed to all.

Q. *When was the Alamo, famous in Texas history, established?*

A. It was founded as the Mission of San Antonio de Valera, on May 1, 1718, by a Spanish expedition led by Governor Martin de Alarcon of Coahuila, Mexico. Two miles upstream, on the San Antonio River, they also founded the Villa of San Antonio de Bejar, now the city of San Antonio.

Q. *Where and when was the first Spanish mission established in what is today the continental United States of America?*

A. In 1659 the Mission of Guadalupe was established at what is now the city of Juarez, on the west bank of the Rio Grande. In 1685, LaSalle established a French colony on the Texas coast. The LaSalle colony appeared as a grave threat to the Spaniards, and after a flurry of exploration, the Mission of San Francisco was established near the Neches River, on the eastern border of Texas. This mission, however, was short-lived. By October 1693 the priests were forced by the Indians to leave. So the church was burned, and the Spaniards fled. For the next twenty years, Texas was abandoned by the Spaniards.

Q. *I have read that hippies have taken over Taos, New Mexico, and that tourists are avoiding that town. Is this correct?*

A. In the late 1960s and 1970s there was an influx of young street people to Taos. Many stayed and made homes there, and have become good citizens, willing to "live and let live," which is the way of Taos people. Many Taos businessmen are now happy that these young people came there. Taos, it may be said in passing, has absorbed many cultures and ethnic groups.

Q. *What design did the first builders of the cowboy chuckwagon follow in its construction?*

A. The chuckwagon was actually just a modification of the wagons used by surgeons in the later years of the Civil War. Those light wagons had a chest of medical supplies on shelves at the rear end, a drop end-gate that was used as an operating table. The wagon had shelving that contained a goodly supply of medicines and surgical equipment. The medical wagons of the Civil War were covered over to keep the interiors dry. They were *not* used as ambulances, except in special cases, but were the "field hospitals" of that time, offering the surgeons a mobile unit which could be moved rapidly to the scene of the battle. The wagons were horse-drawn, of course, with a driver assigned to each wagon to care for the teams. There have been stories of how Charles Goodnight and others "invented" the first chuckwagon. But this is nonsense. The chuckwagon had evolved out of men's experiences in the war, and the Texas men were probably the first to use the wagons on the "cow hunts" in Texas in the 1860s.

Q. *What was a jockey box on a chuckwagon?*

A. Both chuckwagons and freighting wagons had tool boxes that carried farrier's tools, axle grease, tar buckets, and items for repair of wheels or wagons. These boxes were referred to as the jockey box.

Q. *I have heard that the genuine Conestoga wagon was not used by the pioneers traveling west from the Mississippi to the West Coast. True?*

A. A few of these big wagons did serve as freight wagons, but the family-type wagons, particularly the Pittsburg, also made in Pennsylvania, was the favorite of most pioneers who were unable to supply the six to ten oxen needed for the larger outfits.

Q. *What did one of the Peter Shuttler wagons cost in the 1870s?*

A. In the late 1860s and 1870s a wagon cost about $150 to $200. A spring seat cost $20. A wagon cover (jet sheet) cost $10 to $12. By 1910 a good, heavy two-ton capacity farm wagon cost less than $50.

Q. *Why were so many wagon trains lost on the journey from Yuma, Arizona, to Redlands (near San Bernardino), California in the gold rush days?*

A. The terrible sandstorms obliterated trails. Some of the rusted iron parts and dried boards from these old wagon trains are found far off the proper trail, evidence of the many tragedies along and near that old trail.

Q. *Where did the covered wagons get the name "prairie schooners"?*

A. The Conestoga wagons had the appearance of boats and were so constructed to aid in making river crossings. The wagons built for Stephen Austin and Gail Borden were also built in this manner. The resemblance of white wagon sheets to sails probably added to this inventive name for the prairie wagons.

Q. *Where, if anywhere, do they hold reenactments of wagon trains crossing the prairies in the U.S.?*

A. Several states feature such reenactments, usually along the old routes such as the Oregon or Santa Fe trails. The historical societies of the various Western states will give you the information and dates on these trips. The general public is invited to "take a wagon train trip," and fees are low, and much fun en route is reported on these one-week or ten-day trips.

Q. *How much did pioneers on wagon trains pay for supplies at various points en route?*

A. According to John Bidwell, who was with the Bartleson wagon train in 1843, powder was one dollar per cup; lead, one-and-one-half dollars per pound; sugar, one dollar per cup; flour, one dollar per cup; tobacco, two dollars per pound; a butcher knife was one to three dollars; and a gun would bring as much as a good horse.

Q. *Why did ox teams have so much difficulty pulling freight loads across deep-water fords?*

A. Oxen, pulling under a yoke, have to keep their heads low to pull the wagons. In deep water, this caused them to turn their heads sideways, and upward, or their muzzles would be in the water and they could not breathe.

Q. *How many wagons constituted a "freighter's train" in the 1850s and 1860s?*

A. Alexander Majors's trains consisted of twenty-five or twenty-six large wagons, each carrying three to three-and-a-half tons, and drawn by six oxen.

Q. *Who were the personnel of a wagon train?*

A. The personnel of the Majors' train consisted of the wagonmaster, or captain, his assistant, a teamster for each wagon (bullwhacker), a herder for the 320 to 330 extra head of cattle and oxen, a farrier, and two or three extra men to fill vacancies that arose. The trains averaged twelve to fifteen miles daily, loaded and twenty miles per day when empty on the return trips. The oxen could travel 2,000 miles in the season, 1,200 to 1,500 miles of that pulling loaded wagons.

Q. *What types of wagons were used on the Santa Fe Trail for freighting purposes?*

A. The Conestoga, the Pittsburgh, and the Santa Fe were the three most popular. With a load of no more than three tons, four span of mules or oxen could handle the wagon; when weight was added up to five or six tons, two or three span, or yoke, were added to handle the extra weight.

Q. *How did a jerkline work on freight teams?*

A. Usually six to eight span of mules or horses made up a jerkline outfit. The driver rode the left wheel animal. The jerkline extended from his hand, through rings on the left hames of the other left-hand horses, to the bridle bit or halter of the left lead animal. A series of two to four sharp jerks caused the left lead animal to turn to the *right*; a slow pull caused the left lead animal to turn to the *left*. The right lead animal was connected to the left lead animal by a jockey stick attached to its bridle bit or halter and then to the right hame of the left leader. Various hitches and devices were employed, but the above is the general arrangement used for jerkline control.

Q. *In the earliest times, the Spaniards and Mexicans used two-wheeled wooden carts to haul freight from Santa Fe to Mexico City. What were these carts called?*

A. The long, narrow carts were called *carretas*. By piling the merchandise or raw commodities high, and using wooden stakes on the sides, the freighters prevented the articles from falling off. Oddly enough, though hitched to the *front* of the carts, the animals (oxen) actually *pushed* the load; for ox bows were not used and the wagon tongue was lashed to the oxen's horns with leather straps, enabling the animals, by pushing forward, to move the load.

Q. *What originally prompted Josiah Gregg, the early American author, to travel West on the old freighting trails?*

A. Gregg was almost an invalid. In 1831, when he was twenty-five, his doctor advised him to make a trip West to overcome his illness. Gregg remained in Santa Fe for two years, studying the business methods of the people and regaining his health in the high, dry air of what is today New Mexico.

Q. *Was Capt. William Becknell the first to use the Santa Fe Trail?*

A. This trail had been used many, many years before Becknell "discovered" it. The Mexican Comancheros and the Spanish had pretty well established it as a route to Santa

Fe, after the Indians had followed it for many years from hunting ground to hunting ground. Jedediah Smith's grandnephew told how Smith had traveled most of this trail to Santa Fe in 1818. But Becknell is generally given the credit for "discovering" it and for "first using it."

Q. *What is meant by the expression "to neck an animal"?*

A. The term is used, as is the term "yoke an animal," to mean to tie one animal to a gentler animal, to get control over the former.

Q. *What was a "dog trail" in the early West?*

A. Many early "dog trails" became the main travel routes of the West. The trails were made by Indians' dogs, dragging a small *travois*, in the years before Indians had horses. In his *History of Kansas*, Noble L. Prentis states: "All these [dog trails] left their mark in Kansas in the years when it was not an undiscovered country [that is after Coronado's journey in 1541], but lying open and void, waiting for the rise of the Star of Empire." Without doubt, many of the north-south dog trails were laid down upon the same traffic patterns followed by the buffalo in their annual migrations; these are used today as super-highways.

Q. *Is it true that the old Oregon Trail was actually many trails, not just one?*

A. It can hardly be said that there are "many" Oregon Trails, for there is actually only one main road. However, in many places where pioneers thought to make better time, or to avoid bad river crossings, or in other ways to relieve themselves and their animals of harder work than necessary to traverse the country, they would branch away from the main road for a few miles. As a result, some of the better "cut-offs" were formed and later used almost exclusively. The Mormons, for example, followed the north side of the Platte River in Nebraska for quite a few miles, though the main road of the Oregon Trail followed the south side of the river, passing through Mitchell Pass, near present Scotts Bluff National Monument.

Q. *Did Indians have any special word to describe the covered wagons they saw crossing the Plains?*

A. They called them "tepees on wheels," an apt description, or as the Sioux put it, *Hoo-ha Wa-Keh-Ya*, a wheel-tent, or *Te-Yah-dah*, home.

Q. *What was the Lander Cut-Off on the Oregon Trail; why so named and what was its purpose?*

A. In 1857 Congress appropriated funds to improve the Government Road (Oregon Trail) from the Missouri River to Oregon. William F. McGraw got the contract for the work. The following spring, when the road gang was breaking its winter camp on the Popo Agie River, Col. F.W. Lander arrived and took command of the work. Lander then proceeded to improve the road and created the Lander Cut-Off, a new approach to Fort Hall. It began at South Pass, shortening the two previous roads, the old trail that had dipped southwest to Fort Bridger and the newer Sublette Cut-Off, which crossed from South Pass to Bear Lake. Lander's new cut-off headed toward the mountains from South Pass on the Sweetwater River and struck Green River at a much higher point than did the old Sublette road. Colonel Lander negotiated a treaty with Chief Washakie of the Shoshones to cross their boundary lands and to build the new road. The old ruts of the Lander Cut-off are still visible across that sagebrush-covered land.

Q. *What was the expression about cowards on the Western trails?*

A. "The Cowards never started, and the Weak died along the trails."

Q. *When did the cholera epidemic hit travelers on the Oregon Trail route west? Did St. Louis also have such an epidemic?*

A. Yes, cholera hit St. Louis in 1832, 1848, and 1853, and as late as 1873. It was called "asiatic cholera." The disease seemed to follow travelers up the trails in 1848 and 1853.

Q. *What year did Jesse Chisholm lay out the old Chisholm Trail?*

A. Chisholm is believed to have taken supplies down this old Indian trail in 1864 to Council Grove, the site of an old Indian trading post he had formerly operated on the North Canadian River. But it is not correct to speak of him "laying out" the trail, for he was following an older trail that had been used as early as 1834 when the Delaware scout, Black Beaver, guided Army dragoons along this north-south pathway. Nor did Black Beaver "discover" or "lay out" this trail, for it was an ancient trail used by the Plains Indians in following the buffalo migrations during their hunting seasons. The natural terrain and the ease of obtaining water along the streams and natural lakes were factors that first determined where the natural pathways would extend. When Texas cattlemen brought their herds north, they used the established routes. What they called "the Chisholm Trail," after Jesse Chisholm, the old hunter and freighter, was among the best-known trails at the time. Today, that old trail is almost straddled by U.S. Highway 81 across Oklahoma from Terral, Oklahoma, to Caldwell, Kansas. In all ages we seem to cling to the most accessible and easiest routes of travel.

Q. *Has any estimate ever been made of the number of names carved on Independence Rock on the Oregon Trail in Wyoming?*

A. Yes, the Natrona County (Wyoming) Historical Society, in their publication *Independence Rock*, 1930, compiled not just the numbers but the actual names and dates. There were 750 names. They are carved from the top to the bottom of the great marker.

Q. *Is there any worthwhile book written by a person who has,* in recent years, *followed the old Oregon Trail? We plan a trip up that trail next summer and would like to familiarize our family with the subject.*

A. I highly recommend Irene Paden's *Wake of the Prairie Schooner*, published by Macmillan in 1953. Your library or historical society may loan you a copy if you can't buy one. The book tells the interesting story of Mrs. Paden and her family's many experiences on the trail, with excellent historical descriptions and anecdotes. Also consult Merril J. Mattes's *The Great Platte River Road*, published by University of Nebraska Press, 1969.

Q. *How could anyone use bull boats and other boats to bring hides down the Platte River in old times? There was hardly a drop of water in that river when I came down it last fall on Highway 26.*

A. Things change, don't they? The Platte, like many rivers, now has its water flow impounded in several dams for irrigation purposes in places like the Pathfinder Dam near Casper, Wyoming, in the Ogalalla Dam, near Ogalalla, Nebraska, etc. The water is now let into the river channel as needed downstream. You picked a poor season to see the Platte in free flow, for it is a wide and beautiful stream at times.

Q.   *Was there ever actually a woman trail driver?*

A.   Yes, it is well authenticated that Mrs. Margaret Heffernan Barland made the trail drive to Wichita, Kansas, in 1873. She contracted malaria fever on the trip and died in Wichita. The *Victoria Advocate* (Texas) tells her story in volume 88, number 12, page 63. There may have been other women, too, but trail-driving was principally a man's work. There is a record of another lady, Mrs. D. Welborn Barton, accompanying her husband, "Doc" Barton, in a buggy on a trail drive, but I have heard of no others who rode horseback up the trail.

Q.   *When did the last Texas cattle drives to Dodge City take place?*

A.   In 1885. Kansas law forbade Texas herds to cross the state after that because of the danger of tick fever and the settlement of the High Plains country. Drives continued a few years up the National Cattle Trail, along the Colorado-Kansas line.

Q.   *Have there ever been "drives" of other animals comparable to the Texas cattle drives of the 1870s?*

A.   Do fowl count? If so, and if a letter in the August 1852 mail from California can be trusted (as quoted by the *Kansas Historical Quarterly*), then an Illinois man came through Independence, Missouri, with a flock of 2,000 turkeys, "all hale and hearty." The turkeys were bound for Western markets. "He has been offered eight dollars apiece," the letter stated. Sheep, we know, have been driven to and from California by the thousands, and horses in herds of up to and more than 1,000 head have been moved great distances, such as from Texas to Nebraska, and from Oregon to Montana and Wyoming. Barbed wire and railroad transportation ended these numerically large, long-distance drives.

Q.   *I recently read that the genuine joining of the transcontinental railroad did not occur at Promontory, Utah, as is generally attributed by historians, but at some remote place in Colorado. Is this true?*

A.   Yes, when the ceremony of "joining the rails" of the Union Pacific and the line that came in from California was held at Promontory Point, Utah, *there were gaps in the actual transcontinental railroad.* The very *last* of these gaps to be closed was at Strasburg, Colorado. When the Kansas Pacific Railroad bridged the Missouri River, it made Strasburg the actual point of completion of the transcontinental railroad. This event took place August 15, 1870, not in 1869 in Utah. Emma Mitchell, Strasburg, Colorado, author and historian, has been working hard to put this point across to all interested people, particularly historians and railroad buffs.

Q. *What was the Old Wire Trail to Dodge City?*

A. It was the Military Road, running from Fort Dodge to Camp Supply, in the Indian Territory. This road paralleled the military telegraph line. The poles were made of iron to withstand prairie fires, which were allegedly set in the fall of the year by Indians to concentrate the game for their hunts. Occasionally the route was referred to as the Iron Trail.

Q. *How many riders did the Pony Express employ during its active life delivering the mail?*

A. No authoritative list or roster appears to have been left. However, the papers of Maj. William B. Waddell (of Russell, Majors, and Waddell) found in Lexington, Missouri, in 1942, together with other papers, indicate that at least 120 young men were involved in carrying the Pony Express mail. This list, incidentally, *did* include the name of William F. Cody. Russell, Majors, and Waddell carried mail for the U.S. government on a semi-monthly schedule over the western trail to California (via Salt Lake).

Q. *How many Pony Express stations were there between St. Joseph, Missouri, and Sacramento, California?*

A. Approximately 119 stations are reported to have been established on that 1,966-mile-long route. About every 75 to 100 miles on the route was a "Home Station," where a rider could sleep, eat, and rest before starting back.

Q. *Was the Pony Express owned and operated by Wells Fargo & Company?*

A. No. It was created, owned, and operated by Russell, Majors, and Waddell, a major freighting and stage company. Wells Fargo & Company were appointed local agents for the Pony Express at Sacramento and at San Francisco on May 16, 1861. The Pony Express, operated in its final stage by the Overland Mail Company, ceased its operations entirely October 24, 1861. The advent of the telegraph system ended its need for fast communication. The telegraph line was being built even as the Pony Express was in operation, and many travelers, including Mark Twain, have written of these fast couriers passing even the swiftest stagecoaches on their way and waving to the lineman and grunts building the telegraph line.

Q. *What was the average distance ridden daily by a Pony Express rider?*

A. According to Alexander Majors of Russell, Majors, and Waddell, the average distance was thirty-three and one-third miles daily. Three horses were ridden on this run. The stations were ten to twelve miles apart, and the horses changed at each station. Majors was the man who sold the idea of the Pony Express to his partners in the firm.

Q. *What were the stagecoaches called that were suspended on leather thoroughbraces to take up shock and make riding easier?*

A. One of them was called the Passenger Wagon, the other the Yellowstone Wagon. The Passenger Wagon was built to seat nine persons inside; the Yellowstone Wagon to seat eleven passengers inside. The Passenger Wagon was frequently used in place of the Mail coach, the latter of which could be ordered to seat twelve passengers inside and cost $1,200 each. The others sold at $750 and $600. All were Abbot, Downing & Company coaches, made in Concord, New Hampshire, and referred to as "Concord coaches."

Q. *What is the meaning of "Jehu," as applied to stage coach drivers and others?*

A. The word comes from the king of Israel, who was noted for his furious attacks by chariot. A stage driver who drove fast—and recklessly or so it seemed to the passengers —was called a Jehu by old-time editors. The *J* is sounded as a *Y*, so the name comes out "Ya-hoo," the more familiar term in Western language.

Q. *How were the stage stations defended along the old stage and Pony Express lines?*

A. The stronger stage stations, and Pony Express home stations, had more defense points than just the stone or wood walls of the buildings. At three triangular points—

the rear and the two front sides of the buildings and corrals—pits were dug with underground passages connecting them with the building. These rifle pits, covered over with stone and having gun slits in all directions, brought a field of fire to every point surrounding the building and its livestock. Plenty of repeating rifles, Spencers, and Henrys were kept there. Old Fort Wallace (then Pond Creek Station) was fortified in this way.

Q. *How did Horace Greeley make his famous trip West by stagecoach? Did he travel all the way from New York to California by stage?*

A. Greeley's trip by stage started from Manhattan, Kansas. He changed from the mud wagon, as the tarp-sided stagecoaches were called, to a private coach, which he took on to Laramie, Wyoming. From Laramie he rode the regular stagecoaches on to California. He had come by train from New York to Kansas.

Q. *Where did the Sidney, Nebraska to the Black Hills stage route cross the North Platte River?*

A. At a point three miles west of the present town of Bridgeport, Nebraska. Henry T. Clarke from Omaha built the bridge across the river in 1875 and it remained the main crossing thereafter. It was sixty miles east of Fort Laramie, Wyoming, the next closest bridge across the river for many years.

Q. *Where could I have a genuine stagecoach (like in the old days) built for my museum?*

A. Nolan Davis and his son, Larry, of Orange, California, have constructed many genuine Western stagecoaches. Davis's maternal grandfather, a Cherokee Indian from North Carolina, taught him the trade. One of Davis's coaches was used in the noted film, "Stagecoach," featuring John Wayne. Davis has built several for Hollywood film companies.

Q. *Where was the fastest long-distance stage run made? What was the condition of the horses after they had finished the race?*

A. The San Francisco to Atchison, Kansas, run made by the Overland Stage Company was probably the longest "fast" run ever completed. The promoter of this stage line, Ben Holladay, made the complete trip. Time: twelve days, two hours and thirteen minutes. This run beat the old time by five full days. It cost Holladay many horses and several coaches, but he was awarded the Overland mail contract for another year for making fast time. In retrospect, it is sad to think how little consideration was given to animals, particularly man's good friend and helpmate, the horse, in pioneer times. Many men thought no more of riding a fine horse to death than he would have thought of tossing away a short cigar butt when his habit was temporarily satisfied. In *Trails of Yesterday*, a book by John Bratt, Nebraska cattleman of the 1870s and 1880s, there is mention of riding good horses until "... Neither of our horses were worth a dollar after that day's work." (p. 225).

Q. *Did stagecoaches on the prairie routes ever get lost in wind storms or blizzards?*

A. Yes, the *Rocky Mountain News*, Denver, May 31 and June 7, 1865, reported a coach with six passengers lost in a blizzard between Coyote and Denver. The driver stopped, stayed overnight on the Plains. No one froze, though the cold was intense. There were many cases of Kansas stages being held up overnight or lost on the Plains.

Q. *How were the stagecoaches (Concords) brought to the West from New Hampshire?*

A. As the early stage lines developed, most of the Concord coaches went West on their own wheels, after reaching the terminus of the railroads. After 1868, when the transcontinental railroad was finished, many were shipped West. One photo shows a Wells Fargo & Company shipment of many carloads of stagecoaches, heading west on flatcars much as we now ship tractors. It is possible, of course, that some of the first stagecoaches may have also reached California after rounding Cape Horn by sea.

Q. *I have read that in the early days of stagecoach travel Wells Fargo & Company, listed their charges as follows: Sacramento to Omaha, $236; Virginia City, Montana to Omaha, $236; Austin, Texas to Omaha, $225; Sacramento to Cheyenne, $250; Salt Lake City to Bannock, Montana, $120. Could these rates be correct?*

A. Possibly so, but the rates sound doubtful. Why would a

fare from Sacramento to Omaha cost fourteen dollars less than to Cheyenne, Wyoming, when Omaha is at least 400 miles or more *east* of Cheyenne?

Q. *I am taking my family on a tour of ghost towns in the fall, particularly those in the Colorado Rockies. Will my Buick be all right for mountain roads?*

A. No. Most autos are too low for the rutted trails you will need to traverse to get to the old towns in the back roads, but you can always hire a Jeep or Scout in nearby towns. Don't attempt, however, a ghost town trip into the back areas in a car with a transmission and muffler as low as that of your Buick.

Q. *How many types of snowshoes are there? Which is best for cross-country travel in mountains?*

A. I know of at least four types. The Bear Paw is oval-shaped, worn in woods and deep, heavy snow. The Cross Country is long, with a turned up toe, perhaps best for your purpose. The Maine or Michigan snowshoe is similar to the Cross Country, good for hunting and fast trailing. Then there is the Trails snowshoe, also with a turned up toe. These slimmer and longer shoes are best for long-distance travel. For light, unpacked snow, a shoe with a good turnup on the toe and a wide surface is best.

Q. *Trains, we have heard, were ofttimes late on schedule in the West. Which train was the latest, or is there such a record?*

A. We know of no record compilation of late trains, but Ed Syers, a Texas newsman, told of a late run by the old Gulf and Interstate, which ran from Beaumont to Port Boliver (across from Galveston). On September 8, 1900, Engine Number Four was water-soaked and buried in sand, eleven miles short of its terminal, by a great hurricane which flooded the area at that time. *Three years later*, in 1903, the Gulf and Interstate Railroad raised the engine and cars, honored its tickets, and completed the run into Port Boliver!

Q. *Is there a railroad museum in the West where I may see old engines, cars, and other similar items of interest?*

A. The Colorado Railroad Museum between Denver and Golden, Colorado, has locomotives dating back to 1881, as well as the famous "Gallopin' Goose" that was used in western Colorado on the narrow gauge lines. It is run by a nonprofit group and has a most interesting collection. St. Louis, Missouri, also has a large railroad museum.

Q. *When did the Burlington & Missouri Railroad build through the Sandhills of Nebraska?*

A. In 1886-87. It completed the Omaha to Billings, Montana, route later.

Q. *Why were the railroads so favored by pioneer people and the government in the early days?*

A. The country was new and lacked transportation and communication facilities, so the people regarded railway construction as a public benefaction, much as hospitals and community facilities are regarded today.

Q. *Where may I find information on methods of transportation in the Northwest during the pioneer period?*

A. Read *The River Trail and Rail* by Bruce Mitchell of the *Wenatchee Daily World*, Wenatchee, Washington.

Q. *What was a hot box tree?*

A. When the journals of an axle of a railroad car overheat, the axle begins to melt. The "hot box," stuffed with oiled rags, starts dripping the mixture of steel and oil down on to the railroad tracks, or ties. Usually, when a hot box is detected, the car is set off on a siding (if the offending hot box cannot be fixed) and the dripping continues in one place, building up what appears to be a miniature metal Christmas tree. These little formations are called hot box trees. I knew an old railroad brakeman who used them for book ends, and they were most attractive and served their purpose well. Collectors now buy them for up to fifteen dollars each.

Index

Abbot, Downing and Company, *see* stagecoaches
Abbott, E.C., 112
Abilene, Texas, 313
Aboriginal Population of America, North of Mexico, The, 144
Across the Wide Missouri, 95
Adams, Andy, 103; books by, 108-09, 112
adobe, 278
After the Battle of the Little Bighorn (painting), 99
Agua Preita, Chihuahua (Mexico), see "Villa, Poncho"
Agrita bush, 193
Alamo; date established, 314; defense of, 244
Alarcon, Martin de (Gov.), 314
Allison, Clay, 225
Altar Valley, 305
Amaral, Anthony, 64
Amarillo, Texas, 311
American Fur Company, 143; *see also* forts—Fort John
American Quarterhorse Association, 12
American Tract Society, *see English-Dakota Dictionary*
American West magazine (Danker article), *see* windmills
Amerindian and Western Historical Research Assoc., 141, 255
Amerindian and Western Historical Review, 136
"ancapogari," 309
Anderson, "Bloody Bill," 253
Anderson, Gilbert A. (Bronco Billy), 103
Anderson, John, 81
Anderson, L.B. (cowboy), 70

Andreas' History of Nebraska, 306
animals, wild, 25-35
Annals of Kansas, 313
Annihilation of the Fetterman Command (painting), 100
Anthony, Major Scott, 257
Arbuckles' Coffee, 280
Arickara Narrative, The, 136
Arizona, 305
Arizonac, 305
Armijo, Gov. Manuel, 138
Army Register, 246
Army scouts, 258; Theodore Baughman, Kit Carson, Ben Clark, William F. Cody, James H. Cook, Billy Dixon, Tom Donnell, Baptiste Garnier (Little Bat), Wild Bill Hickok, Frank North, Luther North, George Oaks, Baptiste Pourier (Big Bat), Al Sieber, Jack Stillwell, Mose Waters
Arthur H. Clark Company, *see* Drury, Clifford
ash hopper, 279
Athabasca Pass, 246
Atlantic Monthly, 102
Austin, Moses, 274
Austin Statesman, see Thompson, Ben
Austin, Stephen, 106, 315
Austin, Texas, *see* Thompson, Ben
Averill, James, 68
Azara, Felix de, 8-9

"bad actor," 218
badgers, 31
Bad Heart Bull, Amos (Oglala Sioux), 134
Bad Lands, Dakota, 305

Baird, Jim (trapper), 46
Baird, W. David, 158
Baker, Johnny, see rifle shots, best
    of the West
Baldwin, F.D., see Clarke, Ben
Baldwin Ferry Road, see Second
    Texas Infantry
Ball, Eva, 113
"Ballad of Sam Bass," 106
Balme, Col. Aguste de la, 136
Bank of St. Louis, see Austin, Moses
Bank of Vernal (Utah), construction
    of, 55
barbed wire, manufacture, 47, 48,
    66
Barland, Margaret Hefferman,
    321
Barlow, Merris C. (Bill), 99
Barrymore, Maurice, 105–06
Bartholomew, Ed, 199, 200,
    208–09
Bartleson wagon train, 316
Bartlett, Donald, 50
Barton, Mrs. D. Welborn, 321
Barton, "Doc," 321
Barringer, Daniel M., 180
Basketmakers, 146
baskettail, 10
Bassett, Nebraska, see Kid Wade
Battle at Yellow House Draw, see
    Spotted Jack
Battle of Sand Creek, Colorado,
    257
Battle of the Little Bighorn, 10
Baxter, Warner, 95
Beadle, E.F., 112
Beale, Leonard F., see Stacy,
    May H.
Bear Lake, 319
Bear That Scatters (Wazzazi Chief),
    see Grattan Massacre
bears, 27
Beaumont, Texas, 326
Beauregard, Toutant, 14
beaver, 32, 46
Beaver, Oklahoma, 312
Becknell, Wm. (Capt.), 317
Beecher, George Allen (Bishop),
    267
Beecher's Island, see Forsythe,
    George A.

Beeler, Joe, 101
Beer City, Kansas, 310
Beer Mug Ranch, 73
Beeson, Chalkley, 312
Beeson, Mildred, 99
Before Barbed Wire, 97
Behan, John, 206
Belden, Charles, 97
Bell, Ham, 204, 308
bell ox, 15
Ben Hur, 12, 102
Bent's Old Fort, 245
Bent's Stockade, Hidden in the
    Hills (Hurd), 245
Bent's Store, 248
Betsinez, Jason, 152
Beverly, H.M., see Trail City,
    Colorado
Bidwell, John, see Bartleson Wagon
    Train
"biggest man in the West," 273
Bighorn Ranch, Banner County,
    Nebraska, 288
bighorn sheep, 25
Billy the Kid, 221; see also Garrett,
    Pat
Binder, Billy (horsebreaker), 72–73
bingle, 52
Bishop of the Great Plains, A
    (Beecher), 267
bitch light, 279
Black Bart, 227
Black Hills, 59, 304–05
Blasingame, Clara, 90
blinders, 293
Blish, Helen, 134
Blood Indians, see Cypress Hills
    Massacre
"Bloody Benders" (Kansas), 231-32
blowguns, 159–60
Blue Whistler, see firearms
Boarman, Henry, see windmills
Bodie Free Press, 58
Body, William S., 58
Bogardus, A.H., see rifle shots,
    best of the West
Boot Hill Cemetery, 308
boots, cowboy, 299
Borden, Gail, 315
Bordet, Kansas, see Stanton County,
    Kansas

Bothwell, A.J., 68
bounty, 218
bowleggedness, in cowboys, 68
Bowman, Everett, 86, 88
Boxelder Creek, Montana, *see*
    forts—Fort Maginnis
Boy Scout Handbook, 36
Bozeman Trail, 155-56
branding; cryogenic or cryobrand-
    ing ("freezing"), 65; earmarks,
    15-16; effect on sales, 56; irons,
    65; methods of, 66
brands, cattle, 64-66; first regis-
    tered in Texas, 64; most diffi-
    cult, 65-66; most unusual, 66
Bratt, John (Nebraska cattleman),
    81, 112; *see also* Western phe-
    nomena—prairie fires
Bray, Dr. W.H. (Soda), 89
Breakenridge, Billy, 224
Breihan, Carl, 213, 214
Bridger, Jim ("mountain man"),
    182
Bridger, Wyoming, 308
bridle bits, 297-98
Brink, J.W., 210
bronc riding, 11; *see also*
    rodeos
Brooks, William L. (Billy), 205
Brown, (Marshal) George, 215
Brown, Henry, 202-03
Brown, John, 272
Brown, (Marshal) Henry, 158
Brown, Salmon, 272
Bryan, James, *see* Austin, Moses
Buckland's Bridge, *see* forts—Fort
    Churchill
Buckland, Samuel S. (trading post),
    see forts—Fort Churchill
Buckskin Frank Leslie, *see*
    Claiborne Billy
buffalo, 2, 15, 21-24, 144;
    American Bison, 21; bones, 21,
    150; carabao, 22; hides, 24;
    hunting, 21, 23; laws to protect,
    23-24; slaughter of, 24; water
    buffalo, 22
Buffalo hunters, 23; Jim Cator,
    Frank Collinson, Wright Mooar,
    Tom Nixon, Henry H. Raymond,
    Vic Smith

Buffalo Bill, *see* Cody, William F.
Buffalo Bill Museum, 57, 107, 108
Buffalo Bill's Wild West Show, 74;
    see also Cody, William F.
buffalo burr, 194
Buffalo Creek Ranch, 309
buffalo grass, 197
buffalo nickel, 158
"Buffalo Soldiers," *see* Negro
    troops in Union Army
The Buffalo Soldiers (Leckie), 242
Buffalo Vernon (rodeo man), 68
bull boats, 320
bull fights, 22
bull grappling, 66
bullwhacker, 316
Burbank, Henry, 82
Bureau of Indian Affairs, 169, 170
burial customs of Old West—
    "boots," 216
business and commerce, 44-60
*Butch Cassidy and The Sundance
    Kid*, 105, 222-23
Butcher, Solomon D. (photo-
    grapher), 98; *see also* sod dugouts
Butler, Frank, *see* rifle shots, best
    of the West
Butterfield Trail, 303
buzzards, *see* vultures

caballeros, 249
Calamity Jane, 216-17
Calderwood pistol, *see* firearms
Calderwood, William, *see* firearms
Caldwell Standard (Kansas), 76
California and Oregon Trail, The
    (Parkman), 245
Callas, Plutarco Elias, *see* Villa,
    Pancho
camel corps (U.S. Army), 242
Camp Chadbourne, *see* forts—
    Fort Concho
Camp Fletcher, Kansas, 245
Camp Supply, 322
Camp Verde, Texas, *see* camel
    corps
Campbell, Robert, *see* forts—
    Fort John
Cananburg, (Judge) Lewis, *see*
    Kid Wade
Canby, Edward S., 154

331

Canyon of Bones (Sante Fe Trail), 185
Card Catalog of the Dodge City Newspapers (Beeson), 313
Cardenas, Garcia Lopez de (Coronado Scout), *see* Grand Canyon
Carpenter, (Captain) A.B., 249
carretas, 317
Carson, Christopher (Kit), 111,259
Carson River, *see* forts—Fort Churchill
Carter, Harvey L., 111
Carver, George Washington, *see* Votaw
Casper, Wyoming, 308, 309; *see also* Collins, Caspar
Cassidy, Butch, 98
Castenada, 165
Caster, J.G. (Conductor), 218
cattails, 195
cattle, 13–19; brands, *see* brands, branding; cost of grazing, 74; deaths, 89; drives, first in N. America, 75; industry, 52, 55; industry, in Hawaii, 77; maverick, 14, 15, 76; production, 17, 51; raising of, 78; rustling of, 80; screwworms, 52; types of: Aberdeen-Angus, 18; Aurochs, 14; Black Angus, 18; Hereford, 18; longhorn, 2, 13–15, 18, 72
Cattle and Men, 66, 76
Cattle Brands (Adams), 108
Cattle Kate (Ella Watson), 68
cattlemen, 20; association of, 67
Cattle Trails of the Old West, 89
cebadera, see nosebag
center-fire cinch, 264
Champion, Nathan (Nate) (cowboy), 83
Chapman, Amos, 262; *see also* Price, William R.
chapparel cock (roadrunner), 39
Charbonneau, Jean Baptiste, 254
Charbonneau, Toussaint, 254
Chatfield, Harry E., 141, 255
Chattanooga, Tennesee, 240
checkrein, 296

cheese-making, 51
Cherokee Strip, 144–45
Cherokee Strip Live Stock Association, 69
Chicago Tribune, 50
"chicken-pulling," 69
Chief Crazy Horse, sculpture of, 107
chinook winds, 190
Chisholm, Jesse, 156, 319–20
Chisholm, Richard H., 64
Chisholm Trail, 156, 319–20
Chisum, John (cowman), 65
Chivington, Colorado, 257
Chivington, (Colonel) John M., 257
Chivington Massacre, 132, 134
cholera epidemic, 319
Choteau, August, 46
Choteau, Pierre, 46
"chousing the herd," 69, 79
Chrisman, Henry E. (Gene), 291
chuckwagon, 314
Churchill, (General) Sylvester, *see* forts—Fort Churchill
Civil War, Indians serving in, 139–40
Claiborne, Billy (outlaw), 225
Clark Field Collection, 47
Clark, Marion, 311
Clarke, Ben, 259–60
Clarke, Henry T., 324
Clay, Henry, 18
Clayton, New Mexico, *see* Ketchum, Tom
Clayton, S., 255
Clements, Jene (author), *see* Gray, Mabry
Cliff Dwellers, 145–46
Cloquet, Minnesota, *see* prairie fires
Clovis, people, 143
Club Foot George (outlaw), 226
Cochise Station, Arizona, *see* Stiles, Billy
Cody, Wm. F. (Buffalo Bill), 74, 81; artifacts and relics of, 108; books about, 107; death of, 77; financial problems, 57; gravesite, 57, 107–08; politics of, 108; pony express, 322; Scouts' Rest Ranch, 57; sign-

ing of treaty as promotional
stunt, 137–38
Coffeyville, Kansas, bank raids of
1892, *see* Dalton, Frank
Collector's Weekly, *see* hitching
weight
Colley and Manion, owners of
Longbranch, 312
Collins, (Lieutenant) Caspar, 255
Collins, (Colonel) William O., 255
*Colorado Charley: Wild Bill's
Pard*, 75
Colorado-Kansas line, 321
Colorado Live Stock Record, 56
Colorado Railroad Museum, 326
Colorado Rockies, *see* ghost towns
Colt Company, *see* firearms
Columbus, Christopher, 24
Columbus, New Mexico, *see* Villa,
Pancho
Comanche (horse), 10
Comanche Cattle Pool, 69
*Commerce of the Prairies: A Journal
of a Sante Fe Trader* (Gregg),
6, 45
Company M, National Guard
(Holcomb Guards), *see* Talbot,
Claris
*Complete and Authentic Life of
Jesse James*, 213, 214
Concord Stage Coaches, 294–95
Conestoga Wagon, manufacturer,
299–300
Confederate Army, 241
conservation, 38
Cook, (Captain) James H., 250
Cooley, Croyden, E., 311
Cooper, Gary, 95
correa, 297
Coronado, Francisco Vasques de,
10, 75, 141, 159
Cortez, Hernando, 8
Co-Rux-Te-Chod-Ish (Mad Bear),
Sergeant, 260
Costello, David F. (botanist), *see*
Western grasses—life span of
Cottonwood Creek, *see* forts—
Fort Robinson
Cottonwood Springs, Nebraska
Territory, *see* forts—Fort

Cottonwood
cougar, 27
Council Grove, Kansas, 310
Council Oak Tree, 311
"cowards," 319
Cowboy Artists of America, 101
"Cowboy's Shirttail, The," 97
Cowboy Turtles Association, 84–85
cowboys, 63–90; clothing, 77, 81;
of Hawaii, 80; Negro, 70–72;
origin of word, 78; school of,
67; songs about, 109; as a
symbol, 67; way of life, 77, 80
cow chips, 270
Cowman's Southwest, The, 112,
161, 203
cowpoke, 68
coyote (prairie wolf), 28, 29
"crackers," Georgia, 83
Craig, Nute, 137
Crandell, Edward M., 66
cranes, sandhill, 39
Crawford, (Captain) Emmet,
255–56
Creasey, John, 111
"creasing," of horses, 13
Creede Candle, *see* petrified man
Creede, Colorado, *see* petrified man
Cripple Creek, Colorado, 310
Crook, (General) George, 255
"cruppers," 87
Cruzate, Petriz de, 138
culture, 92–115
Culver, Martin, *see* Trail City,
Colorado
Curleymesquite, 178
Curly Bill Brocius, 223, 224
Custer, (Colonel) George A., 10,
99, 100, 134, 135, 166, 211,
249–51
Custer, Mrs. George A. (Elizabeth),
212
Custer County Chief (Nebraska), 72
Cut Nose (Cheyenne), 261
Cypress Hills Massacre, 243, 244

Dahlman, James C. (James Murray),
72
Dakota Cowboy (Blasingame), 90,
214–15

Dakota Old-Time Cowboys Association, 67
Dakota Territory, 306
Dallin, Charles E., 106-07
Dalton, (U.S. Marshal) Frank, 214
damages paid to Indians, 147
Davis, Col. J.C., 154
Davis, Larry, 324
Davis, Nolan, 324
"Day of the Cowboy," 97
Day, R.W., 97
Dead Man's Butte, Wyoming, 309
Dead Man's Canyon, 187
Dead Man's Hand, 211
Dear Old Kit: The Historical Christopher Carson, 111
Death Valley, 34
Death Valley Scotty, 57
deeds of land in the Yukon, 186
deer, 25-26; hunting, 26; skinning, 26
Deger, Larry, 204, 205
Deimling, (Colonel) Francis, 259
Democrat Leader (Cheyenne, Wyo.), 82
dendrochronology, 194-95
Dendrochronology in Mexico (Scott), 194
Denton, John, 106
Denver Republican, 262
Denver Westerner 1962 Brand Book, 260
Denver Westerners, The, 102
DeSoto, Hernando, 9
Desperate Men, 98
devil's claw, 194
Devil's Lake, North Dakota, *see* forts—Fort Totten
DeVoto, Bernard, 95
dewlap, 66
Dick, (Constable) Leroy F., *see* "Bloody Benders"
diseases; ague, 42; cholera, 282, 319; diphtheria, 282, 304; malaria, 42, 321; swamp fever, 42; tick fever, 321; trichinosis, 281; tularemia, 34; yellow fever, 42
Divine, R.M., 73
"Dixie's Land," 140

Dixon, Billy, *see* Price, William R.
Dobie, Frank, 5, 6, 8, 76, 103, 112
Doc Holliday, 223
Dodge, Col. Richard, 24, 176
Dodge City, The Cowboy Capital (Wright), 312, 313
Dodge City, Kansas, 308, 312
"dog trail," 318
"dollar," origin of, 57
Dore, J.J., *see* petrified man
doughie (doggie), 15, 16
Douglas Budget (Wyo.), 79
Dover, Ohio, 253
Dowling, Bernard John (Congressional Medal of Honor), 168
Drannen, Capt. William F., 110
"draw a blank," 86
Drover's Cottage, 313
"Drunk's Hole," *see* Beaver, Oklahoma
Drury, Clifford M., 277
dueling in the Old West, lack of, 234
dugout, sod, 277, 278
Dundy County (Nebraska), 306
Duryea, Dan, 105
Dye, Charlie, 101

Eagan, Robert A. (author), 313
eagle, bald, 39
Early Ford County (Rath), 313
earmarks, 15-16, 65; *see also* brands, branding
Earp, Wyatt, 202, 205-07; relatives of, 207-08, 209
Eastern land grants, 188-89
Eastman, Mary H., 103
ecological process, 40, 48
d'Eglise, Jacques, 143
elk, 26, 27
Elliott, Major, 249
Ellis, Erl H. (lawyer), 238
Ellsworth, Texas, *see* Drover's Cottage
Ellsworth Reporter, see Sheriff Whitney shooting
encomienda, 139
endangered species, 34-35, 39
English-Dakota Dictionary (Williamson), 174

Estavanico, 183
estray, 16–17
Evans, Governor John (Colorado), 257–58
Exploration and Empire: The Explorer and Scientist in the Winning of the American West, 95

Fair God, The, 102
Famous Gunfighters of the Western Frontier, 202
Famous Indians, 170
Farewell's Post, *see* Cypress Hills Massacre
farms; population, 48; production, 49
Farney, Henry F., 99
fence, longest, 66
fences, 284–85
Fetterman Massacre, 155
Fifty Years on the Owl Hoot Trail, 199
films, Western, 95, 104–05; Academy Awards for, 95; actors in, 104–06; Indian, 113
Finlay, Dr. Carlos, 42
firearms, 263–68
Fish Hook, Illinois, *see* "biggest man in the West"
Fisher, John King, 226–27
Fitzsimmons, Bob, *see* "petrified man"
Five Minutes to Midnight (horse), 7–8
Fix, Dr. Georgia Arbuckle, photo 92
flag signal system, *see* frontier wars and tactics against Indians
flanking, of cattle, 17
Fletcher, Colin (hiker), 182
Flintlock pistol, *see* firearms
Flipper, Lieutenant Henry O., 252
"flippin' turds," *see* recreation
folklore, 98
Folsom man, 143
Fontenelle, P., *see* forts—Fort John
food on the prairie, 280–81; candy substitutes, "cornstarch cakes," preserved eggs, fish, "mast crop," shortage of and enjoyability, sourdough starter, "sugar tit," water glass
force-feeding, of cattle, 16
Ford, Bob, 213, 224–25
Ford, Charles, 213
Forgan, Oklahoma, 288
Forsythe, (Major General) George A., 251
Fort A. Lincoln, *see* forts—Fort Rice
Fort Elliot, *see* Mason, Joe
Fort Griffin, Texas, *see* Spotted Jack
Fort Harker, *see* forts—Fort Ellis
Fort Laramie, *see* forts—Fort John
Fort Laramie, Wyoming, 324
Fort Lisa, 46
Fort MacLeod Rodeo, 8
Ford McPherson, *see* forts—Fort Cottonwood
Fort Niobara National Wildlife Refuge, 15
Fort Recovery, 136
Fort Recovery, Ohio, *see* Little Big Horn, Battle of
Fort Riley, Kansas, *see* U.S. Cavalry horses
Fort Riley Riding Club, 262
Fort Scott Daily Monitor (Kansas), 97
Fort Whoop-Up, *see* Cypress Hills Massacre
Fort William, *see* forts—Fort John
Fort Wise, *see* forts—Fort Lyons, Colorado
forts; Bent's Fort, 245; Fort Bridger, 319; Fort Churchill, 247; Fort Concho, 247; Fort Cottonwood, 246; Fort Craig, 239; Fort Dodge, 322; Fort Ellis, 246; Fort Hall, 319; Fort Hayes, 249, *see also* Camp Fletcher, Kansas; Fort Jefferson, 250; Fort John, 246–47; Fort Lyons, 245, 248; Fort McPherson, 256; Fort Maginnis, 245; Fort Mohave, 245–46; Fort Rice, 247; Fort

Robinson, 248; Fort St. Vrain,
245; Fort Steele, 246; Fort
Totten, 247; Fort Union (New
Mexico), 236; Fort Wallace, 249,
251, 324; Fort William, *see*
Fort John; Fort Yates, 311;
"Jasper House," 246; Old Fort
Mitchell, 244-45; Sutter's Fort,
247
forts in defense against Indians, 244
fowl, 38-41; migratory, 38, 40
foxes, 29
Frasca, Charles, 21
Fraser, James Earl, 158
Free, Micky, 258
Freeman, Daniel, *see* Homestead
Law
freemartin, 17
"freighter's train," 316
Fremont, Gen. John C., 206, 306
frogs, 37
Front Street, 308
frontier wars and tactics against
Indians, 243
fur trapping, 46

"Gallopin' Goose," *see* Colorado
Railroad Museum
Garden City, Kansas, see "National
Forest projects"
Garrett, Pat (assassin), 214-15
Gauthrie, James A., 212
geese, 39
gelding, of horses, 8
Geuda Springs, Kansas, *see* Short,
Luke
Georgia State Railroad, *see* Chatta-
nooga
gestation, of cows, horses, rabbits,
sheep, 18
"getting a good draw," 77
Getz, David, 166
ghost towns (tour of), 326
Giddings, Texas, *see* Wild Bill
Longley
gillflirted, 13
ginning, of cattle, 69
Glenn, George (cowboy), 71
Glass Mountains (Oklahoma), 187
goats, 20

Goetzman, William H., 95
gold; Black Hills, 186; coins, 48;
discovery of, 59; mining of, 60;
mines, 58; nuggets, 59; value of,
59-60
Gold Mine Certificates, 57
Goodnight, Charles, 24, 71, 76, 315
Goodnight, Texas, 308
Gore, Louisa, 313
Gorgas, Dr. William, 42
Government Road, *see* Oregon Trail
Grand Canyon, 182
Grand Junction Sentinel (Colorado),
102
Grant, George, 18
Grant, Ulysses S., 24, 140, 253;
attitude toward Indians, 137
Grarr, Ed, *see* Cypress Hills Massacre
Grattan, Lieutenant, 248
Grattan Massacre, 248-49
Gray, Mabry, 227
Great American Desert, 303, 304
Great Plains, 19, 21, 24
Great Platte River Road, The
(Mattes), 320
Great River; The Rio Grande, 95
Great Salt Lake, Utah, 21; forma-
tion of, 188
Great Serpent Mound, 147; *see
also* Indian tribes—Adena
Great Smith auto, 51
Great Train Robberies of the West
(Block), 218
Great Train Robbery, The, 104
Greathouse, Charles H. (rancher),
28-29
Greeley, Horace, 46, 324
Green, Edward and Jess, 215
Green River, 319
Gregg, Josiah, 45, 317
Grey, Zane, 111-12, 113, 196, 276
Grinnell, George Bird, 256
groundhog, 30
grouse, wild, 38
"grubbing loco," 194
grubline gossip, 76
guerilla leader, North Amerca's
greatest, 230
Gunfighters, The, 200
gunfighters in Old West: top ten,

233–34; top twenty, 220
gunny sacks, 295
"Gunsmoke," 111

Hackney, H.A., 51
Haley, J. Evatts, 95, 201
halogeton, 19, 197
Halsey National Forest (Nebraska),
    see National Forest projects
Hambone (Bonella), 262
Hamer, Frank, 204
Hamner, Laura V., 311
Hanyston, John, 101
Hancock, Maj. Gen. Winfield
    Scott, 211
Hand, Dora, 228–29
hand-dug well, 185
hangings, 103–04
Hannibal, Missouri, see Twain,
    Mark
"hard soap," 283
Hardesty, R.J., 308
Hardin, John Wesley (Wes), 212
Harman, Fred, 101–01
harness, parts of, 292
Harper's Monthly, 211
Harrison, Charley, 201–02, 252
harvesting wheat before the com-
    bine, 290
Hawes, Jasper, see forts—Jasper
    House
Hawikuh Ruins, see "Seven Cities
    of Cibola"
hawks, 41
Haycox, Ernest, 111
Hayes, Rutherford B., 206
Hays Tavern, 311
headweight, see "hitching weight"
Heller, Adolph, 166
Hemet, California, see "Maze
    Stone"
Herron, Jim, 205
Hertzler, Dr. Arthur E., 111
Hibbard, Spencer & Bartlett Com-
    pany, see "hitching weight"
Hickock, James Butler (Wild
    Bill), 74–75, 209–13, 215–
    16; verse at gravesite, 114
"hideout," 234
highway, U.S. 26, 309

Higley, Dr. Brewster, 110
Histoire du Far West, 103
Historic Sketches of the Cattle
    Trade of the West and South-
    west, 14
Historical and Statistical Informa-
    tion Respecting the History,
    Condition, and Prospects of the
    Indian Tribes of the U.S., 147
historical dating, 194
History of the American Frontier,
    95
History of Kansas (Prentis), 318
History of the United States, 83
hitching block, see "hitching
    weight"
"hitching weight," 293
Hite, Yost, see Eastern land grants
Hitler, Adolph, influence of Karl
    May on, 173
Hodges, Ben, 308
hogans, 149
Hogg, Ima, 273
Hogg, (Gov.) James S., 273
Holden, William C., 83
"hold-up," 77
Hole-in-the-Wall, 222, 309
Hole-in-the-Wall Gang, 73, 105,
    309
Holladay, Ben, 303, 324
"Home on the Range," 109
Homestead Act, 93
Homestead Law, 272–73
homesteading, 54
Hood, Hazel, 307
"hooey," 87
"Hoo-ha Wa-keh-Ya" (Sioux),
    see "tepees on wheels"
Hooks, Matthew (Bones), 71
"hoolihaning," 87
Hoover Dam (Colorado), 191
Horan, J.D., 98, 214
Horn, Tom, 230
horse, as symbol of freedom, 110
Horse and Buggy Doctor, The, 111
"Horse's Petition, The," 103
horseback through Rocky Moun-
    tains, 184
horsemeat, 3
horses, 2–13, 181; Arabian, 11;

bay, 4–5; bell-mare, 8; chestnut, 4; colts, 2, 5; cutting horse, 11, 79; gelding of, 8; Morgan, 11; mustang, 3, 4, 6; pinto, 4; quarterhorse, 12; roping horse, 11; saddle horse, 5, 6, 7, 9, 12; sorrel, 4; stew bald (stewballed), 4; wild, 3, 13
horseshoes, types of, 12; shoeing as a trade, 49, 75, 279–80
"hot box tree," 327
Houston, Sam (statesman), 273
"How," as greeting origin of, 149
Hoxie, Jack, 104
Huamantla, Mexico, see Walker, Samuel H.
Hudson Bay Company, 46; see also forts—Jasper House
Hughes, Robert E., see "biggest man in the West"
Hunter, J.M., 112
hunting, 21, 23, 25, 26, 27, 34–35, 38
Huntt, (Captain) George Gibson, see forts—Fort Concho
Hurd, C.W. (author), 245

Ikard, Bose, 71, 72
Iliff, John, 19
In the Days of Victorio, 113
Independence, Missouri, see Meeker, Ezra
Independence Rock (Wyoming), 320
Indian artifacts; authentic, 172; blankets, 171; Navajo rugs, 170, 171; war bonnets, 39
Indian battles, number of, 136
Indian burial; customs, 166; mummified, 160
Indian chiefs; Blackbird (Chippewa), 138; Black Heart, Arapahoe, photo 44; Black Kettle, 132, 134, 211; Buffalo (Chippewa), 138; Cloud (Chippewa), 138; Cochise (Chiriacahua Apache), 154–55; Colorow (Ute War Chief), 137; Douglas (Ute Civil Chief), 137; Flat Iron (Sioux), 138; Geronimo (Apache), 152; Joseph (Ny Perce),
155; Left Hand, 135; Little Turtle (Miami), 136; Nokoni (Comanche), 153; Peter Picthlynnn (Choctaw), 158; Quanah Parker (Comanche), 153; Red Cloud (Oglala Teton Sioux), 153, 155–156; Sabeata (Jumano), 143; Sitting Bull (Oglala Sioux), 157; Spotted Eagle, 134; Sweet Bird, 134; Ten Bears (Comanche), 148; Two Moons (Cheyenne), 153; Washakie (Shoshone), 157, 319; Yellow Bear, 153; Yellow Hair (Yellow Hand), 260–61
Indian ceremonials, 172
Indian childbirth, 146
Indian children, treatment of, in schools, 139
Indian Claims Commission, 143, 147
Indian culture areas, 140–41
Indian dress; Apache, Sioux headdress, 164; "breath feathers," 161; sewing needles, 162; war bonnets, 39, 172
Indian "fetish," 160
Indian foods; "bread," 165; maize, 162; Paiute biscuits, 161; preserving meat, 130, 164
Indian giver, origin of, 164
Indian lands, legal "justification" for appropriation of, 148–49
Indian languages, 173–76
Indian, literature on, 170
Indian lodging; earth lodges, 146; tepees, 162
Indian mounds, 147
Indian "mouth fishing," 161
Indian organizations; American Indian Historical Society, 170; Indian Press Association, 170
Indian population; decline of, due to Spanish, 145; prior to advent of white men, 146
Indian powwows, 144, 167
Indian religion, 160, 176
Indian reservations; Allegany reservation, 169; Crow reservation, 168; Eastern, 169; size, 168
Indian scouts, average age of, 136
Indian sign language, 150–51

Indian soldiers in U.S. Armed
Forces, 168
Indian sports, 168
Indian terminology, 149–52
Indian tribe names, 151
Indian tools; mano, 161; metate,
161
Indian trade muskets, see firearms
Indian treaties; broken with Sioux,
138; unbroken, 137
Indian tribes (nations), names of,
151; Adena, 147; Adirondack,
151; Apache, 141, 151, 159;
Aqua Caliente, 168; Aricara,
143; Blackfoot, 136, 142;
Cherokee, 144–45, 160; Chey-
enne, 151, 154; Chippewa, 137;
Choctaw, 160; Comanche, 141–
42, 154, 159; Crow, 142, 151;
Delaware, 151; Hopewell, 147;
Karankawa, 143–44; Kiowa, 141;
Mandan (Sioux), 142–43; Min-
esetperi, 142; "mission," 142;
Modoc, 153–54; Mohawk, 151;
Navaho, 149, 151, 164; Pawnee,
146; Pima, 163; Pueblo, 149;
Seminoles, 147; Sioux, 136, 137,
143, 151–52; Tenewa, 141–42;
Utes, 136–37; Washoe, 143;
Wyandotte, 168; Zuni, 151
Indian Tribes of North America,
The, 144
Indian uprisings; Comanche, 135;
Kiowas, 135; Sioux, 135; Pue-
blo, 180–82, 133
Indian War of 1864, The, 97
Indian weapons; bows, 163;
stunner, 165
Indians, notable; Black Beaver
(Kiowa), 156, 319; Captain
Jack (Modoc), 153–54; Crow
Dog, 153; Pope (Tewa medicine
man), 133; Sequoya (Cherokee),
157; Spotted Horse, 158; Spotted
Tail, 153; Thorpe, Jim, 167–68
Indians Inter-Tribal Indian Cere-
monial, 167
Industrial Revolution, 304
Insects, 41–43; bees, 42; grass-
hoppers, 42–43; locusts, 42;
mosquitoes, 42; scarab beetle,

43; stings, 41; tumblebug, 43
International Boundary Lines
Across Colorado and Wyoming
(Ellis), 238
Introduction to Handbook of
American Indian Languages
(Boas, Powell), 174
Iron Trail, see Old Wire Trail
Ironquill (Capt. Eugene F. Ware),
96–97
Irving, Washington, 114

"jacal," 77
jackrabbits (Great Plains jacks), 33
James, Jesse Woodson, 212
James, Will (Joseph Ernest Neph-
tali Dufault), 64
Jasperson, Elmer, see windmills
Jefferson, Thomas, 46
Jeffords, Capt. Thomas, 154–55
"Jehu," 323
jerkline, 317
Jesse James Was His Name, 214
jet sheet, 315
Jewett, Eva, see Talbot, Claris
jockey box, 315
Johnson, R.B. (Bob), trail boss, 71
Johnson, Sam (cowboy), 72
Johnson and Graham's Lessee vs
William M'Intosh, 148
Johnson County Cattle War, 79
Jones, Bob (cowmen), 65
Jones, Charles J. (Buffalo), 24
Jones and Plummer Trail, 308
Joslyn, Benjamin, 267
Joslyn Arms Company, 267
Journal of May Humphreys Stacy,
Supplemented by the Report of
Edward Fitzgerald Beale (Stacy),
242
Juarez, 314
Judge, Bill (author), 250
Judson, E.C., 256
"June Teenth," 243

Kansas City Museum of History,
140
Kansas City Times, 214
Kansas Historical Quarterly, 321
Kansas Historical Society, 51, 146
Kaw Mission, 311

Kaycee, Wyoming, 309
Kelley, Hal J., 305
Kelly, Charles, 98
Kelly, Ed. O. (assassin), *see* Ford,
    Bob
Kelly, Jim (cowboy), 72
Kelso, Texas, 309
Kennedy, Edward, 205-06
Kennedy, James and Miflin, *see*
    Hand, Dora
Keogh, Capt. Myles, 10, 263
Kerry, Hobbs, 214
Ketchum, (Black Jack) Tom,
    227-28
Kid Wade, 225
killdeer, 40
Kilpatrick, Ben, 224
King, Frank M., 206
Kino, Eusebio Francisco, 306
Kirkpatrick, "Old" John (cow-
    man), 15
Kiskaddon, Bruce, 97
Kosterlitzky, Col. Emilio, 204
Krakel, Dean (director, National
    Cowboy Hall of Fame), 108
Kress, George, 98
krooper (crupper), 297
Krumrey, Kate, 106

*Ladder of Rivers: The Story of
    I.P. (Print) Olive*, 72, 89
La Junta, *see* forts—Bent's Fort
Lake Jasper, *see* forts—Jasper
    House
Lake, Stuart, 103, 207, 208
L'Amour, Louis, 111, 238
lampblack, 77
Lamy of Santa Fe, 95
land, investment, 53
Land of the Pueblos, The, 102
Lander Cut-Off, 319
Lander, (Col.) F.W., 319
"Language des Naondoonessis,"
    174
laprobes, 294
La Ramee, Jacques, *see* forts—
    Fort John
Laramie Boomerang, 56
Laramie Mountains, 305
Laramie Plains, 305

Laramie, Wyoming, 324
lariat ropes, 299
Las Vegas Daily Optic (N.M.),
    135
LaSalle Colony, 314
Lasater, Tom, 78
Last Chance Store, 311
last train robbery, 218
Latham, Dr. Hiram, 19
Lawrence, Kansas, *see*
    Quantrill's Raid
Lead, South Dakota, 310
L'eau qui pleure, see Weeping
    Water
Le Fors, Joe, 205
Le Fors, Nettie, 205
"leg bail," 219
Lemert, Bernard (cowman), *see*
    Western phenomenon—elec-
    tricity
Lemmon, Ed, 81
leppy *(leperos), see* doughie
Lewis and Clark expedition, 30,
    46, 141, 253-54
Lexington, Missouri, 322
Lexington, Virginia, *see* Houston,
    Sam
Liars' Brigade, 239
Liberal, Kansas, 310
Libby, O.G., 136
*Life and Daring Adventures of
    Jesse James and Frank James,
    The*, 213
Lives and Legends of the Sioux, 103
Linn, John J. (Texas historian), *see*
    Gray, Mabry
Lisa, Manuel, 46
"literaries," frontier, 96
Little Bighorn, Battle of, 133-34,
    250; depiction by an Indian,
    133-34; Indian survivors of,
    135; *see also*, Sitting Bull;
    George Custer
livery, description of, 52
Lives and Legends of Buffalo Bill
    (Russell), 260
lobo wolf, 28
Lobo Wolf Park, 28
loco weed, 9, 31
log cabin, construction, 47

340

Log of a Cowboy, 103, 108, 112, 115
Lone Cowboy (James), 64
long distance driving team speed, 294
Longbranch Saloon, 312
Longhaired Jim Courtright, *see* Short, Luke
Longhorns, The, 76, 112
Lookout Mountain, 57
Lopez, Francisca, 49
Los Angeles Corral of the Western-ers, *see* Drury, Clifford
Lost Trails of the Cimarron (Chrisman), 310, 313
Louisiana Purchase, 46
Loveless, A.C., 89
Lovell, Mary, *see* Deimling, Francis
"lunettes," 241
Lyon County, Nevada, *see* forts—Fort Churchill
Lyon, Nathaniel, *see* forts—Fort Lyons

Mackenzie, (Bvt. Maj. Gen.) Ranald S., 252
Madsen, Chris (soldier), 261
Majors, Alexander, 316, 323
"make-do," 278, 291
"Mako Sica," Bad Lands, Dakota
Man Called Horse, A, 104
"Man Eater, The," *see* Packer, Alfred
Man of the Plains: The Recollec-tions of Luther North (Grinnell), 256
The Man Who Walked Through Time (Fletcher), 182
Manhattan, Kansas, 324
Maple Grove Cemetery, 308
Marcos, Fray, *see* "Seven Cities of Cibola"
marijuana, use of, 275
Marshall, James, 49
Marshal, Chief Justice John, 148
Marvin, Lee, 95
Mason, Joe (Dodge City cop), 231
Masterson, Bat (William Bartholo-mew Barclay), 200–02, 208
Mather, Dave, *see* McIntyre, Jim

Mauvaises Terres, see Bad Lands, Dakota
maverick, *see* cattle
Maverick, Samuel A., 14
Maxwell, Pete, *see* Garrett, Pat
May, Karl (author), 173
"Maze Stone," 185
M Bar Ranch, *see* Mason, Joe
McCall, Jack (assassin of Wild Bill Hickok), 75
McCanles, David C., 209–10, 212
"McCarty," 75
McCarty, Claude, 312
McConnell, J., 203–04
McCoy, Joseph, 14, 313
McCreight, M.I. (author), *see* Sutton, E.S.
McDonald, Ranch, *see* forts—Fort Cottonwood
McGinty, Billy, 89, 112; *see also* "petrified man"
McGraw, William F., 319
McIntyre, Jim (Marshal), 215
McJunkin, George (cowboy), 72
McPherson, George, 81
Meanea, F.A. (saddlemaker), 295
meat packing, 51, 53
Medicine Bow: mountains, 305; town of, 305
Meeker, Ezra, 271–72, 307
Meeker Massacre, 136–37
Mendoza, Domingo de, 143
Merritt, (Col.) Wesley, 261
Merwin Hulbert and Company, *see* firearms
Mesa de la Contedena, *see* Val Verde, battle of
Mesa Verde National Park, 145–46
mesa, 187
Meteor Crater (Arizona), 180
Mexican influence on American Southwest, 49
Michigan Department of Conserva-tion, 38
Middleton, "Doc," 115
Midnight (horse), 7–8
"Midnight Call to Arms," 256
Miles, (Gen.) Nelson A., 259
Military Road, 322
Mine 'a Breton, *see* Austin, Moses

miner's washboard, 58
mines; Cornucopia, 58; Lost
    Dutchman, 59; Silver Plume,
    59; Tombstone, Arizona, 58
Minnehaha, 103
mirages, 189
Mission of Guadalupe, see Juarez
"The Mission of San Antonio de
    Valera," see Alamo
Mississippi River, 191
Missouri Company, 143
Missouri Fur Company, 46
Missouri River, 191
Mitchell Bridge, see forts—Old
    Fort Mitchell
Mitchell, Emma, 322
Mitchell Pass, 318
Mix, Tom, 105
mochila, see Mother Hubbard
    Saddle
Mohave, meaning of, 150
Monroe Doctrine, 54
Monticello Township (Kansas), 216
Moody, Joel, 98
Mooney, James, 144
Moore, James, see Thompson, Ben
Moore, (Col.) John C., see Second
    Texas Infantry
Moore Patent Firearms Company,
    see firearms
Mores, Marquis de, 53
Morgan, George (designer of old
    silver dollar), 58

Mormons; on Oregon Trail, 318;
    trade exchange with California,
    54; Utah, and Nauvoo, Ill., 277
Morrison, George D. (Pete), 105
Mother Hubbard (Mother Machree)
    saddle, 295
Mount McKinley (Alaska), 184
"mountain oysters," 82
Mountain States Ranch School, 67
Mountain survival, 184
Mule Mountains, 180
mules (jacks, burros, asses), 9, 10
Munoz, Captain, 138
"muskeg," 150
Mustangs, The (Dobie), 8, 112

Myer, A.J. (Chief signal officer),
    see frontier wars and tactics
    against Indians

names, "prettiest-sounding,"
    306–07
Nan-na-saddie, see Clarke, Ben
Nantaje, see Clarke, Ben
National Arms Company, see
    firearms
National Cattle Trail, 312, 313, 321
National Cowboy Hall of Fame, 108
National Forest projects, 193
Natrona County (Wyoming) Histor-
    ical Society, 320
Nauvoo, Illinois, see Mormons
Navajo Rugs, Past—Present—Future
    (Maxwell), 171
Neal, Edgar, 204
"Nebraska," meaning of, 306
Nebraska Game Commission, 53
Nebraska History Quarterly, 210
Nebraska State Historical Society
    (Sutton), see Sutton, E.S.
Neches River, 314
Negro Cowboy, The, 70
Negro troops in the Union Army,
    241, 243
Neighbors, (Major) R.S., 176
Nelson, Oliver M. (cowboy), 78,
    85, 112, 203
nerve-gas, testing of, 19
Nevada; Territory, 306; State of,
    306, 308
New Haven Arms Company, see
    firearms
New Rockford, North Dakota,
    see forts—Fort Totten
New York Film Critics Award, 95
New York Morning Telegraph, 201
New York Times Book Review, 67
Nichols, "Col." G.W., 211
Nicholson, (Lt.) W.C.F., 262
Nickell, Willie, see Horn, Tom
Nimmo, Joseph (compiler of
    The Nimmo Report), 75
Nixon, Richard M., 29
No Man's Land, 256
North Canadian River, 319
North, (Maj.) Frank, 256

North, Luther, *see* Sutton, E.S.
North Platte, Nebraska, *see* forts—
Fort Cottonwood
nosebag (morral), 296
"nose-paint," 75

Oakley, Annie, *see* rifle shots, best
of the West
Ogalalla Dam, 320
oil; drilling, 50-51; from shale,
49-50; spills, 39
Oil Through Bottom (Arkansas),
279
Old Army Press, 268
"Old Chisholm Trail" (song), 109
Old Fort Bernard, *see* Grattan
Massacre
Old Jules (Sandoz), *see* windmills
Old Oregon Trail, The (Meeker),
272
Old West, The, 89, 112
Old Wire Trail, 322
Olive, Bob, 89
Olive, I.P., 308, 313; *see also*
Trail City, Colorado
Orange, California, *see* Davis, Nolan
Order of the E. Clampus Vitas, 110
Oregon, 305; as frontier land,
305; as state, 305
Oregon Trail, 271-72, 318
Orick, Missouri, *see* "Bloody Bill"
Anderson
Orteza, *see* San Francisco Bay—
discovery of
Otermin, (Governor) Antonio de,
133
Outlaw Trail, The, 98
Outlaws; location of worst gangs,
221; psychology of, 218-19;
women, 217
Outlet, The, 109
Overland Mail Company, 323
Overland Stage Company, 324
Overland Stage Road (Virginia
City, Nevada), *see* forts—
Fort Churchill
overo, see horses—pinto
Owens, Commodore Perry, 212
owls, snowy white (great snowy),
28, 41

*Ox Team, or the Old Oregon Trail,
The* (Meeker), 307
oxen, 12, 15

Packer, Alfred, 229-30
Panhandle City, Texas, 311
panioles, 80
Pathfinder Dam, 320
Pawnee Bill (Maj. Gordon Lillie), 44
Pawnee Scouts, 256
Paxson, Frederick, 95
"Peacemaker," *see* firearms
Pease, Bethaneth, 167
Peeples, Willis (cowboy), 72
Penn, Chris, 200
Penrose, Dr. Charles, 79
Penrose, Colorado, *see* forts—
Bent's Fort
Peshtigo, Wisconsin, *see*
"prairie fires"
pesticides, *see* poisons
"petrified man," 189
pheasant, 38, 39
Philadelphia Enquirer, 50
Philbrook Art Center, 47
Phippen, George, 101, 115
photographers, of cowboys, 97
Pickett, Bill (cowboy), 72
*Pictographic History of the Oglala
Sioux,* 134
pigeon (passenger), 40
"piggin' string," *see correa*
Pinal Apaches, *see* "Free, Micky"
Pinto Horse Association of America,
Inc., 4
Pike, Albert, 140
pioneer; battles vs. Indians, 251-
52; clothing, 114; farm machinery, 284; foods, 280-81;
home equipment, 279; homesteading, 272, 273; life, 93-95;
loneliness, 275; problems,
282-83; recreation, 288; remedies, 282-83; sod homes,
277-78; tools, 284
"piskun," 150
pitch pine, 194
"pitcher and catcher hotel," 279
Platte River, 318, 320
Platteville, Colorado, *see* forts—

Fort St. Vrain
Plummer Gang, 198
poddy, *see* doughie
poisons, 19, 29, 31, 40-41, 53,
pollution, 56
Pond Creek Station, *see* Old Fort
　Wallace
Pony Express, 303, 322
Pope, Gen. John, 137
Popo Agir River, 319
Port Boliver, 326
Portola, Gaspar de, *see* San Fran-
　cisco Bay, discovery of
Potato Creek Johnny (gold miner),
　59
"potlach," 151
Potosi, *see* Austin, Moses
Potter, Jack (cowboy), 89
pottery, Indian, 47
Powers, Bill, *see* Dalton, Frank
Prairie Dog Park, 30
prairie dogs, 30, 31
prairie fires, 276-77
prairie gopher, 33
Prairie Grove Cemetery, 308
prairie swift (kit fox), 28
Preece, Harold, 99
Pretty Cloud, Dolly, 134
Price, (Major) William R., 258-59
Prinz, August, *see* windmills
prostitution in the Old West,
　217-18
Public Service Company of Colo-
　rado, *see* forts—Fort St. Vrain
"pueblo," meaning of, 149
Puget Sound, see "Meeker, Ezra"
Puget Sound Agricultural Co., 46
Pulitzer Prize, for books on the
　West, 95
"pulling leather," 86
puncheon floor, 278
purple sage, 196
Puyallup, Washington, 307
Pynchon, John, 75

Quaker Oats Company, 186
Quantrill's raid, 241-42, 252-53
"Queen City of the Texas Pan-
　handle," 311
quinine, 161

raccoons, 32
Ragsdale, M.C., 97
railroad lines; Burlington and
　Missouri, 327; Fort Worth and
　Denver City, 311; Gulf and
　Interstate, 326; Kansas Pacific,
　322; Rock Island, 310; Union
　Pacific, 302, 305, 321
railroads, refrigerated box cars, 53
Ralston, J.K., 99
ramada, 149
ranch, average size in Southwest, 73
Ranch on the Beach, The, 109
rancheros, 249
Randall, Glen (horse trainer), 12
range wars, cattlemen vs. sheepmen,
　20; Johnson County (Wyo.), 84
Rath, Bob, 23
Rath, Charles, 23
Rath, Ida Ellen, 308
Rath, Jesse, 312
Rath Trail, The (Rath), 313
rats (kangaroo, desert, wood), 33
Rawlins, John A. (Bvt. Maj. Gen.),
　253
Raymond, H.H., 200
"reach," wagon pieces, 294
realism in "Western" fiction, 232
Reaugh, Frank, 15
recreation (on farms, ranches), 288
Red Bluff, 272
Red Canyon, 309
Redlands, California, 315
Reed, Anthony: Cowman, 109
Reed, Dr. Walter, 42
Reese, Estelle Walker, 102
Regimental History of the 5th
　Cavalry, 261
Register Rock (Idaho), 185
Reid, Capt. Mayne, 85
reins (lines), 293
Remington, Frederick, 81-82, 113
rennet, 51
Reno, (Maj.) Marcus A., *see*
　Clayton, S.
repartimiento, 139
Report on the West (1866), 137
*Representative Old Cowboy: Ed
　Wright,* 82
reptiles, 35-38

Reynolds, Charley, *see* gold—
  Black Hills
Reynolds, Joe, 81
Rhode Island, 308
Rhodes, Gene, 103
Rider, Keith, 79
Riders of the Purple Sage, 112
"riding clothespin" or straddle, 275
"riding on the circle," 79
Rienpeyrout, Jean-Louis, 103
rifle shots, best of the West, 261-62
rifles, 324
Ringo, Johnny (outlaw), 225-26
Riordan, Dan, 88-89
Ripley, Tennessee, *see* "Second
  Texas Infantry"
River Trail and Rail, The (Mitchell), 327
roadrunner, 39
Robinson, (First Lt.) Levi H.,
  see forts—Fort Robinson
Rocky Mountain News (Denver),
  325
Rodeo Cowboys Association, 84
rodeo events; Brahma bull riding,
  86; most hazardous, 86; team
  roping, 87; "wild cow milking,"
  83
rodeos, 72, 84-87, association
  saddle, 87; greatest ropers, 88;
  meaning of, 88; origin of, 85;
  school of training for, 86
Rogers, Roy, 12
Roosevelt, Theodore, 65, 155; *see
  also* rifle shots, best of the West
roping, tie-fast, 73
Rosa, Joseph G., 113, 200
Rose's History, 240
Ross, Jim, 73
roundups, 3, 76, 79, 83; largest, 81
Rowan Brothers, *see* firearms
Russell, Charles M., 11, 14, 64, 81-
  82, 89, 99-100, 113
Russell, Don (biographer), 95, 107;
  see also Sutton, E.S.
Russian thistles (tumbleweeds), 196
Rustler Business, The, 79

Sacajawea, 254
sad iron, 278

saddles, 295-300
Saga of the Sawlog, 106
Saguaro Cactus, 188
St. Clair, Gen. Arthur, 136
St. John's Cemetery, *see* Quan-
  trill's Raid
St. Louis Republican, 214
St. Vrain, Ceran, *see* forts—Fort
  St. Vrain
salt, value of, 48-49
saltbush, 195
San Angelo, Texas, *see* forts—Fort
  Concho
San Antonio Exposition, 72
San Antonio, New Mexico, *see*
  Val Verde, battle of
San Antonio, Texas, 314
San Francisco Bay, discovery of,
  181
Sandhills of Nebraska, 327
Sandoz, Mari, 250
Santa Anna, general, *see* Alamo—
  defense of
Sante Fe Trail, 45, 303, 310
Sargent, Randall (Ron), black-
  smith, 291
Sarpy, John B., *see* forts—
  Fort John
Saunders, Charles W. (trail
  driver), 76
"scalded the calf," 88
scalping, origin of, 140
Schoolcraft, Henry R., 146-47
Scotts Bluff National Monument,
  281, 318
Scottsbluff, Nebraska, *see* forts—
  Old Fort Mitchell
scouts, 258
screwworms as threat to cattle
  industry, 52
Second Texas Infantry, 240, 241
Sedgwick, (Maj.) John, *see* forts—
  Fort Lyons
"seeing daylight," 86-87
"seeing the elephant," 219-20
Sergeant Rowdy, *see* Clarke, Ben
set-fast, 10
Settle, William A., 214
"Seven Cities of Cibola," 75, 141,
  183, 189

sheep, 19-21; Dall, 25; industry,
20; shearing, 49; sheepmen, 20;
stone, 25
Shenandoah Valley (Virginia),
see Eastern land grants
Sherburne, Minnesota, bank hoist,
219
Sheridan, Gen. Philip Henry, 23,
251
Sheriff Whitney shooting, 229
Sherman, Gen. William T., 135
Shining Mountains, 187
Shiprock (New Mexico), 190
Short, Luke, 111, 214, 223-24
Show Low, Arizona, 311
Shown (Shaughn), John, 205-06
Sibley, H.H. (Gen.), 254-55
sidesaddle, 275
Sidney, Nebraska to Black Hills
Stage route, 324
sign language, see Indian—languages
"Silent City of Rocks," see Register
Rock
silver; silver dollar, 58; "silver rush,"
305
Simmons' Liver Regulator, 279
Sinaloa Saddle, 196
Sioux, film about, 104
Sioux Dictionary (Warcloud), 174
Sioux Uprising, Great, 132
Sioux Wars, 1865-76, 132-33
Sitting Bull, Chief (Sioux), 134
skunks, 32-33
slaves; last state to abolish, 107;
Indians as, 138; owned by
Indians, 140
sleeper, 15
Smith, Billy, 202-03
Smith, Dr. Clement, 51
Smith, Erwin E., 97
Smith, (Col.) James, 166
Smith, Jedediah, 303, 318
Smith, Soapy, see "petrified man"
Smoky (James), 64
snakes; see also reptiles; coral, 36;
hog nose, 36; rattlesnake, 24,
35, 36, 41
snowshoes, 326
soapwood, 195
SOB stew, recipe for, 88
Socorro County, New Mexico, 178

sod dugouts, 277
sod houses, 277, 278
Sod Walls: The Story of the Ne-
braska Sod House (Welsch), 277
soddy, 278
Solomon's Fort, see   Cypress Hills
Massacre
sombrero, 82-83
Song of the Talking Wire, 99
songs, most popular of 1870-80,
109
"soring," of horses, 13
South Pass, 181, 319
"Spanish bayonet," see soapweed
Spanish Conquistadores, 5
"Spanish Diggin's," 183
spelunkers, 187
"Spotted Jack," 258
Spring, Agnes Wright, 75
Springfield "cap and ball" rifles,
see firearms
Springfield Patriot, 211
Spur Ranch, The, 83
Stacy, May H., see camel corps
Stagecoaches, 323-325; Concord
Coaches, 323; Passenger Wa-
gon, 323; Yellowstone Wagon,
323
stampedes, 14
Standing Rock Agency, 311
Stanton County, Kansas, 312
steel fork on Western saddles, 296
Steele, (Gen.) Frederick, see forts—
Fort Steele
Steele, James, 50
steer roping, 72
Sterling, Illinois, see "biggest man
in the West"
Stevens Arms and Tool Company,
see firearms
Stiles, Billy (train robber), 228
"stomping barn," 279
stone tools in prehistoric times, 192
Story, Nelson (cowman), 83
Strang, (Capt.) Edward J., see
forts—Fort Concho
Strasburg, Colorado, 322
Sublette Cut-Off, 319
Sublette, William, see forts—
Fort John
stumpsucker, 6

sulling, of cattle, 18–19
Sutters Mill, 49
Sutton, E.S. (author), 260
Swallow, Alan, 98
swastika, 173
Sweetwater River, 319
Sweetwater, Texas, 231
Swift, Gustavus F., 53
Syers, Ed, 326

Tabor, H.A.W., 106, 273
Tabor Theater, 106
"tack room," 292
Talbot, Claris, 253
Taney, Roger B., 149
Taos, New Mexico, 314
tapadero, 298
Taylor Grazing Act, 29
Taylorsville, Kentucky, see
    Quantrill's Raid
Tell Them They Lie, 157
Teller Opera House, 106
"Tent City," 310
"tepees on wheels," 318
Tepees to Soddies (Sutton), 306
"terrapin," 297
Territories, 303
Terry, South Dakota, see Calamity
    Jane
tetherweight, see hitching weight
Teton Park, 184
Teton River (Montana), see Cypress
    Hills Massacre
Texas, war for independence, 244
Texas and the Confederacy (Hend-
    erson), 255
Texas Matchmaker, 108–09
Texas Rangers, 204
"Te-Yah-dah" (Sioux), see
    "tepees on wheels"
Thode, Earl, 85
The Thoen Stone (Thomson),
    186
Thompson, Ben, 206, 223, 224
Thompson, Billy, see Sheriff
    Whitney shooting
300 club (Texas), 106
Three-seven-seventy-seven (Mon-
    tana Vigilantes), 232–33
threshing rig, 56

Thrills: 1861 to 1887 (Craig),
    137
throatlatch, 297
Tilden, H.R. (Asst. U.S. Surgeon),
    259
Tilghman, Bill, 204
toad, 37
tobiano, see horses—pinto
Tom Sawyer, see Twain, Mark
Tombstone, Arizona, 308
"Toot" Over, see Mason, Joe
Topperwein, Ad and Plinkey, see
    rifle shots, best of the West
Tour of the Prairies, A, 114
Towne, C.W., 76
toys, 287
Trail City, Colorado, 212, 313
trail drives, doctoring on, 78
Trail Drivers of Texas, The, 6, 69,
    76, 112
trail-driving, peak years, 75
trailering, of horses, 7
Trails of Yesterday, 112, 325
Trans-Missouri Stock Raising, 19
Tri-State Old Time Cowboys
    Assoc., 67
Turkey Creek, see forts—Bent's
    Fort
"turtle," see "terrapin"
turtles, 37
Twain, Mark (Samuel Clemens),
    274, 323

"uncompahgre," 309
U.P. Railroad (Wyoming), see
    forts—Fort Steele
University of California—Davis, see
    pioneer—farm machinery
uranium; as cure for arthritis, 55;
    mining, 54
U.S. Cavalry horses, 262
U.S. Geological survey, 50
U.S. Highway 81, 320
U.S. Post Office Service, 304
Utter, C.H. (Colorado Charley),
    74

Vaca, Cabeza de, 144
Val Verde, battle of, 239
Valentine (Neb.) Fish Hatchery, 41

Valverde, New Mexico, *see* Val
    Verde, battle of
Vancouver, Capt. George, 77
Vaqueros, 249
varmints, 33
Verendrye, Francois, 30
Verendrye, Louis, 30
Verendrye, Sieur de la, 142
Vicksburg, *see* Second Texas
    Infantry
Victoria Advocate (Texas), 321
Videtto, S.S., *see* windmills
vigilante trials, 233
Villa, Luiz Corral de (Pancho
    Villa's wife), 230-31
Villa, Pancho, 64, 242-43
Villistas, *see* Villa, Pancho
Virginia City, Montana, *see*
    Deimling, Francis
Virginian, The, 89, 113
Votaw (Coffeyville, Kansas),
    274-75
Voyage a la Louisiana (Narciss),
    174
vultures, turkey, 40

Waddell, (Maj.) William B., 322
"waddie," 80
Wagon Boss, The, 100
wagons, pioneer, 315-17; Cones-
    toga, 315; Peter Shuttler, 315;
    Pittsburgh, 315; prairie schoon-
    er, 317; Santa Fe, 317
Wake of the Prairie Schooner
    (Paden), 320
Walch Fire Arms Company, *see*
    firearms
Walker Colt Revolver, *see* Walker,
    Samuel H.
Walker, Preston, 102
Walker, (Capt.) Samuel H., 252
Walker, Walter, 102
"walking hill," 181
Wallace, Susan Elston (Mrs. Lew),
    102
"wampum," origin of, 159
Warner, J.H., *see* windmills
Warner, (Col.) Lewis, 252
"Washerwoman's Song," 96-97
Washington, Gen. George, 136

Washita, *see* "Yellow Hair"
"water tanks of the desert," 188
wattle, 66
Watt, Thomas A., 57
Wayne, Gen. "Mad Anthony,"
    136
Wayne, John, 95, 105
We Pointed Them North, 112
Webb, C.G., *see* Mormons—Utah
Webb, Walter Prescott, 103
Weeping Water (stream), 308
Weld County seat, *see* forts—
    Fort St. Vrain
Wellman, Horace G., 210
Wellman, Paul, 214
Wells Fargo and Company, 322,
    325; *see also* Concord Stage
    Coaches
Welsch, (Prof.) Roger L., *see*
    sod dugouts
Welty, Levi, 310
Wentworth, Edward N., 76
Wesley, John, 202-03
West, The, 256
"West, The," area of, 179-80
West Turkey Creek Canyon, 226
Western grasses; life span of, 195;
    seed viability, 195; species, 196
Western medicines; Chokecherry
    bush, 282-83; cures for insect
    stings, 284; pioneer remedies,
    colds, 283; prunis virginiana,
    283; whiskey, 282
Western phenomena; animals and
    vegetation in Death Valley, 191;
    cities with highest elevation, 192;
    cities with most sun, 192; elec-
    tricity (physical), 189; prairie
    fires, 191; spring on the central
    prairieland, 193; temperature in
    Death Valley, 191; transition of
    Plains grasslands to mountain
    pine forests, 192
Western place names, "prettiest-
    sounding," Amarillo, Texas,
    306; Atascadero, California,
    306; Broken Bow, Nebraska,
    307; Capulin, New Mexico,
    306; Cimarron, 307; Coeur d'-
    Alene, Idaho, 306; Ovando,

Montana, 306; Scottsbluff, Nebraska, 307; Sierre Madre, 306; Tonopah, Nevada, 306; Uravan, Colorado, 306
Western Writers of America, Inc., 111
"Westerns," organizations of, 101
Wheeler, Ben, 202
When You and I Were Young, Nebraska (Chrisman), 1
Whetstone Indian Agency, 142
whiffenwoffle, *see* hitching weight
whips, 298
White Buffalo Council of American Indians, 166
"White Chief," *see* North, Frank
"White City," *see* "Tent City"
"White Eyes," 159
White, (Marshal) Fred, *see* Curly Bill Brocius
white stallion of the Plains, 6
Whitney, Sheriff, 206, 229
Why the West Was Wild (Miller and Snell), 220, 313
Wibaux, Pierre (cattleman), 80
Wichita Beacon, 207
Wild Bill Hickock, 245
Wild Bill Longley (outlaw), 226
Wild Bunch, The, 98
wild hay, 193
Wilkins, William, 306
Will James, the Gilt Edged Cowboy (Amaral), 64
Williams, Anna W. (profile on old silver dollar), 58
Williams, J.R., 101
"Williamsburg of the West," *see* Mormons—Utah
Wilmot Company, *see* firearms
Wimot, Nathaniel N., *see* firearms
Wilson, Thomas, 82
Wilson, Woodrow, *see* Villa, Pancho
windmills, 285–87
Winona, North Dakota, 311
Wister, Owen, 103, 113
Wolf Point, Montana, 308

wolves, 28
woodchuck, 30
work-swapping, 52
Wounded Knee, S.D., cause of Indian occupation, 133
Wright, Burris (cowboy), 181
Wright, Ed, 82
Wright, Robert M. (author), 308, 312
Writer's Project Book on Wyoming, 309
writers, of Western books, 111–13
Wyandotte (Kan.) *Gazette*, 21
Wyatt Earp: Frontier Marshal, 207, 208
Wyatt Earp: The Untold Story, 199, 200, 205
Wyoming Peace Officer, 205
Wyoming Stock Growers Association, 68
Wyoming wilderness, 184

XIT Ranch (Texas), 309

"Yahoo," *see* "Jehu"
Yeager, L.J.F. (Billy the Bear), 74
"Yellow Hair" (Custer), 249
Yellowhead Pass, 246
Yellowstone Park, 182–83, 184
Yellowtail, Mrs. Zuzie (Mrs. Indian America), 139
yeomanry, 249
Yoakum, Bob, 22
York, (Dr.) William H., *see* "Bloody Benders"
Young Cattle Kings, The, 109
yucca plant, *see also* soapweed; importance to Indians, 149; value in grass areas, 196
Yuma, Arizona, 307

Zimmerman, Frederick C. (homesteader), 273
Ziolkowski, Korczak, 107
Zuni, New Mexico, *see* "Seven Cities of Cibola"